Who's Who
in Alaskan Politics

Who's Who
in Alaskan Politics

*A Biographical Dictionary of Alaskan
Political Personalities, 1884—1974*

Compiled by
Evangeline Atwood
and
Robert N. DeArmond

Published by
Binford & Mort
2536 S.E. Eleventh • Portland, Oregon 97202

for the
Alaska Historical Commission

Foreword

The goal of the Alaska Historical Commission is to assure accurate, inclusive, and comprehensive data about the Great Land. Efforts at achieving this are four-fold: information retrieval and dissemination; education in historical methodology and interpretation; research; and publication. From May, 1973, when its office was first established, through statute, the Commission envisioned research and publication directed at producing references, chronicles, and narratives. Initial emphasis has been upon research tools and the development of an historical methodology series to encourage citizen participation in researching community history and biography.

Who's Who In Alaskan Politics is the first hardbound publication produced by the Commission. Each of its authors has served on the Commission, having won nomination by the membership of the Alaska Historical Society and appointment by the Governor. Evangeline Atwood and Robert DeArmond chose to support the Commission's program by presenting the manuscript to the State of Alaska. All proceeds from the sale of this volume will accrue to the State and be deposited for further projects to the Alaska Historical Commission's special account requested by the Governor and passed by the Ninth Alaskan Legislature in 1976 as SB521am. A generous grant by an Alaskan foundation supplied two-thirds of the printing and binding cost.

The State of Alaska and its Historical Commission is most grateful for the presentation of the completed manuscript and the publication grant. All entries received careful editing by Charles Michael Brown. The Commission's secretary, Deborah Jo Coffel, assisted proofing the final copy.

Robert A. Frederick
Executive Director
Alaska Historical Commission

Preface

Compilation of biographical information in this volume is drawn from thirty years of research by the authors. The major portion has been gleaned from old newspapers, magazines and government documents. In addition, hundreds of letters and telephone calls have provided information on present-day political figures.

In order to furnish a resource tool for historical researchers, abbreviated biographies were decided upon so that the material could be printed as soon as possible. Even as such, it has taken a year to make the compilation. Subsequent volumes, already in organizational form, will provide more extensive biographies of various individuals who made major contributions to Alaska's political history.

An appendix, consisting of tables of categories is included to enable the researcher to more easily relate the individual to his time, place and service. The categories include governors, secretaries, judges, district attorneys, U.S. marshals, legislators, delegates to the constitutional convention, territorial and state commissioners, attorneys general, and directors of departments, plus a miscellany of personalities who have made substantial imprints on Alaska politics.

The year 1884 was chosen as the starting point because it was in that year that the U.S. Congress accorded Alaska a formal civil government. During the previous seventeen years of American ownership, Alaskans were left to fend for themselves in finding ways to maintain law and order and transact day-to-day activities.

Accuracy and objectivity have been our primary goals; derogatory data has been deliberately omitted.

It is hoped that this basic research tool will inspire further biographical studies which will help to interpret Alaska's past, give understanding to its present and inspiration for its future.

The Authors

Table of Contents

Table of Abbreviations

A.A.	Associate Arts		BLM	Bureau of Land Management
AAAS	American Association for the Advancement of Science		BPR	Bureau of Public Roads
			BPW	Business and Professional Women
AAUW	American Association of University Women		br.	branch
			brig.	brigadier
A.B.	Arctic Brotherhood		bro.	brother
ABC	American Broadcasting Corporation		bros.	brothers
acad.	academy		B.S.	Bachelor of Science
acct.	accountant		B.S.E.E.	Bachelor of Science in Electrical Engineering
ACS	Alaska Communication System			
adjt.	adjutant		bur.	bureau
adm.	administrative, administrator, administration		bus.	business
adv.	advisory		c.	circa.
AEC	Alaska Engineering Commission		CAA	Civil Aeronautics Administration
A.E.F.	American Expeditionary Force		CAB	Civil Aeronautics Board
AFB	Air Force Base		Calif.	California
A.F. of L.	American Federation of Labor		Can.	Canada
AFN	Alaska Federation of Natives		cand.	candidate
AFWC	Alaska Federation of Women's Clubs		capt.	captain
Ala.	Alabama		CCC	Civilian Conservation Corps
Alta.	Alberta, Canada		C. of C.	Chamber of Commerce
Am.	America, American		chmn.	chairman
AMA	American Medical Association		CIO	Congress of Industrial Organizations
Am. Leg.	American Legion		co.	company, county
AMU	Alaska Methodist University		col.	colonel
ANB	Alaska Native Brotherhood		coll.	college
ANS	Alaska Native Service		Colo.	Colorado
AP	Associated Press		com.	commission, committee
appt.	appointed		comdr.	commander
Apr.	April		comr.	commissioner
ARC	Alaska Road Commission		conf.	conference
Ariz.	Arizona		Cong.	Congress, Congressman
Ark.	Arkansas		Conn.	Connecticut
arr.	arrival, arrived		const.	constitution, constitutional
ARRC	Alaska Rural Rehabilitation Corporation		consult.	consultant
			constr.	construction
ASHA	Alaska State Housing Authority		cont.	continued
assoc.	associate		conv.	convention
assn.	association		corp.	corporation
asst.	assistant		CPA	Certified Public Accountant
atty.	attorney		cr.	creek
Aug.	August		ct.	court
aux.	auxiliary			
ave.	avenue		d.	daughter
			DAR	Daughters of the American Revolution
B.	born			
B.A.	Bachelor of Arts		Dak.	Dakota
B.A.A.	Bachelor of Applied Arts		D.C.	District of Columbia
B.B.A.	Bachelor of Business Administration		D.D.	Doctor of Divinity
B.C.	British Columbia, Canada		D.D.S.	Doctor of Dental Surgery
B.C.E.	Bachelor of Civil Engineering		Dec.	December
B.D.	Bachelor of Divinity		dec.	deceased
bd.	board		D.Ed.	Doctor of Education
B.D.S.	Bachelor of Dental Surgery		Del.	Delaware
B.E.	Bachelor of Engineering		del.	delegate, delegation
B.Ed.	Bachelor of Education		Dem.	Democrat
B.E.E.	Bachelor of Electrical Engineering		dept.	department
B.F.	Bachelor of Forestry		dep.	deputy
BIA	Bureau of Indian Affairs		DEW	Distant Early Warning System
bk.	bank		dir.	director
bldg.	building		dist.	district
B.LL.	Bachelor of Laws		div.	divorced, division
B.Litt.	Bachelor of Literature, or Letters		D.Litt.	Doctor of Letters

Dr.	Doctor, Drive
D.Sc.	Doctor of Science
D.Th.	Doctor of Theology
ed.	editor
elem.	elementary
engr.	engineer
engring.	engineering
estab.	established
etc.	et cetera
exec.	executive
FAA	Federal Aviation Agency
FAO	Food and Agriculture Organization of the United Nations
FBI	Federal Bureau of Investigation
FCC	Federal Communications Commission
Feb.	February
fed.	federal, federation
FHA	Federal Housing Administration
Fla.	Florida
found.	foundation
Fr.	Friar
frat.	fraternity
ft.	foot
Ga.	Georgia
GAR	Grand Army of the Republic
gen.	general
Gov., gov.	Governor, governor
govt.	government
grad.	graduate, graduated
gr. sc.	grade school
GSA	General Services Administration
hdqrs.	headquarters
hist.	historian, historical, history
hon.	honorary
hosp.	hospital
H.R.	House of Representatives
h. sc.	high school
HUD	Housing and Urban Development
I.	island, islands
Ia.	Iowa
Ida.	Idaho
Ill.	Illinois
incorp.	incorporated
Ind.	Indiana
ind.	independent
inst.	institute
insur.	insurance
internat.	international
IOOF	International Order of Odd Fellows
IRS	Internal Revenue Service
ISEGR	Institute of Social, Economic and Goverment Research
ITT	International Telephone and Telegraph
IWW	Industrial Workers of the World
Jan.	January
J.D.	Doctor of Jurisprudence

J.P.	Justice of the Peace
jr.	junior
jud.	judicial
Kan.	Kansas
K.C.	Knights of Columbus
K.P.	Knights of Pythias
K.T.	Knights Templar
Ky.	Kentucky
La.	Louisiana
leg.	legislature, legal
Lit.D.	Doctor of Literature
Litt.B.	Bachelor of Letters, or Literature
LL.B.	Bachelor of Laws
LL.D.	Doctor of Laws
LL.M.	Master of Laws
lt.	lieutenant
Ltd.	Limited
LWV	League of Women Voters
m.	married, marriage
M.A.	Master of Arts
maj.	major
Man.	Manitoba, Canada
Mass.	Massachusetts
M.B.A.	Master of Business Administration
M.C.L.	Master of Civil Law
M.C.P.	Master of City Planning
M.D.	Doctor of Medicine
Md.	Maryland
M.D.S.	Master of Dental Surgery
Me.	Maine
M.E.	Mining Engineer
med.	medical, medicine
M.Ed.	Master of Education
mem.	member
M.F.	Master of Forestry
mfg.	manufacturing
mgr.	manager
mi.	miles, mile
Minn.	Minnesota
misc.	miscellaneous
Miss.	Mississippi
mo.	month
Mo.	Missouri
Mont.	Montana
mos.	months
M.S.	Master of Science
N.	North, Northern
NAACP	National Association for the Advancement of Colored People
nat.	national
NAT & T Co.	North American Trading and Transportation Company
N.B.	New Brunswick, Canada
NBC	National Broadcasting Company
N.C.	North Carolina
N. Dak.	North Dakota
NEA	National Education Association of the United States
Neb.	Nebraska
Nev.	Nevada
N.H.	New Hampshire

N.J.	New Jersey		Sen.	Senator
N. Mex.	New Mexico		Sept.	September
No.	Number		sgt.	sergeant
Nov.	November		soc.	society, social
NPS	National Park Service		SPEBSQA	Society for the Preservation and
N.W.T.	Northwest Territories, Canada			Encouragement of Barber Shop
N.Y.	New York			Quartets in America
N.Y.C.	New York City		SS	steamship
			st.	street
O.	Ohio		stat.	statute
Oct.	October		stud.	student, studied
OEO	Office of Economic Opportunity		supt.	superintendent
Okla.	Oklahoma			
Ont.	Ontario, Canada		Tel. & Tel.	Telephone & Telegraph
OPA	Office of Price Administration		temp.	temporary
OPM	Office of Power Management		Tenn.	Tennessee
Ore.	Oregon		terr.	territorial, territory
OSS	Office of Special Services		Tex.	Texas
			treas.	treasurer
Pa.	Pennsylvania			
Ph.B.	Bachelor of Philosophy		U.	University
Ph.D.	Doctor of Philosophy		UA	University of Alaska
Phila.	Philadelphia		UCLA	University of California, Los Angeles
P.I.	Philippine Islands		UN	United Nations
prac.	practice		UNESCO	United Nations Educational,
prep.	preparatory			Scientific, and Cultural
pres.	president			Organization
prof.	professor		unm.	unmarried
prop.	proprietor		U.S.	United States
pt.	point		USAAF	United States Army Air Force
PTA	Parents and Teachers Association		USARAL	United States Army, Alaska
pub.	publisher, publishing		U.S.E.D.	Unites States Engineers Division
pvt.	private		USFS	United States Forest Service
PWA	Public Works Administration		USGS	United States Geological Survey
			USNR	United States Naval Reserves
Que.	Quebec, Canada		USSR	Union of Soviet Socialist Republics
			Ut.	Utah
r.	river			
RCA	Radio Corporation of America		Va.	Virginia
reg.	regular, regional		VFW	Veterans of Foreign Wars of the
Rep.	Republican			United States
rep.	representative		vol.	volume
res.	resigned, resident		vols.	volumes
ret.	retired, returned		v.p.	vice president
R.I.	Rhode Island		vs.	versus
Rev.	Reverend		Vt.	Vermont
RFC	Reconstruction Finance Corporation			
R.R.	Railroad		Wash.	Washington
Rt.	Route		WCTU	Woman's Christian Temperance
Ry.	Railway			Union
			WICHE	Western Interstate Commission on
S.	South, Southern			Higher Education
SAR	Sons of the American Revolution		Wis.	Wisconsin
Sask.	Saskatchewan, Canada		WPA	Works Progress Administration
Sat.	Saturday		W. Va.	West Virginia
SBA	Small Business Administration		Wyo.	Wyoming
sc.	school			
S.C.	South Carolina		YMCA	Young Men's Christian Association
S. Dak.	South Dakota		Y.T.	Yukon Territory, Canada
sec.	secretary		yr.	year
			yrs.	years

Who's Who in Alaskan Politics

A

ALBRECHT, Conrad Earl, physician. B. in Bruder-heim, Alta., Can., June 25, 1905; s. Charles Augus-tus and Elizabeth (Biedelman) A.; B.A., Lehigh U., 1926, Moravian Coll., 1926; B.D., Moravian Theological Seminary, 1928; M.D., Jefferson Med. Coll., 1932; hon. LL.D., Moravian Coll., 1951; hon. D.Sc., UA, 1964; m. Blanche Rebecca Smith in Anchorage, July 1935 (div.); children: Jane Eliza-beth, John Richard; m. 2d, Margery Jones in Phila., Pa., May 4, 1964; res. physician, Abington Memorial Hosp., Abington, Pa., 1932-35; asst. supt., Alaska R.R. hosp., Anchorage, June 1935-; head med. officer, Matanuska Valley colonization project, Palmer, July 1935-41; gen. surgeon and hosp. adm., U.S. Army hosp., Ft. Richardson, at-taining rank of col.; terr. comr. of health, 1945-56; prof., dept. of preventive med., O. State Med. Sc. and asst. dir., O. state dept. of mental hygiene & correction, 1956-58; dep. sec., Pa. state dept. of health, 1958-63; prof. of preventive med., Jef-ferson Med. Coll., 1961-71; part-time med. prac., Anchorage, 1971-73; coordinator for health profes-sional education, Alaska, and consult., Alaska Man-power Corp., 1973-. Mem., bd. regents, UA, 1949-57. Address: 1736 Dolina Circle, Anchorage.

ALBRECHT, Maj. George W., lawyer. B. in Ky., Nov. 12, 1855; served in Spanish-Am. war; pvt. law prac. and U.S. Comr., Iditarod, 1912-; pvt. law prac., Fairbanks, 1920s and 1930s; pres., 4th div. Rep. club, Fairbanks, 1927-28; cand., Rep. Nat. Com., 1928; U.S. Comr., Fairbanks dist., 1930-35; died in Fairbanks, Oct. 4, 1939; survived by wife and 2 daughters. Mem., Tanana Valley Bar Assn. (pres., 1939). Republican.

ALDRICH, Frank A.T., miner. B. in Fort Wayne, Ind., Sept. 22, 1857; gr. sc., Chicago, Ill.; unm.; fought in Sioux Indian wars, Mont., 1876-78; gold miner, Mont., 1879-92; moved to Juneau, 1893; joined gold stampede to Dawson, 1896; miner, Seward Peninsula and Siberian coast, 1899-1917; prop., 60-Mile roadhouse, New Eldorado dist., 1899-; terr. H.R., 1913-15, Sen., 1915-19, 1923-27; game warden, north section, 1st jud. div., 1917-. Mem., terr. bd. of education, 1925-; Pioneers (grand pres., 1914). Democrat, Republican and Inde-pendent.

ALEXANDER, George Forest, judge. B. in Gallatin, Mo., Apr. 10, 1882; s. Joshua W. and Rose Ann (Richardson) A.; LL.B., U. Mo., 1905; m. Lola Mae Surface, Apr. 27, 1907; children: George F., Jr. (killed in France, 1944), Lillian (Mrs. Dean Sher-man), Julia Jane (Mrs. William Arthur Lavery); city atty., Gallatin, 1907-12; pvt. law prac., Portland,

Ore., 1912-33; U.S. Marshal, Ore., 1917-21; nominee for circuit judge, Multnomah Co., 1922; U.S. dist. judge, 1st jud. div., Juneau, 1933-47; died in Portland, Ore., May 16, 1948. Mem., Elks, Masons, Shrine. Christian Church, Democrat.

ALEXANDER, John, government administrator. B. in 1937; served with U.S. Army, Alaska, 1960; speech grad., UA; employe, Alaska dept. of labor, 1965-74, employment interviewer, wage and hour inspector, coordinator of fed. labor programs, asst. comr. in charge of Anchorage office; appt. state comr. of labor, July 1, 1974, becoming first black cabinet officer in Alaska. Mem., Bartlett Dem. Club, Anchorage (pres., Jan. 1974). Democrat.

ALLAN, Allan Alexander (Scotty), businessman, dogmusher. B. in Allanbrae, Scotland, June 5, 1867; m. (dec. 1933); children: Fay, George; employe, Hudson Bay Co., Can., 1887, Nome, 1900; delivered mail by dogteam between Valdez, Fair-banks, Nome; in 8 sweepstakes dog races, he won 3 firsts, 3 seconds and 2 third places; mem., Nome sc. bd.; transported and trained 400 dogs for use by A.E.F. in French Alps, WWI; terr. H.R., 1917-21; moved to Calif., 1920, engaging in dogfood manu-facture; miner, B.C., Can.; tech. adviser, Para-mount Pictures; adviser to Admiral Byrd before his departure for Antarctic; died in San Francisco, Calif., Dec. 1, 1941. Republican.

ALLEN, William Prescott, newspaper editor-publisher. B. in Olympia, Wash., Mar. 1, 1897; m.; children: William Prescott, Jr., Mrs. Samuel D. Cowan; ed.-pub., Laredo (Tex.) TIMES, 1926-65; Montrose (Colo.) PRESS; ALASKA DAILY EM-PIRE, Juneau, 1955-59; sold EMPIRE to Don Rey-nolds, Las Vegas; died in his home, Laredo, Oct. 19, 1965. Awarded Order of Aztec Eagle and Military Order of Merit by Mexican govt., 1942, in recognition of his efforts to improve U.S.-Mexico relations.

ALLYN, Clifford Merit, miner. B. in Trip, N. Dak., Dec. 22, 1892; s. George R.A.; m. Lena in Nome, Aug. 11, 1923; children: Connie (Mrs. Donald G. Creamer), Marvel (Mrs. Richard R. Lines); dep. U.S. Marshal, Nome; terr. H.R., 1931-33; pres., Northwest Alaska Fair Assn., Nome, 1937; employed at Ladd Field, 1943. Republican.

ALMQUIST, Gustaf Edward, tailor. B. in Orebro, Sweden, Apr. 26, 1878; employed in tailor shop, Sweden, until 1902 when he emigrated to U.S.; em-ployed in tailor shops, N.Y., Conn.; moved to Seattle, 1905, and opened tailor shop; m. Hulda Welin; d. Edna Linnea (Mrs. Dean Williams); naturalized U.S. citizen, 1911; Juneau res., 1926-30, 1938-53; Seattle res., 1930-38; terr. H.R., 1947-51; moved to Stockholm, Sweden, 1953; died there, Dec. 10, 1959; survived by wife Ebba. Democrat.

ANDERSON, Abel, marine engineer. B. in Madison, Minn., c. 1893; s. P.A. Anderson; parents moved to Alaska, c. 1898; reared in Juneau-Douglas area, where his father operated small boats; m. Mrs. Eleanor Grace Potterson, May 25, 1946; terr. H.R., 1949-51; operated small gasboats and cannery tenders. Democrat. Address: Juneau (1974).

ANDERSON, Carl Dewey, businessman. B. in Ord, Neb., May 24, 1905; s. Albert Andrew and Mary (McKisecek) A.; h. sc. grad.; attended commercial sc., 2 yrs.; m. Eunice Wallin, 1925; children: Ina Mae, Joyce; salesman, Los Angeles, Calif., 1926-31, 1936-41; salesman and mem. Wash. state liquor control bd., Seattle, 1931-36; in charge of U.S. Army Transport Service Office, Seward, 1941-43; mgr., Lomen Commercial Co., Nome, 1943-49; Nome city councilman; terr. H.R., 1947-49; moved to Calif.; mgr., Sears Roebuck stores and acct., Kaiser Engineering Co.; mgr., Werner Furniture & Appliance Co., June 1959; died in Seward, Nov. 1, 1960; survived by wife Mary Anne. Republican.

ANDERSON, Clarence L. (Andy), biologist. B. in Seattle, Wash., 1895; early youth in Dawson and Fairbanks, where father, Louis C. Anderson, was partner of Andrew Nerland in furniture bus.; B.A., 1912, M.A., 1924, U. Wash.; m. Bertha; s. Dale C.; employe, U.S. Bur. of Fisheries, several yrs. on Atlantic and Pacific coasts; instructor, sc. of fisheries, U. Wash., 5 yrs.; studied fisheries industry, Norway, 1921-22; employe, Wash. state dept. of fisheries, dir., 1930s and 1940s; first and only dir. of Alaska terr. dept. of fisheries, 1949-57; dir., Alaska dept. fish and game, 1957-59; Alaska state comr. fish and game, 1959-61; ret. to Seattle, 1961; died in Seattle hosp., Apr. 22, 1966. State-owned fish and game purse seiner was named in his honor, 1962.

ANDERSON, Edward M., miner. B. in Karlskrona, Lykeby, Sweden, Nov. 23, 1878; emigrated to U.S., 1902; worked in iron mines, Ashpaiming, Mich., 2 yrs., then in pipe factory, Kewanee, Ill.; gold miner, Seward Peninsula, 1906-47; naturalized U.S. citizen, 1912; m. Anna Samuelson, May 24, 1914; Nome city councilman, 1937-41, mayor, 1942-45; terr. H.R., 1945-47, Sen. 1949-53; died in Nome, Nov. 30, 1954. Democrat.

ANDERSON, Jacob P., horticulturist. B. in Nebraska City, Neb., 1874; unm.; stud., U. Neb.; B.S., Ia. State Coll., Ames, M.A., 1916; hon. D.Sc., UA, 1940; teacher in rural Neb. and Ia.; horticulturist, Sitka Agricultural Experiment Station, 1914-17; operated florist shop in Juneau, 1917-37; terr. H.R., 1937-41; terr. dir. of census for Alaska, 1940; asst. curator, herbarium, Ia. State Coll.; died in Rochester, Minn. hosp., Feb. 16, 1953. Author of book on Alaska flora, 1940s. Democrat.

ANDERSON, James H., U.S. Signal Corps. U.S. Signal Corps operator at various places in Alaska terr.; Nome postmaster, 1925-28; terr. Sen., 1929-33; re-enlisted in Signal Corps, 1933-34; died after lingering illness in VFW hosp., San Francisco, Calif., Feb. 23, 1935. Republican.

ANDERSON, Robert Hamilton, railroad executive. B. in Emporia, Kan., Sept. 2, 1909; s. Oscar and Rosa (Boller) A.; B.A., Bethel Coll., Newton, Kan., 1930; stud., Inst. for Management, Northwestern

U., 1956; m. Bernice E. Gates, Feb. 27, 1938; d. Rosalie V.; employe, Atchison, Topeka & Santa Fe R.R., 1926-42, 1945-52; ry. operating battalion, U.S. Army, Europe, 1942-45; mayor and city councilman, Newton, Kan., 1942, 1946-47; gen. suppt. of transportation, Chicago, Rock I. & Pacific R.R., Elmhurst, Ill., 1952-58, 1960-; gen. mgr., Alaska R.R., 1958-60. Mem., Masons, Rotary. Protestant.

ANDERSON, Roy, journalist. B. in Ketchikan, Sept. 21, 1905; s. Adolph and Andrea (Andersen) A.; h. sc. grad., Ketchikan; stud., U. Wash., 1924-25, 1934; m. Oleta McDaniel, July 17, 1932; worked on newspapers in Seattle and Olympia, Wash., Portland, Ore., Stockton, Calif., N.Y.C., Minneapolis, Minn.; reporter, Ketchikan CHRONICLE ed. 1924, ed. and gen. mgr., 1930s and 1940s. Mem., Elks, Masons. Address: Seattle, Wash. (1974).

ANDERSON, Tury F., miner. B. in Colo., Dec. 6, 1904; h. sc. grad.; m.; children: Bud, Garth; operated Ford agency, Wyo.; machinist, Seattle, Wash., 1939-40; employe, Wolf Creek Mining Co., Fairbanks, 1940; U.S. Army Engrs., 1941-45; hardrock miner, Fairbanks area, 1946-67; state H.R., 1967-71. Republican. Address: Fairbanks.

ANDREWS, Clinton Thom, journalist. B. in Hickory, N.C., Apr. 29, 1933; s. Clinton T. and Faye A.; gr. and h. sc., Hickory, 1951; stud., U. of N.C., 1955; m. Susan Katharine Stoffel in Anchorage, Nov. 25, 1960; children: Christina Faye, Clinton T., III, Paul Christian, Christopher; reporter, Hickory DAILY RECORD; radio station news staff, WIRC; Sun. ed., Rocky Mount (N.C.) TELEGRAM, 1955-58; city ed., Anchorage DAILY NEWS, 1958-59, managing ed., 1959-62; ed., WEEKLY HERALD, Pullman, Wash., 1962-65; reportorial staff, CHRONICLE ADVERTISER, Mansfield, Nottinghamshire, England, 1965-66; managing ed., Burlington (Vt.) FREE PRESS, 1967-73; managing ed., Anchorage DAILY TIMES, 1973-. Mem., Rotary, Am. Field Service foreign exchange stud. program (organizer and Alaska chmn., 1959-62). Episcopalian.

ANGERMAN, Frank, machinist. B. in Germany, Jan. 27, 1903; emigrated to U.S., 1911; gr. sc., Cordova; apprentice machinist, Copper River & Northwestern Ry.; moved to Fairbanks, Oct. 15, 1928; machinist, Fairbanks Exploration Co., until his death; terr. H.R., 1949-51; died Nov. 16, 1956; survived by wife, Lillian, inspector for terr. dept. of labor, Fairbanks; mother, Mrs. Pete Sather, Nuka Island, Alaska; 2 step-children, Charles R. Hoyt and Mrs. Katherine Wilky.

ANTIOQUIA, Clarence (Clay), government administrator. B. in Sitka, 1940; gr. and h. sc., Sitka; stud., Sheldon Jackson Jr. Coll.; m. Patricia; 3 children; mem., Civil Service Com., 2 yrs., U.S. Coast & Geodetic Survey, 4 yrs.; asst. technician, BIA, Anchorage, Juneau, Seattle; acting supt., BIA, Nome; moved to Juneau, 1967; equal employment opportunity rep., Civil Service Com., Seattle, 1970-72; asst. area dir., BIA, Juneau, 1972-73, area dir., 1973-.

AREND, Harry O., judge. B. in Spokane, Wash., Oct. 26, 1903; s. William Frederick and Ida August (Schimanski) A.; LL.B., 1927, M.A., 1930, U. Wash.; m. Mrs. Laree Clark Spencer, June 29, 1940; children: Otis, Erling, Rebecca, Frederick David; teacher, Wash. and Alaska, 1927-35; pvt. law prac., Fairbanks, 1935-37; asst. dist. atty., Fairbanks, 1937-44; U.S. dist. atty., 4th jud. div., Fairbanks, 1944-49; trial atty., U.S. Justice Dept., anti-trust div., Los Angeles, Calif., 1949-55; pvt. prac., Fairbanks, 1955-59; superior ct. judge, Fairbanks, 1959-60; state supreme ct. justice, 1960-64; solicitor, Dept. Interior, Anchorage, 1965-66; died in Anchorage, June 28, 1966. Mem., Rotary, Elks. Mormon, Democrat.

ARMSTRONG, Rev. Robert Rolland, minister. B. in Grapeville, Pa., Oct. 21, 1910; s. Robert and Charlotte Horne (Kinnear) S.; h. sc., Pawtucket, R.I.; B.A., Grove City Coll., Pa.; stud., Princeton Theological Seminary, Louisville Presbyterian Theological Seminary; ordained Sept. 18, 1937, Buckhorn Presbytery, Ky.; hon. D.D., Whitworth Coll., 1953; hon. DHL, UA, 1962; m. Katherine Ratcliff, Hyden, Ky., Dec. 3, 1938; children: Mrs. Allison Anne Keef, Mrs. Mary Charlene Whitney; Sun. school missionary, Buckhorn, Ky., 1937-38, Charlevoix, Mich., 1938-40; pastor, 1st Presbyterian church, Fairbanks, 1940-42, Anchorage, 1942-50; field rep., Presbyterian Bd. of Nat. Missions, Juneau, 1950-53, asst. sec., 1953-56; del.-at-large, const. conv., Fairbanks, 1955-56; pres., Sheldon Jackson Jr. Coll., Sitka, 1956-66; field adm., Presbyterian Synod of Ariz., Ft. Defiance, 1966-72; consult. in ministries, Synod of N. Mex., Roswell, 1972-. Mem., terr. bd. health (chmn., 1943-50); del., White House Conf. Church & Youth, 1951, 1956; Rotary. Address: 115 East Lewis St., Roswell, N. Mex. 88201.

ARNOLD, Winton Cumberland, lawyer. B. in Walla Walla, Wash., Apr. 11, 1903; s. John Schuyler and Minnie (Blackard) A.; stud., U. Ida., 1920-24; m. Minnie Wiley, Nov. 4, 1927 (dec.); children: Winton Cumberland, Jr., Alice Anne (Mrs. John S. Calvert); m. 2d, Vivien Click, Oct. 19, 1961; admitted to Ida. bar, 1924, Alaska bar, 1927, Wash. bar, 1945; pvt. prac., Grangeville, Ida., 1925-27, Hyder and Ketchikan, 1927-45, Seattle, Wash., 1945-60, Anchorage, 1960-; U.S. Comr., Hyder and Ketchikan, 1927-33; dir. and lobbyist, Alaska Canned Salmon Industry, 1945-60. Mem., adv. com. on fisheries, Dept. of State, 1954-63; adv. com. on fisheries and conservation, Dept. Interior, 1939-41, 1955-60; adv. com., American Section, Internat. Northern Pacific Com., 1953-62; Alaska Temporary Claims Com., 1964; Alaska and Anchorage C. of C. (dir.); Kappa Sigma, Phi Alpha Delta, Masons, Elks, Rotary, Petroleum (Anchorage) Club, Wash. Athletic Club, Arctic (Seattle). Episcopalian, Republican. Address: Lathrop Bldg., Anchorage 99501.

ASHER, Jack O'Hair, lawyer. B. in Paris, Ill., May 21, 1930; s. John R. and Ruth Frances (O'Hair) A.; B.S., U. Ill., 1954, J.D., Tulane U., La., 1957; admitted to La. bar, 1957, Ill. bar, 1967; m. Jane Fitzgerald, Miami, Fla., Aug. 25, 1957; children: Duffey Ann, William; asst. atty. gen., Juneau, 1957-59; state dist. atty., 1st jud. div., Juneau, 1960-67; appeals atty., Selective Service, 1961-66; returned to Paris, Ill., 1967; mem., law firm of Dillavou, Overaker, Asher & Bonaldi. Mem., Juneau Bar Assn. (v.p., 1960-65); del., Dem. Nat. Conv., 1964. Address: 236 W. Court St., Paris, Ill. 61944.

ASPLUND, John M., businessman. B. in Minneapolis, Minn., Aug. 15, 1913; grad., h. sc., Minneapolis, 1932; extension courses, U. Minn.; owner-operator, J.M. Asplund Trucking Co., 1933-37; owner, Arrow Tire Co., 1938-40; manufacturers' rep., San Francisco, Calif., 1941-46; m. Ida Moberg in Carson City, Nev., 1942; children: John E., Larry C., David R., Karen Susan; moved to Anchorage and estab. John M. Asplund Co., dealing in maintenance supplies and equipment, 1946-; chmn., Greater Anchorage Wholesale Trade Com., 1953; dir., Greater Anchorage C. of C., 1954-57; mem. and pres., Spenard Public Utility Dist. Bd., 1956-63; Anchorage Ind. School Dist. bd., 1960-63; chmn., Greater Anchorage Area Borough, 1964-73, retired. Address: 4001 Northwood Dr., Anchorage 99503.

ATKINS, Barton, U.S. Marshal, businessman. B. in Buffalo, N.Y., 1826; m. Eliza Russell, 1850; children: Arthur R., 1 daughter in Marquette, Mich., 1865; owner-capt., small lake steamer, Duluth, Minn., 1870; R.R. agent, St. Paul, Minn., 1876; U.S. Marshal, Dist. of Alaska, Sitka, 1885-89; agent, Reading R.R., Buffalo; died in Buffalo, early 1901. Mem., Buffalo Hist. Soc. Author, "Modern Antiquities" and "The River Niagra". Democrat.

ATWOOD, Robert Bruce, newspaper editor-publisher. B. in Chicago, Ill., Mar. 31, 1907; s. Burton Homer and Mary (Stevenson) A.; B.A., Clark U., Worcester, Mass.; hon. LL.D., AMU, 1967; m. Evangeline Rasmuson in Winnetka, Ill., Apr. 2, 1932; children: Marilyn Jeanette (Mrs. Milton W. Odom), Sara Elaine; ct. reporter, Ill. STATE JOURNAL, Springfield, 1929-33, Worcester (Mass.) TELEGRAM, 1933-35; ed.-pub., Anchorage DAILY TIMES, 1935-; Norwegian consul, 1959-; chmn., Alaska Statehood Com., 1949-59; trustee, AMU, 1960-70; pres., Anchorage-Westward Hotel Corp., 1960-73. Awarded first "Alaskan of the Year", 1967; Distinguished Citizen, Nat. Municipal League, 1970. Mem., Rotary (pres.); state com. on jud. qualifications, 1968-74; Nat. Municipal League (dir., 1969-); Allied Newspapers (dir., 1973-); Am. Soc. Newspaper Editors, 1951-; bd. of advisors, Geophysical Inst. of UA, 1970-; trustee, Pacific Northwest Newspapers Assn., 1974-; Am. Polar Soc., Explorers' Club, Sigma Delta Chi, Nat. Press Club, Am. Newspaper Publishers' Assn., Internat. Press Inst., Inter-Am. Press Assn., Pioneers, U.S. Public Health Service Adv. Com., 1956-64. Presbyterian, Republican. Address: Box 40, Anchorage 99510.

AWES, Dorothy, lawyer. B. in Moorhead, Minn., Oct. 3, 1918; d. George S. and Decia E.A.; B.A., J.D., U. Ia.; m. Ragnar Haaland, 1956; children: Roger, Jane; atty., OPA, Juneau and Ketchikan, 1945-47; U.S. Comr., Cordova, 1947-48; pvt. prac., Anchorage, 1948-49; law research clerk, 3d jud. div., 1949-53; pvt. prac., Anchorage and Palmer, 1953-60; del., const. conv., 1955-56; terr. H.R., 1957-59; asst. dist. atty., Jan. 11, 1960-; asst. atty. gen., Anchorage, 1970-. Mem., LWV, Sons of Norway. Catholic, Democrat.

AYER, Fred M., mining engineer. B. in Atchison, Kan., Feb. 12, 1874; h. sc., Salt Lake City, Ut.; stud., Stanford U., 3 yrs., Northwestern U., 1 yr.; m. Ann Sullivan, July 13, 1933; employe, Wild Goose Mining Co., Nome, 1900-, later gen. mgr.; terr. Sen., 1923-27 (pres., 1925); southern Calif. res., 1925-30; mgr., Lomen Bros. drug store, Nome, 1930-33; mgr., Keith Roberts store, Deering, 1933-, Steel Creek roadhouse, 1939-40; dep. adm., War Finance Com. for Alaska, 1941-43; in charge of dragline operations on Quartz Creek, Kougarok dist., 1940s; moved to Lima, O., 1950s; died there. Mem., terr. bd. education, 1925-. Won Solomon Dogteam Derby 5 successive yrs., 1913-17, Bordon Cup, 1918, 1919, 1921.

B

BADGER, Harry Markley, farmer, miner. B. in Wyoming, Minn., Nov. 24, 1869; farmer, Minn., Calif., Wash., until 1900; miner, Bonanza Creek, Dawson, Can., 1900-03, Fairbanks area, 1903-; town recorder, estab. Badger & Woodward, brokers; farmed and became known as "the strawberry king"; terr. H.R., 1945; moved to Pioneers' Home, Sitka, where he lived for several yrs.; died Oct. 11, 1965. Democrat.

BAGGEN, Dr. Edgar I., dentist. B. in Petersburg, 1913; m. Mertie Johnson, Petersburg (dec. 1968); children: Edward (Abe), Wendy, Laurel, Jill (Mrs. Jensen); mem., Petersburg sc. bd., 2 yrs.; Fairbanks res., 1941-, mayor, 1953; mem., Fairbanks sc. bd., 10 yrs.; state H.R., 1961-65. Mem., state bd. dental examiners, 7 yrs., com. jud. qualifications, Elks, Pioneers. Republican. Address: Fairbanks.

BAILEY, Eben Gordon, businessman. B. in Georgetown, Mass., Aug. 3, 1896; s. Eben A. and Mary Elizabeth (Gordon) B.; naval officers' training, Harvard U.; U.S. Navy, until 1921; salesman, 1921-29; moved to Calif. with wife, Caroline, and son, Gordon Lee; employe, Douglas Aircraft Shipbuilding Corp., Santa Monica, Calif.; helped build yacht harbor at Santa Monica, and served as its first harbor master; moved to Anchorage, estab. Shady Acre Trailer Ct., Mountain View, and Hi-way Diner, 1945; del., Dem. Nat. Conv., 1948; terr.

H.R., 1956; died at Elmendorf AFB hosp., Dec. 13, 1972. Mem., bd. dirs., Chugach Electric Assn., 1951-59, Alaska Dept. of Veterans WWI (1st comdr., 1962).

BAILEY, Douglas B., lawyer. B. in Evanston, Ill., Feb. 1937; stud., U. Ill.; B.A., Beloit Coll.; J.D., U. Ill., 1964; children: Drew Frazier, Reeve; went to Alaska with USGS, 1957; field geologist, Pan Am. Petroleum, Anchorage, 1960-61; returned to law sc.; asst. atty. gen., Juneau, 1964-67; state dist. atty., Anchorage, 1968-69; U.S. atty. for Alaska, Anchorage, 1969-71; pvt. prac., Anchorage, 1971-74; adm. asst. to Gov. Hammond, 1974-. Republican. Address: 3035 Madison Way, Anchorage.

BAILEY, Joseph, director of customs for Alaska, 1965-.

BAKER, Forbes L., mechanic. B. in South Bend, Wash., Jan. 1, 1893; moved to Skagway with family, 1902; Fairbanks res., 1905-10; U.S. Army, 1911-16, U.S. Navy, WWI; m. Bertha Niddrie, Jan. 1, 1920; children: Bertha Evelyn (Mrs. John Melville), Forbes D., Helen Slifer; returned to Alaska, 1921, settled in Fairbanks; mechanic, Alaska R.R., Fairbanks Exploration Co., Northern Commercial Co., Wien Airlines, Alaska Airlines, CAA; mem., city council and sc. bd., Fairbanks; state H.R., 1961-62, 1963-64. Mem., Alaska Game Com., 1947-59; grand chef de gare, 40 & 8, 1953; Am. Legion (dept. comdr., 1954-55); Scottish Rite Masonry (elevated to 33d degree, 1961).

BALDWIN, Capt. George B., miner, riverboat captain. Arr. Circle City, 1894; joined stampede to Nome, 1900; Nome city councilman, 1908-; chairman, terr. Rep. central com., 1912-16; Valdez res., 1912-. Republican.

BALFE, Joseph D., lawyer. B. in 1933; J.D., Willamette U., 1964; m. Janet Crabtree, Juneau, Aug. 24, 1973; state trooper, Juneau, 1956-64; pvt. prac. and asst. dist. atty., Morrow Co., Ore., 1964-70; asst. dist. atty., Juneau, 1970; dist. atty., Juneau, 1971-73, Anchorage, 1973-. Democrat.

BALL, Mottrone Dulany, lawyer, collector of customs. B. in Fairfax Co., Va., June 23, 1835; M.A., William and Mary Coll.; children: Sally Stuart (Mrs. James Clarkson Gillmore), M. Corbin; teacher until outbreak of Civil War; Confederate Army, 1861-65; law prac., Alexandria, 1865-72; ed.-pub., VIRGINIA SENTINEL, Alexandria; collector of customs, Sitka, 1878-81; elected first unofficial del. to Cong. from Alaska, Sept. 5, 1881; U.S. dist. atty., Sitka, 1885-87; died aboard southbound steamer, Sept. 13, 1887. Episcopalian, Democrat.

BALLINGER, Richard Achilles, lawyer. B. in Boonesboro, Ia., July 9, 1858; s. Richard H. and Mary E. (Norton) B.; prep. education, U. Kan. and Washburn Coll., Williams Coll., 1884; admitted to bar, 1886; LL.D., 1900; m. Julia A. Bradley, Oct. 26, 1886; 2 sons; city atty., Kankakee, Ill., New Decatur, Ala.; pvt. prac., Port Townsend, Wash., 1889-97, Seattle, 1897-; U.S. ct. comr., 1890-92; superior ct. judge, Jefferson Co., Wash., 1894-97;

mayor, Seattle, 1904-06; comr., Gen. Land Office, Wash., D.C., 1907-09; Sec. of Interior, 1909-11; pvt. prac., Seattle, 1911-22; died June 6, 1922. Author: "Ballinger on Community Property," 1895 and "Ballinger's Annotated Codes & Statutes of Wash.," 1897. Republican.

BALONE, Thomas J., lawyer. B. in Detroit, Mich., July 16, 1929; grad., h. sc., Farmington, Mich., 1945; U.S. Army, WWII, 1946-48; stud., Wayne State U. night sc. and salesman, machine and tool co.; received law degree, 1960; 5 children; arr. Fairbanks, 1960; employe, Taylor & Crace law firm; moved to Nome, 1961; pvt. prac. and city atty., Nome; mem., Alaska Boundary Com., 1963; state H.R., 1965-66, 1967-68. Address: Nome.

BANFIELD, Mildred Harshburger, teacher, social worker, accountant. B. in Fremont, Neb.; stud., Midland Coll., 1931-35, U. Chicago bus. sc., 1945; m. Norman Banfield, atty., in Las Vegas, Nev., Jan 26, 1951; children: Nancy, Elizabeth, Julie; teacher, Neb., 1935-37; matron, children's homes, 1937-45; moved to Juneau, 1946; acct. and book-keeper, Juneau Cold Storage, Alaska Coastal Airlines, Columbia Lumber Co.; vice chmn., Rep. state central com., 1956; vice chmn., Rep. House dist. com., 1963; appt. to state Sen., 1963-65; state H.R., 1967-75. Mem., Mental Health Assn., St. Ann's Guild, Girl Scouts adv. council, Community Action program (chmn.), Rotary. Chosen Woman of the Year, Rotary, 1966. Lutheran, Republican. Address: 320 Whittier St., Juneau 99801.

BARBER, Edward G., commercial fisherman. B. in Ontario, Ore., July 17, 1910; s. Guy B. and Fanni B.; Valdez res., 1911-17, Anchorage, 1917-; grad., Anchorage h. sc., 1928, LaSalle Extension U.; records management officer, Alaska R.R., 1928-60; m. Janet Borges, 1939; children: Edward G., Hugh F., Richard L.; mem., city council, 1947-50; commercial fisherman, 1960-73; lobbyist, Cook Inlet Fishermen's Assn., 1964-70; terr. H.R., 1971-75. Mem., sc. adv. bd., 1952-58, Elks (past state pres.), Pioneers (life mem.), Rotary, Masons, Sportsmen's Assn. Presbyterian, Democrat. Address: 1001 E St., Anchorage.

BARNES, Doris Marian, saleswoman. B. in Portland, Ore., Aug. 27, 1891; d. Oakes M. and Jessie B. (Kribs) Plummer; stud., Portland Acad., 1908-10, U. Ore., 1910-12; m. Franklin Scott Barnes, Mar. 20, 1912 (dec. 1940); children: Frank Plummer, Marian Elizabeth (Mrs. Clarence E. Henning), Dori-anne (Mrs. Arthur C. Salonek); moved to Wrangell, 1912; owner-mgr., Barnes Insur. Agency, Wrangell, 1940-72; city council, 1944-46, mayor, 1946-50, 1960-64; terr. H.R., 1949-53, Sen., 1953-57; Rep. Nat. Com., 1954-58, 1964-68; moved to Everett, Wash., Oct. 1972. Mem., Rep. state central com., 1959-64 (vice chmn., 1960-64); Presbyterian Synod of Wash. (vice moderator, 1958-59); adv. com., Sheldon Jackson Jr. Coll.; Arctic Inst. of North Am.; Alaska Insur. Agents Assn. (exec. bd. 1955); Alaska electoral coll.; Wrangell C. of C. (pres.), AFWC (pres.), Alaska BPW (pres.), Chi Omega, Beta Sigma Phi. Republican.

BARNETT, Cecil Glen, carpenter. B. in Miami, Ariz., Sept. 24, 1916; s. Earl W. and Hetty (Classen) B.; h. sc., Anchorage; placer miner, 1935-38, trucking and constr., 1938-40, carpenter, 1940-; U.S. Army, 1943-45; arr. Anchorage, 1922; terr. H.R., 1947. Mem., Elks. Democrat. Address: 607 W. 12th Ave., Anchorage.

BARONOVICH, F. Joseph, fisherman, businessman. B. at Karta Bay, Prince of Wales I., May 15, 1879; s. Charles Vincent B.; gr. and h. sc., Ketchikan; stud., Coll. Our Lady of Lourdes, near Seattle, Wash., 2 yrs., Wilson's Bus. Coll., 1 yr.; 1 son; fisherman, southeastern Alaska for yrs., Irving Packing Co., Karheen, 3 yrs.; sand and gravel bus., Ketchikan, 1934-; terr. H.R., from Ketchikan, 1933-37; moved to Seattle, 1946, later to Berkeley, Calif. Democrat.

BARR, Frank, U.S. Marshal, aviator. B. in Lawrence Co., Ill., Aug. 22, 1903; attended public schools, Ill. and Ia.; m. Mary K. Sands in Atlin, B.C., Can., 1937; children: Sharon Alaska, Lynn Frances; commercial pilot with U.S. Cavalry in Mexico; Army Air Service, Tex. and Calif.; test pilot and radio technician, Detroit, Mich., 1926-32; bush pilot, Atlin, Juneau, Fairbanks, 1932-38; dispatcher and pilot, Alaska Airlines, Fairbanks, 1938-; terr. Sen., 1949-53, 1955-59; del., const. conv., 1955-56; U.S. Marshal, 4th jud. div., Fairbanks, 1951 (Mar.-Aug.); mem., Alaska Aeronautics Com.; left Alaska, May 1956; purchased trailer park, Portland, Ore. Democrat.

BARRY, Jefferson B., government administrator, teamster. B. in Wenatchee, Wash., Dec. 14, 1915; public sc., Wenatchee; stud., U. Wash., 1934-37; m.; 3 children; m. 2d, Mrs. Warren (Della) Colver, June 1970; camp mgr. and paymaster, Morrison-Knudson Constr. Co., Anchorage; teamster, 1956-58; active in teamsters' union, 1958-60; mgr., state dept. of revenue, Anchorage, 1960-62; dir., div. of field services, motor vehicle licenses, state dept. of revenue, Anchorage, 1962-64; exec. asst. to Gov. Egan, 1964-66; employe, British Petroleum Corp., Anchorage, 1970-. Democrat. Address: 2123 Hillcrest Place, Anchorage 99503.

BARTLETT, Edward Lewis (Bob), journalist, miner. B. in Seattle, Wash., Apr. 20, 1904; s. Edward and Ida (Doverspike); grad., Fairbanks h. sc., 1922; stud., U. Wash., 1922-24, UA, 1924-25; hon. LL.D., UA, 1960; m. Vide Marie Gaustad, Aug. 14, 1930; children: Doris Ann (Mrs. Burke Riley), Susan Bernice (Mrs. Larry James Peterson); reporter and assoc. ed., Fairbanks NEWS-MINER, 1927-33, 1934-35; sec. to Del. to Cong. Anthony J. Dimond, Wash., D.C., 1933-34; gold miner, Circle dist., 1934-35, 1936-37; public dir., social security bd., Juneau, Feb.-Oct., 1937; chmn., Alaska Planning Council, Juneau, Oct.-Nov., 1937; chmn., Unemployment Compensation Com., Juneau, Dec. 1937-39; Sec. of Alaska, 1939-44; Del. to Cong., 1944-59; U.S. Sen., 1959-68; died in Cleveland, O. hosp., Dec. 11, 1968; funeral service, Fairbanks, Dec. 14, 1968; statue unveiled in Statuary Hall,

Capitol Rotunda, Wash., D.C., May 6, 1969. Mem., Elks, Pioneers. Awarded "Alaskan of the Year," Mar. 29, 1968. Episcopalian, Democrat.

BAYER, George A., law enforcement officer. B. Sept. 24, 1911; m.; 2 children; dep. U.S. Marshal, Nome, 1937-60, chief dep., 1942; clerk of Superior Ct., 2d jud. div. and dep. clerk, U.S. dist. ct., Nome, 1960-61; U.S. Marshal, Dist. of Alaska, Anchorage, 1961-69. Democrat.

BAYLESS, William S., lawyer. Rep. Nat. Committeeman, 1912-16; law partner of Louis P. Shackleford, Juneau. Republican.

BEARDSLEY, Robert L., businessman. B. in Seattle, Wash., 1925; grad., U. Wash.; m. Patricia; 2 children; dir., commercial and industrial sales, Wash., Natural Gas Co., Seattle; mgr., industrial program, John Graham Co., Seattle, architectural and engineering firm; state comr. of highways, Alaska, 1969-71. Republican.

BEAUMONT, Maj. George D., U.S. Signal Corps. B. in Lima, O., 1878; telegraph operator, Alaska R.R., Anchorage, 1916-17; 401st telegraph battalion, U.S. Army, France, 1917-18; Seattle, Wash., res., 1918-21; U.S. Marshal, 1st jud. div., Juneau, 1921-25; moved to Los Angeles, Calif., 1925; connected with movie industry several yrs., also Union Pacific R.R., 1928, Southern Pacific R.R., 1929; died in Los Angeles, June 18, 1935. Republican.

BEGICH, Nicholas John, educator. B. in Eveleth, Minn., April 6, 1932; s. John and Ann B.; B.S., St. Cloud State Coll., 1952; teacher, St. Cloud h. sc., 4 yrs.; M.A., U. Minn.; post-grad. stud., U. Colo., U. N. Dak.; moved to Anchorage, 1956; labor relations, U.S. Army dist. engineers and boys' counselor, West h. sc., 1956-57; m. Pegge Jean Jendro in St. Cloud, Minn.; children: Nichelle Josephine, Nicholas John, Thomas Scott, Mark Peter, Stephanie Lynn, Paul Michael; dir., stud. personnel, Anchorage sc. dist., 1957-59; principal, Ursa Minor sc., Ft. Richardson and instructor, UA branch, Elmendorf AFB, 1959-63; supt., Ft. Richardson schools, 1963-67; state Sen., 1963-67, 1967-71; U.S. Congressman, 1971-72; lost on airplane flight, Oct. 16, 1972; re-elected posthumously to U.S. Cong., Nov. 7, 1972. Chosen "Alaskan of the Year," 1973; elected to 49er Hall of Fame by Alaska Press Club, 1973. Catholic, Democrat.

BEIRNE, Dr. Helen, pathologist. B. in St. Maries, Ida., 1922; d. Henry John and Mamie F. Dittman; B.A., U. Ida.; M.A., Ph.D., speech and hearing pathology, U. Denver; m. O. Thomas Beirne, March 17, 1962; scholarship to U.S. Army's physical therapy sc., Brigham City, Ut.; U.S. Army med. corps, 23 mos.; U.S. Army's hosp., Jama, Japan, 1 yr.; stud., Stanford U., 1 summer; "psychiatrist," Chester gen. hosp., Pa., 2 yrs.; stud., speech therapy, U. Ore., 1 semester, Dr. Phelps' sc. for cerebral palsy, Cockeysville, Md., 1 yr.; arr. Anchorage, May 1956; speech and physical therapist, Alaska Crippled Children's Assn. treatment center, dir., Sept. 1956, res., May 1968; state H.R., 1969-70, 1973-77; project mgr., Bur. Education for

Handicapped, study of children hearing problems. Mem., White House Conf. on Youth, 10 yrs.; All-Women Am. Leg. Post, No. 21 (past comdr.); Anchorage Inter-Agency Council for Exceptional Children (organizer); Anchorage Altrusa Club (organizer); Alaska Hist. Soc., Rotary Ann. Republican. Address: Box 4BB, Spenard 99503.

BEIRNE, Dr. Michael Francis, physician, pathologist. B. in Towanda, Pa., Nov. 22, 1925; s. Col. John F. and Helen (Kelly) B.; B.A., U. Scranton, 1947; M.D., St. Louis U., 1951; U.S. Army, 1954-56; m. Corinne A. Rowe; children: Beverly, David, Mark, Paul, Sally, Barry, Gregory, George; moved to Anchorage, Jan. 1957; estab. Alaska Med. Laboratories, Anchorage and Fairbanks, Lake Otis Clinic, Anchorage; state H.R., 1967-68. Mem., Toastmasters Club (pres., 1957); Flying Physicians (past pres.); Anchorage Med. Soc. (pres., 1960); Anchorage Rep. Club (pres., 1965); American Med. Political Action Com. (pres., 1966), Alaska chapter; Blood Bank of Alaska (organizer and dir.); Alaska Mutual Savings Bk. (organizer and dir., 1961); Alaska assemblyman, Nat. Assembly, Coll. Am. Pathologists; Elks, Lions, Am. Leg. Catholic, Republican. Address: 936 W. 10th Ave., Anchorage.

BELTZ, William Earnest, carpenter. B. in Haycock, Apr. 17, 1912; s. Jack Skyles and Susie (Goodwin) B.; home study course for h. sc. diploma; apprentice carpenter, Nome, Unalakleet, Fairbanks; m. Helen B. Merrifield, Nov. 18, 1934; children: George E., Carolyn Lee, Wanda Fay (Mrs. John Collins); m. 2d, Arne Louise Bulkeley, Nov. 28, 1953; children: Mark Albert, William, Katherine, Axel; pres. and bus. agent, Carpenters' Local No. 1243, Fairbanks; terr. H.R., 1949-51; Sen., 1951-60 (pres., 1959); died in Alaska Native Service hosp., Anchorage, Nov. 21, 1960. Vocational sc. in Nome named in his honor, 1965. Mem., Eagles, Democrat.

BENJAMIN, Charles O., miner, merchant. B. in Edwardsburg, Mich., Oct. 7, 1873; m. Miss Lilly McCulley in Tacoma, Wash., Feb. 27, 1911; children: Lloyd, Marjorie; m. 2d, Mary; miner, Cook Inlet area and Yakataga beach, 1903-07; operated mercantile store, Wrangell, 1907-39; city councilman for many yrs.; terr. H.R., 1927-29, Sen., 1929-33; died in Wrangell, Nov. 12, 1939. Mem., Elks, Redmen, All-Alaska C. of C. (v.p., 1929); Wrangell hosp. bd. (chmn.). Republican.

BENNETT, Burton Ellsworth, lawyer. B. in North Brookfield, N.Y., Apr. 17, 1863; s. Samuel Rhoades and Mary Hill (Loomis) B.; grad., Brookfield Acad.; regents' diploma, U. State of N.Y., 1881; B.S., D.Sc., LL.D., Cornell U.; unm.; law prac., Utica, N.Y., then Seattle, Wash., 1887-95; mem., bd. park comrs., Seattle, 1892-95; U.S. dist. atty. for Alaska, Sitka, 1895-98; Alaska comr., Internat. Mining Cong., 1898; ret. to Seattle, Wash.; comr., Buffalo Exposition, 1901; writer on Masonic subjects. Mem., Masons (33d degree). Episcopalian, Democrat.

BENNETT, Robert L., lawyer. B. on Oneida Indian reservation, Wis., Nov. 16, 1912; Catholic parochial sc., Haskell Inst., 1931; earned law degree in

Wash., D.C.; m. Lucille A. Martell of Turtle Mountain Chippewa Tribe, 1933; children: John, William, Leo, Joanne, David, Robert; employe, BIA, Vt., 1933-, transferred to Wash., D.C.; U.S. Marine Corps, 1941-43; asst. supt., Navajo reservation, 1943-46; staff mem., Veterans Adm., Phoenix, Ariz., 1946-49; placement officer, BIA, Aberdeen, S. Dak., 1949-52; program officer, BIA, Wash., 1952-54; supt., Consolidated Ute Agency, Ignacio, Colo., 1954-56; asst. area dir., BIA, Aberdeen, S. Dak., 1956-61; area dir. for Alaska, BIA, Juneau, 1961-66; U.S. Comr., BIA, Wash., D.C., 1966-69. Received Indian achievement award of Indian Council Fire, 1962; Indian of the Year, Indian Exposition, Anadarko, Okla., 1966. Mem., Am. Leg., Lions, Nat. Cong. Am. Indians, Am. Acad. Political and Social Science, Am. Soc. for Public Adm. Republican.

BENSON, Henry A., fisherman. B. in Ill., 1910; m. Irene Bliss; children: Terry, Dennis; m. 2d, Mrs. Pauline Sanders in Juneau, Sept. 1, 1958; commercial fisherman based in Seattle, Wash.; moved to Alaska, 1930; fished several seasons in southeastern Alaska waters; U.S. Army, Pacific theatre, 1942-45; partner and acct., Kenai Packing Co., Anchorage, 1945-46; terr. labor comr., 4 consecutive terms, 1946-59; moved to Anchorage, 1959; cand., U.S. Cong.; appt. labor comr., 1970, res., 1972; labor law compliance officer, Anchorage; consult., joint labor-management com. for painting industry. Mem., VFW, Am. Leg. Republican.

BENSON, Monte, miner. B. in West Haverstraw, N.Y., 1876; m. Ina J. Honganey in Douglas, Sept. 8, 1905; 3 children; part-time miner and employe, White Pass & Yukon Ry. and Alaska Central Ry., 1898-1904; employe, Treadwell gold mine, 1904-18; terr. H.R., 1917-18; employe, Tacoma, Wash. smelter, 1918-20; moved to Calif.; died of pneumonia, San Francisco, May 13, 1920. Mem., Odd Fellows, Masons (32d degree), Shrine. Republican.

BERRY, Montgomery P., collector of customs, printer, miner. B. in Ky., c. 1824; m.; 1 son; served in Mexican and Civil wars, rank of maj. in latter; co. sheriff and supt. of state prison, Mo.; U.S. collector of customs for Alaska, Sitka, 1874-77; cont. in customs service; died in Sitka, Dec. 28, 1898.

BETIT, Joseph, military officer, government administrator. B. in 1923; m. Ethel; 7 children; U.S. Army, ret. lt. col., 1943-67; adm. officer, state dept. of health and social services, 1967-70, dep. comr., 1968-69, comr., July 1969-70, res., Apr. 1970 to become comr. of social welfare, Vt., his home state.

BETTINGER, Lee Crawford, businessman. B. in Pendleton, Ore., 1905; s. Harold E. and Neva (Rogers) B.; grad., Stanford U.; m. Rose Felan, 1924; children: Lee Felan, Mildred Marqueta; moved to Kodiak, 1940; partner-mgr., Kodiak Bottling Works and Kodiak Candy Co.; agent, Ry. Express; city councilman, Kodiak, 1944-45, mayor, 1946-1950s; moved to Wash., D.C.; remarried.

BINGHAM, Frank C., lawyer. Former Mont. educator; U.S. Comr., Nome, 1940s; appt. U.S. dist. atty., 2d jud. dist., Nome, June 1944; removed from office, Aug. 31, 1951; pvt. law prac., Missoula, Mont., May 1951. Democrat.

BINKLEY, Charles M. (Jim), riverboat pilot, tour operator. B. in Wrangell, May 16, 1920; s. Charles M. and Fannette B.; father operated riverboats on Stikine River; stud., UA, 1940-41, 1948-49; m. Mary Hall, Portland, Ore., June 15, 1947; children: Charles M., III, James, John, Marilee; Fairbanks res., 1940-; tourist bus., Alaska Riverways, Inc., using sternwheeler "Discovery" for cruises on Chena and Tanana rivers; state H.R., 1961-65. Mem., bd. dirs., Fairbanks and Alaska C. of C., state centennial com., Nat. Civil Rights Com., 1953-61; Rep. central dist. com. (chmn.), Pioneers. Republican. Address: Drawer G, College 99710.

BIRCH, Ronald G., lawyer. B. in 1942; J.D., Columbia U., 1965; law clerk, Supreme Ct. justice, Fairbanks, 1965-66; asst. atty. gen., Juneau, 1966-67; state dist. atty., 1st jud. div., Juneau, 1967-68; staff atty., Alaska's U.S. Sen., Wash., D.C., 1968-71; pvt. law prac., Anchorage, 1971-. Address: 401 K St., Anchorage 99501.

BISHOP, Harry A., businessman. B. in Ia., c. 1869; m. Grace Vrooman in Des Moines, Wash., 1911; moved to Alaska, 1896; Sheep Creek, near Juneau; employe, Juneau Water Co., mgr., 1910-14; sec., Dem. Terr. Central Com., 1910-12; mayor, Juneau, 1912-13; U.S. Marshal, 1st jud. dist., Juneau, 1914-17, res. due to ill health; moved to farm near Des Moines, Wash.; died there, May 12, 1920. Mem., Elks (exalted ruler). Democrat.

BLAKE, Arthur G., civil engineer. B. in Calif., c. 1867; went to Nome, 1900; bro. H.L. Blake was one of three men who first discovered gold on Anvil Creek; dep. mineral surveyor, mayor, Nome; terr. H.R., 1933-35; died in Nome, Nov. 25, 1935; buried there. Republican.

BLISS, Cornelius Newton, businessman. B. in Fall River, Mass., Jan. 26, 1833; s. Asahel Newton and Irene Borden (Luther) B.; gr. and h. sc. education; m. Elizabeth Mary Plummer, Mar. 30, 1859; dry goods merchandising; N.Y. partner, 1866, in house of J.S. & E. Wright of Boston, operators of larger textile mills; firm later became Bliss & Fabyan, with Bliss at its head until his death; chmn., Rep. state com., N.Y., 1887; treas., Rep. Nat. Com., 1892-1904; Sec. of Interior, 1897-98; pres., Fourth Nat. Bk.; died Oct. 9, 1911. Republican.

BLODGETT, Robert R., mechanic, trader. B. in Preston, Ia., Aug. 2, 1920; s. Mrs. Mildred B., Creston, Ia.; stud., U. Colo., 1 yr., UA, 1 yr.; LaSalle U. extension course in law; U.S. Army Air Corps, 1941-45; employe, Arctic Contractors, Pt. Barrow, and later DEW line, 1946-53; m. Helen M. Simmons in Pt. Barrow, Dec. 28, 1950; s. Richard; purchased gen. store, Teller, 1955; Nome res., 1956-60; ret. to Teller, 1960; state H.R., 1959-64, Sen., 1965-70. Democrat.

BOARDMAN, William K., businessman. B. in Nevada, Ia., Feb. 3, 1915; stud., Grinnell Coll., 3 yrs.; B.A., Drake U.; m. and div.; m. 2d, Florence Pratt; d. Mrs. Nancy Eklund; m. 3d, Genie Chance (Mrs. Winston C.), Sept. 23, 1971; investment banker, Des Moines, Ia., 1935-42; U.S. Coast Guard Acad., New London, Conn., U.S. Coast Guard service, Ketchikan, Aleutian Is., 1943-46; agent, Pan Am. Airlines, Ketchikan, 1946-50, part-time mgr., C. of C., 1948-66; underwriter, Northern Life Insur. Co., 1950-; terr. H.R., 1953-55, state H.R., 1961-71, speaker, 1968-69. Mem., Elks, Masons, Toastmasters, Am. Leg., Moose, Eagles, Rotary, VFW. Methodist, Republican. Address: Ketchikan.

BOGAN, James J., businessman. B. in Leadville, Colo., Feb. 25, 1893; s. James J. and Annabelle (Gallagher) B.; h. sc., Nome; law stud., Hugh J. O'Neill office, Nome; m. Nancy D. Maples in Nome, Oct. 15, 1919; children: James Jr., Robert Allan; U.S. Army, 1917-18; water wholesaler and retailer, Nome; terr. H.R., 1919-21; moved to Seattle, Wash., early 1920s; operator, gas station, employe, Fidelity Electric Co. Democrat.

BONE, Scott Cordelle, journalist. B. in Shelby Co., Ind., Feb. 15, 1860; s. Alfred P. and Louisa (Deacon) B.; grad., Shelbyville h. sc., 1876; m. Mary Worth, June 15, 1887; children: Paul Myers, Roger Morse, Scott Worth, Carroll Alfred, Robert Douglas, Mildred (Mrs. John Ford Starr), Marguerite (Mrs. Alfred B. Wilcox); reporter, Cincinnati COMMERCIAL, Indianapolis JOURNAL, Indianapolis SENTINEL, 1881-88; news ed.-managing ed., Wash. POST, 1888-1905, Chicago TRIBUNE, 1905-06; ed.-owner, Wash. HERALD, 1906-11; ed.-in-chief, Seattle POST-INTELLIGENCER, 1911-18; publicity dir., Rep. Nat. Com., N.Y.C., 1918-21; Gov. of Alaska, 1921-25; ed.-in-chief, AMERICANIZATION MAGAZINE, Atascadero, Calif., 1925-; died in Santa Barbara, Calif., Jan. 27, 1936. Republican.

BONEY, George Frank, lawyer. B. in Savannah, Ga., July 3, 1930; s. Clark Howell and Evelyn (Anerson) B.; 2 bros., 1 sister; grad., Andrew Jackson h. sc., Jacksonville, Fla.; B.A., U. Ga., 1951; LL.B., Harvard U., 1954; m. Sarah Estelle Boozer, Feb. 21, 1955; children: Catherine Lynn, George Frank, Jr., Angela Carol; judge advocate gen. corps, U.S. Air Force, Lackland AFB, Tex., 1954-56, Elmendorf AFB, 1956-58; asst. U.S. atty., Anchorage; partner, Burr, Boney and Pease law firm, Anchorage, 1959-68; appt. assoc. justice of Alaska Supreme Ct., Dec. 2, 1968, appt. chief justice, May 8, 1970; drowned in boating accident on Cheri Lake, north of Palmer, Aug. 30, 1972; buried at China Hill, Telfair Co., Ga. Mem., Mason. Methodist, Republican.

BOOCHEVER, Robert, lawyer. B. in N.Y.C., Oct. 2, 1917; s. Louis Charles and Miriam (Cohen) B.; gr. and h. sc., Ithaca, N.Y.; B.A., 1939, LL.B., 1941, Cornell U.; m. Lois Colleen Maddox in St. Johns, Newfoundland, Apr. 22, 1943; children: Barbara K. (Mrs. Craig Lindh), Linda Lou (Mrs. Steve Tyler), Ann Paula (Mrs. Dick Stenson), Miriam Deon; U.S. Army, 1941-46; asst. U.S. atty., Juneau,

1946-47; partner, Faulkner, Banfield, Boochever & Doogan law firm, Juneau, 1947-72; sworn in as assoc. justice, state supreme ct., Juneau, Mar. 22, 1972; mem., terr. development bd., 1951; dir., 1st Nat. Bk., Juneau, 1955-61. Mem., adv. bd., Nat. Bk. Alaska; Juneau Planning Com., 1956-61; Alaska Bar Assn. (pres., 1962), Rotary (pres., 1966), Am. Judicature Soc., Juneau C. of C. (pres., 1952-55), Explorers. Democrat.

BORER, Richard R., businessman. B. in Forsyth, Mont., Sept. 10, 1926; attended Forsyth h. sc.; m. Patricia Jean Emard (div. 1966); 7 children; U.S. Navy, 1942-46; bk. employe, Minn. and Seattle, Wash., 1946-51; purchased 1st Bk. of Cordova, 1953; estab. R.R. Borer insurance agency; pres., bd. dir., Cordova Community Coll.; state H.R., 1967-71. Catholic, Republican.

BOSWELL, John C., mining engineer. B. in Vale, Ore., 1905; gr. and h. sc., Vale; stud., U. Ore., 2 yrs.; B.A., UA, 1929; children: John, Robert, Marian; employe, U.S. Smelting, Refining & Mining Co., Fairbanks, mgr., for yrs.; del., const. conv., 1955-56.

BOUCHER, Emily, newspaper editor-publisher, civic leader. B. in Nome, 1907; d. Antonio and Mary Polet; grad., U. Wash., 1928; m. Wilfred Amede Boucher, 1932; children: Wilfred (Bill), Mary Jeanne, Rodney; ed.-pub., Nome NUGGET, 1943-63, sold in Sept. 1963; Sun. sc. teacher; organist for community Methodist church; part-time librarian; notary public; N.Y. TIMES correspondent; rep., Dunn and Bradstreet; died in Seattle, Wash. hosp., Nov. 28, 1963.

BOUCHER, Henry Aristide (Red), businessman. B. in Nashua, N.H., Jan. 27, 1921; s. Henry Aristide and Helen Isabel (Cameron) B.; placed in St. Vincent's orphanage, Fall River, Mass. after father's death, 1930; grad., h. sc., 1936; U.S. Navy, 1937-57; m. and div.; 1 daughter; m. 2d, Alfheidur (Heida) Valgardsdottir Blondal, Apr. 1, 1958; children: John Leonard, Johanna, Jamie, Jacqueline, Jennifer; estab. Fairbanks sporting goods store, Pan Alaska Inc., 1958; organizer-mgr., Alaska Goldpanners baseball team; city councilman, Fairbanks, 1961-64; mayor, 1966-70; dist. sales mgr., Alaska Airlines, 1964-67, asst. v.p., 1967; sales mgr., Interior Airways, 1968 (Jan.-July); exec. dir., Fairbanks Industrial Development Corp., 1969; res. as field mgr., Alaska Goldpanners, March 1970; Alaska's first Lt. Gov., 1970-74. Democrat.

BOWMAN, Willard L., labor relations officer. B. in Grand Rapids, Mich.; attended public sc., Toledo, O.; U.S. Navy, 1938-45; stud., Calif. Coll. Fine Arts, San Francisco, 1946-49; m. Maria Graves, 1950; children: Willard, Gregory; moved to Anchorage, 1950; constr. worker, 1950-63; lobbyist for civil rights, 1962-63; exec. dir., State Com. Human Rights, 1963-70; state H.R., 1971-77; labor relations officer, Surfcote, Northwest Co. Received VFW Outstanding Com. Service award, 1969; Alaska Press Club Outstanding Citizen award, 1964. Mem., Anchorage Manpower Development & Training Assn., 1965-69; civilian-military equal employment adv. com., 1964-70; Laborers' Local No. 341, exec. bd., 1950-70; YMCA (v.p., bd. dir.). Democrat. Address: 1112 E. 69th Ave., Anchorage 99502.

BOYCE, John J., lawyer. Atty., Nome, 1900; ret. to Calif.; elected state Sen. from Berkeley; U.S. dist. atty., 1st jud. dist., Juneau, 1903-10; ret. to Calif.; associated with U. Calif., Berkeley. Republican.

BOYER, David Newton, rancher, hotel-motel owner-operator. B. in Nashville, Tenn., Feb. 22, 1915; s. David Washington and Daisy Ann (Williams) B.; attended gr. and h. sc., Cairo, Ill.; stud., various colleges; studied law in Alaska under clerkship provision; m. Katherine, 1948; children: Lancet Ann and s.; m. 2d, Maxine Veronica Wheeler, 1959 (div. 1960); m. 3d, Louise Gantt Kienel, 1962 (div. 1965); m. 4th, Maibeth Woodward Thompson, 1968; joined Ill. Nat. Guard, 1934; U.S. Army Reserves until 1961; honorably discharged as lt. col.; moved to Alaska, Nov. 1952; teacher, Koyukuk, Kenai, homesteaded at Anchor Point; built and operated Colony Inn, Ninilchik; mgr., Harbor View hotel-motel, Kenai; cand., terr. H.R., 1956, state H.R., 1958, State Sen., 1959, U.S. Cong., 1960, Gov., 1962, U.S. Sen., 1966. Mem., Ill. Nat. Guard Assn., 1938-48; Am. Leg., Elks, Eagles. Methodist, Democrat. Address: Box 86, Anchor Point.

BOYKO, Edgar Paul, lawyer. B. in Vienna, Austria, Oct. 19, 1918; s. Dr. Myron David and Florence B.; stud., U. Vienna, 1936-38; B.S., U. St. Andrews, Scotland, 1940; J.D., U. Md., 1945; LL.M., George Wash. U., 1948; m. Blanche Kahn, April 10, 1940 (div.); 2 children; m. 2d, Georgie Lee Turner, Nov. 28, 1969; BLM, Wash., D.C., 1945-47; pvt. law prac., Wash., D.C., 1947-52; reg. chief counsel, BLM, Anchorage, 1952-53; corp. counsel, Chugach Electric Assn., 1954-57; pvt. law prac., Los Angeles, Calif., 1957-67; atty. gen., Juneau, 1967-68; pvt. law prac., Anchorage, 1968-. Mem., Rotary, bd. dir., Alaska Acad. Trial Lawyers; Anchorage Unitarian-Universalist Fellowship (charter). Democrat.

BOYLE, Frank A., lawyer. B. in Mt. Pleasant, Pa., June 1, 1877; s. John D. and Nora (Brannan) B.; LL.B., Georgetown U., 1909; m. Jane Morris, Jan. 3, 1933; slate picker, 1888; asst. locomotive engr., 1891; teacher, 1897-98; quartz miner, 1899-1902; placer miner, 1903-04; clerk, U.S. Land Office, Wash., D.C., 1909-11; registrar, U.S. Land Office, Juneau, Anchorage, 1912-24; U.S. Comr., 1926-29; pvt. law prac., Juneau, 1924-32; cand., del. to Cong., 1924; terr. H.R., 1931-32; terr. auditor, 1932-50; died in his home, Juneau, Dec. 15, 1950. Catholic, Democrat.

BOYLE, Dr. Frank M., physician. B. in N.Y.C.; s. Col. Arthur R. B.; pub. sc.; grad., Medico-chirurgical Coll., Phila., Pa.; post-grad., N.Y. Polyclinic Coll.; m. Mary Stevens (div.); fought in Spanish-Am. war, 1897-98; joined gold stampede to Dyea and Skagway, 1898-1901; city councilman and mayor, 1910, Valdez; medical prac. and operated drug stores, Valdez, Seward, Katalla, Cordova; Valdez postmaster, 1904-08; terr. H.R.,

1913-15; operated drug store and medical prac., Anchorage, 1917-20; city councilman and pres., C. of C., Anchorage; special surgical work, San Francisco hosp., 1 yr.; died in Seattle, Wash., Nov. 6, 1922.

BRADNER, Mike, journalist. B. in Wash., D.C., 1937; B.A., UA, 1964; m. Janet; children: Michelle, Bonnie, Heather, Heide; Yukon River towboat pilot and mate, Yutana Barge Lines, Nenana, 1957-62; reporter, Fairbanks DAILY NEWS-MINER, 1962-65; ed., JESSEN'S DAILY, Fairbanks, 1967-68; operated Alaska Information and Research Services, and pub., Alaska Economy Report and Alaska Series, 1968-; state H.R., 1967-77, minority leader, 1973-75, speaker, 1975. Democrat. Address: Box 2183, Fairbanks.

BRADSHAW, Howard C., merchant. B. in Newark, N.J., Nov. 7, 1908; m. Edith; children: William, Maureen; U.S. Navy, Sitka, 1936; after discharge, commercial fisherman in Sitka; owned men's clothing store; city councilman, bd. of public utilities, 5 yrs.; chmn., hosp. bd., 5 yrs.; state Sen., 1959-71, res., 1971; dir., Sitka Pioneers' Home, 1971-. Mem., Elks, Moose, Pioneers, Sitka Alaska Native Brotherhood (hon.). Democrat. Address: Box 56, Sitka.

BRADY, Carl Franklin, businessman. B. in Chelsea, Okla., Oct. 29, 1919; s. Kenneth A. and Pauline B.; h. sc., Springdale, Ark.; stud., U. Wash., 1 yr.; m. Carol E. Sprague, 1941; children: Carl Jr., Linda, James; U.S. Army Air Corps, 1942-46; estab. commercial helicopter service, Yakima, Wash., 1946-48; employe, USGS, Alaska, 1948; estab. ERA Helicopters of Alaska, Inc., Anchorage, 1956; moved family to Anchorage, 1959; state H.R., 1965-66; state Sen., 1967-68; sold ERA Helicopters, Inc. to Rowan Drilling Co., Houston, Tex., remaining pres. of ERA Helicopter, Inc., 1967; corporate v.p., Rowan Companies, Inc., and pres., ERA Aviation Caribe, Inc., 1973; hon. consul for Belgium, 1974. Mem., Nat. Helicopter Assn. (past pres.), Anchorage C. of C. (past pres.), Alaska Crippled Children's Assn. (past pres.), Petroleum Club (past pres.), Rotary, Am. Leg., Elks, Alaska Mutual Savings Bk. (trustee), Alaska Bk. of North, Anchorage Natural Gas Co. (dir.), Alaska Pipeline Corp. Methodist, Republican. Address: 2727 Iliamna Ave., Anchorage.

BRADY, John Green, clergyman, lawyer, businessman. B. in N.Y.C., May 26, 1847; B.A., Yale U., 1874; D.D., Union Theological Seminary, 1877; ordained Presbyterian minister, 1878; m. Elizabeth Jane Patton in Sitka, 1887 (dec. 1951); children: John Green, Jr., Hugh P., Sheldon Jackson, Mary Anna (Mrs. Beattie), Elizabeth P.; missionary, Sitka, 1878-79; operator-owner, sawmill, trading post, steamship co., fur trade, Sitka, 1879-; admitted to Alaska bar, 1885; U.S. Comr., Sitka, 1885-88; Gov. of Alaska, 1897-1906; dir., treas., Reynolds-Alaska Development Co., Boston, Valdez, N.Y.C., Sitka, 1904-07; ret. to Sitka after Reynolds Co. bankruptcy, 1907-10; export-import bus. with China, N.Y.C., 1910-14; estab. vocational school, Canton, China, 1914-16; ret. to Sitka with wife and daughter, Mary, who taught in govt. sc., 1916; died in Sitka, Dec. 17, 1918; buried in nat. cemetery, Sitka.

BRADY, Kenneth L., general contractor. B. in Chelsea, Okla., Aug. 15, 1921; s. Kenneth A. and Pauline B.; grad., Okla. State Coll.; U.S. Marine Corps, 1942-46; m. Dorothy; 7 children; carpenter, Anchorage, 1947; founded own bus. and brought family to Anchorage, 1951; estab. Ken Brady Constr. Co., Inc., 1955; state H.R., 1967-68. Mem., reg. adv. council, SBA, 1970-; state jud. council, 1969-; Alaska Mutual Savings Bk. (trustee), Petroleum Club (dir.). Republican. Address: 2727 McCollie Ave., Anchorage.

BRAGAW, Robert S., businessman. B. in Rathdrum, Ia., May 2, 1889; public sc., Spokane, Wash.; stud., U. Ida.; m. Evelyn Johnson in Spokane, Wash., 1912 (dec.); m. 2d, Mrs. Myrtle (Edwin L.) Everett; moved to Anchorage, 1918; estab. photography bus. and gift shop; ranger, Mt. McKinley Park, 6 mos., 1923; terr. Sen., 1931-35; city clerk, treas., Anchorage, 1935-44; moved to Sumner, Wash., 1944; real estate bus., Whidbey I.; died at Oak Harbor, Wash., Feb. 10, 1969; entombment in Masonic Ct. Garden mausoleum, Whidby I. Mem., Anchorage C. of C. (perpetual sec., pres., 1927, 1932), Rotary (1st pres.), Anchorage Power & Light Co. (asst. mgr., sec.), Alaska Guides (organizer-pres.), Masons, K.T., Eastern Star, Shrine, All-Alaska C. of C. (pres., 1941), unemployment compensation com., 1937-41. Republican.

BRAMSTEDT, Alvin Oscar, businessman. B. in Cosmopolis, Wash., May 9, 1917; s. Oscar and Ruth B.; grad., Grays Harbor Jr. Coll.; stud., U. Wash., 3-1/2 yrs.; m. Rosa Lea Bailey, July 16, 1940; children: Susan (Mrs. Robert Mellin), Janet (Mrs. Ivan W. Felton, Jr.), Alvin O., Jr., Shelley; radio announcer, Aberdeen, Wash.; announcer, KFAR station, Fairbanks, 1940, mgr., 1944; moved to KENI station, Anchorage, gen. mgr. and sec.-treas. of network, 1955; bought state-wide network, Midnight Sun Broadcasting Co., 1960, including: 2 radio-television stations (Fairbanks and Anchorage), KINY radio-television station (Juneau), KTKN radio-television station (Ketchikan), all affiliated with NBC and ABC nat. networks; key booster in Walter J. Hickel's gubernatorial campaign, 1966; state chmn., United Citizens for Nixon, 1968; chmn., Keith Miller's gubernatorial campaign. Elected to Alaska Press Club 49er Hall of Fame, 1968; Outstanding Alaskan of the Year by Alaska State C. of C., 1968; awarded Gold Pan by Anchorage C. of C., 1971, for distinguished community service. Mem., Alaska-Nippon Kai (chmn.), Lions (pres.), Fairbanks sc. bd., 1949-55, Alaska Japan Trade Mission (chmn., 1969), Alaska Bus. Council (chmn.). Methodist, Republican. Address: Lathrop Bldgs., 4th Ave., Anchorage 99501.

BRAYTON, Lawrence M. (Larry), newsman, photographer. B. in Fort Wayne, Ind., Oct. 12, 1927; s. Lawrence M. and Maxine B.; gr. and h. sc., Ft. Wayne; m. Rosita Shifman in Moscow, U.S.S.R., Dec. 17, 1963 (div. 1968); U.S. Navy, WWII; went to Alaska, 1945; fisherman, longshoreman, constr.

worker; bus. mgr., Am. Fed. of Technical Engrs., Fairbanks, 1960; newsman with radio, television and newspapers, Fairbanks, 1961-66; cand., U.S. Sen., 1960, 1966; pub., daily morning NEWS BULLETIN, Fairbanks, 1965-66; exec. dir., Alaska State Community Action Program, 1967-69; producer, Alaska films, 1971-. Mem., Americans for Democratic Action in Alaska (founder), Fellowship of Reconciliation & Cong. on Racial Equality; Internat. Printing Pressman (former organizer). Unitarian, Republican. Address: Anchorage.

BRENNEMAN, Franklin Russell, U.S. Marshal, miner. B. in Columbia City, Ind., Mar. 21, 1876; m. Helen Peterson, June 14, 1908; children: Elinor M., Dorothy, Bernice; mem., 160th Ind. Volunteers, Spanish-Am. war, 1896-98; joined gold stampede to Nome, 1900; prospector-miner, Kodiak I.; dep. marshal, Kodiak, 1901-06, Katalla, 1906-13; U.S. Marshal, 3d jud. dist., Valdez, 1913-22; moved to Long Beach, Calif.; real estate bus. and dep. sheriff, Long Beach, 1922-42; died there, Nov. 13, 1942. Mem., Masons. Democrat.

BREUER, Leo W., educator. Sc. teacher, 1919-; supt. sc., Nome, 1926-28, Cordova, 1928-29; terr. comr. education, 1929-30. Republican.

BREWER, Max Clifton, geologist, geophysicist. B. in Blackfalds, Alta., Can., 1924; B.S., Wash. U., St. Louis; grad. stud., U. Calif., Wash. U.; hon. D.Sc., UA, 1965; m. Marylou; children: William, Linda, Karen, Paula, John; U.S. Army Air Force, 1942-44; employe, USGS, conducting permafrost studies, Fairbanks area, 1948; chief, Arctic Ice and Permafrost Project, USGS, Pt. Barrow, Sept. 1950-; dir., Arctic Research Laboratory, operated by UA for Office of Naval Research, 1956; responsible for U.S. occupied Arctic ice station, Arlis II; head of state dept. of environmental conservation, 1971-74. Received Sweeney medal, Explorers Club, 1971; U.S. Navy Distinguished Public Service Award. Mem., Tau Beta Pi (engr. hon.), Sigma Xi, AAAS, Am. Geophysical Union, British Glaciological Soc., Arctic Inst. North America (fellow).

BRITT, William E., pharmacist. B. in Norway, Sept. 12, 1868; B.S., U. Christiana; m. Sophia Lind, 1904; s. Jacob William; emigrated to U.S., 1893; settled in Chicago as pharmacist; joined Klondike gold stampede, 1898; estab. drug store, Skagway; mem., sc. bd., city council, sc. treas., city magistrate, Skagway; moved to Juneau, 1913, estab. pharmacy; city councilman, 1914; pres., terr. bd. of pharmacy, 1913-17; terr. hist. library and museum com., 1930-32; terr. H.R., 1915-17, Sen., 1919-23; Norwegian vice consul for southern Alaska, 1914-32, knighted by King of Norway; killed in automobile accident, Juneau, Apr. 29, 1932. Mem., Masons, Elks. Democrat.

BRONSON, Lester, businessman. B. in Vallejo, Calif., Dec. 23, 1905; served in U.S. Coast Guard; went to Nome, 1929; m. Rose Gray, 1932; children: Dean, Tess (Mrs. Tex Sparks); estab. water delivery service, gen. contractor firm, Pilgrim Hot Springs hotel; terr. H.R., 1955, state H.R., 1969-70, state Sen., 1959-64; chmn., legislative council; organized

Civil Air Patrol and rose to lt. col.; dir., civil defense for Nome area, 20 yrs.; city councilman, 8 yrs.; chmn., northwestern dist., Dem. com. and mem., state central com., several yrs.; died in his home, Nome, Jan. 24, 1972. Democrat.

BROOKS, James W., biologist. B. in Erie, Pa., Aug. 6, 1922; B.S., 1953, M.A., 1954, UA; unm.; left Mich. for Alaska, 1940; commercial fisherman, commercial pilot, heavy equipment operator; joined dept. of fisheries, 1954, first assigned to marine mammal investigation, later in charge of div. predator investigation and control; head of div. fur and game, dept. fish and game, 1957-59; dir., div. of game, dept. fish and game, 1959-67; U.S. Fish & Wildlife Service, 1967-72; comr., dept. of fish and game, Aug. 1, 1972-. Mem., Boone & Crocket Club, N.Y.C.

BROOKS, John M. (Jack), miner. B. in Mich., 1874; drifted to mining camps in West; went to Juneau, 1897, later to Dawson; city councilman, Juneau, 2 terms; joined stampede to Tanana; wood and ice bus., 1904-10; gold prospector, Fortymile country; Socialist cand., del. to Cong., from Jack Wade, 1914. Mem., Western Fed. of Miners.

BROSIUS, Cal M., miner. B. in Alliance, O., Jan. 4, 1870; joined gold stampede to Fortymile, 1894; miner, Dawson, Nome, Valdez; lived in Whitehorse, Y.T., Can.; moved to Seward, 1904, estab. lumber bus.; terr. H.R., 1931; m. Mrs. Helen Dennis in Seattle, Wash., May 1938; died in accident at his lumber mill, Oct. 8, 1942. Mem., Masons, A.B., Odd Fellows, Pioneers (Grand Pres., 1930). Republican.

BROWN, Charles Wesley, Jr., miner, accountant. B. in Lewiston, Mont., Aug. 28, 1893; s. Charles W. B.; Nome public sc.; m.; s. Charles W.; Nome res., 1901-25; estab. home in Seattle, Wash., going north for summers; U.S. Navy, 1917-18; terr. H.R., 1921-23, Sen., 1923-29; rep., Mass. Mortgage Co., Seattle. Mem., terr. bd. education, 1926-; Odd Fellows, Moose, Elks. Independent.

BROWN, Frederick Merrill, judge. B. in Brooklyn, N.Y., May 7, 1864; stud., Brooklyn Polytechnic U.; law stud., Dak. Terr.; m.; children: Richard Field, Harry R., Helen (Mrs. Rathbun), Estelle (Mrs. Totten), Mildred (Mrs. Warren); m. 2d, Mrs. Mayme Murman Wheat (formerly of Valdez), Oakland, Calif., Feb. 3, 1927; step-s., Horace Wheat; pvt. law prac., Deadwood, S. Dak.; city atty., Rapid City, S. Dak.; pvt. law prac., Valdez, 1901-13; mayor, Valdez; U.S. dist. judge, 3d jud. div., Valdez, 1913-21; moved to Oakland, Calif., 1921, pvt. law prac. until 1926; died in Oakland, 1946. Mem., Masons, Eagles, Moose, Pioneers (hon.). Democrat.

BROWN, Harold D., lawyer. State dist. atty., 1st jud. dist., Ketchikan, 1971-73. Democrat.

BROWN, Lyle K., government administrator, aviator. B. in Pearl, Ill., 1918; m. Dorothy; children: Rex, Linda; U.S. Army Air Corps, fighter pilot and flight instructor, 1943-46; airways operator special-

ist, FAA, Cincinnati, O., traffic control center, 1946-57; chief of operations, FAA, Indianapolis, Ind., 1957-61, Kan. City, Kan., 1961-65; mgr., FAA, Minneapolis, Minn., 1965-67; reg. adm., FAA, Anchorage, 1967-70, 1973-; in charge of Great Lakes area, FAA, Chicago, Ill., 1970-73. Pres., Anchorage Fed. Exec. Assn., 1969-70, 1974-75. Methodist.

BROWN, Melville Cox, judge. B. Kennebec Co., Me., Aug. 16, 1838; s. Enoch and Sarah (Reed) B.; stud., Hallowell (Me.) Acad., Colby Coll., 1 yr.; law stud., Boise, Ida.; m. Miss Filmore in Laramie, Wyo., May 20, 1874; children: Adelaide (Coburn), Melville E. (dec. childhood), Ethel (Mearns), Susan Helen; mining and merchandising near Marysville, Calif., 1856; moved to Ida. terr., 1862; mem., Ida. legislature, 1864; asst. assessor, 1864; assessor of internal revenue, Ida., 1867; moved to Cheyenne, Wyo.; first mayor, Laramie, Wyo.; passed bar and estab. pvt. law prac.; pres., Wyo. const. conv., 1890; appt. dist. judge for Alaska, April 1900; appt. to 1st jud. div., June 6, 1900, res., 1904; moved to Seattle, Wash.; senior mem., Brown, Leahy & Kane law firm, Seattle, until 1908; pvt. law prac., Laramie; died April 9, 1928. Presbyterian, Republican.

BROWN, Norman Cole, journalist. B. in Brooklyn, N.Y., Oct. 4, 1901; s. Clarence S. and Susan H. (Cole) B.; grad., h. sc., Snohomish, Wash.; stud., sc. of journalism, U. Wash., 3 yrs.; m. Blanche Sutherland in Valdez, May 28, 1930; children: Susan Elizabeth (Mrs. Rene Jacques Cappon), Norman Cole, Jr.; ed., Langley (Wash.) IS-LANDER, 1925; went to Valdez, 1929; city ed., Cordova DAILY TIMES, 1932-37; managing ed., Anchorage DAILY TIMES, 1937-45; organized Northern Pub. Co., pub. of Anchorage DAILY NEWS, Jan. 1, 1946; sold the NEWS, Sept. 6, 1967; moved to Sun City, Ariz., 1972. Mem., Rotary, Elks, Lambda Chi Alpha. Republican.

BROWNELL, Don Carlos, businessman. B. in San Francisco, Calif., Mar. 17, 1882; s. A.M.J. Brownell; public sc., San Francisco; went to Skagway with parents; operated hardware store, Valdez, 1902; moved to Seward with parents, 1903; m. Alice Murphy, Sept. 29, 1927; owner-mgr., movie theatre, Seward, 1926-50s; mgr., Seward Light & Power plant; mayor, Seward, 9 consecutive terms, 1930-39; terr. Sen., 1941, 1945-49; died in Seward, July 2, 1952. Mem., Taxpayer's Assn. (pres.). Methodist, Democrat.

BROWNING, Dr. Levi M., physician. B. in Benton, Ill., Sept. 3, 1904; public sc., Benton; M.D., U. Ill., 1929; m. Sally; no children; pvt. prac., Milwaukee, Wis., 1931-36; joined U.S. Army, 1936; grad., flight surgeon's school, 1940; served at Ladd Field, Fairbanks, 1949-50; hosp. comdr., Elmendorf AFB, 1951-52; ret. to Elmendorf, 1959, after duty tours in Md. and Colo.; hosp. head, Elmendorf, 1959-62, ret.; state comr. health and social services, 1963-67; pvt. prac., Anchorage, with home in Matanuska Valley, also coordinator, Wash-Alaska reg. med. programs, 1967-68; died at Lackland AFB, San Antonio, Tex., July 30, 1968. Awarded Anchorage C. of C. Gold Pan posthumously for originating Alaska Cobalt

Center for cancer treatment, Providence hosp., Anchorage. Mem., A.M.A., Military surgeons, Explorers', Masons, Elks.

BRUBAKER, John K., lawyer. B. in 1938; J.D., U. Va.; asst. atty. gen., Juneau, 1963-65; dist. atty., Anchorage, 1965-66; pvt. law prac., Anchorage, 1966-. Address: 360 K St., Anchorage.

BRUCE, Miner W., lawyer. Rep. Nat. Committeeman, Juneau conv., 1889; unofficial del. in Cong., 1889-90; pvt. law prac., Skagway, 1897-99, Nome, 1900-. Mem., A.B. (Nome). Author, "Alaska," N.Y., 1899. Republican.

BRUNELLE, Maurice E.S., office clerk. B. in Red Lake Falls, Minn., Sept. 9, 1895; s. George and Eugenie (Marchand) B.; stud., Coll. of St. Thomas, St. Paul, Minn., 1915-17; m. Matilda K. Kolbenson, Nov. 27, 1923; children: Patrick E., Gretchen Maureen, Linda Jane; commissary clerk, Alaska Gastineau Gold Mining Co., Perseverance mine, Juneau, 1917-18; U.S. Army, 1918-19; timekeeper, Kennecott Copper Corp., Kennecott, 1912-22; chief clerk and dispatcher, Copper River & Northwestern Ry., Cordova, 1922-37; terr. Sen., 1935-39; employe, Northern Commercial Co., Fairbanks, 1937-38; clerk, U.S. dist. ct., 3d jud. div., Valdez and Anchorage, 1938-53. Mem., terr. C. of C. (pres., 1935-37), Elks (past exalted ruler, Cordova), dist. dep. of Grand Lodge, western Alaska, 1932-33. Democrat.

BRUNER, Elwood, lawyer. B. in Zanesville, O., Sept. 27, 1854; s. Rev. Joseph A. and Margaret (Morris) B.; B.A., U. Pacific, Santa Clara, Calif.; moved to San Francisco with parents, 1856; dist. atty., Sacramento Co.; pvt. law prac., Sacramento, Calif.; m.; 4 daughters; Calif. state assemblyman, 1880s-1890s; joined bro. Alvin J. in law prac., Nome, 1904; 3d bro., J. Allison, later joined law firm; terr. Sen., 1913-15; died in Byron Hot Springs, Calif., Jan. 15, 1915. Republican.

BUCKALEW, Seaborn Jesse, Jr., lawyer. B. in Dallas, Tex., Dec. 6, 1920; s. Seaborn J. and Lorene B.; B.A., Tex. A. & M. Coll., 1942; J.D., John B. Stetson U., 1949; m. Marcy Hudel, 1947; children: Seaborn J., III, Robert John; U.S. Army, 1942-46, Army reserves, 1946-51, U.S. Air Force, 1951-52; moved to Anchorage, 1950; dist. atty., later U.S. atty., Anchorage, 1952-53; pvt. law prac., Anchorage, 1953-71; terr. H.R., 1955-57, 1957-59; del., const. conv., 1955-56; state Sen., 1960; asst. adjt. gen., Air Nat. Guard, 1965-67, 1971-73; U.S. dist. atty., 3d jud. dist., 1971-73; appt. superior ct. judge, 3d jud. dist., Anchorage, July 9, 1973. Mem., com. on jud. qualifications (chmn., 1971), Am. Leg. Episcopalian, Democrat. Address: 3124 Antioch Circle, Anchorage.

BUGBEE, John S., lawyer. B. in Sackville, N.B., Can., 1840; s. Sumner C.B.; grad., Harvard U., 1862; m. Anna Maxwell (dec. 1895); 3 sons, d. Bessie; atty., San Francisco, Calif., 1862-89; asst. city and co. atty., 1885-87; interested in brewing bus., 2 yrs.; U.S. dist. judge, Alaska, 1889-92; pvt. law prac., Juneau, 1892-96; wrote extensively for nat. publications; connected with *Overland Monthly;* artist in water color and crayon; died in Juneau, May 16, 1896. Republican.

BULLOCK, Donald M., radio-television announcer. B. in Seattle, Wash.; gr. and h. sc., Cleveland, O., Grand Rapids, Mich.; grad., U. Ida.; m.; 3 children; U.S. Navy, WWII; circulation mgr., DAILY IDAHONIAN, Moscow, Ida.; ed., Oak Harbor (Wash.) NEWS, Grays Harbor WASHINGTONIAN, Hoquiam, Wash.; news dir., KBKW radio station, Aberdeen, Wash.; mgr., Grays Harbor Gold & Country Club, Aberdeen, 1953-55; news dir., KFAR radio and television stations, Fairbanks, 1955-; appt. adm. asst. to Gov. Stepovich, July 22, 1957; studied for ministry; Rector, St. John's and St. Elizabeth's Episcopal Churches, Ketchikan, 1974. Episcopalian.

BULLOCK, Edith R., businesswoman. B. in Red Lodge, Mont., April 4 (no year given); stud., U. Wash., 1 yr.; m. and div.; m. 2d, John L. Bullock, Dec. 12, 1940 (div. 1966); went to Nome, 1939; bookkeeper, secretary, bank teller, Nome; freighter and miner, Teller and Kougarok, 1945-48; moved to Kotzebue, and operated mailboat; estab. B & R Tug and Barge service, freighting and lighterage, 1951; obtained Standard Oil distributorship; merged B & R Tug and Barge with Pacific Inland Navigation Co., Inc., Seattle, 1969, of which she is a dir.; terr. H.R., 1953-57, Sen., 1957-58; moved to Anchorage, 1969. Received state C. of C. "Outstanding Alaskan" award, 1967. Mem., Surgeon Gen.'s Adv. Com. Indian Health, Adv. Com., BLM, 1964; bd. regents, UA, 1967-75; bd. dir., state C. of C., 1968. Republican. Address: 221 E. 7th Ave., Anchorage 99501.

BUNNELL, Charles Ernest, lawyer. B. in Dimock, Pa., Jan. 12, 1878; s. Lyman Walton and Ruth Naomi (Tingley) B.; B.A., 1900, M.A., 1902, LL.D., 1925, Bucknell U.; m. Mary Ann Kline at Winfield, Pa., July 24, 1901; d. Jean; teacher, Wood I., Alaska, 1900-01, Kodiak, 1901-03, Valdez, 1903-07; admitted to Alaska bar, Nov. 21, 1908, at Valdez; pvt. law prac., Valdez, 1908-15; cand., del. in Cong., 1914; U.S. dist. judge, 4th jud. div., Fairbanks, 1915-21; pres., Alaska Agricultural Coll. & Sc. Mines (UA), 1921-49; pres. emeritus, UA, 1949-56; died in Burlingame, Calif., Nov. 1, 1956. Mem., Pioneers, A.B., Masons, Elks. Episcopalian. Democrat.

BUNESS, Everett W., businessman. B. in 1924; m. Hattie; U.S. Army, 1941-48; part-time stud., Wash. State Coll., Stanford U.; B.A., U. Wash., 1951; pres., C. of C., city councilman, planning com. and hosp. bd. mem., Wrangell, 1951-67; dep. comr. of economic development, 1967-70, comr., 1970-71; dir., U.S. Dept. of Commerce, bus. service field office, Anchorage, Aug. 1972.

BURDICK, Charles G., forester. B. in Glendive, Mont., Feb. 11, 1894; s. Gilbert N. and Mary (Rock) B.; stud., U. Mont.; m. Martha Marie Buhrer, July 14, 1926; entered USFS, Beaverhead Nat. Forest, Mont., 1923; transferred to Alaska, 1926; asst. reg. forester, USFS, 1946, ret.; estab. investment service bus., Juneau, 1956; cand., U.S.

Cong., Alaska-Tenn. Plan, 1956; moved to Mont., 1960; died there, Feb. 8, 1965. Mem., Am. Leg., Elks, Terr. Sportsmen, Inc., Boy Scouts of Am., Rep. central com. of Alaska (sec.). Republican.

BURGESS, Lloyd Albert, civil engineer. B. in Culver, Ore., Oct. 4, 1917; B.S., Ore. State Coll., 1939; m. Dorothy, 1940; s. Jason; m. 2d, Wanda Marie Gregory; children: Elizabeth Ann, Gregory Scott, Jeffrey Lloyd; lt. comdr., USN, civil engr. corps, 1942-46; Burgess Constr. Co. hdqrs. moved from Astoria, Ore. to Fairbanks, 1951, to Phoenix, Ariz., 1972, to Anchorage, 1974. Mem., Rep. Nat. Com., 1964-69. Republican.

BURGH, Sydney Henry, proprietor. B. in Detroit, Mich., Jan. 1, 1870; m. Margaret Curran, Nome; children: Ernest E., Margaret (Ballard), Henrietta (Safoulis); spent youth in Mont.; went to Dawson, Can., with first gold rush; moved to Nome during gold rush; prop., Nevada Bar; city councilman, mayor, Nome; terr. H.R., 1929-31; died in Nome, May 18, 1936. Mem., Nome Brass Band, 1900-36. Republican.

BURKE, Edmond Wayne, judge. B. in Ukiah, Calif., Sept. 7, 1935; s. Judge and Mrs. Wayne P. Burke; B.A., M.A., Humboldt State Coll., Arcata, Calif., 1953-58; J.D., Hastings Coll. of Law, Calif., 1964; m. and div.; d. Kathleen Rose; m. 2d, Mrs. Gene A. (June) Hock, Anchorage, Jan. 21, 1970; science teacher, jr. h. sc., Sonoma, Calif., 1958-61; pvt. law prac., Red Bluff and Santa Rosa, Calif., 1964-67; asst. atty. gen., Juneau, 1967-68; Anchorage, 1968-70; superior ct. judge, Anchorage and Kodiak, 1970-75; assoc. justice, state supreme ct., 1975. Mem., state com. on jud. qualifications, 1973-. Presbyterian, Republican. Address: Box 1367, Kodiak 99615 and 941 4th Ave., Anchorage 99501.

BURNS, William T., miner. B. in Carthage, Mo., July 16, 1876; public sc., Portland, Ore.; m. Blanche L. Miller of Bellingham, Wash., Jan. 31, 1910; children: William T., Jr., Frank, Robert; miner, Nizina dist., Dawson, Fairbanks dist., Little Eldorado Cr., 1904-21; terr. H.R., 1913-19; chmn., Dem. terr. com., 1916-21; died in Fairbanks, Feb. 24, 1921. Mem., Fairbanks Miners' Union, bd. dir., 1st Nat. Bk., Fairbanks. Catholic, Democrat.

BURR, Donald A., lawyer. B. in Gurley, Neb., 1923; stud., U. Neb.; J.D., Creighton U., 1952; m. Joy; U.S. Army Air Corps, 1945-47, 1951-53; judge advocate's office, Alaska Air Command, Elmendorf AFB, 1953-56; asst. U.S. atty., Anchorage, 1956-58; pvt. law prac., Anchorage, 1958-66; atty. gen., 1966-67; pvt. law prac., Anchorage, 1967-. Mem., bd. dir., Alaska Title Guaranty Co. Catholic, Republican.

BURROUGHS, Edward W., railroad executive. B. in Chagrin Falls, O., Oct. 11, 1849; engaged in railroading, 25 yrs.; went to Nome, 1898; prospector, Kotzebue Sound reg.; settled in Nome; mgr., Seward Peninsula R.R., asst. bank cashier, asst.

postmaster, Nome; terr. H.R., 1920; died in Seattle, Wash., Mar. 2, 1921, 5 days before legislature convened. Mem., A.B., Masons, Shrine. Democrat.

BUTCHER, Harold J., lawyer. B. in Ogden, Ut., May 17, 1906; grad., Southeastern U., Wash., D.C., 1936; m.; children: 1 s. and d. Paula (Mrs. Howard Bliss); purchasing and contracting dir., BPR, during constr. of Alaska highway; moved to Anchorage, serving as OPA dir.; pvt. law prac., 1945-, Anchorage, superior ct. judge, 3d jud. div., family ct., Anchorage, July, 1967-. Mem., bd. gov., Alaska bar assn., 1957-60; state jud. council, 1962-65. Mormon, Democrat. Address: 1073 W. 23d, Anchorage.

BUTROVICH, John, businessman. B. Fairbanks Creek, Alaska, Mar. 22, 1910; s. John and Zada B.; grad., Fairbanks h. sc., 1929; stud., Wash. State Coll., UA, each six mos.; m. Grace Marguerite Meggitt, May 16, 1936; d. Jane (Mrs. Robert Almquist); area salesman, Standard Oil Co. of Calif., 1930-36; estab. Alaska Insur., Inc., Dec. 8, 1936; city councilman, Fairbanks, 1940-42; utilities bd. mem., 3 yrs.; terr. Sen., 1945-57; cand., terr. Gov., 1958; state Sen., 1963-79, pres., 1967-68. Mem., Elks, Pioneers. Republican. Address: 1029 5th Ave., Fairbanks.

BYER, George Henry, mail carrier. B. in Artesian, S. Dak., June 22, 1912; h. sc., Sherrial, N.Y., 1930; m. Mrs. Helen Jane Baker in Anchorage, Sept. 1963; U.S. Army, 1942-46; went to Alaska, 1947; laborer in bush and longshoreman in Anchorage; mail carrier, Anchorage, 1951-59; first full-time Anchorage mayor, 1959-61; cand., state Gov., 1962; city councilman, 1963-66; mem., borough assembly, 1964-66; cand., state Sen., 1964; acting postmaster, Anchorage, Nov. 1966-Apr. 1967; almost singlehandedly initiated and directed movement for All-American City status for Anchorage, 1956, 1965; introduced original soft drink, Ah-Ha, 1967; left Alaska, July 1968; ranger, NPS, Sheridan, Wyo., 1970; res., Monterey Park, Calif., 1973-. Awards: Man of the Hour, Anchorage C. of C., 1956; Man of the Year, VFW, 1957; postmaster emeritus award, Anchorage post office employees 1967. Mem., Fed. Govt. Employees Council (past pres.), Anch. C. of C. (hon. lifetime), Elks. Protestant, Democrat.

BYINGTON, Glen, acting U.S. Marshal, 1st jud. div., Nome, Feb. 1953-Mar. 1954. Republican.

C

CAIN, Augustine Benedict, newspaper editor. B. in Cain City, Kan., Mar. 3, 1884; s. Roger M. and Catherine (Corrigan) C.; stud., Wesleyan Coll., Kan.; m. Mrs. Alice Lowe, Seattle, Wash., 1947; step-sons, William A. and Albert D. Lowe; stenographer, clerk, news reporter, Portland, Ore., 1906-30; sales rep., EXTENSION MAGAZINE (Catholic), Alaska, 1930-32; ed., THE ALASKA CATHOLIC, Juneau, 1936-46; clerk and sgt.-at-arms, terr. H.R., 1937-39-43-44; terr. H.R., 1945-46; moved to Seattle, Wash., 1946; toured country with Alaska movies to illustrate lectures; died in Seattle, Apr. 8, 1963.

CALE, Thomas, law enforcement officer, farmer, miner. B. in Underhill, Vt., Sept. 17, 1848; s. Patrick and Catherine (Shanley) C.; attended dist. sc. and Bell Acad., Underhill Flat, Vt.; m. Maggie Rooney, Fond du Lac, Wis., 1872; 7 children; moved to Ft. Edward, Wash. Co., N.Y., 1866; sc. teacher, near Underhill Center, Vt., 1867-68, Fond du Lac Co., 1869-; farmer near Eden, Wis.; town clerk, Eden, 1881-84; mem., bd. of co. comrs., 1884-86; co. under-sheriff, 1886-88; co. sheriff, 1888-90; farm machinery salesman, then Pinkerton detective, traveling extensively throughout Midwest and far western states; went to Y.T., 1896, to Dawson, 1898; prospector-miner, Fairbanks dist., 1904-07; elected Alaska's del. in Cong., 1906, for long term on Ind. ticket, 1907-09; farmer, Puget Sound area, 1909-10, McLaughlin, S. Dak., 1910-15, Stevens Point, Wis., 1915-20; ret. to Fond du Lac; died there, Feb. 3, 1941; internment in Calvary cemetery. Catholic, Republican.

CALLAHAN, Daniel, miner, freighter. B. in Ft. Dodge, Ia., Aug. 12, 1865; grad., gr. sc.; m. Ernia Ellen Pavloff in Circle City, 1904; children: Richard, Helen; logger, Mich., 1878-82; miner and freighter, Colo., 1882-92; hod carrier, Portland, Ore. and Revelstoke, B.C., Can., 1892-95; miner and freighter, Sitka, Dawson, Circle, Nome, Fairbanks, Innoko, Ruby, Valdez, Cordova, 1896-1930s; city councilman, Fairbanks, 9 terms, 1906-15; assoc. ed., Fairbanks TIMES, 1907; terr. H.R., 1923; died in Pioneers' Home, Sitka, Nov. 9, 1935. Catholic, Independent.

CAMPBELL, Bruce Adolph, civil engineer. B. in Binghampton, N.Y., Jan. 23, 1931; s. Julian A. and Viola L. (Bordeaux) C.; B.Sc., Union Coll., Schenectady, N.Y.; m. Marl J. McCurdie, June 21, 1958; children: Robert, Richard, Katherine, James; engr., ARC, 1952-57, BPR, 1957-60; chief road design engr., state dept. of highways, 1960-62, preconstr. engr., 1962-64, special asst. to comr. of high-

ways, 1964-67; Campbell & Assoc., constr. engrs., 1967-68; exec. v.p., Burgess Constr. Co. and pres., Burgess-Houston Co., Fairbanks, 1968-71; state comr. of highways, 1971-74. Mem., Elks, Lions.

CAMPBELL, James R., businessman. B. in Phila., Pa., Mar. 2, 1887; children: Weldon, Marcin; went to Dawson, Can., 1899, Fairbanks, 1903, Anchorage, 1915; owner-operator, 2 pastime parlors, Anchorage; terr. Sen., 1933-37; moved to San Francisco, Calif., 1941; died there, Sept. 11, 1943. Democrat.

CANNON, Frank B., hotel proprietor. B. *c.* 1863; justice of the peace, Black Hills, S. Dak.; joined gold stampede to Dawson, Can., 1898; prop., Pioneer roadhouse, Knik, 1908-18; terr. H.R., 1917-19; farmed Wasilla homestead, 1918-23; U.S. Comr. (Jan.), postmaster (Mar.), Wasilla, 1923; died in his home, Wasilla, June 15, 1923. Mem., Odd Fellows, Pioneers. Democrat.

CARLSON, Chester C. (Red), fisherman. B. in Elgin, Wash., 1892; grad., h. sc. and bus. coll.; m. Alice M. Ollis, 1943; bridge carpenter, Copper River & Northwestern Ry., Cordova, 1916-17; U.S. Navy, 1917-18; commercial fisherman, Cordova, 1918-; city councilman, 1922; terr. H.R., 1949-53. Mem., Fishermen's Union (past pres.), Am. Leg. (past dept. comdr.), VFW, Moose, Masons, Pioneers. Democrat.

CARLSON, M.O., acting U.S. Marshal, 4th jud. div., Fairbanks, Mar.-June, 1933. Democrat.

CARLSON, Victor D., lawyer. B. in Sand Lake, Mich., May 20, 1935; s. Fred C. of Greenville, Mich.; B.B.A. and LL.B., U. Mich., 1962; U.S. Navy, 1957-59; asst. atty. gen., Juneau, 1962-63; asst. dist. atty., Fairbanks, 1963-65; asst. city atty., Anchorage, 1965-66; pvt. law prac., Anchorage, 1966-69; head of Alaska's public defender agency, 1969-70; atty., Greater Anchorage Area Borough, 1969-70; superior ct. judge, Sitka, 1970-.

CARR, Bernard Joseph, Sr., machinist, businessman. B. in Eckly, Pa., Nov. 25, 1898; m. Bernice Fitzgarrald; children: Bernard J., Jr., Lawrence J. (Larry), Mrs. Louis (LaMoine) Oppelt, Mrs. Ted (Mary) Piaskowski; stud., Mining and Mechanical Inst., Freeland, Pa.; machinist, Santa Fe R.R., ret., 1954; joined sons in grocery bus., Anchorage, 1954-64, sec.-treas., dir. of personnel and public relations, 10 yrs.; state H.R., 1965-66; died in Anchorage, Feb. 24, 1967. Mem., K.C., McKinley Lions, Alaska Hist. Soc. (charter). Catholic, Democrat.

CARR, Lawrence John (Larry), businessman. B. in Albuquerque, N. Mex., July 28, 1929; s. Bernard Joseph and Bernice (Fitzgarrald) C.; grad., St. Bernadine's h. sc., San Bernardino, Calif., 1947; went to Anchorage, 1947; worked in commissary warehouse, Alaska R.R., and Thrifty drugstore; estab. grocery bus. with bro., Bernard J., Jr., Feb. 1950; m. Wilma Ruth Moseley, June 25, 1950; children: Gregory, Jacqueline, Brian; estab. supermarkets in Anchorage, Fairbanks, Eagle River, Kenai, 1952-74; chmn., 1965-67, and mem., ASHA

Bd.; campaign mgr. for Mike Gravel in U.S. House race, 1966; appt. Nat. Defense Exec. reservist, Office of Emergency Planning; mem., Nat. Adv. Council, SBA; cand., state Gov., 1970. Catholic, Democrat. Address: Anchorage.

CARROL, Selwyn, educator. B. in Sanford, Fla., Oct. 28, 1931; s. George and Bessie (Tyson) C.; B.A., UA, 1969; m. Ruth Blassengale, Fairbanks, Mar. 17, 1972; children: Karen, Selwyn; U.S. Army, 1950-60; social worker, juvenile counselor, sc. attendance supervisor, Fairbanks, 1965-70; h. sc. social studies teacher, Main jr. h. sc., 1970-72; state H.R., 1973-75; dir. of customer development, Alaska Bk. of North, 1973-; chmn., North Pole Unification study group, Fairbanks Borough. Mem., Kiwanis, Veteran's Club, NEA, NAACP. Republican. Address: 425 "B" St., Fairbanks 99701.

CARROLL, Capt. James, steamboat captain. B. in Ireland, 1840; came to U.S. as child; sailed on Great Lakes, 1857-60; went to sea on sailing ships; steamboat captain, 1870; commanded *Great Republic* on Pacific coastwise run; began Alaska run, *c.* 1880, Pacific Coast Steamship Co. boats, *Idaho, Ancon, Mexico, Queen;* interested in gold mines (Bear's Nest Mine, Douglas I.) a wharf and other Juneau properties, 1880s; while skipper of *Queen,* elected del. to Cong., non-partisan conv., Juneau, Oct. 8, 1890; gained some notoriety by offering Fed. Govt. $14 million for Alaska; agent, steamship and fisheries cos., Seattle, Wash., *c.* 1902-; died following stroke, Seattle, May 20, 1912.

CARROLL, Thomas P., accountant. B. in Edgmont, S. Dak., 1919; m. Kathleen Roberts of Londonderry, Ireland, 1946; children: Michael, Thomas, William and Kevin (twins); U.S. Army, 1941-46; earned Silver Star, Purple Heart with oak leaf cluster, Bronze Star with cluster; accountant, Alaska R.R., Anchorage, 1946-50; joined Nat. Guard when first organized, 1950; mem., Nat. Guard, Edgmont, S. Dak., 1937-; maintenance div., Reeve-Aleutian Airways, 1950-55; maintenance officer, Nat. Guard, 1955-57; appt. adjt. gen., Alaska Nat. Guard with rank of brig. gen. by Pres. Eisenhower, Dec. 1958 (had been serving in that capacity since Nov. 1957); first head of state dept. of military affairs, Sept. 1959; killed on flight near Valdez inspecting earthquake damage, Apr. 25, 1964; Nat. Guard training site, Ft. Richardson, named Camp Carroll, Feb. 17, 1968. Mem., Am. Leg. Republican.

CASEY, William W., businessman. B. in Theresa (later, Watertown), N.Y., June 26, 1859; m.; children: William W., Jr., Russell; moved to Mont., 1876; res., Glendive, Mont., 1881-88; estab. furniture bus., Seattle, Wash., 1888; bus. destroyed by fire, 1889; moved to Everett, Wash.; trainman, Great Northern R.R.; freighter, Dyea to Chilkoot Pass, 1897-98; moved to Juneau, 1898, and entered hotel bus.; founded Juneau Transfer Co.; interested in hardware store; dir. of bank; mem., sc. bd., several terms; bd. trustees, Pioneers' home, Sitka; chmn., 1st div., Dem. com., 1918; Dem. Nat. Committeeman, 1908-09; terr. H.R., 1917-21; died in Ketchikan, Oct. 19, 1924. Mem., Elks, Masons, Odd Fellows. Democrat.

CASHEL, Frank E., carpenter, fisherman. B. in Douglas, Alaska; grad., Douglas h. sc.; stud., UA; m. Myrtle Hollywood at Sitka (div.); m. 2d, Betty Kibby; children: David, Phillip, Lori Irene; U.S. Navy base inspector, commercial fisherman, constr. worker, plumbing bus., Sitka, 1941-64; state H.R., 1959-65; dir., employment & security div., dept. of labor, Douglas, 1965-68, 1971-75; bldg. official, city and borough of Juneau, 1968-71. Mem., Alaska Council of Carpenters (pres.). Democrat.

CELLA, Joseph J., lawyer. Grad., Regis Coll., Denver, and U. Colo.; admitted to Colo. bar, 1933; criminal div., U.S. Dept. of Justice, Wash., D.C., 1941-64; U.S. dist. atty. for Alaska, Anchorage, June-Oct., 1964. Author, 4-vols. work on model indictments for fed. lawyers. Democrat.

CERNICK, Clifford, journalist. B. in Cle Elum, Wash., July 14, 1918; s. Frank and Alma (Radosevich) C.; B.A., journalism, U. Wash., 1949; m. Patricia Hervey, Feb. 4, 1956; children: Nancy Anne, Clifford, Jr.; U.S. Army, Ft.Richardson, 1942-45; reporter, Anchorage DAILY NEWS, 1949-50, managing ed., 1950-58; ed., Fairbanks DAILY NEWS-MINER, 1958-61; education ed., Santa Barbara (Calif.) NEWS-PRESS, 1961-62; asst. public affairs officer, FAA, Los Angeles, 1962-68; chief, employee information div., FAA, office of information services, Wash., D.C., 1968-. Author, children's book on Alaska, Little Golden Book series, 1961. Mem., Alaska Press Club, Anchorage chapter (charter, hon. life, pres., bd. chmn.).

CESSNUN, E.J. (Peter), aviator. B. in Council Grove, Kan., Aug. 2, 1918; grad. h. sc.; worked in Kan. City; m. Anna Lee, 1945; children: Gregory, Mike, Deborah, Patty; moved to Ketchikan, 1946; owner-operator, Webber Air, Inc., Ketchikan; state H.R., 1967-68. Republican.

CHAMBERLAIN, Erford Elle (Al), miner, businessman. B. in Waushara Co., Wis., July 2, 1863; grad. h. sc., Berlin, Wis.; newspaper reporter, Neb., until 1888; real estate bus., Tacoma, Wash., until 1897; freighted over White Pass trail from Skagway; agent, Chilkoot Tramway Co., 1897-98; prospector, Klondike, 1898-1900; prospector-miner, Seward Peninsula, organized Bluestone and Kougarok mining dists., 1900-08; settled in Seward; city councilman, 19 yrs., mayor, 3 terms, Seward; guide, U.S. govt. expeditions to Matanuska coal fields and elsewhere, 5 yrs.; terr. Sen., 1921-25; tax collector, Bristol Bay, 1923; U.S. Comr., McCarthy, 1926-36; died in Seward hosp., May 27, 1948. Mem., Pioneers, K.P. Presbyterian, Republican.

CHAMBERLIN, Arthur M., journalist, businessman. B. in Chicago, Ill., Apr. 17, 1905; public sc., Chicago, Salt Lake City, Seattle; m. Mrs. Elizabeth P. Magids in Seattle, June 1, 1931; children: Patricia Ann (Mrs. A.W. Clark); sports writer, AP and POST-INTELLIGENCER, Seattle, 1922-30; operated trading post, Deering, 1931-35; terr. H.R., 1935-36; Nat. Resources Planning Bd., Wash., D.C., 1936-41; USNR, 1941-45; field rep., U.S. Dept. Labor, retraining and re-employment adm., Alaska and West Coast, 1946-56; reg. dir., Bur. of Veterans' Re-employment Rights, Dept. Labor, Seattle, 1956-. Democrat.

CHANCE, Genie, public relations consultant. B. in Dallas, Tex., Jan. 24, 1927; d. A.S. and Jessie Broadfoot; stud., Paris Jr. Coll., East Tex., Teachers' Coll., S. Methodist U.; B.S., North Tex. State U., 1946; grad. stud., Baylor U.; m. Winston C. Chance, 1947 (div. 1971); children: Winston, Albert, Jan (Mrs. Charles L. Blankenship); m. 2d, W.K. (Bill) Boardman of Ketchikan, Sept. 23, 1971, on Mercer I., Wash.; instructor, speech and radio, N. Tex. State U., 1946-49; moved to Anchorage, May 1959; newscaster and editorialist, KENI-radio-television and KFQD-radio, 1962-64; estab. public relations firm, Sept. 1964; state H.R., 1969-74; state Sen., 1975-79. Recipient of McCall Magazine's Golden Mike top award, 1965; Camp Fire Girls of Tex. Distinguished Lady of the Year, 1969; Distinguished Alumnus of the Year, N. Tex. State Coll., 1969. Mem., Alaska Press Women (pres., 1966); Defense Adv. Com. on Women in Military Service (DACOWITS), 1967-70. Protestant, Democrat. Address: Box 2392, Anchorage 99510.

CHANDLER, Catherine, lawyer. B. in Anchorage, 1946; d. William E. and Elladeen (Hayes) Bittner; gr. and h. sc. (1962), Anchorage; B.A., Georgetown U., 1966; law stud., George Wash. U.; LL.B., U. Calif., San Diego, 1969; m. Dr. James Chandler in Anchorage, June 1965; asst. U.S. dist. atty., San Diego, 1969-72; asst. state atty. gen., Fairbanks, 1972-74; state dist. atty., 4th jud. dist., Fairbanks, 1974-. Mem., Phi Beta Kappa. Democrat.

CHAPADOS, Frank Xavier, businessman. B. in Juneau, Jan. 18, 1914; s. James E. and Monica (Flabby) C.; stud., U. Wash. and UA, 1936-39; m. Leona Chernenko, Jan. 23, 1948; children: Katherine, Marcia, Gregory; dep. U.S. Marshal, Fairbanks, 1942-43, 1946-47; U.S. Navy, 1943-46; owner-operator, transfer bus., 1947-48; U.S. Fish & Wildlife enforcement agent, McGrath, 1948-51; U.S. Marshal, 4th jud. dist., Fairbanks, 1951-53; partner, H. & S. Warehousing Assn., Fairbanks, 1953-; state H.R., 1959-63. Mem., Am. Leg., Citizens Adv. Com. on Alaska Highway Study (chmn., 1963). Catholic, Democrat.

CHAPMAN, Oscar Littleton, lawyer. B. in Omega, Va., Oct. 22, 1896; s. James Jackson and Rosa Archer (Blount) C.; stud., Randolph-Macon Acad., Bedford, Va., 1918, U. Denver, 1922-24, U. of N. Mex., 1927-28; LL.B., Westminster Law Sc., Denver, 1929; LL.D., Colo. State Coll. of Education, Augustana Coll.; m. Olga Pauline Edholm, Dec. 21, 1920 (dec.); m. 2d, Ann Kendrick, Feb. 24, 1940; s. James; U.S. Navy, 1918-20; probation officer, juvenile ct., Denver, 1922-27; admitted to Colo. bar, 1929; asst. Sec. of Interior, 1933-46; Undersecretary of Interior, 1946-49; Sec. of Interior, 1949-53. Mem., Am. Leg., Phi Alpha Delta, Am. Judicature Soc., VFW. Methodist, Democrat.

CHAPMAN, Dr. Wallace John, physician. B. in 1928; M.D., UCLA, 1958; U.S. Navy, 1941-45; m. Jean, also physician; s. Evan; pvt. prac. with wife,

Cordova; founded Cordova med. clinic, 1962-66; med. dir., state workman's compensation center, San Francisco, Calif., 1966-67; state comr. of health and welfare, Alaska, 1967-68; moved to Anchorage to open "family medicine" center, June 1968. Republican.

CHAPPLE, Emery W., Jr., law enforcement officer, aviator. B. in Phoenix, Ariz., May 20, 1928; stud., U. Wash., UA, FBI Nat. Acad., Northwest Traffic Inst.; m. Mrs. Lydia Arlene Van Conia in Fairbanks, March 1971; children: Dale Gordon, Kent Joseph; went to Alaska, 1941; he and father sold plumbing bus., Fairbanks, 1953; patrolman, terr. police, 1954-67; pilot, Wien Consolidated Airlines, 1967-69, Interior Airways, 1969-71; state comr. of public safety, res. to return to aviation, 1971-74. Mem., Masons, Pioneers, Internat. Assn. Chiefs of Police, Alaska Peace Officers Assn. Address: Fairbanks.

CHARLES, Sidney Dean, journalist. B. in St. Cloud, Minn., Sept. 6, 1870; s. John B. and Agnes (McPherson) C.; public sc., Red Bluff, Calif.; m. Mary Anne Burden in Portland, Ore., Dec. 22, 1901; children: Eileen (Mrs. Herbert Kittilsby), Alice (Mrs. Herbert Vick), Paul Stuart, Marjorie (Mrs. George Sarvela); reporter or ed.: Portland TELEGRAM, Seattle NEWS, Seattle TELEGRAPH, Tacoma LEDGER, Tacoma UNION, Tacoma NEWS, Red Lodge (Mont.) WEEKLY, Salt Lake TRIBUNE, Spokane SPOKESMAN REVIEW, Rossland (B.C.) MINER & NEWS, St. Louis GLOBE DEMOCRAT, Chicago TRIBUNE, Omaha (Neb.) BEE, 1887-1904; founded SOUTHERN OREGONIAN (Medford, Ore.); went to Fairbanks via Valdez trail, Feb. 1904; reporter or ed.: Fairbanks NEWS, Fairbanks TIMES, Cordova TIMES, Cordova NORTH STAR, Juneau DISPATCH, Juneau EMPIRE, Anchorage TIMES, Alaska DAILY CAPITAL (Juneau), Ketchikan CHRONICLE; founded weeklies: Alaska PIONEER, Alaska MAGAZINE (monthly), Juneau SPIRIT, Sitka TRIBUNE, Ketchikan WEEKLY; purchased Petersburg REPORT (renamed Petersburg HERALD), Alaska FISHING NEWS (renamed Ketchikan DAILY FISHING NEWS, now Ketchikan DAILY NEWS and owned by s. Paul); dep. U.S. Marshal, McCarthy, 1913; died in Ketchikan, Jan. 25, 1959; buried there. Mem., Pioneers. Episcopalian, Republican.

CHASE, Dr. Will Henry, physician. B. in Warsaw, N.Y., Jan. 19, 1874; s. Leander and Almeda (Mallison) C.; h. sc., Warsaw; stud., med. technician sc., Bellvue Hosp., N.Y.C., emphasis in natural hist.; m. Ellen Fraisure, Nov. 1920; d. Lorraine (Mrs. James H. Kelly); res., Skagway, Dyea, Dawson, 1897-1903, Fairbanks, 1903-04, Valdez, 1905-06, Katalla, 1907, Cordova, 1908-; mayor, Cordova, 24 terms; dep. comr. of health, 3d div.; died in Seattle, Wash., Oct. 1, 1965. Mem., Alaska Med. Assn. (organized with Dr. J.H. Romig, 1906); Alaska Game Com., 1925-31 (chmn., 1927-31); Masons, Pioneers (grand pres., 1938). Author, "The Sourdough Pot," 1943, "Capt. Billie Moore," "Pioneers of Alaska," 1951. Received JESSEN'S WEEKLY Distinguished Service award, 1948. Methodist, Republican.

CHENEY, Zina Reville (Zack), lawyer. B. in Garden City, Minn., July 25, 1870; moved to Medalia, Minn.; law degree, U. Minn., 1893; m. Pearl Ziegler in Seattle, Wash., June 10, 1909; admitted to bar, prac. in Worthington, Minn.; served in Spanish-Am. war and in China during Boxer Rebellion; went to Alaska, 1900; prospector-miner, Porcupine dist.; estab. law office, Douglas; mem., sc. bd.; moved to Juneau, 1907, associated with R.W. Jennings, and later with A.H. Ziegler; chmn., Dem. central com., 1908-13, Dem. Nat. Com., 1913-16; died in Seattle, Wash., July 11, 1919; buried in Masonic plot, Juneau. Mem., Alaska Bar Assn. (v.p., 1919). Democrat.

CHILBERG, Joseph, miner. Res., Olympia, Wash.; miner, Seward Peninsula, 1897-1907; bro. John Edward was partner in Pioneer Mining Co., Nome, and pres., Scandinavian-Am. Bk., Seattle, Wash.; estab. small gen. mercantile store, Nome, 1907; Labor cand., del. in Cong., 1908; prop., Alaska Museum, Silver Spray Pier, Long Beach, Calif., 1923-; lived in San Bernardino, Calif., 1928-; died in Los Angeles, Calif., Apr. 1, 1935.

CHRISTIANSEN, Raymond C., aviator. B. in Eek, Alaska, April 13, 1922; Moravian Children's Home Mission sc., on Kwethluk R.; m. Tillie; children: Carol, Ray, Christine, David; worked in family's trading post, Kwigillingok; U.S. Army, 1942-46; stud., flying sc., Anchorage, Seattle, 1946-48; bush pilot, Bethel, 1948-; state H.R., 1961-67; state Sen., 1967-73; chmn., Dem. state central com., 1969-70; pres., bd. dir., Calista corp., 1973-. Democrat. Address: Box 35, Bethel.

CLARK, Henry Wadsworth (Eskey), lobbyist, author, public relations director. B. in Wrangell, Apr. 11, 1899; s. Willoughby and Georgiana (Choquette) C.; prep. sc., Seattle, and Phillip Exeter, N.H.; B.A., magna cum laude, 1923, M.A., 1928, Harvard U.; m. Evelyn Rockwell, N.Y.C., Oct. 18, 1946; children: Merle Rose Klotz, Joan Den, Henry W. Clark, Jr., Janet Whalen, Mary Sprang, Karen Morris; instructor, Harvard U., 1926-35, Lafayette Coll., 1936-42; U.S. Army, 1942-46; gen. mgr., Alaska Development Bd., 1946; pres., Pacific Maritime Assn. (labor relations), 1946-52; v.p., Alaska SS Co., Wash., D.C., 1952-70. Author: "A History of Alaska," MacMillan, 1930, "Alaska, The Last Frontier," Grosset & Dunlap, 1936, "Alexander, Buck Choquette," pvt. pub., 1960. Mem., Harvard Clubs of N.Y., Boston, San Francisco, Wash., D.C., Hawaii; Overseer of Harvard, Rotary, Arctic Soc., Phi Beta Kappa. Catholic. Address: 14513 Elmham Ct., Silver Spring, Md. 20906.

CLARK, Walter Eli, journalist. B. in Ashford, Conn., Jan. 7, 1869; grad., Conn. Normal Sc.; principal, gr. sc., Manchester, Conn.; stud., Williston Seminary, East Hampton, Mass.; B.A., Wesleyan U., 1887-94; m. Lucy Harrison Norvell, 1898 (dec.); m. 2d, Mrs. Juliet Staunton (Buckner) Clay, Aug. 13, 1929; reporter, Hartford POST, 1894; Wash., D.C., correspondent: N.Y. SUN, N.Y. COMMERCIAL-ADVERTISER, New Haven REGISTER, Hartford COURNAT, Seattle POST-INTELLIGENCER, 1897-1909; Gov. of Alaska,

1909-13; moved to Charleston, W. Va., and purchased Charleston MAIL; died in Charleston, Feb. 4, 1950. Mem., Elks, A.B., Nat. Rose Soc. (pres., 1928-29). Presbyterian, Republican.

CLASBY, Charles J., lawyer. B. in Monroe, Wash., 1910; J.D., U. Wash., 1933; m. Hazel Bruce in Fairbanks, 1939 (dec. 1962); children: Carolyn Theresa (Mrs. James J. Lennon), Robert; pvt. law prac., Seattle, Wash., 1933-36, Fairbanks, 1936-39, 1945-; U.S. dist. atty., 2d jud. dist., Nome, 1939-44; special U.S. atty., Anchorage, 1944-45. Mem., C. of C., Elks, Eagles, Rotary, 1st Nat. Bk. (bd. dir.), Usibelli coal mines (bd. dir.). Republican. Address: Fairbanks.

CLAYTON, Monroe N., lawyer. State dist. atty., 4th jud. dist., Fairbanks, 1971-74; pvt. law prac., Merdes, Schaible & DeLisio law firm, Fairbanks, 1974-. Democrat. Address: 300 Barnette St., Fairbanks 99701.

CLEGG, Cecil Hunter, lawyer. B. in Sion Mills, Co. Tyrone, Ireland, June 9, 1873; B.A., honors, Toronto U., Can., 1897; m. Jessie Magelalance Johnston, May 11, 1903; m. 2d, Miss Louise Parcher, Aug. 27, 1935; law stud., office of Charles Toll, Denver, Colo., then admitted to Colo. bar, 1897-1900; law clerk, office of Charles S. Johnson, pvt. law prac., Nome, 1900-03; asst. U.S. atty., 3d div., Valdez and Nushagak, 1903-07; sec. to Judge Gunnison, Juneau, 1907-08; pvt. law prac., Fairbanks, 1908-09; asst. U.S. atty., 4th jud. dist., Ruby and Fairbanks, 1909-13; city atty., Fairbanks, 1918-20; U.S. dist. judge, 4th jud. dist., Fairbanks, 1921-32; U.S. dist. judge, 3d jud. dist., Valdez, 1932-34; pvt. law prac., Fairbanks, 1934-49; ret. to Calif., Oct. 1949; died in Santa Barbara, Calif., May 24, 1956. Mem., Pioneers (grand pres., 1919), Masons, Elks. Episcopalian, Republican.

CLEMENTS, J.M., lawyer. U.S. dist. atty., 2d jud. dist., Nome, 1919-21; res., Helena, Mont. Democrat.

CLUM, Maj. John P., postal inspector, lawyer. B. on farm near Claverick, N.Y., 1851; grad., Hudson River Inst.; stud., Rutgers Coll., 1870; U.S. Meteorological Service, Santa Fe, N. Mex., 1871-74; m.; children: Woodworth, Caro (Mrs. Peter Vachon); m. 2d, in N.Y., Oct. 1914; U.S. agent for Apache Indians, San Carlos, Ariz., 1874-77; captured Apache chief Geronimo at Ojo, Caliente, N. Mex., Apr. 22, 1877; admitted to bar, Pinal, Ariz.; prop.-ed., Tucson CITIZEN, 1877-80; owner-ed., Tombstone EPITAPH, 1880-82; postmaster, Tombstone, Ariz., 1880-82, 1885-87; first mayor of Tombstone, 1881-82, during which Wyatt Earp, peace officer, and Clanton boys met in O.K. Corral shooting; employe, office of chief inspector, Post Office Dept., Wash., D.C., 1882-85; real estate bus., San Bernardino, Calif., 1887-90; post office inspector, Rio Grande border, 1891-93; employe, office of chief inspector, Post Office Dept., Wash., D.C., 1893-98; special duty organizing and extending postal service in Alaska, 1898-1906; appt. chief post office inspector, 1900, ret. to Alaska; estab. 40 post offices in Alaska; spent summers, Alaska, and winters, Wash. and N.Y.; installed and operated hydraulic dredge, Nome dist., 1903; cand., Alaska gov., 1905; Ind. cand., del. to Cong., 1908; died in Los Angeles, Calif., May 1932.

COBB, John H., lawyer. B. in Tex.; m. Emma Joy; s. E. Lang; went to Alaska, 1898; pvt. law prac., Juneau, 1902-08, Valdez, 1908-09; terr. counsel (predecessor to atty. gen.), 1913-17; moved to Santa Barbara, Calif.; died there, Dec. 23, 1924. Democrat.

COBLE, Allison F. (Joe), businessman. B. in Flora, Ill., Mar. 2, 1901; m. Helen Alexson, 1928; children: Ronald, Gary, Lloyd; U.S. Marine Corps, 1918-22; car repair shop work, Tacoma, Wash., 1922-26; part-owner, restaurant, Seattle, Wash., 1926-31; misc. jobs, Seattle and Cordova, 1931-36; mined 2 yrs., purchased and operated Pioneer Cab Co., city councilman, Fairbanks, 1936-53; terr. H.R., 1947; mem., Fairbanks sc. bd., 1948; terr. Sen., 1951-53; moved to Seattle, March 1953; died in his home, May 10, 1953. Mem., K.T., Masons. Republican.

COCHRAN, Orville D., lawyer. B. in Virgil City, Mo., Mar. 10, 1871; h. sc., Parsons, Kan., 1887; J.D., U. Ore., 1898; m. Mrs. Inez Hontoon, Nome, Nov. 11, 1908 (dec. 1933); R.R. employe, Kan. and Ore., 1890-98, law stud., in evenings; pvt. law prac., Portland, Ore., 1898-1900, Nome, 1900-48; counsel, Hammon Consolidated Gold Corp.; mayor, 1910-14, city atty., Nome; terr. H.R., 1921-23, Sen., 1937-47; died in Nome, Jan. 30, 1948. Mem., bd. regents, UA, 1939-48; Alaska C. of C. (pres., 6 yrs.). Democrat.

COFFEY, Edward Daniel, businessman. B. in Chelsea, Okla., July 15, 1897; s. Daniel and Mattie (Creason) C.; grad., h. sc., St. Joseph, Mo.; m. Ruth Yost Kelly, Nov. 11, 1936; s. Daniel Kelly; traveling salesman, Kan. City, Kan., Los Angeles, Calif., 1914-23; U.S. Army, 1917-18; employe, Alaska-Juneau Gold Mining Co., Juneau and Hirst; fisherman, Cordova, Kodiak, Bristol Bay; sec., United Fishermen's Union of Alaska, 1923-35; commissary supervisor, Palmer, 1935-37; estab. insurance agency, Anchorage, 1937; terr. H.R., 1937-41, Sen., 1941-49; finance chmn., Dem. Party, Alaska; sold insurance agency, moved to Palm Springs, Calif. Mem., Rotary, Elks, Am. Leg. Democrat.

COGHILL, John Bruce (Jack), businessman. B. in Fairbanks, Sept. 24, 1925; s. William Alexander and Elizabeth Winifred (Fortune) C.; h. sc., Nenana; m. Frances Mae Gilbert, Nenana, June 18, 1948; children: Patricia Mae, John Bruce, Jr., James Alexander, Jerald Francis, Paula, Jeffrey; U.S. Army, 1943-46; partner in family bus., Nenana, 1946-; terr. H.R., 1953-57; del., const. conv., 1955-56; state Sen., 1959-65; cand., Alaska gov., 1962; mayor, Nenana, 1962-63; chmn., Rep. state central com., 1972-. Mem., Alaska sc. bd. assn. (organizer, 1st pres., 1956-57), VFW, Nenana sc. bd. (pres.). Episcopalian, Republican.

COLE, Charles E., salesman. Served U.S. Army, Aleutian I., 1944-46; salesman, Standard Oil Co., Seward, 1946-63; state H.R., 1963-64; city council-

man, Seward, 2 yrs. Mem., Moose Pass Sportsman's Club, Seward Volunteer fire dept., Lions, Elks, Am. Leg., Boy Scout (chmn., adv. bd.). Republican.

COLE, Clarence Cash, businessman. B. in Henderson Bay, Wash., Feb. 12, 1891; s. Cornelius Philip and Marcella (Clark) C.; gr. and h. sc., Juneau; stud., U. Minn.; m. Ruby Worth, June 23, 1915; children: James C., Thomas P., Gerald; m. 2d, Ruth Marcella (Marsh) Gudbranson, Jan. 20, 1945; moved from Tacoma, Wash., to Juneau with parents, 1893; transfer and contracting bus., Juneau, 1912-44; Am. Ry. Express agent, 1917-32; terr. H.R., 1921-23, speaker, 1923; won popular vote on referendum for Alaska gov., 1923; terr. auditor, 1929-32; moved to Vashon I., near Seattle, 1958; died in Bellingham, Wash., hosp., Nov. 8, 1959. Mem., Pioneers, Elks. Presbyterian, Republican.

COLLETTA, Michael J., businessman. B. in Chicago, Ill., Sept. 1, 1927; stud., Seattle U., 1 yr.; m. Peggy Overstreet of Kosciusko, Miss.; s. Michael J., Jr.; U.S. Marine Corps, 1944-46; founded Colletta Corp., cleaning supplies and equipment, Anchorage, 1953; state H.R., 1971-72; state Sen., 1975-79. Mem., Lions, Rotary, Moose, VFW, Anchorage C. of C. (bd. dir.). Catholic, Republican. Address: 380 Oceanview Dr., Anchorage.

COLLINS, Ernest Bilbe, miner, lawyer. B. in Farmland, Ind., July 19, 1873; s. William John and Elizabeth (Robbins) C.; grad., Chico (Calif.) State Normal Sc., 1896; studied law in atty.'s office, Chico, 1896-1904; m. May Imogene Kimball, Nov. 26, 1900; d. Margaret Henshaw (Mrs. Robert Cooper); m. 2d, Mrs. Jenny Tilleson Larson, Jan. 23, 1936; gold miner, Fairbanks area, 1904-18; terr. H.R., 1913-15-19, speaker, 1913-15; admitted to bar, May 31, 1915; terr. Sen., 1921-23, 1947-51; special asst., U.S. atty., Fairbanks, 1921-33; pvt. law prac., 1933-50; mayor, Fairbanks, 1934-39; del., const. conv., 1955-56; res., Pioneers' Home, Sitka, 1961-67; moved to Pioneers' Home, Fairbanks, May 1967; died Sept. 28, 1967. Mem., Elks, Masons, Rotary, Pioneers (Grand Pres., 1951-53), Alaska-Yukon Pioneers. Methodist, Republican.

COLLINS, Grenold, aviator. B. in Tacoma, Wash., Mar. 24, 1907; s. Glenville A. and Enid (Jones) C.; stud., Principia (Calif.) Military Acad., U. Wash., Stanford U.; m.; d. Robin; m. 2d, Mrs. Dorothy Booth Tibbs, Sept. 28, 1941; pilot-agent, U.S. Fish & Wildlife Service, 1936-41; pilot, Morrison-Knudsen Co., 1941-45; terr. Sen., 1945-47; estab. and operated Collins charter airplane service and big game guide service after 1945; western Alaska rep., salmon div., Libby, McNeill & Libby Co., 1945-; temp. res., Alaska, 1925-31, permanent res., 1931-. Mem., Delta Chi, Elks. Episcopalian, Democrat.

COLVER, Warren C., lawyer. B. in Fenton, Mich., Jan. 19, 1925; stud., UA, 1950-52; B.A., J.D., Willamette U., 1952-56; m. Della E. (div., May 1970); children: John W., James C., Jane; m. 2d, Rita M. (div., June 1973); U.S. Navy, 1942-46; dep. U.S. Comr., Anchorage, 1956; pvt. law prac., Anchorage, 1957-59; asst. atty. gen. and state dist.

atty., 3d jud. dist., Anchorage, 1959-60; pvt. law prac., 1960-61; U.S. atty. for Alaska, 1961-64; state atty. gen., 1964-66; pvt. law prac., 1967-. Mem., Elks, Lions, Am. Leg. (comdr., Alaska dept., 1973). Democrat. Address: 750 W. 2d Ave., Anchorage.

CONNOR, Roger George, lawyer. B. in N.Y.C., Apr. 23, 1926; father died and mother moved to Juneau, 1932; mother (Frances Worobec) remarried, employed at Juneau public library; public sc., Juneau and Douglas, 1933-43; grad., Western Reserve Acad., Hudson, O., 1944; electronic technician's mate, U.S. Navy, 1944-46; worked on various vessels in Alaska, rising to 1st and 2d mate on ocean-going tugs, 1946-51; stud., U. of B.C., 1 yr.; B.A., political science, U. Wash., 1947-51; LL.B., U. Mich., 1951-54; admitted to Alaska bar, 1955; m. Anabel Simpson in Seattle, Wash., Nov. 19, 1959 (div., May 2, 1969); 2 children; atty., Faulkner, Banfield & Boochever law firm, Juneau; U.S. dist. atty., 1st jud. dist., Juneau, 1956-59; exec. asst., criminal div., U.S. Dept. of Justice, Wash., D.C., 1959-61; pvt. law prac., Juneau, 1961-68; pvt. law prac., Anchorage, 1968; appt. assoc. justice, state supreme ct., Dec. 2, 1968, voters' certification, Nov. 1972. Mem., Alaska Bar Assn. (pres., 1967-68). Republican.

CONNORS, James Joseph, miner, merchant. B. in Halifax, Nova Scotia, Can., Apr. 27, 1876; s. James Joseph and Isabell Louise (Williams) C.; orphaned at early age; self-educated; m. Katherine Ann Collins of Kent, Wash., July 1907; s. James J., Jr.; 2 step-children: Capt. Leo J. Collins, Mrs. Minard Mill; emigrated to U.S., 1893; worked in lumber camp, lineman and constr. foreman for telephone co., mine-operator, mercantile bus., Nome, Candle, and prop., hotel, Council, 1902-14; owner-operator, Connors Motor Co., Juneau, 1915-33; Hyder res., 1914-15; Juneau city councilman, 1918, 1922-24, mayor, 1925-26; Dem. Nat. Com., 1928-34; collector of customs, 1933-51; died in Seattle, Wash., Dec. 16, 1951. Mem., Elks, Pioneers. Catholic, Democrat.

CONRIGHT, Jack Dudley, businessman. B. in Tacoma, Wash., July 7, 1919; h. sc., Tacoma; m. Daisy Hutson, 1936; children: Jack Leslie, Rebecca Susan; meat cutter, Juneau, 1940-42; U.S. Army, 1942-44; estab. furniture and appliance store, Anchorage, 1946; terr. H.R., 1949, 1951; died at U. Wash. clinic, Seattle, Oct. 8, 1965. Democrat.

COOK, Frank, tax consultant, big game guide. B. in Silver Springs, N.Y., Sept. 4, 1925; grad., h. sc., Silver Springs, 1942, Rochester Bus. Inst., 1948; B.S., U. Denver, 1951; m., div.; s. Craig A.; U.S. Navy, 1943-46; moved to Alaska, 1951; estab. tax and bus. consult. firm; cand., U.S. Sen., 1962. Holder of world record for Dall sheep, and Sagamore Hill Trophy, Boone & Crockett Club. Mem., Alaska Bd. of Fish & Game (chmn., 1969), Alaska Big Game Trophy Club (organizer and pres., 4 terms), Anchorage Izaak Walton League (past pres.), Mt. McKinley Lions (past pres.), Anchorage Rep. Club, Boone and Crockett Club (since 1965), Masons, Sportsman's Assn., Am. Leg. Republican. Address: 109 6th Ave., Anchorage.

COOMBS, Nathan H., businessman. B. in Napa, Calif., Dec. 19, 1880; grad., Napa h. sc., 1898; m. Olive Storey, Nome, 1909; children: Nathan Storey, Allison Shelton; ship chandlery bus., San Francisco, 1898-1900; moved to Nome with mother, 1900; prop., drug store and gen. merchandise store, Nome, 1912-15; employe, clerk of ct. and dist. atty.'s office, 1912-15; clerical position, Wild Goose Mining Co.; terr. H.R., from Council City, 1915-19; moved to Napa, Calif., early 1920s; prop., gas station, 1928; cand., assessor, 1930. Mem., A.B., Pioneers. Republican.

COOPER, George D., businessman. B. in Cotopaxi, Colo., Dec. 24, 1923; h. sc., Edmonds, Wash.; m. Phyllis McCrea, 1944; children: Kathryn, Marilou, George, Jr., Gregory; pilot, U.S. Army Air Corps, 1942-46; dispatcher for ready-mix concrete, Seattle, Wash.; moved to Alaska, 1949; estab. sand and gravel bus., Northern Ready-Mix, Inc., Fairbanks; del., const. conv., 1955-56; chmn., Rep. central com., 1960-63; Fairbanks sc. dist. bd., 1957-60. Mem., Masons, Shrine, Elks, Kiwanis. Methodist, Republican.

COOPER, Joseph Earl, lawyer. B. in Guymon, Okla., Feb. 18, 1907; h. sc., Montebello, Calif.; stud., Los Angeles Coll. of Law; LL.B., Pacific Coast U., 1931; m. Bess Tilford, 1940; children: Susan Jane (Mrs. Paul Martin Schmidt), James Earl; BIA sc. teacher, Ketchikan and Levelock, 1939-42; area dir., War Manpower Com., U.S. Dept. Labor, Anchorage, 1942-44; dir., civilian personnel, Corps of Engineers, Anchorage, 1944-46; asst. U.S. atty., Anchorage, 1946-49; U.S. atty., 3d jud. dist., Anchorage, 1949-52; U.S. dist. judge, 2d jud. dist., Nome, 1952-53; pvt. law prac., Anchorage, 1953-59; terr. Sen., 1955-59; state superior ct. judge, Anchorage, 1960-62; died in his home, Nov. 26, 1964. Mem., Lions, Anchorage Community Theater. Presbyterian, Democrat.

COOPER, Stephen, lawyer. B. in Mt. Holly, N.J., Dec. 17, 1937; s. Frederick and Katherine (Sixt) C.; B.A., UA, 1959; LL.B., U. Calif., 1965; unm.; dep. atty. gen., Calif. dept. of justice, 1965-69; asst. atty. gen., Juneau, 1969; state dist. atty., 4th jud. div., Fairbanks, 1969-71; asst. U.S. atty., Fairbanks, 1971-. Address: Box 2815, Fairbanks 99701.

COPPERNOLL, William D., lawyer. B. c. 1865; prac. law, Chicago, Ill., 1887-1900; moved to Nev., 1900; mem., Nev. legislature, 1912; went to Juneau, Seward, 1912-17; atty., U.S. Shipping Bd., Seattle, Wash., 1917-18; U.S. Comr., McCarthy, 1919-24; U.S. dist. atty., 3d jud. div., Valdez, 1926-29; suffered stroke and taken to Elks' Nat. Home, Bedford, Va., 1931; died there, Dec. 1937. Republican.

CORNELIUS, Stanley P., lawyer. B. in Bremerton, Wash., Oct. 15, 1941; s. Starling P. and Virginia (Sloat) C.; went to Alaska with parents, 1954; res., Big Delta, Fairbanks, Kodiak, Kenai, Anchorage; stud., Kodiak h. sc., 1957; grad., West h. sc., Anchorage, 1958; stud., Wash. State U., U. Ore.; B.A., AMU, 1964; J.D., U. N. Mex., 1967; m. Mary Ann Randall, Feb. 12, 1964; m. 2d, 1972; son b.,

Feb. 12, 1973; admitted to Alaska bar, Oct. 18, 1968; pvt. law prac., Anchorage, 1968-74; state H.R., 1969-70. Presbyterian, Republican. Address: 601 E. 15th Terrace, Anchorage.

CORRIGAN, Philip, miner, labor union official. Sec.-treas., 1908, pres., 1917, Western Fed. of Miners, Nome Local No. 240; terr. H.R., from Nome, 1917-19; died c. 1933; buried near Ventura, Calif. Democrat.

CORSON, John W., lawyer. B. in Me., 1861; stud., Kent's Hill Acad., Wesleyan U.; read law with Baker, Baker & Cornish; m. Jane Perley of N.H., 1893; moved to Seattle, Wash., 1889; miner and lawyer, Nome, 1900; atty. for Guggenheim interests; cand., del. in Cong., 1908; died in his home, Salem, Ore., Dec. 8, 1916. Republican.

COUNCIL, Mary Lee, secretary. B. in Seattle, Wash., May 2, 1915; d. Dr. Walter Wooten and Martha Virginia (Scurry) C.; h. sc., Berkeley, Calif.; stud., U. Calif., Berkeley; sec., Pan-Am. World Airways, 1937-40; adm. asst. to Del. Anthony J. Dimond, Wash., D.C., 1940-45; adm. asst. to Del. E.L. Bartlett, Wash., D.C., 1945-59, U.S. Sen. Bartlett, 1959-67, ret. Mem., Commonwealth Club, San Francisco. Received Alaska Press Club award for weekly newsletter from del. and sen. office. Democrat. Address: 5101 River Road, N.W., Wash., D.C. 20016.

COUNCIL, Dr. Walter Wooten, physician. B. in Council, N.C., May 25, 1882; s. John Pickett and Johnnie (Wooten) C.; stud., U. of N.C., 1899-1902; M.D., U. Va., 1905; m. Martha Virginia Scurry, 1907 (div.); children: Nancy, Mary Lee; m. 2d, June Murray, 1927 (dec.); m. 3d, Ruby Alleine Apland, 1934; d. Carol Ann; surgeon, Ellamar Mining Co., 1906-11; surgeon, Copper River & Northwestern Ry., Cordova, 1911-27; asst. surgeon, U.S. Public Health Service, 1916-27; terr. comr. of health, Juneau, 1933-43; estab. Juneau Med. and Surgical Clinic, Juneau, 1936; died in Juneau, Nov. 13, 1943. Mem., Elks, K.P., Moose. Episcopalian, Democrat.

COURTNEY, E.N. (Al), office administrator. B. in Sequim, Wash., May 9, 1928; gr. sc. and h. sc., Sequim; m. Rosanne Dalton (dec.); children: Ralph, Laurie Ann, Michael; m. 2d, Joan Arletta Senour at Carmel, Calif., Jan. 25, 1968; U.S. Air Force, 1946-49; res., Seattle, Wash., 1949-52; dispatcher, Pacific Northern Airlines, Anchorage, 1952-57; real estate salesman, Anchorage, 1957-59; joined Title Insur. & Trust Co., 1959-61; city councilman, Anchorage, 3-1/2 yrs.; Greater Anchorage Borough Assemblyman, 1-1/2 yrs.; exec. dir., ASHA, 1961-65; comr. of commerce, 1965-66; dir., ASHA, 1966-67; chmn., Anchorage centennial com., 1967-68; owner-mgr., City Fuel Co., 1968; mgr., housing development, Napa Valley, Calif., apartment complex, Portland, Ore., 1968-72; gen. mgr., Skyway Realty, Anchorage, 1972-. Mem., Elks, Lions, Rotary.

CRADDICK, Marrs, lawyer. State dist. atty., 1st jud. dist., Ketchikan, 1962-63.

CRANE, Fred D., lawyer. B. in 1896; asst. dist. atty., Boise, Ida.; special asst. to U.S. dist. atty., Fairbanks, 1924; prac. law, Fairbanks, Nome, Kotzebue, 1930-1950s; state dist. atty., 2d jud. dist., Nome, 1965-69; acting dist. atty., Fairbanks, May-Sept., 1968; died in Nome, Mar. 8, 1969.

CRESSWELL, Thomas J., engineer, aviator. B. in Greenwood, Miss.; B.E., George Wash. U., 1956; flight instructor, U.S. Navy, 1946-48; engr., Aluminum Co. of Am., Pittsburgh, Pa., 1956-58; staff asst. and supervisory safety engr., GSA, Wash., D.C., 1958-59; adm. aide, U.S. Treasury Dept., Wash., D.C., 1959-61; safety engr., office of personnel and training, 1961-68, dir. of training div., FAA, 1968-71; reg. adm., Anchorage, 1972-73; dir., FAA Aeronautical Center, Okla. City, 1973-.

CROFT, Leland Chancy, lawyer. B. in Jennings, La., Aug. 21, 1937; s. Leland and Dorothy C.; law degree, U. Tex., 1961; m. Anita Toni Ruth Williamson in Midland, Tex., July 8, 1963; children: Eric, Kimberly, Lee; USNR, 1954-62; prac. law, Odessa, Tex., 1961-62; assoc. with Burr, Boney & Pease, Anchorage, 1962; state H.R., 1969-70; state Sen., 1971-79, pres., 1975-76; chmn., Pipeline Impact Com. Democrat. Address: 1511 G St., Anchorage.

CROSS, Elizabeth Patricia (Bess) nee Berger, merchant. B. in Winnipeg, Man., Can., 1897; m. Samuel Magids, 1915 (dec. 1929); children: Letty Jean, Emily Alice; m. 2d, Arthur M. Chamberlin, June 1, 1931; d. Patricia Ann (Mrs. A.W. Clark); m. 3d, John Milton Cross, 1937 (div. 1947); moved to Kotzebue, 1915; prop., trading posts, Deering, Kotzebue, Fairhaven, Kobuk, Noatak and fox farm, Noatak; terr. H.R., 1945-47; entered Sitka Pioneers' Home, late 1960s; transferred to Fairbanks Pioneers' Home, June 1968; died in Seattle, Wash., Apr. 14, 1971. Democrat.

CROSS, John Milton, aviator, businessman. B. in Goddard, Kan., 1895; s. Edwin Dallas and Mittie (Reece) C.; B.S., U. Ottawa, Can., 1919; m.; children: Milton, Edwin, Gordon Cooper, Harry; m. 2d, Elizabeth Chamberlin, 1937 (div. 1947); m. 3d; d. Mary Elizabeth; Air Service Signal Corps, Ft. Worth, Tex., 1917; served later at Ft. Riley, Kan.; test pilot, Swallow Aircraft, Kan., stunt flyer on weekends, 1918-34; pilot, Cordova Air Service, 1934-35; Wien Consolidated Airlines, Kotzebue, 1935-37, 1947-64; owner-operator, Northern Cross, Inc., Deering, 1937-47; U.S. Army Air Corps, 1941-45, Ladd, Elmendorf, Naknek, King Salmon and Aleutians; del., const. conv., 1955-56; ret. lt. col., USAF Reserve, 1965. Mem., aeronautics and communications com., 1939-53; WWII Vets bd., 1946-53; Kotzebue Electric Assn. (pres., 9 yrs.); Alaska Jud. Council, 1940s; Order of Daedalians. Democrat. Address: Kotzebue.

CROSSLEY, James J., lawyer. B. on farm, Madison Co., Ia., 1869; B.A., post-grad. law stud., Ia. State U., 1 yr.; Ph.D., Yale U.; m., 1910; children: Mrs.

Jane Mudd, Mrs. Hannah Pinkstaff, Mrs. Alice Currin, Mrs. Cherry Richards, Mrs. Helen Dosser, Mrs. Helen Alfredson; m. 2d, Mrs. Minerva Brown in Seattle, Wash., May 2, 1934; prac. law, Winterset, Ia., 1900-08; Ia. state Sen., 9 yrs.; U.S. dist. atty., 3d and 4th jud. div., Valdez and Fairbanks, 1908-14, res.; moved to Portland, Ore., 1914; Rainbow Div., U.S. Army, 1917-18, rank of col.; died in Portland, Ore., Oct. 1957. Presbyterian, Republican.

CUDDY, Warren N., lawyer, banker. B. in Abbington, Md., Oct. 11, 1886; s. George L. and Sarah (James) C.; B.A., U. Puget Sound, Tacoma, Wash., 1911; m. Lucy Hon, 1917; children: David Warren, Daniel Hon; clerk, Rhodes dept. store, Tacoma, 1911-14; mgr., later owner, Valdez Mercantile Co., 1914-21; clerk, dist. ct.; 1921-29; studied law; U.S. dist. atty., 3d jud. dist., 1929-33; pvt. law prac., Anchorage, 1933-; discont. law prac., pres., First Nat. Bk. of Anchorage; died at Providence hosp., Anchorage, Sept. 9, 1951. Mem., Elks, Rotary, Masons. Methodist, Republican.

CURRALL, Geoffrey G., lawyer. B. in Brunswick, Me., July 10, 1944; s. William Griffin and Catherine Agatha (Bender) C.; Holy Trinity h. sc., Westfield, N.J.; B.A., U. Coll. of Holy Cross, Worcester, Mass.; J.D., Seton Hall U., N.H., 1969; m. Sandra Hedrick, Ketchikan, June 8, 1974; s. Nathaniel Sadler; employe, state div. of taxation, N.J., 1969-70; law clerk, Supreme Ct. Justice Dimond, Juneau, 1970-71; asst. dist. atty., Ketchikan, 1971-73; dist. atty., Ketchikan, 1973-. Address: Box 1564, Ketchikan 99901.

CURRAN, Thomas E., Jr., lawyer. B. in Boston, Mass., 1938; B.A., Wesleyan U.; J.D., Cornell U., 1963; m. Mary Jane; children: Thomas E., III, Maeve, Desmond Doherty; pvt. law prac., Portland, Ore., 1963-64; asst. dist. atty., Fairbanks, 1964-65; asst. dist. atty., Anchorage, 1965-66; state dist. atty., Anchorage, 1966-67; pvt. law prac., Anchorage, 1967-; special counsel on consumer protection for state, 1967. Democrat. Address: 642 K St., Anchorage.

CURTIS, John E., legislator. State H.R., from Kotzebue, 1959-61. Republican.

CUSHMAN, Edward E., lawyer. B. in Louisa Co., Ia., Nov. 26, 1865; s. Henry and Elizabeth (Newell) C.; h. sc., Brighton and Ia. City, Ia.; read law under L.A. Riley, Wappello, Ia.; m. Alice Louise Sommer, Laramie Co., Wyo., 1888; 2 sons (one named Arthur W.); prac. law, Rock and Polk Cos., Neb., 1889-92, Tacoma, Wash., 1893-1900; asst. U.S. atty., Tacoma, 1900-04; special asst. to atty. gen., 9th circuit ct., San Francisco, Calif., 1904-09; U.S. dist. judge, 3d jud. dist., Valdez, 1909-12, res.; appt. fed. judge, Tacoma, July 1912; died in Tacoma, Jan. 14, 1944. Republican.

D

DAFOE, Don M., educator. B. in Sheyenne, N. Dak., Jan. 15, 1915; B.A., State Teachers' Coll., Valley City, N. Dak., 1936; M.S., U. Ida., 1947; D.Ed., Stanford U., 1961; m. Lois E. Smith, May 1938; d. Judy (Mrs. William Hopkins); educator, Ida., 1936-51; asst. supt. of sc., Anchorage, 1951-53; terr. comr. of education, 1953-59; field rep., div. of state sc. system, U.S. Office of Education, Dept. of Health, Education and Welfare, Wash., D.C., 1959-61; supt., Anchorage Ind. Sc. Dist., 1961-66; dean, Anchorage Community Coll., provost, UA, Anchorage, and prof. of education, 1966-69; exec. sec., council of state sc. officers, Wash., D.C., 1969-71; v.p. for public service, UA, Fairbanks, 1971-. Mem., Masons, Elks, Rotary, Z.J. Loussac Found. (bd. dir., 1963-), Nat. Reading Council, 1970; Alaska Humanities Forum (chmn., 1972-), WICHE, 1973-. Methodist.

DALE, Mrs. Essie Rock, educator, businesswoman. B. in Mankato, Kan., Feb. 1, 1881; d. John and Harriette (Stone) Rock; Kan. Normal Sc.; B.S., U. Wyo.; m. Ford J. Dale, June 1, 1908 (dec. 1951); children: Inez (Mrs. Jack Ferguson), Dorothy McCullock, Henri Ford; newspaper ed.-pub., Kan., Okla., Wyo.; lecturer, WCTU, Kan., 1907-15; sc. teacher, Kan., Wyo., 1901-30; co. supt. sc., Teton Co., Wyo., 1930-37; estab. women's dress shops, Fairbanks, 1937; joined by husband, son, and d. Dorothy in bus., Dale Enterprises, 1942-, including men's sportwear shop, fishing lodge on Paxson Lake; Dem. Nat. Committeewoman, 1948-52; terr. H.R., 1949; mem., bd. regents, UA, 1951-53; died in Fairbanks, June 14, 1965. Mem., Soroptimists es.), BPW, Fairbanks Woman's Club, Rebeccas, vation Army (adv. bd.). Methodist.

DALY, Alfred J., lawyer. B. in Troy, N.Y., Mar. 18, 1873; B.A., Williams Coll., 1893; m.; 2 children; stud. law in lawyer's office; admitted to bar, Troy; dep. clerk of dist. ct., Sitka, 1894-96; asst. U.S. atty., Juneau, 1896-1900; pvt. law prac., Nome and Iditarod, mining successfully part-time; spent winters in Seattle; Dem. Nat. Com., 1909-12; committed suicide aboard Yukon R. steamer, Aug. 11, 1912. Democrat.

DALY, James Patrick, miner. B. in Troy, N.Y., June 6, 1872; grad., Troy h. sc., 1888; m. Emma Ring, Dec. 8, 1932; went to Alaska, 1898; successful miner, Dawson; settled in Nome area, where bro. Alfred J. was lawyer; appt. clerk to U.S. dist. atty., Nome, 1909; operated dredges, Kougarok, 1910-22; agent, Alaska SS Co., Nome, 1922-36; terr. H.R., 1915-21, 1923-25; chief clerk, H.R., 1921 session;

ret. to Seattle, Wash., 1936; died there, Oct. 24, 1937. Mem., Pioneers (grand sgt.-at-arms, 1920). Democrat and Independent.

DAVENNY, Robert Alton, businessman. B. in Boise, Ida., 1915; m. Kate; children: Diane Dee, Jaclyne Jean, Robert Alton, Jr.; m. 2d, Dorothy Hilda McGinn, Aug. 1971; moved from Boise to Fairbanks, 1950; wholesale bldg. supply bus.; moved to Anchorage, 1965; chmn., Rep. central com., 1965-69; Rep. Nat. Com., 1969-72; selling logs to S. Korea, 1974. Republican. Address: 2414 Susitna Dr., Anchorage 99503.

DAVIDSON, Charles Edward, surveyor. B. in Fort Jones, Calif., Mar. 7, 1873; m. Mrs. Fred Peters, nee Helen Beede, in Cordova, Mar. 24, 1912; children: Ethel Belle, Charles Edward, Jr., James Gerald; joined survey crew, Juneau, 1896-98; stud., surveying, Calif., 1898-1900; pvt. surveyor, Juneau, 1900-07, Nome, 1 season, Fairbanks, 1907-13; appt. surveyor-general and ex-officio sec. of Alaska, 1913-19; chmn., Dem. central com., early 1912; Dem. Nat. Com., 1912-13; drowned at Taku Inlet when he slipped from deck of small cruiser, Aug. 8, 1919. Democrat.

DAVIES, John Haydn, mariner, businessman. B. in Plymouth, Pa., Feb. 8, 1875; m. Ann Museth in Douglas, Nov. 10, 1910; children: John, Thomas; moved to Tacoma, Wash. in early youth; purser on small steamers, mate on tugs, Puget Sound; purser on mail steamer, Juneau to Sitka, 1903; dep. U.S. Marshal, Ketchikan, 1910-15, res. to enter cannery and insur. bus.; city councilman, several terms, mayor, Ketchikan, 1932; terr. H.R., 1919-21; died in Ketchikan, Apr. 30, 1935. Republican.

DAVIS, Edward V., lawyer. B. in Aberdeen, Ida., Dec. 15, 1910; s. Edward L. and Hazel (Van Ornum) D.; B.A., Gooding (Ida.) Coll.; LL.B., U. Ida., 1935; m. DeEtte C. Scholberg, Jan. 9, 1937; children: Edward Lloyd, Charles Lee, Donald Lynn; probate judge, Ida. Falls, Ida., 1936-39; pvt. law prac., Anchorage, 1939-59; del., const. conv., 1955-56; state superior ct. judge, 3d jud. dist., 1959-73, presiding judge, 1959-64, ret., June 30, 1973; served on bench, part-time, 1974-. Mem., Greater Anchorage Area sch. bd. (pres.); Anchorage C. of C. (pres., 1946); Alaska Bar Assn. (pres.); bd. of govs., Am. Judicature Soc.; Am. Bar Assn., del. H. of Del.; Lions; Alaska Rhodes Scholarship Com., 1960-. Episcopalian, Democrat. Address: 546 W. 10th Ave., Anchorage 99501.

DAVIS, James V., businessman. B. in Friday Harbor, Wash. Terr., Oct. 13, 1887; s. Rowland Edwin and Amelia (Haroldson) D.; m. Grace Delight Hoover, Anacortes, Wash., April 1909 (div.); children: Grace Vivian (Mrs. David Ramsay, dec.), Mrs. J.E. Ohrbeck; m. 2d, Anna Bergstrom, Nov. 19, 1930 (dec., March 23, 1945); children: Anna Lois (Mrs. Don S. Smith), Demaris (Mrs. Orland Dean), James V., Jr., Rowland Edwin, II; m. 3d, Mrs. Alyce Schultz in Seattle, Feb. 27, 1951 (div. 1962); attended sc., Anacortes, Wash.; went to Alaska, 1910, with father, spent 9 mos. at Kasaan Bay and Ketchikan; canner, Tee Harbor, 1911; fish-

ing and transportation bus., Juneau; built and operated mailboat Estebeth, running between Juneau, Haines and Skagway; organizer, Marine Airways (became Alaska Coastal Airlines, merged with Alaska Airlines); terr. H.R., 1937-45, speaker, 1943; moved to Seattle area, late 1940s, to Whidbey I., where living in 1974.

DAWES, Dr. Leonard Pratt, physician, surgeon. B. in Adams Co., Wis.; s. George Frank and Sarah (Phelps) D.; grad., U. Ill. Med. Sc., 1905; m. Miss Effie Lenore Buzard, Albany, Mo., Dec. 31, 1914; sc. teacher, Wis., 1896-99; assoc. prof., Chicago Coll. of Medicine and Surgery, attending physician, St. Mary's hosp., Chicago, 1905-10; pvt. prac., Wrangell, 1910-12; internship, St. Mary of Nazarene hosp., Chicago, 1912-14; pvt. prac., Juneau, 1915-46, flight surgeon, Dept. of Commerce, 1934; ret., 1946; terr. Sen., 1947-51; died in Juneau, Nov. 12, 1951. Mem., terr. bd. of med. examiners (pres.), Am. Coll. of Surgeons (fellow). Republican.

DAWNE, Edward J., judge. Appt. U.S. dist. judge for Alaska, July 21, 1885; replaced, Dec. 3, 1885; from Salem, Ore., with wife and children; was in Sitka briefly, then disappeared on trip to Wrangell; family ret. to Salem. Democrat.

DAWSON, Lafayette, lawyer. B. c. 1841; m., 1886; 1 d. and s. (John M.); prac. law, Maryville, Mo., 1860s-; prosecuting atty., Mo.; U.S. dist. judge for Alaska, Sitka, 1886-88; ret. to Mo.; died, 1897.

DAY, Charles Marion, businessman. B. in Petaluma, Calif., Feb. 28, 1863; public sc., Ukiah, Mendochin Co., Calif.; unm.; rancher, Calif., for many yrs.; went to Wrangell, 1898; ret. to Calif.; went to Nome, 1900, to Valdez, 1902; owner-operator, Seattle Hotel, 1912-; co-owner, THE COMMONER, weekly newspaper; city councilman, Valdez; passenger transportation bus., Prince William Sound; terr. H.R., 1915-19 (non-partisan Wickite, 1914; Progressive Dem. Wickite, 1916); ret. to Calif., early 1920s. Mem., Pioneers, Valdez Igloo (pres., 1912-15), Native Sons of Golden West (Calif. order, pres.).

De ARMOND, Robert Neil, journalist, historian. B. in Sitka, July 29, 1911; s. Robert William and Elizabeth (Davidson) D.; grad., Stadium h. sc., Tacoma, Wash.; stud., U. Ore., 1931-33; m. Dale F. Burlison, July 29, 1935; children: William Davidson, Jane Paisley; reporter, STROLLER'S WEEKLY, Juneau, Seattle STAR, 1933-34; employe, Sitka Cold Storage, free-lance writer, 1934-38; city councilman, Sitka, 1937-38; bookkeeper, postmaster, radio operator, Pelican, 1938-44; city ed., Ketchikan DAILY NEWS, 1945-49; part-owner, Sitka Printing Co.; political columnist, Juneau EMPIRE, Ketchikan NEWS, Anchorage NEWS, Fairbanks NEWS-MINER, radio stations KFAR, KENI, KJNO, KABI, 1949-53; adm. asst. to Gov. B. Frank Heintzleman, 1953-57; exec. ed., Alaska Sportsman, 1962-66; researcher, Alaska Hist. Library, 1957-73; ed., Alaska Journal, 1971-. Mem., Pioneers (grand. pres.). Republican.

DECKER, Rev. Richard D., minister, lawyer. B. in Grand Rapids, Mich., May 30, 1888; stud., U. Puget Sound, U. Wash., U. Mich., theological seminary, San Francisco; stud. law; admitted to bar, 1922; m. Florence Marianne Price, 1920; ordained, 1914; pastor, Federated Church, Nome, 1919-; terr. H.R., 1923-25. Mem., K.P., Eagles. Methodist, Independent.

DEGNAN, Charles O., legislator. B. in Unalakleet, June 23, 1941; s. Frank A. and Ada; B. Ed., UA; m. Virginia Margaret Breedlove of Unalakleet, Sept. 10, 1965; 2 children; U.S. Army, 1966-68; field rep., Rural Development Agency, gov. office; state H.R., 1971-75. Mem., Arctic Native Brotherhood, Bering Straits Native Assn., AFN, Rotary (Nome). Democrat.

DEGNAN, Frank A., businessman. B. in St. Michael, Alaska, July 7, 1901; public sc., Nome, Koyuk, Holy Cross; m. Ada; 2 sons, 4 daughters; when teenager, riverboat steward and deckhand between Nenana and St. Michael; constr. worker, Calif.; dredgeman, Nome area; terr. H.R., 1951-53; station mgr., Wien Air Alaska, Unalakleet, 1960s; owner-operator, taxicab co., Unalakleet, 1970s. Mem., Unalakleet Village Council (pres.), AFN (co-founder, officer), State Rural Affairs Com., Alaska Bd. Fish and Game, Native Industries Cooperative Assn. (dir.). Received Citizen of the Year award, AFN, 1974; hon. Dr. of Public Service, UA, 1975. Catholic, Democrat. Address: Unalakleet 99684.

DELANEY, Arthur K., lawyer. B. in Fort Ticonderoga, N.Y., Jan. 10, 1841; common sc., acad.; read law; admitted to bar, 1865; m. Anna J. Wallwork, 1865; children: Kathryn (Mrs. Terell, then Mrs. Abrams), Alma (Mrs. Teal); state assemblyman, 1869, supt. sc., 1873, state Sen., Wis., 1879; U.S. atty., Milwaukee, 1884-86; cand., U.S. Cong., 1886; U.S. collector of customs, Sitka, 1887-90; law prac., Juneau, 1890-92, Everett, Wash., 1893-94; U.S. dist. judge for Alaska, Sitka, 1895-97; Dem. Nat. Com., Juneau, 1897-1904; 1st city councilman, 1st mayor, Juneau, 1900-; died in Paso Robles, Calif., Jan. 21, 1905. Democrat.

DeVANE, Thomas Jones, businessman. B. in Bladen Co., N.C., Jan. 22, 1887; s. Dr. James D. and Elizabeth (Jones) D.; grad., Clarkton Military Inst., N.C.; m. Anna D. von Ruth Willis, Ruby, Feb. 28, 1928; children: Harvey, Coralyne (Mrs. Delaney); telegrapher, Atlantic Coastline R.R., 1906-08; U.S. Signal Corps, Fairbanks, 1908-11, res.; estab. telegraph system, Ruby, 1911; operated gen. mercantile store; agent for petroleum products; prop., fur trading post, Kokrines, 1920-39; U.S. Comr., Ruby, 1913-21; terr. H.R., 1933-35; sold bus. to Northern Commercial Co., moved to Seattle, 1939; airport mgr., chief dispatcher, Pan-Am. Airways, Seattle; died, Aug. 1, 1956. Mem., Elks. Democrat.

DEVEAU, Peter Maurice, fisherman, businessman. B. in Olympia, Wash., Nov. 16, 1917; s. Frederick and Nellie (Dunthorn) D.; m. Minnie Lentz, Seattle, Wash., Nov. 6, 1945; d. Lena Lou (Mrs. Herbert Carpenter); fished with father, Seldovia, 1932-39;

moved to Kodiak, 1939; U.S. merchant marine, 1942-45; radio technician, CAA, Woody I., 1946-48; organizer-pres., Island Seafoods, Inc., 1949-58; sold cannery interest; estab. electronics and electrical co., Kodiak; state H.R., 1959-63, 1969-70; mayor, Kodiak, 1963-68; chmn., Alaska King Crab Marketing Control bd., 1965-70; ret. as supt. and v.p., King Crab, Inc., cont. electronics bus.; moved to Sequim, Wash., June 1973. Mem., Elks, Pioneers. Democrat. Address: Rt. 4, Box 1133, Sequim, Wash. 98382.

DeVIGNE, Dr. Harry Carlos, physician, author. B. in Havana, Cuba, Sept. 3, 1876; s. Henri C. and Maria (Solano) D.; M.D., Hahnemann Med. Coll., San Francisco, 1904; m. Martha Charlotte Maller, Feb. 24, 1906; d. Dana; Med. Corps, WWI; pvt. prac., Wrangell, Juneau, 31 yrs.; comr. of health, 1922-33; sec., Alaska Bd. Med. Examiners, 1914-34; ret. to Santa Barbara, Calif., cont. med. prac. Author: "Pole Star" (with Stewart Edward White), "The Time of My Life." Mem., Am. Leg., Masons. Unitarian.

DeVINE, John F., miner, businessman. B. in Scranton, Pa., Jan. 19, 1883; stud., St. Michael Coll., Toronto, Can.; m.; prospector, Nev., until 1904; miner, Nome, Tin City, and Kobuk dist., 1904-25; owner-operator, Lincoln Hotel, Nome, 1925-35; terr. Sen., 1935-39; died in Portland, Ore., Aug. 4, 1939.

DEWEY, Karl F., accountant. B. in Manchester, Ia., Aug. 22, 1901; gr. and h. sc., Manchester; m. Eda Jacobson of Bellingham, Wash., July 16, 1924; U.S. Navy, 8 yrs.; employe, IRS, Louisville, Ky.; freight agent, Lomen Commercial Co., Nome, 1943-45; employe, U.S. Smelting, Refining & Mining Co., 1945-53; terr. tax comr., Juneau, 1953-58; cand., sec. of state, withdrew before gen. election, 1958; special investigator, U.S. Dept. Interior, Guam, 1959. Republican.

DIAMOND, Joseph Bernard, grocer. B. in Gateshead, Durham City, England, Aug. 23, 1877; pvt. bus., Phil., Pa., for yrs.; m. Katherine Farrell, 1898; children: Charles E., Mrs. Ann D. Swift; hotel bus., Seattle; employe, Alaska Northern Ry., Seward, 1914; employe, Alaska R.R., Anchorage, 1915; prop., Diamond grocery store, Anchorage, 1920-33; jail guard, 1933-45; terr. H.R., 1945; died in Seattle hosp., Oct. 1, 1945. Catholic, Democrat.

DICKSON, Dr. William Maclean, educator. B. in Lordsburg, N. Mex., Dec. 15, 1925; B.A., U. Minn., 1949; M.A., U. Ut., 1953; Ph.D., Stanford U., 1962; m. and div.; 3 children; U.S. Army, 1943-46, 1950-55; salesman, Pillsbury Mills, Salt Lake City, 1956-60; organization analyst, Lockheed Corp., 1960-62; asst. prof., dept. of bus., U. Ut., 1962-63; assoc. prof., dean, coll. of bus., economics and govt., UA, 1963-65; state comr., economic development, 1965-67; prof., Bellingham, Wash., 1968. Mem., gov. employment adv. com. (chmn., 1964), emergency resources planning com. (chmn., 1964).

DIMOCK, Mrs. Barbara D., secretary. B. in Seattle, Wash., Nov. 22, 1914; public sc., Long Beach, Calif.; grad., Southwestern U. Sc. of Law, Los

Angeles, 1946; timekeeper-sec., Ryan Sc. of Aeronautics, Hemet, Calif., 1940-42, mgr., San Diego, 1942-47; m. Edmond T. Dimock, June 14, 1947 (dec., Seattle, Sept. 29, 1967); owner-prop., Bethel roadhouse, 1947-49; legal secretary, Davis & Renfrew, attys., Anchorage, 1949-50; adm. asst. in charge of RFC, 1950-51; husband-wife bus., LaBow Haynes insur. agency, 1950-66; terr. H.R., 1953-55; cand., del. to Cong., 1954; res., Arlington, Va., 1970s; appt. U.S. del., Inter-Am. Com. on Women, Oct. 1972. Mem., Anchorage Rep. Women's Club (pres., 1957), Soroptimist (pres., 1961); state fed. of Rep. women (pres., 1962). Republican.

DIMOND, Anthony Joseph, lawyer. B. in Palatine Bridge, N.Y., Nov. 30, 1881; s. John P. and Emily (Sullivan) D.; stud., St. Mary's Inst., Amsterdam, N.Y.; m. Dorothea Frances Miller, Valdez, Feb. 10, 1916; children: Sister Maria Therese, John Henry, Ann Lillian (Mrs. Rom Reilly); teacher, rural N.Y., 1898-1905; prospector-freighter, Copper River valley, Alaska, until injured by accidental gunshot, 1905-11, stud. law and passed bar, 1913; U.S. Comr., Chisana, 1913-14; joined Tom Donohoe in law prac., Valdez, 1914-32; mayor, Valdez, special asst., U.S. dist. atty., 1920-21; terr. Sen., 1923-31; del. to Cong., 1932-45; U.S. dist. judge, 3d jud. dist., Anchorage, 1945-52; died in Anchorage, May 28, 1953. Mem., Elks, Moose, Eagles, Pioneers (grand pres., 1926). Catholic, Democrat.

DIMOND, John Henry, lawyer. B. in Valdez, Dec. 28, 1918; s. Anthony J. and Dorothea F. (Miller) D.; grad., St. John's Coll., Wash., D.C., 1936, Catholic U., Wash., D.C., 1941; LL.D., Catholic U., 1948; m. Roberta Jane Dooley in Anchorage, Jan. 11, 1946; children: Anthony Joseph, II, Patricia Helen, Timothy Robert; joined Gerald Williams in pvt. law prac., Anchorage, 1948; asst. atty. gen., Juneau, 1949-53; joined father in law prac., 1953 (Apr.-July); ret. to Juneau after father's death; city magistrate, Juneau, 1955-56; joined Banfield, Boochever & Doogan law firm, 1956; appt. assoc. justice, state supreme ct., July 1959; ret. from bench for reasons of health, Nov. 30, 1971. Catholic, Democrat. Address: 506 5th Ave., Douglas 99824.

DISCHNER, Lewis M., carpenter, labor union official. B. in San Pedro, Calif., c. 1918; m. Yvonne Marie; children: Lois, Lewis M., Jr., Vanessa, Yvonne Marie; supt., Chris Berg Constr. Co., Fairbanks, 1950; active in union affairs, Fairbanks, 1954; pres., Alaska fed. of carpenters; business mgr., carpenters' Fairbanks local union; v.p., state fed. of labor; state comr. labor, 1959-60; rep., teamsters' union, southeastern Alaska, Apr. 1960; legislative dir., Alaska teamsters' union and dir., Dem.-Rep. Ind. Voter Education (DRIVE, teamsters' political organ), 1960s-1970s. Mem., Dem. central com., 4th jud. dist., 1960s; state workmen's compensation bd., 1964-74. Democrat.

DISTIN, Gen. William Langmead, surveyor. B. in Cincinnati, O., Feb. 9, 1843; s. William L. and Anna Semenetta (Lehmanowsky) D.; m. Laura L. in Keokuk, Ia., Nov. 22, 1865; d. Mrs. L.E. Emmons, Jr.; gen., Civil War, 1861-65; Ill. Nat. Guard, Quincy, Ill.; aide-de-camp to 3 O. gov-

ernors; surveyor-gen. and ex-officio sec. of Alaska, 1897-1913; ret. to Quincy, Ill., 1913; died in Chicago, Ill., Nov. 20, 1914. Mem., Masons, K.T., Mystic Shrine, K.P. (past chancellor), GAR (grand comdr.).

DITMAN, Robert Irwin, teamster, fisherman. B. in Bakersfield, Calif., Apr. 6, 1927; s. Hans and Mary (Griffith) D.; gr. sc., Chitina, Valdez, Anchorage; grad., Juneau h. sc., 1945; m. Florence Dobson, 1945 (div. 1962); children: Donna, Diana; m. 2d, Elizabeth Ann Frank, 1963; children: Lynn, Richard, Robert; exec., trucking industry, Valdez and Copper Center, 1951-73; city councilman, Valdez, 3 yrs.; state H.R., 1961-67, 1971-73; legislative asst. to Gov. Egan, 1973-74. Mem., Valdez charter com., Pioneers. Episcopalian, Democrat. Address: Valdez.

DODGE, William Sumner, collector of customs, newspaper publisher. Served as "agent of customs," U.S. Dept. of Treasury, Sitka, 1867-68; first mayor, Sitka, 1867; owner, THE SITKA TIMES newspaper and successor THE ALASKA TIMES; moved to Calif.; real estate bus. for some yrs.

DONNELLEY, Harry, miner, businessman. B. in Phila., Pa., Dec. 25, 1877; s. Dudley A. and Elizabeth (Hoey) D.; m. Mary S. Coolidge, 1916; mined and engaged in various businesses, including hand laundry, Nome, 1904-10; operated dredge and mercantile bus., pres., Miners & Merchants Bk., Iditarod, 1910- ; moved interests to Flat; owner, Erskine merchandise bus., Kodiak, 1948- ; terr. H.R., from Flat-Iditarod dist., 1929-33; ret. to Bellevue, Wash., 1949; died in Seattle, Dec. 21, 1960. Republican.

DONOHOE, Thomas Joseph, lawyer. B. in Ireland, 1874; m. Rosalie Miller in Tacoma, Wash., Oct. 31, 1901; children: Ruth, Thomas Miller; studied law in bro.'s office, Willows, Calif.; lawyer-gold miner, Nome area, 1900-02; estab. law office, Juneau, 1902-03, Valdez, Cordova, 1903-30; 1st law partner, John Y. Ostrander, 2d, Anthony J. Dimond, 3d, s. Thomas (Stanford U. grad.), Valdez and Cordova; mem., Dem. Nat. Com., 1916-28; moved to Menlo Park, Calif., early 1930s; died in Atherton, Calif., Jan. 17, 1934. Democrat.

DOOGAN, James Patrick, businessman. B. in Douglas, Nov. 3, 1914; s. Theodore and Mary D.; gr. and h. sc., Douglas; stud., UA and Anchorage Community Coll.; m. Geraldine Feero of Skagway, 1941; children: Margaret, James Patrick, Jr., G. Michael, Maureen, Daniel, Kathleen; city councilman, Fairbanks, 6-1/2 yrs.; del., const. conv., Fairbanks, 1955-56; exec. asst., ASHA, Fairbanks and Anchorage, 1962-69; moved to Anchorage, 1964; public relations rep., Alaska Oil & Gas Assn., 1969-71; appt. dir., state Alcoholic Beverage Control bd., Anchorage, Apr. 1971. Mem., UA alumni assn. (bd. dir.), Anchorage Little League (pres.), Elks, Pioneers, Catholic, Democrat. Addess: 906 10th Ave., Anchorage.

DORSH, Albert Fuller, agronomist. B. in Great Falls, Mont., July 25, 1911; h. sc., Fromberg, Mont.; B.S., UA; m. Jane Robertson of Juneau, in

Fairbanks, Dec. 27, 1936; children: Albert F., III, Lynne R.; went to Fairbanks, 1932; supt., experimental farm, UA, 1936-; U.S. Marshal, 4th jud. div., Fairbanks, 1953-59. Mem., Masons, Shrine, Lions, Alaska Peace Officers Assn. Presbyterian, Republican.

DOWD, Walter J. (**Jack**), radio operator. B. in Madrid, N.Y., 1898; m. Helen; children: Marilyn (Neil), Elinor (Hatcher), Alfred John, Frank, Walter; signal man, field artillery, Can. forces, WWI, 3 yrs.; radio operator, U.S. Signal Corps, Nome, 1927-; radio operator for Ferguson stores and U.S. Comr., Kotzebue, 5 yrs.; terr. H.R., from Kotzebue, 1939-41; dep. U.S. Marshal, Nome, 1940; terr. liquor enforcement officer, 2d div., 1944, also U.S. Comr.; food reserve dir. for western and northern Alaska, WWII; moved to Seattle, Wash., after war; died in Hillsboro, Ore., May 12, 1973.

DOWNES, Thomas Keily, businessman. B. in Bovill, Ida., Jan. 17, 1916; s. Thomas Emmett and Mary Helen (Keily) D.; m. Eleanor Frances Randlett, Kirkland, Wash., Oct. 28, 1939; children: Thomas K., Jr., Gile R., Theresa Whitesell, Marina Holmes; went to Alaska, 1937; employe, Northern Commercial Co., Unalaska, 1941-42, Fairbanks, 1942-68, branch mgr., 1959; state jud. councilman, 1967-68; dep. comr. of commerce, 1968-69; comr. of admin., 1969-71; owner-mgr., Caslers Men's Wear, Juneau, 1971-. Mem., Elks, Pioneers. Catholic, Republican.

DOWNING, Richard Alle, engineer. B. in Cordova, Mar. 13, 1917; s. Walter E. and Vera (Harris) D.; gr. and h. sc., Cordova, 1922-34; B.S., UA, 1940; m. Hazel Isobel Mathison, Apr. 6, 1941; children: Richard E., Michael W., Meredith Lee, Laurel Ann, Deborah Lynn; U.S. Army, Corps of Engineers, Ladd and Eielson AFB, 1940-54; supervising engr., Morrison Knudson Constr. Co., Fairbanks, 1954-59; state comr. highways, comr. public works, 1959-67; dir., public works, West Cameroon, Africa, 1967-68, Monrovia, Liberia, Africa, 1968-70. Mem., Elks, Shrine (past pres., Fairbanks), Sportland Pony League baseball team (mgr., Fairbanks, 2 yrs.). Address: Los Angeles, Calif. (1973).

DRAGER, Karl Allen, lawyer. B. in Seattle, Wash., July 16, 1891; m. Carlotta; children: Eunice, Courtland, Karl Allen, Jr.; U.S. Navy, WWI, res. 1922; arr. Kodiak with Navy, 1920; supt., terr. fish hatchery, Seward, 1922-25; merchandise bus., Union Oil Co. agent, policeman, law stud., pvt. law prac., Ketchikan; sec., Alaska Boxing Com., 1930; terr. H.R., from Anchorage, 1939-41; city magistrate and city atty., Anchorage, until 1943; U.S. Navy, 1943-44; died following heart attack, Anchorage, May 18, 1945. Mem., VFW, Am. Leg., Forty and Eights, Elks. Democrat.

DRISCOLL, Daniel, baker. B. in Morristown, Ill., June 4, 1862; s. Michael and Anna (Donavan) D.; m. Mary Obye, Yamhill, Ore., 1890; left Ia. home, 1876; farmer, 2 yrs.; logger, farmer, streetcar motorman (7 yrs.), Yamhill; miner, baker, Dawson, 1900-06; estab. Tanana Bakery, Fairbanks, 1906-17; city councilman, 5 terms, mayor, 1912,

Fairbanks; terr. H.R., 1913-17; ret. to ranch near Portland, Ore., 1917; died in McMinnville, Ore., Dec. 1934. Democrat.

DUFFIELD, Theodore Castleman, aviator. B. in Neb., Mar. 31, 1908; stud., U. Calif., 2 yrs.; m. Edith Turner, Nome, 1949; U.S. Air Force, 1942-44; bush pilot, station mgr., Alaska Airlines, Anchorage, Homer, Nome, 1944-48; U.S. Comr., Nome, 1948-51; mgr., Gaasland Constr. Co., Nome, 1951-52; station mgr., Alaska Airlines, Nome, 1952-; terr. H.R., 1953-55. Democrat.

DUGGAN, Sherman, lawyer. B. in Honey Creek, Ia., Feb. 19, 1879; s. John Henry and Ellen (Carey) D.; stud., S. Dak. Agricultural Coll., 1900-05; LL.B., U. of S. Dak., 1906; m. Iva McKennett of Webster, S. Dak., Oct. 21, 1915; pvt. law prac., Waubay, S. Dak., 1907- co. judge, Day Co., S. Dak., 1909-13; U.S. dist. atty., 3d jud. div., Valdez, 1921-25; pvt. law prac., Ketchikan, 1926-. Mem., Elks, K.P. Christian Science, Republican.

DUNN, John H., lawyer. B. in Fa.; grad., U. Pa. law sc.; m. Miss Carrie L. Sutherland in Nome, Oct. 16, 1906; pvt. sec. to Judge Alfred S. Moore, later chief dep. clerk of ct., Nome, 1902-; U.S. Comr., Council City, several yrs.; U.S. Marshal, 2d jud. div., 1904-05; clerk of dist. ct., Nome, 1905-. Protestant, Republican.

DUNN, John William, lawyer, miner. B. in Nicholsville, O., June 27, 1875; public sc., Denver; stud., U. Denver Law Sc.; served in Philippines, Spanish-Am. War; miner, logger, merchant, Fairbanks area, 1905-08; joined stampede to Ophir, 1908; prospector, teamster, lawyer, Iditarod, 1909-11; moved to Ruby, 1911; postmaster, Ruby, 1913-18; terr. H.R., 1919-21, Sen., 1923-31; mem., terr. bd. education, 1925-; died in Juneau, Mar. 19, 1931. Independent.

E

EASLEY, George W., engineer. B. in Williamson, W. Va., Mar. 14, 1933; s. Dr. George W. and Isabel Woodson (Saville) E.; stud., U. Richmond, 1952-55, Northwestern U., 1960; m. Alice Marie Bland Smith, Oct. 25, 1952; children: Bridget Bland, Saville Woodson, Marie Alexis, Roxanne Isabel, George W.; m. 2d, Paula Elizabeth Pence, Jan. 3, 1970; step-children: Kathy Clark, Laura Dean; U.S. Army Reserves, 1956-74; Va. dept. of highways, 1952-62; traffic engr., Anchorage, 1962-68; chmn., Alaska Transportation Com., 1966-67; asst. city mgr., Anchorage, 1968-69; consult., nat. transportation system for Australia, 1969; consulting engr., Wilbur Smith & Assoc., Los Angeles, 1969-71; state comr. of public works, Juneau, 1971-74; exec. v.p., Burgess Constr. Co., Anchorage, 1974-. Received Outstanding Young Man of the Year Award, 1964, Anchorage Jr. C. of C. Mem., Rotary, Navy League, Nat. Guard Officers' Assn., Anchorage and Alaska C. of C., Assoc. Gen. Contractors, Am. Public Works Assn., Inst. for Municipal Engring., Inst. of Traffic Engrs., Petroleum Club, SKAL Internat., Pi Kappa Alpha. Address: Box 4-2520, Anchorage 99509.

EASTAUGH, Frederick Orlebar, lawyer. B. in Nome, June 12, 1913; s. Edward Orlebar and Lucy Evelyn (Ladd) E.; grad., U. Wash., 1937; m. Carol Benning Robertson, Aug. 8, 1942; children: Robert Ladd, Jane, Alison; freight clerk and asst. purser, Alaska SS Co., 1937-41; traffic agent and acct., Pan-Am. Airways, 1941-46; cont. study of law, Juneau, 1946; admitted to bar, 1948; mem., Robertson, Monagle & Eastaugh law firm; city magistrate, Juneau, several yrs.; terr. H.R., 1953-55; Norwegian and French consul for southeastern Alaska. Mem., Pioneers. Protestant, Republican. Address: 217 Second St., Juneau 99801.

EDES, William Cushing, engineer. B. in Bolton, Mass., Jan. 14, 1856; s. Richard S. and Mary (Cushing) E.; B.S., Mass. Inst. Technology, 1875; m. Mary Burnham, Jan. 1901; Mass. Census Bur., 1875; Spring Valley Water Co., Calif., 1876-77; surveys for Southern Pacific R.R., 1877-81; gen. engr. prac., Mass., 1882-86; asst. engr., Southern Pacific and Atchison, Topeka and Santa Fe Rys., Calif., 1886-1907; chief engr., Northwestern Pacific R.R., 1907-14; chmn., AEC, 1914-19, const. engr., 1919-20, consulting engr., 1920-22; ret. due to ill health; died in Calif., May 26, 1922.

EDMONDSON, A. Cameron, journalist. B. in 1928; B.A., La. State U.; m. Ruth; 1 child; staff mem., 2 petroleum magazines, "Drilling" and "Oil," New Orleans and Houston; gen. reporter, Anchorage DAILY TIMES, 1959-64; experimented in creative writing while serving as winter watchman, Seldovia-Port Graham Consolidation marine ways, Seldovia, 1964-66; bus. and resources ed., Anchorage DAILY NEWS, 1966-70; contributing ed., *Alaska Industry* magazine, 1969-71; ed., "Alaska Scouting Services," weekly report on petroleum activities, 1971-73; state dep. comr., economic development and planning, 1973-74, comr., 1974-.

EDWARDS, G. Kent, lawyer. B. in Fresno, Calif., Oct. 3, 1939; s. George E.; B.A., Occidental Coll., Los Angeles, Calif., 1962; J.D., U. Calif., Berkeley, 1964; m. Barbara, 1960; children: Scott, Stacy; m. 2d, Patricia Ann Brown, Sept. 16, 1972; counsel, Legislative Affairs Agency, Juneau, 1964-66; pvt. law prac., Anchorage, 1966-67; dep. atty. gen., Juneau, 1967-68; state atty. gen., 1968-70; consult., state dept. of law, Juneau, 1970-71; U.S. dist. atty. for Alaska, Anchorage, 1971-. Republican. Address: 2113 Duke Dr., Anchorage.

EGAN, William Allen, businessman. B. in Valdez, Oct. 8, 1914; s. William Edward and Cora (Allen) E.; gr. and h. sc., Valdez; m. Desdia Neva McKittrick in Valdez, Nov. 16, 1940; s. Dennis; misc. jobs, including truck driver, bartender, gold miner, fisherman, aviator, 1932-43; U.S. Army Air Corps, WWII, 1943-46; mayor, Valdez, prop., gen. merchandise store, Valdez, 1946-56; terr. H.R., 1941-45, 1947-53, Sen., 1953-56; pres., const. conv., 1955-56; Tenn. Plan U.S. "Sen.", 1956-58; Alaska Gov., 1959-66, 1970-74; sales rep., Equitable Life Insur. Co., Anchorage, 1966-67; pres., West Coast Mortgage & Investment Co., Inc., and Security Income Corp., Seattle, 1967-69. Received Alaskan of the Year award, 1971; hon. LL.D., UA, 1972. Mem., Pioneers. Catholic, Democrat. Address: 2700 Arlington Dr., Anchorage 99503.

ELIASON, Richard Irving, fisherman, pipefitter. B. in Seattle, Wash., Oct. 14, 1925; s. George and Elsie (Preisach) E.; h. sc., Sitka; m. Betty Mae Gemmell, 1950; children: Greta Lee, George R., II, Ida Marie, Richard, Jr., Stanley Dean; went to Sitka, commercial fisherman and pipefitter, Sitka, 1927; U.S. Navy, WWII; Sitka city councilman, mayor, Greater Sitka Borough assemblyman, public utilities bd.; terr. H.R., 1969-71, 1973-75. Mem., Am. Leg., VFW, Elks, Moose, Masons. Republican. Address: Box 143, Sitka 99835.

ELLIOT, Albert D., surveyor. Surveyor-gen. and ex-officio sec. of Alaska, Sitka, July 26-Aug. 7, 1897. Democrat.

ELLIOTT, Henry Wood, artist, author. B. in Cleveland, O., Nov. 13, 1846; s. Reuben and Sophia A.E.; public and pvt. sc.; m. Alexandra Melovidov on Pribilof I., July 12, 1872; children: John S., Narene (Mrs. Benjamin B. Mozee); employe, Smithsonian Inst., Wash., D.C., 1861-78; mem., Collins Overland Telegraph Expedition, 1865-66; artist, USGS, Alaska, 1869-70; special agent, U.S. Treasury Dept., Pribilof I., 1872-74; consult., U.S. delegation, internat. fur seal conf., campaigned for 1911 treaty; noted water colorist; lobbied against terr. form of govt. for Alaska; died in Seattle, Wash., May 25, 1930. Author, "Our Arctic Province," N.Y., 1886.

ELLIOTT, John J., miner. Married; s. Calvin Coolidge (b. in Nome, Mar. 4, 1925); terr. H.R., from Haycock, 1925-27. Republican.

ELLIOTT, Malcolm, engineer. Pres., ARC, 1927-32.

ELLIOTT, Tolbert E., government administrator. B. in 1918; m.; s. Roger; realtor, N.Y.C.; mgr., housing projects, Yuba City and Berkeley, Calif.; entered public housing field; U.S. Army Air Corps, 1943-45; exec. dir., city housing authority, Benicia, Yuba City, Martinez, Calif.; asst. dir., urban renewal, ASHA, Anchorage, 1961-63, exec. dir., 1963-66; exec. dir., Okla. City housing authority, 1966. Democrat.

ELLIS, Robert Edmund, aviator. B. in St. Albans, Vt., Jan. 2, 1903; s. Charles H. and Mathilde E. (Deschenes) E.; gr. and h. sc., St. Albans, 1909-20; stud., U.S. Naval Acad., Annapolis, Md., 1920-22; m. Margaret E. Roehr, Mar. 8, 1930; children: Peter R., Michael R., Sabra P.; lumber exporting bus. and pilot training, Seattle, Wash., 1922-29; pilot, Alaska-Wash. Airways, Alaska Southern, Pan-Am. World Airways, 1929-36; estab. Ellis Airlines, pres., 1936-1950s; U.S. Navy, 1942-46; mayor, Ketchikan, 1946-48; terr. Sen., 1955-59; ret. v.p. in charge of sales, Alaska Coastal Ellis Airlines; went to Seattle to purchase 54-ft. yacht as future home, 1962; bd. dir., Alaska Airlines, 1970s. Mem., Am. Leg., Elks. Democrat. Address: Ketchikan.

ELMORE, William S., aviator. B. in Goldthwaite, Tex., Apr. 26, 1915; gr. and h. sc., Shoshone, Wyo.; learned to fly, 1936; barnstorming pilot and carnival stunt flyer, Wyo.; m., 1938; s. William J. (killed in automobile accident, Fairbanks, May 1961); m. 2d, Kathryn Yakley; step-children: Earline, Kathryn; children: Morgan Robert, Foster Sollie (Mrs. Thomas J. Coco), Charles Westley; U.S. Army Air Corps, 1942-46; operated air taxi service and flight sc., Casper, Wyo., 1946-49; homesteaded at Rabbit Creek, near Anchorage; joined Alaska Nat. Guard, pilot, 1954, flight training supervisor, 1955, base detachment comdr., 1956, head of Kulis Air Nat. Guard, Anchorage, 1959; adjt. gen., Nat. Guard, hdqrs. Juneau, 1964-67, air operations officer, Nat. Guard, and flight inspector, FAA, 1967-71; adjt. gen., Nat. guard, with state-conferred rank of maj. gen., 1971-73; asst. operations officer, internat. airport, Anchorage, 1973-. Received Alaska Distinguished Service medal by Gov. Egan, for work in Nat. Guard since 1954. Mem., Nat. Guard Officers' Assn. (pres.). Democrat. Address: Elmore Rd., Rabbit Creek.

ELSNER, Richard E., mechanic. Maintenance supt., Copper River & Northwestern Ry., Cordova, for yrs.; terr. H.R., 1921-23. Republican.

EMBERG, Truman C., fisherman. B. in Proctor, Minn., 1909; m. Maxine; went to Alaska, 1935; Dillingham res.; bus. agent, Bristol Bay Fish Pro-

ducers' Assn., 1950s; bus. mgr., Western Alaska Cooperative Marketing Assn., 1960s; mem., const. conv., 1955-56; labor rep., employment security com., 1955-59; write-in cand., state H.R., 1970. Protestant, Democrat.

ENGEBRETH, Gunnard Marshall, businessman, school teacher. B. in Chicago, Ill., Jan. 19, 1909; gr. and h. sc., Hawkins, Wis., 1915-27; stud., State Teachers' Coll., River Falls, Wis., 1927-31; employe, Savings & Loan Assn., Seattle, Wash., 1931-33; employe, Alaska R.R., Anchorage, and BIA teacher, Eklutna, 1933-36; m. Violet Swanson, 1935; children: Karen, Kristin, Evelyn, Roger, Robert, Nancy; husband-wife BIA teachers, Kaltag, 1935-39; estab. hardware store, Anchorage, 1939-46; sold hardware bus.; estab. Engebreth Appliance Co., Maytag franchise, Anchorage, 1946-51; terr. Sen., 1947-51, pres., 2 terms; died in Swedish hosp., Seattle, Wash., July 14, 1951; buried in Minneapolis, Minn. Lutheran, Republican.

ENGSTROM, Elton Egedeous, Sr., fish broker. B. in Wrangell, June 6, 1905; s. Adolph and Amelia (Nelson) E.; gr. and h. sc., Wrangell, 1911-23; stud., U. Wash., 1923-26; fish broker, Wrangell; m. Thelma Catherine Wait, June 13, 1928; children: Elton E., Jr., Allan; fish broker, Juneau, 1928-63; Sen., 1951-55, 1957-63; chmn., Rep. centennial com., 1936-46; city councilman, 1939-43, mayor, 1943-44, Douglas; died in St. Ann's hosp., Juneau, Jan. 30, 1963. Mem., Pioneers, Sons of Norway, Masons, Moose. Presbyterian, Republican.

ENGSTROM, Elton Egedeous, Jr., fish broker, lawyer. B. in Juneau, 1935; s. Elton E. and Thelma (Wait) E.; B.A., U. Ore., 1958; law degree, Harvard U., 1960; m. Sally, 1963; d. Catherine Nora; mgr., Engstrom Bros., fish broker bus., Juneau, 1963; state H.R., 1965-67, Sen., 1967-71. Republican.

ENGSTROM, Thelma Catherine, educator. B. in Seattle, Wash., Sept. 19, 1905; d. Herbert M. and Marit (Thyve) Wait; grad., U. Wash., 1926; sc. teacher, Neppel, Wash., 1926-27, Wrangell, 1927-28; m. Elton E. Engstrom, Sr., June 13, 1928; children: Elton E., Jr., Allan; sc. teacher, Douglas, daily columnist, Alaska DAILY PRESS, Juneau, 1930-38; mem., Douglas sc. bd., 1938-44; terr. H.R., 1947-49; died in Rochester, Minn., Feb. 7, 1957. Mem., Juneau Woman's Club, Women's Volunteer Service, Eastern Star, Sons of Norway, Pioneers' Aux. Presbyterian, Republican.

ERICKSON, Everett Russell, educator. B. in Everett, Wash., 1904; s. Richard and Clara G. (Baardson) E.; B.A., 1926, M.S., 1938, post-grad., 1933, 1935-36, U. Ida.; stud., Stanford U., 1944-45; unm.; sc. teacher, Ida., 1926-32; head, dept. English, public sc., Juneau, 1932-37; prof., education, UA, 1937-50; dep. comr. education, 1950-51, comr., 1951-53. Mem., Nat. Assn. Journalism (dir., 1934-37), World Fed. Education Assns. (U.S. del., Tokyo, 1937), Nat. Congress PTA (rep., 1938-42), NEA (dir., 1936-42), Alpha Tau Omega, Kappa Delta Pi, Delta Sigma Rho, Masons (Shriner, Scottish Rite, K.T.), Eastern Star, Elks. Episcopalian.

ERWIN, Guy Burton, lawyer. B. in Mt. Pleasant, Minn., June 20, 1872; s. Richard R. and Margaret Isabelle (Reading) E.; law stud., U. Chicago; m. Lillian M. Coyle in Minneapolis, Minn., Oct. 15, 1895; employe, bldg. and loan assn., Minneapolis; joined Klondike stampede, going to Dawson via Chilkoot trail, Jan. 1898; moved to Fairbanks, 1904; admitted to Alaska bar, 1905; U.S. Comr., Fairbanks, 1906-08; pvt. law prac., 1908-21; U.S. dist. atty., 4th jud. dist., 1921-24; left Fairbanks for med. treatment, Jan. 1929; died in Seattle, Wash., May 15, 1929; interment in family plot, Mazeppa, Minn.; survived by widow.

ERWIN, Lewis T. (Stubbs), miner, businessman. B. in Cartersville, Ga.; mem., Ga. legislature; moved to Chattanooga, Tenn., 1884; state assemblyman, Tenn., 1886-88; moved to Everett, Wash., 1892; U.S. Indian agent, Yakima, Wash. reservation, 1893-97; estab. Erwin & Coburn Transportation Co., Dawson, Can., 1897-1904; m. and div. (1902), leaving wife with 5 children, Yakima, Wash.; m. 2d and div.; m. 3d, Hattie Belle Burrell, 1919; moved to Fairbanks, 1904; city magistrate, 1905-07, city clerk, 1905-10, Fairbanks; attended terr. and nat. Dem. conv.; U.S. Marshal, 4th jud. dist., Fairbanks, 1913-21; cancer patient, Mayo clinic, Rochester, Minn., March 1922; died in Mayo clinic, March 28, 1923; survived by 2 sons, 3 daughters. Democrat.

ERWIN, Robert Cecil, lawyer. B. in Seward, Dec. 29, 1934; s. William C. and Hazel (Matthews) E.; B.S., U. Colo., 1956; LL.B., U. Wash., 1959; m. Monica Louise Boucher, Nome, Oct. 21, 1961; children: Janet, Kristina, Roberta, Michel, Andrew; law clerk and asst. atty. gen., Juneau, 1959-60; dist. atty., 2d jud. div., Nome, 1960-62; dist. atty., 4th jud. div., Fairbanks, 1962-63; dist. atty., 3d jud. div., Anchorage, 1963-64; pvt. law prac., Anchorage, 1964-70; supreme ct. justice, 1970-. Catholic, Democrat. Address: 701 W. 20th Ave., Anchorage.

ERWIN, William Matthews, lawyer. B. in Seward, Mar. 23, 1933; s. William C. and Hazel (Matthews) E.; gr. and h. sc., Seward; B.A., U. Colo., 1955; law degree, U. Wash., 1965; m. Sheila Ruth O'Brien in Nome, May 11, 1962; children: Lynn and Eileen (twins), Maureen, Patrick; sc. teacher, Seward, 1957-59, Nome, 1960-61; pvt. law prac., Anchorage, 1968-69; asst. atty. gen., Anchorage, 1969-. Mem., Elks. Catholic, Democrat. Address: 1033 W. 6th Ave., Anchorage 99501.

F

FAGERSTROM, Charles E., construction worker. B. at Golovin Bay, Alaska, Oct. 29, 1905; stud., Chemawa Indian sc., Salem, Ore., 1922-28; m.; 5 daughters, 2 sons; heavy equipment operator, U.S. Smelting, Refining & Mining Co., Nome, 1928-39, dredge master, 1954; U.S. Army Corps Engrs., 1940-48; employe, Gaasland Constr. Co., 1950-53; mem., Nome sc. bd.; terr. H.R., 1953-57, 1959-60; died in ANS hospital, Anchorage, Jan. 2, 1962; buried in Nome. Mem., Arctic Native Brotherhood (pres., 3 times). Democrat.

FAHRENKAMP, Bettye, housewife. Democrat Nat. Committeewoman, 1972-; m. G.H. Gib Fahrenkamp, carpenter (dec. 1974). Address: 4013 Evergreen Ave., McKinley Acres, Fairbanks.

FALL, Albert Bacon, rancher, miner, lawyer. B. in Frankfort, Ky., Nov. 26, 1861; s. William R. and Edmonia (Taylor) F.; public sc., Nashville, Tenn., but mainly self-educated; worked in cotton factory, Nashville, at age 11; sc. teacher; law stud.; admitted to bar, 1891; m. Emma Garland Morgan, May 7, 1883; 4 children; law prac., Las Cruces, N. Mex., specialty in Mex. law; engaged in mining, lumber, real estate, railroads, farming and stock-raising enterprises, N. Mex. and Mexico; terr. H.R., 1891-93; appt. judge, 3d jud. dist., assoc. justice of N. Mex. Supreme Ct., 1893; terr. atty. gen., 1897, 1907; mem., terr. const. conv., 1911; U.S. Sen., 1912-21; changed party affiliation, Dem. to Rep., c. 1900; U.S. Sec. of Interior, 1921-23; central figure in Teapot Dome oil scandal, forcing resignation; found guilty of bribery, 1929; prison inmate, 1931-32 (served 9 mos., 19 days); ret. to ranch, Three Rivers, N. Mex.; died in El Paso, Tex. hosp., Nov. 30, 1944. Quaker, Republican.

FARMER, Elvis M., military officer. B. in 1927; mem., Nat. Guard bureau, Wash., D.C.; dir., personnel section, 1952-54, asst. adjt. gen., 1954-56, adjt. gen., acting, 1956-57, Nat. Guard, Alaska.

FARRELL, Martin A., lawyer. B. in N.Y.C., May 9, 1930; B.A., Fordham U.; LL.B., Catholic U. of Am., 1965; m. Shirley; children: Ellen, Michael, James, David; U.S. Marine Corps, 1948-50; partner, Hahn, Jewell & Farrell law firm, Anchorage, 1959-71; terr. H.R., 1971-73; dir. and legal counsel for Lost River, city created by 1971-72 legislature, hdqrs., Anchorage. Democrat. Address: 1215 W. 8th, Anchorage.

FAULKNER, Herbert Lionel, lawyer, lobbyist. B. in Maitland, Nova Scotia, Can., Nov. 14, 1883; s. John Stephen and Elvira (Pratt) F.; law stud., office of

Charles G. Ingersoll, Ketchikan; m. Miss Roma Jameson in Aberdeen, Wash., May 8, 1911; children: Jean (Mrs. Remington Low), Malcolm; clerk, Tongass Trading store, and dep. U.S. Marshal, Ketchikan, 1903-09; moved to Juneau, 1909; dep. U.S. Marshal, until 1911, U.S. Marshal, 1st jud. dist., 1911-14; admitted to Alaska bar, 1914; naturalized U.S. citizen, 1925; Norwegian vice consul for southeast Alaska, 1934-; ret. to Oakland, Calif., 1959; died in San Francisco, June 28, 1972. Mem., terr. bd. education, 1933-45 (pres.), Pioneers, Scottish Rite, Masons, Elks, Moose, Am. Bar Assn., Wash. Athletic Club. Presbyterian, Republican.

FENTON, Thomas Edgar, Jr., lawyer. B. in Orange, N.J., July 23, 1934; s. Thomas Edgar and Maude Anna (Gegenheimer) F.; B.A., 1956, LL.B., 1961, Trinity Coll., Hartford, Conn.; m. Nancy Keahi Iaea, Fairbanks, Dec. 18, 1965; children: Tercia, Porcia, Marcia, Jaylen, Helen Anna, Thomas Edgar, III; claims examiner, Prudential Insur. Co., Newark, N.J., 1956-58; law clerk, dept. of labor, Juneau, Aug. 1961; right-of-way agent, div. of highways, Juneau, Sept. 1961-Aug. 1962; law clerk, state dept. of law, Fairbanks, 1962-63; asst. atty. gen., Fairbanks, Feb.-Nov., 1963; state dist. atty., 1st jud. div., Ketchikan, 1963-64; state dist. atty., 4th jud. div., Fairbanks, 1964-67; pvt. law prac., Fairbanks, 1967-. Mem., Rotary, Petroleum Club. Covenant Church, Democrat. Address: Suite 206, 1919 Lathrop St., Fairbanks 99701.

FERGUSON, Charles B., fisherman, miner. B. in Fultonham, N.Y., c. 1858; reportedly shipwrecked on Alaska coast, c. 1900, and settled on Prince of Wales I.; terr. H.R., from Craig, 1925-29; employe, Sulzer copper mines, for yrs.; moved to Kent, Wash., 1930; associated with Olympic Gen. and Lapidary Co., 8812 Aurora Ave., Seattle, Wash., 1934. Republican.

FERGUSON, Frank R., aviator. B. in Kotzebue, July 14, 1939; s. Archie R. Ferguson, Kotzebue; h. sc., Lathrop, Fairbanks; m. Phyllis White, Jan. 31, 1959; m. 2d, Sophie; 3 children; U.S. Army, 1963-65; state H.R., 1971-75. Mem., state council of libraries, legal services bd., Northwest Alaska Native Assn. (bd. dir.). Democrat, 1970, Independent, 1972. Address: Box 131, Kotzebue 99752.

FINK, Thomas A., lawyer, businessman. B. in Peoria, Ill., Aug. 26, 1928; s. B.J. and Kathleen F.; youth on farm; B.S., Bradley U., Peoria, 1949; LL.B., U. Ill., 1952; m. Patricia Israelson, 1951; children: Debra, Ann, Maureen, Mark, Michael, Kathryn, Tom, Mathew, Joshua, Johanna Lynn, Kelly Elizabeth; clerk, Kay, Robison & Moody law firm, Anchorage, 1952-53; v.p., City Nat. Bank, 1953-55; bus. mgr., Nukar Sales & Big Three Motors, 1955-57; estab. insur. agency, Friendly Finance Co. (later known as Thomas A. Fink Insur. Agency); gen. agent, Pacific Nat. Life Assurance Co.; certified insur. underwriter, 1957-; state H.R., 1967-75, speaker, 1973-74. Mem., K.C., Lions, Operation Statehood, Jr. C. of C. (pres., 1959). Catholic, Republican. Address: 1320 23d Ave., Anchorage.

FISCHER, Helen Marie, housewife. B. in Sleepy Eye, Minn., June 2, 1912; d. William and Anna Schmid; stud., St. Mary's Sc., Sleepy Eye h. sc., Northwest Coll. of Speech, U. Minn.; m. Edward Anthony Fischer, 1933; children: Richard W., David, Linda (Mrs. Charles Parr, Jr.); moved to Anchorage, 1946; del., const. conv., 1955-56; Dem. Nat. Committeewoman, 1956-63; Alaska H.R., 1957-61, 1971-75. Mem., nat. bd., Women's Med. Coll. of Pa., BPW, Anchorage Woman's Club, Operation Statehood. Catholic, Democrat. Address: 2023 Wildwood Lane, Anchorage 99503.

FISCHER, Victor, town planner, professor. B. in Berlin, Germany, May 5, 1924; s. Louis and Markoosha F.; B.A., U. Wis., 1948; M.C.P., Mass. Inst. Technology, 1950; m. Gloria Rubenstein, 1944; children: Anne, Gregory, Joseph; town planner, Peterborough, N.H., 1949-50; townsite planner, BLM, Anchorage, 1950-52; planning dir., Anchorage, 1952-55; exec. sec., League of Alaskan Cities, 1953-56; community planning consult., Anchorage, 1955-57; del., const. conv., 1955-56; terr. H.R., 1957-59; dir., planning and urban renewal, and asst. exec. dir., ASHA, 1957-61; Littauer Fellowship in public adm., Harvard U., 1961-62; asst. adm., U.S. Housing & Home Finance Agency and dir., office of metropolitan development, U.S. HUD, Wash., D.C., 1962-66; dir., ISEGR, UA, and prof., political science, UA, Fairbanks, 1966-. Mem., Am. Inst. of Planners (bd. gov., 1971-74), Am. Soc. Planning Officials, Alaska Native Foundation (bd. dir.). Democrat. Address: UA, Fairbanks 99701.

FISHER, James Elliott, lawyer. B. in Cleveland, O., 1927; s. Robert M. Fisher, Dallas, Tex.; grad., Woodrow Wilson h. sc., Dallas; grad., Southern Methodist U. law sc.; m. Mrs. Helen Louise Neet in Anchorage, April, 1960; d. Sally; U.S. Marine Corps, WWII, and Corps of Engrs., Korea; employe, Morrison-Knudson Constr. Co., DEW line, Alaska, 1955; insur. adjuster; admitted to Alaska bar, 1956; pvt. law prac., Anchorage, 1958; moved to Kenai, 1961; Kenai city atty. Mem., Am. Bar Assn., Kenai C. of C. (pres., 1962-64). Democrat. Address: Box 397, Kenai.

FISHER, Walter G., miner, sawmill operator. B. in Chippewa Falls, Wis., c. 1887; unm.; miner on Dome Cr., near Fairbanks, 1903-; sawyer, Ind. Lumber Co.; estab. sawmill, Tolovana dist.; ret. to mining, Grant Cr., near Tanana; terr. H.R., 1927-31; died at his mining camp, Grant Cr., July 10, 1946. Independent.

FISHER, Walter L., lawyer. B. in Wheeling, Va., July 4, 1862; s. Daniel Webster and Amanda D. (Kouns) F.; stud., Marietta (O.) Coll., 1878-79, Hanover (Ind.) Coll., 1879-83, LL.D., 1913; m. Mabel Taylor, Apr. 22, 1891; pvt. law prac., Chicago, 1888, 1911, 1913; Sec. of Interior, 1911-13; special counsel in transportation matters, Chicago, 1906-11, 1914-; died Nov. 9, 1935. Mem., exec. com., Municipal Voters' League (sec., 1901-06, pres., 1906); Conservation League America (pres., 1908-09); Nat. Conservation Assn. (v.p., 1910-11); R.R. Securities Com., 1910-11. Republican.

FITZGERALD, James Martin, lawyer. B. in Portland, Ore., Oct. 7, 1920; s. Thomas and Florence (Linderman) F.; grad., Jefferson h. sc., Portland, 1940; B.A., 1950, LL.B., 1951, Willamette U.; grad. stud., U. Wash., inst. public affairs, 1951-52; m. Karin Rose Benton in Albany, Ore., Jan. 1950; children: Dennis, Denise, Debra, Kevin; U.S. Army, 1940-41; U.S. Marine Corps, 1942-46; asst. U.S. dist. atty., 1st and 3d jud. dist., 1952-55; city atty., Anchorage, 1956-59; legal counsel to Gov. Egan, Apr.-Nov., 1959; comr. public safety, Sept.-Nov., 1959; superior ct. judge, 3d jud. dist., Anchorage, 1959-72; assoc. justice, Alaska Supreme Ct., 1972-74; U.S. dist. judge, 1975-. Elected to Alaska Press Club's 49er hall of fame, 1964. Mem., Alaska and Oregon Bar Assns.; Anchorage Parks and Recreation bd., 1965-72; com. on jud. qualifications (chmn., 1971-72). Democrat. Address: 1346 M St., Anchorage.

FITZGERALD, Joseph Harold, government administrator. B. in Los Angeles, Calif., Mar. 20, 1909; B.A., U. Mont., 1931; Rhodes scholar, Oxford U., 1932-35, B.A. Jurisprudence, 1934, Bachelor of Common Laws, 1935; m. Ruth Milliken; children: Dr. Helen F. Cserr, Mrs. Jean F. Jackson, Joseph K., Mrs. Susan F. Othmer; reg. atty., CAA, Anchorage, 1949-51; dir., CAB, Anchorage, 1951-53; dir., bur. of air operation, CAB, Wash., D.C., 1953-58; gen. mgr.-pres., Ozark Airlines, St. Louis, Mo., 1958-63; exec. dir., state public service com., Anchorage, 1963-64; dir., state reconstruction program, Anchorage, 1964-65; chmn., fed. field com. for development planning in Alaska, Anchorage, 1965-69; dir., community affairs, Atlantic Richfield Oil Corp., Anchorage, 1969-71; mem., Joint Fed.-State Land-Use Planning Com. (fed. rep.), Anchorage, 1973-.

FITZPATRICK, Mrs. Marjorie Grace (Margee), housewife. B. in St. John, N.B., Can., Feb. 18, 1918; d. Margaret Albin; registered nurse, received training King's Co. hosp., N.Y.; U.S. Army Nursing Corps, 1941-46; m. Dr. James Joseph Fitzpatrick (dec. 1970); d. Kathleen (Mrs. Richard Bishop); moved to Anchorage from Boise, Ida., 1957; mem., southcentral Rep. dist. com., 1963-68; Rep. Nat. Committeewoman, 1968-70. Mem., Women's Aux., Anchorage Med. Assn. (pres., 1959-60); Am. Nurses' Assn., Anchorage Rep. Club. Republican. Address: 1200 L St., Anchorage 99501.

FLAKNE, Joseph T., government administrator. B. in Beltrami, Minn., Nov. 10, 1900; s. Knud O. and Julia (Orvella) F.; gr. sc., Holt, Minn., h. sc., Minneapolis, Minn.; B.S., UA, 1934; m. Irene Hodges in Fairbanks, June 2, 1934; no children; salesman, Standard Oil Co., Minneapolis, 1922-29; foreman, U.S. Biological Survey, 1929-34; supt., UA farm, Fairbanks, 1934-36; agriculture extension agent, Matanuska Valley, 1936-37; dir., U.S. Employment Service for Alaska, 1937-42; Alaska specialist, War Manpower com., 1942-44; U.S. Army, 1944-45; chief, Alaska branch, div. of terr., Dept. of Interior, 1946-. Mem., Rotary, Masons. Lutheran.

FOLTA, George William, lawyer. B. in Pittsburgh, Pa., Mar. 14, 1893; s. Adam and Anne (Sabo) F.; grad., Beutel's Bus. Coll., Tacoma, Wash., 1912; m. Marion Sutton in Juneau, Apr. 26, 1916; s. George; m. 2d, Ruth M. Coles in Seattle, Mar. 6, 1928; children: Claire (Mrs. Louis Rainery, m. 2d, Mrs. Ray Wipperman), Richard; steno-clerk, Steamboat Inspection Service, Dept. of Commerce, Juneau, 1913; clerk-sec. to Alaska gov., 1915-21; ct. reporter to U.S. dist. judge, 1921-27; admitted to bar, 1927; asst. dist. atty., 1st jud. dist., Juneau, 1927-40; solicitor, Dept. of Interior, 1940-47; U.S. dist. judge, 1st jud. dist., Juneau, 1947-55; died of heart attack while on bear-hunting trip, near Yakataga, June 5, 1955.

FORBES, Vernon D., businessman, lawyer. B. in Wahpeton, N. Dak., May 22, 1905; s. Joseph G. and Mary Catherine F.; special stud., U. N. Dak.; studied law in father's office, Wahpeton; admitted to bar, 1936; prac. law, Wahpeton, and prosecuting atty., Richland Co., 1940-50; m. Ruth Peterson of Fergus Falls, Minn.; d. Catherine Jane (m.); U.S. dist. judge, 4th jud. dist., Fairbanks, 1954-60; v.p. and trust officer, Alaska Nat. Bk., 1960-; pres., Mt. McKinley Mutual Savings Bk.; pres., 1st Fed. Savings & Loan Assn. Received Award of Merit from DAR in recognition of interest in naturalization ceremonies in his ct., 1957. Mem., IOOF, Eagles, Alaska Airlines (bd. dir.), Nat. Assn. Mutual Savings Bks. (bd. dir.). Republican.

FOSTER, Don C., government administrator. B. in Kingfisher, Okla., Sept. 23, 1898; s. George D. and Connie F.; B.S., Okla. A. & M.; post-grad., N. Mex. State Coll., 1 yr.; m. Katie Lee Mahaffey, Jan. 22, 1922; children: Don Max, Kara Lee; U.S. Army, 1917-18; livestock rancher, Kingfisher, 1922-28; sc. teacher, Floyd, N. Mex., 1928-31; co. agent, Quay Co., N. Mex., 1931-35; entered Indian Service, Warm Springs, Ore., 1935; supt., Carson Indian Agency, Nev., 1940-44; transferred to Alaska, 1944; gen. supt., ANS; died May 1, 1971. Mem., Am. Leg., Lions, Alpha Zeta, Lambda Chi Alpha, Masons. Methodist.

FOSTER, Frank H., lawyer. B. in Seattle, Wash., Dec. 6, 1878; s. George and Nettie (Low) F.; grad., Stanford U. law sc., 1901; law prac., eastern Wash. and Seattle; m.; 5 children: Marian, Mrs. E.E. Schroeder, Frank, Jr. (dec. 1939), et al.; admitted to bar, Olympia, Wash., 1906; went to Alaska, 1911; prac. law, McCarthy, Valdez, Cordova; miner, Nizina dist.; terr. H.R., 1923-25, 1929-33; U.S. dist. atty., 3d jud. dist., 1925-26; city atty., Cordova, 15 yrs.; moved to Juneau, 1931; cand.; terr. atty. gen.; moved to Olympia, Wash., 1944; state atty. gen.'s office, pvt. prac.; died in Olympia, Wash., Feb. 1952; survived by wife, 3 daughters. Mem., Mayflower Soc., SAR, A.B., Elks, Odd Fellows. Episcopalian, Republican.

FOSTER, Neal W. (Willie), aviator, miner. B. in Chickasha, Okla., Aug. 2, 1916; m. Jane, 1940; children: Richard, James, Jean, Iris; miner, Seward Peninsula, until 1941; U.S. Air Force, 1941-46; worked at tin mine, Lost River, near Nome; driller-prospector, U.S. Smelting, Refining and Mining

Co.; pilot, Bill Munz, Wien and Alaska Airlines; part-time prospector, wife and children operate family gold mine; estab. own flying service bus.; mem., terr. aeronautics and communications com., 1949-54; Alaska Sen., 1955-59, 1963-67; dir., air commerce, Public Service Com., 1960-61.

FRAME, Arthur, lawyer. B. near Sheldon, Ia., 1880; moved with parents to S. Dak., 1895; stud., Yankton Coll., 1896-99; read law in office of Judge Bartlett Tripp, Yankton, 1898-1901; m. Miss Carrie Ganter in San Francisco, Calif., Feb. 1918; prac. law, S. Dak., 1901-03; assoc., law firm of Hoyt & Haight, Seattle, Wash., 1903-04; assoc., ARC and White Pass & Yukon Ry., Skagway, 1905-06; assoc., McGinn & Sulivan, Fairbanks, 1906-12; U.S. Comr., Fairbanks, 1909-10; res., San Francisco, 1912-19; pvt. law prac., Anchorage, 1919-35; terr. H.R., 1921-23, Sen., 1927-31; cand., Rep. Nat. Com., 1924; went to San Francisco for med. care, Feb. 1935; died there, Apr. 17, 1935. Mem., Masons. Republican.

FRAME, John W., journalist. B. in McComb, Ill., Feb. 7, 1857; sc. teacher, Ia. and Neb., 1876-89; grad., Ia. State U. law sc., 1889; m. Susan Annetta Carpenter, Council Bluffs, Ia., July 20, 1882 (dec. 1933); children: John William, Jr., Grover, Ira, Park; prac. law, Snohomish, Wash., 1890-98; Wash. terr. legislator, 1891-93; newspaper pub., Dawson, 1898; moved to Fortymile and Nome, 1900-02; newspaper pub.: ALASKA RECORD-MINER, Juneau, ALASKA WEEKLY TRANSCRIPT, Juneau, THE ALASKAN, Cordova, THE TRUTH, Cordova, MINER, Cordova, THE COMMONER, Valdez, THE WEEKLY ALASKAN, Anchorage, THE FORTY-NINTH STAR, Valdez and Anchorage, DAILY HERALD, Cordova, THE PATHFINDER (monthly for Pioneers), THE ALASKA EXAMINER, Ketchikan; U.S. Comr., Hyder, 1922-23; elected Rep. Nat. Committeeman, Apr. 1924, but Nat. Com. refused to seat him; attended Dem. terr. conv., 1934; died in Ketchikan, Nov. 6, 1939. Republican and Democrat.

FRANCIS, David Rowland, merchant. B. in Richmond, Ky., Oct. 1, 1850; s. John Broaddus and Elizabeth Caldwell (Rowland) F.; B.A., U. Wash., 1870; LL.D., U. Mo., 1892, Shortleff Coll., 1903, St. Louis U., 1904, Wash. U., 1905; m. Jane Perry, 1876; 6 sons; employe, com. house of Shryock & Rowland; estab. own com. house, grain merchants; pres., merchants exchange, 1884; mayor, St. Louis, Mo., 1885-89; Gov. of Mo., 1889-93; Sec. of Interior, 1896-97; Ambassador to Russia, 1916-18; died Jan. 15, 1927. Mem., Mo. Hist. Soc., St. Louis Art Museum (dir.). Democrat.

FRANKEL, Marvin S., lawyer. B. in O., 1920; grad., Wharton Sc. of Bus., U. Pa., UCLA law sc.; m. Candee in Cleveland, O., 1957; owned chain of motion picture theatres, O.; pvt. law prac., Los Angeles, Calif., asst. U.S. dist. atty. for Alaska, Anchorage, 1966-68; U.S. dist. atty. for Alaska, Anchorage, 1968-69. Mem., Ind. Theatre Owners of O. (bd. dir., 10 yrs.), Temple Beth Shalom, Catholic

Charities, Inc. of Alaska (chmn., bd. dir.), Boys Clubs of Alaska (bd. dir.), Anchorage chapter, Fed. Bar Assn. (v.p.). Democrat.

FRANKLIN, Glen D., accountant, miner. B. in Wash., c. 1914; s. C.F. Franklin, Forest Grove, Ore.; B.A., UA, 1936; m. Vieno Wahto, Fairbanks, Apr. 23, 1938; acct. and office mgr., Alluvial Gold, Inc. and Gold Placers, Inc., Coal Creek; employe, Alaska Freight Lines, 2 yrs.; miner on Kuskokwim, Fortymile, Yukon rivers; terr. H.R., from Fairbanks, 1949-53. Democrat.

FRANZ, Charles J., aviator, fisherman, trapper. B. on Nelson Lagoon, near Port Moller, 1911; s. of Latvian sailor and Eskimo-Russian mother; fisherman, trapper, pilot (winter), Alaska Peninsula and Aleutians; attended Indian sc., Wash. and Ore., public sc., Bellingham, Wash.; state H.R., from Port Moller, 1959-61. Democrat.

FRATIES, Gail R., lawyer. State dist. atty., 1st jud. dist., Juneau, 1969-70. Republican.

FRAWLEY, James, lawyer, miner. B. in Madison, Wis., Jan. 26, 1860; public sc., Madison; B.A., LL.B., U. Wis., 1884; m. Marian M.; miner, Black Hills, S. Dak., 1871-77; lawyer-miner, Deadwood, S. Dak., 1884-1900, Nome, 1900-37; U.S. Comr., 1914-17; promoted large capital investments in gold mining, Seward Peninsula; terr. Sen., 1919-23, 1933-37, pres., 1919; died following operation, Pasadena, Calif., Mar. 3, 1938. Mem., Pioneers. Wickersham-Democrat.

FREEDING, Conrad F., miner, merchant. B. in Sweden, 1869; went to Chicago, Ill., 1876; worked in mercantile bus.; joined Stikine stampede, 1898; went to Dawson via Chilkoot Pass; m. Ida Anderson in Nome, Dec. 7, 1907; 1 d.; gold prospector, discovered the famous "Anvil No. 4"; mayor, Nome, 1907-08; terr. Sen., 1913-15; interested in Barker Hotel, Pike St., Seattle, Wash., 1913, sold out, 1916; ret. to Alaska and purchased store on Taylor Cr.; froze to death in snowstorm, Nov. 1917; buried in Nome, March 1918. Democrat (although elected on non-partisan ticket).

FREEMAN, Oral E., merchant. B. in Ut., Nov. 24, 1915; m. Fay; 2 children; went to Alaska, 1945; commercial fisherman and terr. policeman; estab. Alaska Outboard Services, supply bus. to fishing and logging industries near Ketchikan; state H.R., 1959-61, 1973-75; Gateway Borough assemblyman, 3 yrs., city councilman, 6 yrs., mayor, 3 yrs., Ketchikan. Mem., Alaska jud. council, Alaska Municipal League (dir.). Democrat. Address: 2743 3d Ave., Ketchikan.

FREER, Richard W., accountant. B. in Middleport, N.Y., Oct. 7, 1913; s. Grant Blaine and Mary Minerva (Wilcox) F.; stud., U. Wash., 1935-38; m. Roberta Jane Rushmore, Fairbanks, July 26, 1941; children: Michael (dec.), David, Peter, Cherry; moved from Yakima, Wash. to Fairbanks, 1938; clerical, accounting, paymaster, foreman positions, 1931-49; bus. mgr., terr. dept. health, 1949-55; terr. budget dir., 1955-59; dir., state div. of budget and management, 1959-70; dep. comr., dept. adm., 1971-74, comr., 1974 (Apr.-Dec.), dep. comr., 1975-. Democrat.

FRENCH, Peter, collector of customs, Sitka, 1884-87.

FRIEDRICH, Robert A., lawyer. B. in Ky., c. 1849; m. Miss Proebstel of Ore.; 1 d.; enlisted in Union Army, 1862, lt. col., 1864; moved to Topeka, Kan., 1872; law prac., 1887; brig. gen., Kan. Nat. Guard, adjt. gen., 4 yrs.; prac. law, San Francisco, Calif., 1889-98; U.S. dist. atty. for Alaska, Sitka, 1898-1900; U.S. dist. atty., 1st jud. dist., Sitka, 1900-02; died in Juneau, Dec. 31, 1902. Mem., Union Veterans Union (1st dep. comdr. in chief, 1889), Army & Navy Rep. League of Calif. (comdr. in chief, 1895-97), Union League Club, San Francisco (pres., 1897), A.B. Repubican.

FRIEND, Elmer A., newspaper editor. B. in Eau Claire, Wis., June 4, 1874; public sc., Seattle, Wash.; m., dec. 1948; children: William, Phyllis (Mrs. Arthur Adams); reporter, Seattle POST-INTELLIGENCER, Seattle STAR; went to Skagway, 1900; agent, Alaska SS Co.; reporter, Skagway ALASKAN, Skagway NEWS; correspondent, Dawson DAILY NEWS; ret. to Seattle; ed., Seward GATEWAY, 3 yrs.; city ed., managing-ed., sometimes advertising and circulation mgr., ALASKA DAILY EMPIRE, Juneau, 1916-56; died in Juneau, Dec. 2, 1959; cremation, Seattle, Wash.

FRITZ, Dr. Milo Herbert, physician. B. in Pittsfield, Mass., Aug. 25, 1909; B.A., Columbia Coll., N.Y., 1931; M.D., Columbia U., 1934; internship, Brooklyn, N.Y.; residence, Duke U., in eye, ear, nose and throat; m. Miss Elizabeth Berry in Tioga, Pa., June 15, 1937; children: Jonathan R., Pieter X.; U.S. Army reserve, 1936-41, active, 1941-46; res., Ketchikan, 1940-46; went to Dartmouth Eye Inst., Hanover, N.H.; pvt. prac., N.Y.C., 1946-48; moved to Anchorage, 1948; learned to fly and conducted hundreds of health clinics throughout bush country for natives; elected terr. Sen., but withdrew for "family considerations," 1958; cand., Alaska gov., 1962; state H.R., 1967-69, 1973-75. Mem., Alaska Med. Assn. (pres., 1955), Am. Acad. Ophthalmology & Otolaryngology (since 1946), Arctic Inst. North Am., Cook Inlet Hist. Soc., Flying Physicians, Elks. Republican. Address: Providence Professional Bldg., Anchorage and Anchor Point.

FULLER, Frederick Ernest, lawyer. B. in West Auburn, Pa.; Mar. 27, 1868; s. Charles and Retta May (Raub) R.; B.A., Wesleyan U., Middletown, Conn., 1890; LL.B., 1902, LL.M., 1903, Nat. U., Wash., D.C.; atty., Indian Affairs office and office of clerk of ct. of claims, Wash., D.C.; unm.; prac. law, Juneau, 1897-98, Skagway, 1898-99, N.Y., 1899-1900, Nome, 1900-12; U.S. Comr., Nome, 1906-09; U.S. dist. judge, 4th jud. dist., Fairbanks, 1912-14; prac. law, Los Angeles, Calif., 1914-18, with Peter Overfield, former Alaskan jurist; res., Seattle, Wash., 1918-53; died in Seattle rest home, Nov. 8, 1953. Republican.

FURNESS, Milton John, government administrator. B. in Everett, Wash., May 8, 1903; s. John and Jenny A. (Peterson) F.; stud., sc. of forestry, Ore. State Coll.; m. Nancy Gulley, Sept. 3, 1931; children: Milton John, Jr., Ann Sutton; USFS Snoqualmie Nat. Forest, 1923-26; Snohomish Co. dep. game warden, Everett, 1928-33; Wash. state game protector, 1933-34; U.S. game management agent, in charge Ore. state dist., Portland, 1934-36; adm. asst., div. game management, U.S. Biological Survey, Wash., D.C.,1936-38; adm. asst., Omaha, Neb., and adm. officer, Minneapolis, Minn., until 1943; mem., Alaska Game Com., Juneau, 1943-; adm. officer, Fish & Wildlife Service, Juneau, 1944-. Mem., Nat. Fed. of Fed. Employees (exec. bd. mem., Juneau), Lions. Lutheran.

G

GAFFNEY, Thomas, miner. B. in Ireland, Nov. 12, 1866; res., Chicago, Ill., until 1897; joined Klondike gold stampeders to Dawson; moved to Nome, 1900; game warden and special officer for suppression of liquor among Indians, 2d div., 1916-18; m. Miss Gertrude Whalen, Cordova, Dec. 1919; terr. H.R., 1913-15, 1927-29; cand., del. in Cong., 1928; U.S. Marshal, 2d jud. div., Nome, 1933-37; died in Seattle, Wash., Dec. 9, 1937. Mem., Pioneers (1st grand v.p., 1928). Catholic, Democrat.

GAGNON, Elmer Eugene, government administrator. B. in St. Joseph, Kan., June 7, 1904; gr. and h. sc., Visalia, Calif.; stud., U. Neb.; m. Rosalina (Mrs. Lee, Mrs. Miles Bowen); step-children: Stanley Bowen, Mrs. Georgia Ann Fifield, Mrs. Jacqueline Woods, Mrs. Ellen Vasakis, Mrs. Genevieve Alter; U.S. Army Air Corps, 1922-25; rental agency and project management bus. with father, Visalia, 1926-40; project mgr., Housing Authority, Richmond, Calif., 1940-50; U.S. Navy, Philippines, 1945-46; Am. Red Cross, China-Burma theater, WWII, 18 mos.; project mgr., urban renewal dept., ASHA, Anchorage, 1950-58, Fairbanks, 1958-62; state dir., FHA, Anchorage, 1962-70; real estate broker, Anchorage, 1970-73; died of cancer, Nov. 20, 1973. Mem., Am. Cancer Soc., Anchorage unit (pres., 1969), Lions (pres., Fairbanks, 1961-62), Elks, Order of Red Men, Nat. Assn. Housing Officials, Nat. Assn. Community Planners. Catholic, Democrat.

GALEN, James L., businessman. B. in Helena, Mont., Mar. 29, 1872; s. Hugh F. and Matilda (Gillogy) G.; gr. and h. sc., Helena; B.A., U. Notre Dame; m. Kathryn Monohan in Valdez, 1917 (div.); rep., Anaconda Mining Co., Nome; U.S. Comr., Teller, 1900; rep., Anaconda Mining Co., Valdez and Cordova; supt., Glacier Nat. Park, Mont., 1912-14; owner, Alaska Transfer Co., Cordova, 1918; helped estab. Richardson Highway Transportation Co., 1921-25; cand., del. in Cong., 1922;

pres., gen. mgr., co-owner, Mt. McKinley Tourist & Transportation Co., 1925-39; died in St. Vincent's hosp., Portland, Ore., Jan. 15, 1939; interment, Helena, Mont. Republican.

GARFIELD, James Rudolph, lawyer. B. in Hiram, O., Oct. 17, 1865; s. James Abram (future U.S. Pres.) and Lucretia (Rudolph) G.; B.A., Williams Coll., 1885; LL.B., Columbia U., 1888; O. Sen., 1896-99; mem., U.S. Civil Service Com., 1902-03; comr., U.S. Dept. of Commerce & Labor, 1903-07; Sec. of Interior, 1907-09; pvt. law prac., Cleveland, O., 1909-; cand., O. gov., Progressive Party ticket, 1914; chmn., Com. on Conservation and Public Domain, 1920; died in Cleveland, Mar. 24, 1950. Republican.

GARNICK, Anita, businesswoman. B. in Fort Collins, Colo., Mar. 18, 1910; d. Frank and Clara (Herner) G.; gr. and h. sc., Juneau; studied violin under Willis E. Nowell, a leading Am. violinist; m. George Kodzoff in Juneau, Dec. 3, 1955; owner-operator, Garnick's Grocery (estab. by her mother, 1938); terr. H.R., 1947-49, Sen., 1949-53 (first woman sen.); cand., terr. auditor, 1952. Mem., Women of the Moose, LWV, Eastern Star, Am. Leg. Aux., Pioneers' Aux., Soroptimists, BPW, Am. Fed. of Musicians' Local (sec.-treas., 1941-51), central labor council, Juneau, 1940-50s, Rifle & Pistol Club, Alaska Sportsmen's Assn. Republican.

GARRISON, Kenneth A., businessman. B.A., theology, Southwestern Bible Coll., Waxahachie, Tex.; m. Velma; mgr., Northern Commercial Co. store, Ft. Yukon, 1954-60, res., Dec. 1960; state H.R., 1961-63 (elected by write-in vote); lay-leader of Church of God, Ft. Yukon; ferrying bus., Yukon and Porcupine rivers out of Ft. Yukon. Democrat.

GARRISON, William W., lawyer. B. in Minn., 1939; lived near Bethel, during childhood; LL.B., U. Minn., 1966; U.S. Navy, Kodiak Naval Air Base, WWII; lived in Anchorage, 1941; stud., law sc.; pvt. law prac., Montevideo, Minn.; state dist. atty., 2d jud. dist., Nome, 1970-.

GARY, George M., government administrator, engineer. B. in Oakland, Calif., Feb. 27, 1918; B.S., U. Calif., 1940; m. Florence (Flo) Kubecka, 1948; children: Sandra, George, Jr., Bret; U.S. Army, 1940-46; airport engr., CAA, Austin, Tex., Little Rock, Ark., Seattle, Wash., San Francisco, Los Angeles, 1946-61; chief, airports div., south reg., FAA, Atlanta, Ga., 1961-65; reg. adm., FAA, Anchorage, 1965-67; dir., eastern reg., N.Y.C., 1967-73, ret. to Calif. Mem., Soc. Am. Military Engrs., Anchorage Fed. Exec. Assn. (pres., 1966).

GASSER, George William, agronomist. B. in Youngstown, O., Dec. 10, 1875; s. John and Verena (Gysell) G.; gr. and h. sc., Manhattan, Kan.; B.S., Kan. State Coll., 1905; hon. D.Sc., UA, 1955; m. Minnie Beatrice Peck in Rampart, Aug. 12, 1909; supt., experiment station, Rampart, 1907-21; dir., experiment station, UA, 1921-45; developed varieties of wheat and barley suitable for growing in Alaska which bear his name; prof. agriculture and dean of men (intermittently), UA, 1928-45; 1st comr., terr.

dept. of agriculture, 1945-49; terr. H.R., 1951-53; died in Fairbanks, Jan. 26, 1962. Mem., Rotary, Fairbanks Golf & Country Club, Arctic Inst. of Am., AAAS. Methodist, Republican.

GATZ, Peter, government administrator. B. in 1909; m.; employe, IRS, Seattle, Wash., 1939-42; head of IRS office, Fairbanks, 1942-59; state comr. of revenue, Juneau, 1959-62, res. Democrat.

GAUSTAD, Ole Peter, journalist, miner, businessman. B. in Hammar, Norway, Aug. 15, 1873; emigrated to U.S., 1884; settled in Hillsboro, N. Dak.; employe, Hillsboro BANNER, managing ed., 1884-94; chief dep. sheriff and city auditor, 1894-98; m. Violet L. Simmons, 1903; d. Violet Marie "Vide" (Mrs. E.L. Bartlett); joined gold stampede to Dawson, 1898; moved to Cleary Cr., near Fairbanks, 1906; terr. Sen., 1915-19; mining interests in Tolovana dist.; assoc. with J.A. Gustafson, bankers and merchants, Brooks, owner, Cascaden tramway (11 mi.), Brooks area, living there during summer and in southern Calif. during winters, 1916-24; stockholder and gen. mgr., Fairbanks NEWS-MINER, Aug. 1915-Apr. 1916; owned automobile sales agency, Fairbanks, early 1920s; received, Wash.-Alaska bd., Fairbanks, 1924-26, res.; moved to the states; died in Pioneers' Home, Sitka, Jan. 4, 1945. Mem., terr. bd. education, 1917-, Pioneers (charter mem., Fairbanks Igloo), A.B., K.P. Republican.

GEBHART, Maurice G., real estate broker, land developer. B. in Dayton, O., June 3, 1915; s. Harry M. and Iva G.; gr. and h. sc.; m.; children: Thomas Jay, Patricia Ann (Mrs. Avery); m. 2d, Mrs. June Spears Guthrie, Anchorage, Dec. 1, 1961 (dec. 1964); step-d. Stephanie; m. 3d, Mardy; contracting bus., Houston, Tex.; field engr., Chrysler Corp.; real estate broker-land developer, Anchorage, 1950-55; exec. dir., ASHA, Anchorage, 1955-63; part-owner and pres., Gebhart & Peterson Real Estate Appraisers, Anchorage, 1963-. Mem., Elks, C. of C., Lions (pres., Spenard), Am. Soc. Public Adm., Am. Soc. Planning Officials. Methodist, Democrat. Address: 700 H St., Anchorage 99501.

GEMMILL, Lynn James, lawyer. B. in Sheridan, Ore., Jan. 5, 1904; s. William Huey and Ellen (Elliott) G.; B.A., 1926, J.D., 1928, U. N. Dak.; admitted to N. Dak. and Wash. bars, 1928; m. Lucile Ragsdale, Feb. 5, 1937; moved to Wenatchee, Wash.; pvt. prac., dep. prosecuting atty., 1933-36; prosecuting atty., Chelan Co., 1936-38; asst. U.S. atty., 1st jud. div., Juneau, 1940-42; atty., OPA, 1943-44; U.S. dist. atty., Juneau, 1944-45, resigned.

GEORGESON, Charles Christian, agriculturist. B. Is. of Langeland, Denmark, June 26, 1851; s. J.C. and Jorgine (Hansen) G.; public and pvt. sc., Denmark; emigrated to U.S., 1873; B.S., M.S., Mich. State Coll.; m. Margaret Thompson Lovett, N.Y., Jan. 2, 1882; children: Rosemary, Dagmar; ed., THE RURAL NEW YORKER, N.Y., 1878-80; prof., agriculture and horticulture, Tex. State Agricultural & Mechanical Coll., 1880-83; prof., agriculture,

Imperial Coll. of Agriculture, Imperial U., Tokyo, Japan, 1885-89; prof., agriculture, Kan. State Agricultural Coll., 1890-97; in charge, Alaska experiment stations, U.S. Dept. Agriculture, 1897-1928, ret.; died in Seattle, Wash., Apr. 1, 1931.

GETCHELL, George Elbert, mining engineer. B. in Nevada City, Calif., Nov. 16, 1872; m. Alfreda Billings, Juneau, May 21, 1921; mining engr., Calif.; arr. Alaska, *c.* 1912; U.S. Army Corps Engrs., 1917-18; security guard, ACS, Juneau; terr. H.R., 1921-23; city councilman, Juneau, 1920-21; dep. U.S. Marshal, Douglas, 1921-23; chief of police, Juneau, 1923-26; power house operator, Alaska-Juneau mine, 1927-40; died in Juneau, May 29, 1947. Mem., Masons, Elks, Am. Leg. Republican.

GETCHELL, Walter Waite, miner. B. in St. Cloud, Minn., May 28, 1868; Minn. Normal Sc., St. Cloud; unm.; freight agent, St. Paul-Duluth R.R., West Superior, Wis., later Duluth, 1886-89; real estate bus., West Superior, 1889-91, Everett, Wash., 1892-97, also chief of police; mushed over Dyea trail, 1897; miner, Dawson; dep. U.S. Marshal, 2d jud. div., Nome, 1900-, serving also Nulato, Candle and Shungnak; part-time prospector-miner; terr. H.R., on Ind. ticket, 1915-17; miner, Kenai Peninsula, 1915-17; miner, near Medford, Ore., 1917-22; dep. U.S. Marshal, Nome, 1922-24; died of heart attack near Serpentine Springs, Aug. 5, 1924. Mem., Pioneers (charter mem., Nome). Republican.

GETMAN, Frank P., heavy duty marine engine operator and mechanic. B. in Minn., Dec. 31, 1932; gr. and h. sc., Scappoose, Ore.; completed h. sc. course by correspondence, while employed in Ketchikan; m. Nancy; children: Philip, Peter; moved to Ketchikan with parents, 1940s; worked on various boats; U.S. Navy, 1951-55; outboard motor mechanic, U.S. Public Health Service, Mt. Edgecumbe, Sitka, 1955-58; employe, Alaska Lumber & Pulp Co., 2 yrs.; employe, Sitka Engine & Equipment Co., which he later purchased and added to own shop, Jamestown Bay Marine, Sitka; borough assemblyman and borough chmn., 1963; state H.R., 1967-69. Democrat. Address: Box 359, Sitka.

GHIGLIONE, Angelo Francesco Skinner, civil engineer. B. in Seattle, Wash., May 29, 1909; s. Dr. August Joseph and Estelle (Skinner) G.; B.A., U. Wash., 1931; M.A., Mass. Inst. Technology, 1932; m. Alice Genevieve Palmer, Juneau, June 2, 1939 (dec. Jan. 1, 1974); children: Ann Palmer (Mrs. Timothy Ratner), Kay Estelle (Mrs. Tom Yost), Susan Maria; dist. engr., Anchorage, 1933-34; engr. in charge bridge constr., ARC, 1934-40; U.S. Navy, 1941-46; asst. engr., Anchorage, 1946-47; chief of operations, Juneau, 1947-50; terr. comr. of roads, 1951-56; acting reg. engr., BPR, 1956-57; asst. comr., BPR, Wash., D.C., 1957-68; dep. dir., Fed. Highway Adm., Wash., D.C., 1968-70. Mem., Cosmos Club, Wash., D.C., Broadmoor Club, Seattle. Episcopalian. Address: 5518 N.E. Ann Arbor, Seattle, Wash. 98105.

GIBSON, Dr. Harry V., physician. B. in 1898; grad., Wash. U. Med. Sc., St. Louis, Mo.; postgrad., U. Mich., John Hopkins U.; m. Ruth; children: Harry D. (M.D.), Edward, Mrs. John Greaves; health officer, Great Falls, Mont.; dep. terr. comr. of health, Juneau, 1956-57, comr., 1957-59; city-co. health officer, Great Falls, Mont., and later Nev., ret., 1970; died in his home, Rollins, Mont., June 23, 1973. Mem., Am. Bd. Preventive Medicine & Public Health.

GIERSDORF, Joseph Robert, businessman. B. in Thompson Falls, Mont., Feb. 24, 1935; s. Joseph R. and Genevieve (Nicolas) G.; grad., U. Ore.; m., 1953; children: Deborah Gay, David Allen; m. 2d, Mrs. Peggy (Derr) Strazi, June 1959; m. 3d, Lorraine Heinle, May 24, 1969; went to Alaska, 1951; dist. sales mgr., senior v.p., gen. sales mgr., Alaska Airlines, Fairbanks, 1959-72; organizer-pres., Alaska Tour & Marketing Services, Inc., 1972; state H.R., Jan.-Dec. 1959, Sen., Dec. 26, 1959-Jan. 29, 1960 (res. because underage); appt. state H.R., Feb. 2, 1960. Mem., Sigma Chi, Lions, Alaska Travel Promotion Assn. (past pres.), Alaska Visitors' Assn., Western American Conv. & Travel Inst. Democrat. Address: Kent, Wash.

GILBERT, Hubert Anthony, lawyer. B. in St. Cobb, Okla., 1915; h. sc., Carnegie, Okla.; LL.D., Okla. City U., 1939; m. Lucille M. Thomas in Okla.; d. Jean Ann (Mrs. Frank Hoggan); admitted to Okla. bar; Nat. Guard, 1940-42, commissioned, assigned to judge advocate's office, 1942-46; employe, BLM and RFC, Anchorage, 1946-47; pvt. law prac., Sitka, 1947-48; U.S. Army, Elmendorf AFB, 1948-50; asst. U.S. dist. atty., Fairbanks, 1950-52; pvt. prac. and city magistrate, 2 terms, Fairbanks, 1952-59; terr. H.R., 1955-57; state Sen., 1959; superior ct. judge, Nome, 1959-63, Anchorage, 1963-68, Ketchikan, 1968-73, ret. Dec. 31, 1973. Participant, Nat. Council of State Trial Judges, U. Colo., 1966. Mem., Rotary, Moose (past gov.), VFW, Am. Leg., Lions. Presbyterian, Democrat.

GILL, Oscar Stephen, businessman. B. in St. Lawrence, Pa., Apr. 3, 1880; s. Samuel and M. (Wagner) G.; gr. sc. grad.; m. Emma Dohrmann, 1905; children: Victor, William, Philip, Louise (Mrs. Harry Frederickson); moved to Seward, 1907, to Susitna, *c.* 1909; operated sawmill; moved to Knik; carried mail by dogteam from Seward to Susitna and Iditarod; employe, Alaska R.R., and lighterage bus., Anchorage, 1916-23; estab. automobile garage bus., 1923; mem., sc. bd., 3 yrs.; city councilman, 1929-32; mayor, 1934-36; terr. H.R., 1945-49, speaker, 1947; died after making speech at Elks meeting, Nov. 18, 1947. Mem., Elks, Pioneers. Catholic, Republican.

GILLILAND, Jack T., architectural and engineering consultant. B. in Spokane, Wash., 1918; public sc., Spokane; m. Marion; no children; went to Anchorage, 1947; pres. and first mgr., Spenard Public Utility Dist., 5 yrs.; cand., sec. of state, 1962; bldg. inspector, Greater Juneau Borough, 1966. Republican.

GILMORE, Patrick Joseph, Jr., lawyer. B. in Ketchikan, Jan. 10, 1911; s. Patrick Joseph and Elizabeth Ann (Guinan) G.; public sc., Ketchikan; St. Martin's Coll. h. sc., Lacey, Wash.; Ph.B., Gonzaga U.; LL.B., Georgetown U.; m. Lena Marjorie Waldecker, Feb. 1, 1938; d. Anne; employe, PWA, Wash., D.C., 1933-39; asst. U.S. atty., 1st jud. div., Ketchikan and Juneau, 1939-43; U.S. Navy, 1943-46; U.S. dist. atty., 1st jud. div., Juneau, 1946-54; prac. law and managed family property (hotel, bldgs.), Ketchikan, 1954-. Mem., Am. and Juneau Bar Assns., Lions, Elks. Catholic, Democrat.

GILMORE, William Addison, lawyer. B. in Berkeley, Calif., Jan. 19, 1870; public sc., Portland, Ore.; B.A., Monmouth Coll., 1891; stud., Northwestern U., Chicago, 3 yrs.; LL.B., Lake Forest U., 1897; m. Carrie Iola Thompson, Tacoma, Wash., Nov. 6, 1891; children: George V., Robert M., Dorothy Belle; sc. teacher, Vancouver, Wash.; law stud.; pvt. law prac., Seattle, 1897-1900, 1914-50; prac. law, Nome, 1900-14; mayor, Nome, 1911-13; cand., del. to Cong., 1912; moved to Seattle, 1914; cand., Wash. gov., on LaFollette ticket, 1924; died in Seattle, Mar. 1, 1950; interment, Washelli cemetery. Mem., Wash. Press Club, Seattle, lifetime because he published EGG ISLAND YELLOW JOURNAL while one of 800 passengers aboard SS Ohio, June 1900, quarantined for 2 weeks on Egg I., near mouth of Yukon R., as 2 cases of smallpox had been discovered before they reached Nome; A.B. (Arctic Chief of Camp Nome, 1905); Eagles, Woodmen of the World, Modern Woodmen of Am., Seattle Athletic Club. Republican.

GODING, Maurice Wilfred, government administrator. B. in Skagway, 1911; s. Maurice R. and Blenda E. (Lindahl) G.; h. sc., Skagway, 1929; B.A., Yankton (S. Dak.) Coll., 1933; stud., George Wash. U., 1940-43; m. Harriet Kirk, Nov. 6, 1941; teacher, Napamute terr. sc., 1936-38; staff, Del. in Cong. Anthony J. Dimond, 1940-42; asst. to chief, Economic Potential Div., Bd. of Economic Warfare, 1942-43; asst. to chief, Economic Intelligence Div., Foreign Economic Adm., 1943-44; asst. chief and chief, Alaska br., Div. of Terr., 1944-53; adm., Office of Terr., 1954-60; staff, Sen. Interstate Commerce Com., 1960-61; High Comr., Trust Terr., Saipan, Mariana I., 1961-68. Mem., Phi Delta Phi. Presbyterian, Democrat.

GONNASON, Warren C., civil engineer. B. in Seattle, Wash., 1926; civil engineering degree, U. Calif.; lt. col., U.S. Marine Corps reserve; asst. engr., Hamilton AFB, Calif., 4 yrs.; dir., public works and city engr., Fremont, Calif., 2 yrs.; engr., King Co., Seattle, 1965-67; comr. of highways, Juneau, 1967-68; pres., Harstad Assoc., Inc., Seattle, consulting and engineering firm, 1969-. Republican.

GORDON, Frank Stark, businessman. B. in Wishaw, Lanarkshire, Scotland, Jan. 6, 1872; s. James and Jane (Stark) G.; gr. sc. and apprenticed to dry goods bus., Aberdeen, Scotland, 1882-87; emigrated to Hamilton, Can., 1887-95; res., Grand Forks, N. Dak., 1895-1900, Billings, Mont., 1900-03, Seattle, Wash., 1903-05; went to Fairbanks with his first

shipment of goods, via Valdez winter trail, Mar. 1905; m. Marguerite Myrtle Pauli in Fairbanks, Dec. 21, 1909; children: Donald S., Jane Fournier (Mrs. Milton Herbert Ashkins); involved in public utilities, theatres, women's apparel shops, Fairbanks; mayor and city councilman, Fairbanks, 1911-15; left Fairbanks, 1919; moved to Anchorage, 1920; estab. women's apparel shops, Anchorage, Fairbanks, Seward, Juneau, Ketchikan, 1920s; terr. H.R., 1939-43, Sen., 1943-47. Mem., A.B., Pioneers, Elks. Democrat.

GORE, Lester Otto, lawyer, banker. B. in Hunter, Ore., Nov. 18, 1890; s. Charles Eugene and Jennie (Gorseline) G.; public sc., Kalama, Wash.; stud., U.S. Naval Acad. prep sc., Annapolis, Md.; LL.B., U. Wash., 1914; m. Irene M. DuHamel in Ketchikan, Feb. 7, 1921; children: Charles Millard, Robert Randolph, Nancy Rena (Mrs. Frank Murkowski), Diane DuHamel; admitted to Alaska bar, 1915; joined Grover Winn in pvt. law prac., Juneau, 1915; jr. officer, Merchant Marines, 1918; appt. asst. dist. atty., Ketchikan, 1921, res.; pvt. law prac., Ketchikan, 1923; U.S. dist. judge, 2d jud. div., Nome, 1932-34; can., del. in Cong., 1936; pvt. law prac., Ketchikan, 1934-65; dir., Ketchikan public sc., 1938-44; juvenile judge, 1941-45; city atty., 1938-; fish trap operator; v.p., Miners & Merchants Bk.; v.p., J.R. Heckman Co.; died in Ketchikan, Nov. 3, 1965. Mem., Am. and Ketchikan bar (pres.), Rotary, A.B., Elks, Pioneers (Grand Pres., 1958), Nat. Bk. of Alaska (bd. dir.), Red Men. Congregationalist, Republican.

GORSUCH, John F., businessman. B. in Gambier, O., Oct. 30, 1899; m. 2d, Sally Jones; 3 sons; WWI veteran; coll. and legal education; moved to Anchorage, 1944; estab. Anchorage Bus. Coll.; rep., Kellogg telephone supplies co.; estab. realty firm; terr. Sen., 1953; died July 6, 1954. Mem., Anchorage Ind. sc. dist. bd. (pres., several yrs.), Am. Leg., Kiwanis, Alaska Council of Boy Scouts (v.p.).

GORSUCH, Norman Clifford, lawyer. B. in Pittsburgh, Pa., Oct. 3, 1942; s. Clifford and Helen (Berzac) G.; h. sc., Raleigh, N.C.; B.A., U. of N.C.; LL.B., Columbia U.; m. Marjorie Jean Menzi, Sept. 1966; children: Elizabeth, Keith, Jennifer, Deborah; partner, Ely, Guess & Rudd law firm, Anchorage, 1967-71; dep. atty. gen., 1971-73; state atty. gen., 1973-74; mem., state budget review com. (exec. br.), 1971-73; mem., interstate Oil & Gas Compact com., 1971-73. Mem., Anchorage Young Democrats (pres.). Democrat.

GOTTSTEIN, Bernard J., businessman. B. in Des Moines, Ia., Dec. 30, 1925; s. Jacob Bernard and Anna (Jacobs) G.; gr. sc. and h. sc. (3 yrs.), Anchorage; grad., h. sc., San Jose, Calif.; B.A., U. Wash.; m. Natalie Werner, Sept. 8, 1946 (div. 1969); children: Sandra Lee, James Barry, Ruth Ann, Robert William, David Richard; U.S. Army Air Corps, 1944-45; mgr., father's wholesale grocery bus., J.B. Gottstein Co., 1950 (bus. estab. in Anchorage, 1915); owner, grocery store, drug store, liquor store, shopping center chain, Anchorage, Kenai, Fairbanks, also office bldg., Anchorage;

chmn., Dem. state finance com., 1964, 1968. Mem., state human rights com., Elks. Jewish, Democrat. Address: 6441 C St., Anchorage.

GOTWALS, John C., civil engineer. B. in Norristown, Pa., Nov. 4, 1884; s. Abraham G. and Mary (Logan), G.; unm.; grad., 1906, C.E., 1907, Pa. State Coll.; engr., Pa. R.R.; commissioned 2d lt., Corps of Engrs., U.S. Army, 1913, capt., 1916, maj., 1917; organized and commanded 56th Engrs., France, 1917 to close of war; appt. chief engr., ARC, July 1, 1920; chief engr. and mem., Policy Bd. of Alaska R.R.; ret. to Washington, D.C. on regular Army duty, 1924; died in St. Louis, Mo., Jan. 16, 1946. Awarded Distinguished Service Medal, 1923. Mem., Am. Leg. Presbyterian.

GRANT, Whitaker McDonough, lawyer. B. in Seale, Ala., Apr. 26, 1851; s. Thomas McDonough and Mary J. (Benton) G.; LL.B., U. Ia., 1873; m. Kate W. Weagley, Jacksonville, Ill., Oct. 9, 1878; children: Alice Cory, Kate Weagley, Marguerite Whitaker; prac. law, Davenport, Ia., 1873-87; mem., Ia. legislature, 1884-85; U.S. dist. atty. for Alaska, Sitka, 1887-89; prac. law, Okla., 1893-; mem., Dem. Nat. Com., 1896-99; 1st mayor, Okla. City, under new charter, 1911-15; died Dec. 10, 1927. Democrat.

GRANT, William D., miner. B. in Newark, N.J., Nov. 20, 1856; public sc., Newark; moved to Junction City, Kan., 1872; dep. U.S. Marshal, Wrangell, 1898-1912; children: Brigham Young, Steven, Kate (Mrs. S.D. Blackburn); miner and gen. contractor; Wrangell city councilman; terr. H.R., 1923-27; del., Rep. Nat. Conv., 1900, 1904; died in Seattle, Wash., Oct. 16, 1951. Mem., Elks, Pioneers. Universalist, Republican.

GRAVEL, Maurice R. (Mike), businessman. B. in Springfield, Mass., May 13, 1930; s. Alphonse J. and Maria (Bourassa) G.; Assumption Prep. Sc., Assumption Coll., Worcester, Mass.; stud., Am. Internat. Coll., Springfield, Mass.; B.S., Columbia U., N.Y.C., 1956; m. Rita Jeanette Martin, Apr. 25, 1959; children: Martin Anthony, Lynne Denise; U.S. Army Intelligence, Germany and France, 1952-54; employe, Bankers' Trust Co., N.Y., while attending Columbia U.; taxi driver; salesman, Northern Realty, Anchorage, 1956; mgr., Turnagain Realty, Anchorage, 1957-58; estab. M.R. Gravel Real Estate Development, Inc., April 1958; selected by U.S. Jr. C. of C. to tour nation urging tax reform, Jan.-Apr. 1959; state H.R., 1963-67, speaker, 1965-66; U.S. Sen., 1968-80. Unitarian, Democrat. Address: Box 2283, Anchorage 99510.

GRAY, Clinton, printer. B. in Nome, Apr. 22, 1916; m.; children: Clinton, Jr., Nancy Lynn, James Allen; terr. H.R., from Nome, 1957-59; printer, Nome NUGGET, 1950s, Fairbanks NEWS-MINER, 1960s.

GRAY, Hugh Douglas, government administrator, businessman. B. in Mont., June 12, 1908; s. Felix and Jetta G.; gr. and h. sc., Douglas; grad., U.S. Navy Acad., Annapolis, Md., 1931; m. Mae Fraser in Douglas; children: David, Allan, Cathleen; sc.

teacher, Wrangell and Juneau, 1931-36; U.S. game warden, 1936-42; U.S. Navy, 1942-47; prop. with bro., Gordon, Hotel Juneau, 1947-71; employe, BIA, BPR; mgr., dist. office, BLM, Juneau, 1965; Alaska H.R., 1957-61; del., const. conv., 1955-56.

GRAY, Robert D., miner, businessman. B. in Jefferson, Tex., c. 1857; active in Populist politics, Wash.; moved to Juneau, 1896; clerk, Koehler & James store; moved to Skagway, 1898; miner, Atlin, Can.; wharf and shipping bus., Katalla; U.S. Comr., Katalla, 1913-14; terr. H.R., 1913-15; died in Tex., summer 1917. Democrat.

GREEN, Daniel L., hotel proprietor. B. in Quebec, Can., c. 1883; 1st wife died in Fairbanks, 1940; m. 2d, Charlotte Myers, Kirkland, Wash., 1946; res., Seattle, Wash., 1891-98; moved to Dawson, 1898; operated Green's Cafe; steamboat captain on Yukon R.; prop., hotel, Manley Hot Springs, early 1920s - 1941; drove dog team, Hot Springs to Ruby, in serum relay to Nome, 1925; terr. H.R., 1937-39; ret. to Seattle, Wash., 1941; died there, Mar. 13, 1963. Mem., K.C., Elks, Eagles, Alaska-Yukon Pioneers. Catholic, Democrat.

GREEN, Joseph Kelso, miner. B. in Menlo, Ia., Dec. 31, 1882; gr. and h. sc., Lake City, Ia.; m. Josephine Johnson in Ruby, 1911 (dec. 1946); wandered westward, stopping at Cripple Creek, Victor, Leadville, Denver, camp cook in various mining camps; employe, YMCA, Salt Lake City, Ut.; went to Valdez, 1907; prospector-miner, Hot Springs, Innoko, Iditarod, Ruby, 1908-; employe, Alaska R.R., Nenana, 1917-19; miner, dep. marshal, Hyder, 1919-30s; terr. H.R., from Hyder, 1933-39; tax collector, office of terr. treas., 1937-; terr. Sen., from Haines, 1945-49; died in Juneau, Feb. 3, 1951. Mem., Elks, Pioneers.

GREIMANN, Paul, businessman. B. in Ill., 1902; s. Louis and Catherine (Dalhaus) G.; gr. sc. grad.; employe, Ill. Central R.R., 1918; stud., Rahe Auto & Tractor Sc., Kan. City, Mo.; m. Flora Schnuecke, Feb. 14, 1929; children: Paul, Jr., Katherine (Mrs. Hummell), Malcolm, Judith (Mrs. Moore), Willis; moved from Greenville, Ill., to Alaska, 1923; garage bus., Fairbanks, 1924-; estab. Alaska Coachways, commercial bus service over Alaska Highway, 1932-52; city councilman, Fairbanks, 5 yrs.; owner, Standard garage with Plymouth-Chrysler agency, Fairbanks, Greimann hotel, and office bldg.; with Charles B. West, converted 400-man barracks, Port Chilkoot, into tourist hotel, 1952; state Sen., 1961-63. Mem., Lions, Eagles, Odd Fellows, Pioneers (past pres.). Presbyterian, Republican.

GREUEL, Richard J., radio announcer, businessman. B. in New Holstein, Wis., Apr. 18, 1928; h. sc., Sheboygan, Wis.; m. Viola (Val) J. Forth, Oct. 13, 1951 (div.); d. Paula Ann; m. 2d, Patricia Swaggerty, 1962; children: Lisa Marie, Laura, Peter, Michael; U.S. Army, Ladd Field, 1947, discharged, 1949; announcer, program dir., KFAR, Midnight Sun Broadcasting Co., Fairbanks, until 1953; sales mgr., Alaska Propane Gas & Oil Co., 1953-55; newspaper ad salesman, 1955-; city councilman, Fairbanks, 1951-57; Alaska H.R., 1953-

61, speaker, maj. leader, chmn., legislative council; dep. dir., state div. veterans affairs, Fairbanks reg., 1963; mem., state reapportionment bd., 1971; cand., U.S. Sen., 1974; real estate broker, Fairbanks. Presbyterian, Democrat. Address: 1106 Sunset Dr., Fairbanks 99701.

GRIER, Benjamin A., miner. B. in Nevada, Mo., *c.* 1882; moved to Alaska, *c.* 1911; m. Blanche Garrison in Kanatak, summer 1923; m. 2d, Mrs. Mary Hamilton in Juneau, May 12, 1925; storekeeper, Brown & Hawkins, Seward, 1911-; miner, Cache Cr., near Talkeetna, 1920-; in charge Ray C. Larson lumber yard, Kanatak, 1923-24, Larson lumber yard, Anchorage, 1924-27; terr. H.R., from Anchorage, 1925-27; moved to San Pedro, Calif., 1927; reportedly a concessionaire, bathhouse and cafe, Cabrillo Beach, near Los Angeles, 1935. Republican. .

GRIFFIN, Edward Wellington (Ned), merchant. B. in Chicago, Ill., Apr. 2, 1869; m. Katherine Simmons in Minneapolis, Minn., 1890 (dec. 1930); interested in copper bus., Butte, Mont.; auditor, gen. supt., N.A.T. & T. Co., Dawson, Nome, Chena, Fairbanks, purchased N.A.T. & T. Co. stores, Chena, 1903, Fairbanks, 1905, Ruby, 1914; sold bus. to Northern Commercial Co., 1916; herring packing bus., Halibut Cove, 1918-; operated saltery, Three Saints Bay, Kodiak I., 1920-22-; assoc. with W.J. Erskine in mercantile bus., Kodiak, 1922-31; med. treatment, Chicago, 1931-33; Sec. of Alaska, 1933-38; died in Juneau, Dec. 30, 1938; interment, Seward, beside wife. Kodiak hosp. named in his memory by legislative action, Feb. 1939. Democrat.

GRIFFITH, Morris W., miner, store proprietor. B. in Wash., D.C., 1865; res., Nome, 1900-25; interested in mining properties; employe, Geise Hardware Co.; U.S. Marshal, 2d jud. dist., 1921-25 (Pres. Harding personally handed him his credentials and in return Griffith presented the Pres. a carved ivory umbrella handle); died in Nome, Apr. 21, 1925. Republican.

GRIGSBY, George Barnes, lawyer. B. in Sioux Falls, S. Dak., Dec. 2, 1874; s. Col. Melvin and Fannie (Kingsbury) G.; grad., Sioux Falls Coll., 1893; law stud., Sioux Falls and Chicago; admitted to S. Dak. bar; law prac., Sioux Falls, 1896; m. Elizabeth A. Chapman in Nome, Nov. 23, 1904; children: Melvin, George B., Jr., Elizabeth (Mrs. Hastings), Jane (Mrs. McKnight, then Mrs. Dudley); m. 2d, Patricia Crowley, Jan. 30, 1934; Spanish-Am. War, 1898; hard rock miner and atty., Joplin, Mo., Cripple Cr., Victor, Colo., Butte, Mont.; asst. U.S. atty., Nome, 1902-08; dist. atty., Nome, 1908-10; pvt. law prac., city atty., mayor, Nome, 1910-16; terr. atty. gen., Juneau, 1916-19; del. in Cong., 1919-20; pvt. prac., Ketchikan, 1920-30s, Juneau, 1930s-40, Anchorage, 1940-59; moved to Calif., 1959; died in Santa Rosa, Calif., May 9, 1962. Mem., Pioneers, Eagles, Anchorage Bar Assn. (pres.). Republican, Democrat, Independent.

GRIGSBY, Melvin, lawyer. B. in Wis., 1845; grad., Wis. State Normal Sc., Platteville, Wis.; law stud.; m. Fannie Kingsbury; children: George Barnes,

Sioux K., John T., Fannie; enlisted in Union Army, 1861; col., "Grigsby's Rough Riders," 3d U.S. Volunteer Cavalry, Spanish-Am. War; dist. atty., Nome, 1902-04; life-time res., Sioux Falls, S. Dak.; mem., Dakota terr. legislature; supported Bryan for U.S. Pres., 1896; atty. gen., S. Dak., on Fusion ticket, 2 yrs.; died in Birmingham, Ala., Feb. 15, 1917. Republican, Democrat.

GROH, Clifford John, lawyer. B. in Ramapo, N.Y.; s. Marcel and Helen (Jaworski) Grohoski; h. sc., Tuxedo, N.Y.; B.S., St. Lawrence U., Canton, N.Y., 1948; LL.D., U. N. Mex., Albuquerque, 1951; m. Lucy Bright Woodruff, Aug. 22, 1949; children: Clifford John II (Ford), Paul Woodruff, Lucy Elizabeth; U.S. Navy, 1943-46, 1950-52; admitted to N. Mex. bar, moved to Anchorage, admitted to Alaska bar, 1952; chmn., dir., Security Title & Trust Co.; 1st pres., Operation Statehood, 1953; chmn., Alaska const. research com., 1955; mem., Anchorage ind. sc. bd., 1955-59, 1962-63, pres., 1958-59; city councilman, Anchorage, 1963-67; assemblyman, Greater Anchorage Area Borough, 1964-66; chmn., Anchorage charter com., 1969-70; state Sen., 1971-75; partner, Groh, Benkert & Walter law firm, 1970-. Mem., Fellow Am. Bar Found., Alaska Bar Assn. (bd. gov., 1958-61, pres., 1959-60), Am. Judicature Soc. Episcopalian, Republican. Address: 430 C St., Anchorage 99501.

GROSECLOSE, Robert B., electrical contractor. B. in Radford, Va., Sept. 4, 1915; h. sc., Welch, W. Va.; stud., Syracuse U.; m. Jane Sawyer, Nov. 7, 1945; children: Peggy, Robert B., III, Janet, Thomas (Mrs. S., Janet and Thomas killed in auto collision, July 1968; Peggy killed in airplane wreck, Feb. 1972); worked in Puerto Rico; moved to Fairbanks, 1943; chmn., Rep. central com., 1945-60. Republican.

GROWDEN, William N., U.S. Signal Corps. B. in Clarksville, Tenn., Aug. 18, 1892; m. Gwendolyn Margaret Edmonton Fisher in Ruby, June 21, 1921 (div. 1943); children: William, Robert, James, Andrew; U.S. Army Signal Corps, Nome, Ketchikan, Ruby, 1914-34; terr. H.R., 1935-37; U.S. Comr., Fairbanks dist., 1935-42; city councilman, 1936-40, mayor, 1940-42, Fairbanks; U.S. Air Force, 1942-46; living in Riverside, Calif., 1961. Mem., WWI Vets (comdr.), Am. Leg. Democrat.

GRUENING, Ernest, journalist, author. B. in N.Y.C., Feb. 6, 1887; s. Dr. Emil and Phebe (Fridenberg) G.; grad., Hotchkiss Sc., Lakeview, Conn., 1903; B.A., 1907, M.D., 1912, Harvard U.; m. Dorothy Elizabeth Smith, Nov. 19, 1914; children: Ernest, Huntington Sanders, Peter Brown; reporter, feature writer, ed., various Boston newspapers, 1911-17; managing ed., N.Y. TRIBUNE, 1918; pres., gen. mgr., The Prensa Printing Corp. (only Spanish-Latin-Am. daily in U.S.), 1919-20; managing ed., THE NATION magazine, 1920-24; nat. publicity dir., LaFollette Progressive pres. campaign, 1924; founder-ed., Portland (Me.) EVENING NEWS, 1927-32, contributing ed., 1932-37; gen. adviser to U.S. del., Pan-Am. Conf., Montevideo, 1933; ed., N.Y. EVENING POST, 3 mos., 1934;

dir., Div. Terr. & I. Possessions, U.S. Dept. Interior, 1934-39; Alaska Gov., 1939-53; mem., Alaska Internat. Highway Com., 1942-46; Tennessee Plan U.S. Sen., 1956-58; U.S. Sen., 1958-68; died of cancer at Doctor's Hosp., Wash., D.C., June 26, 1974; cremated and ashes strewn on slopes of Mt. Gruening on Glacier highway opposite his Eagle River cabin, near Juneau. Mem., Phi Beta Kappa, Rotary, Harvard Club, N.Y.C., St. Botolph, Boston, Cosmos, Wash., D.C. Author: "These United States," ed., 1923; "Mexico and Its Heritage," 1928; "The Public Pays," 1931; "The State of Alaska," 1954; "An Alaskan Reader," ed., 1967; "Vietnam Folly" (co-author Herbert W. Beaser), 1968; "Many Battles: an Autobiography," 1973. Democrat.

GUERTIN, Floyd L., government administrator. B. in Chewelah, Wash., 1914; childhood in Cheney, Wash.; h. sc., Spokane, Wash.; stud., Eastern Wash. Coll. of Education, U. Wash., Wash. Coll. of Law, Wash., D.C.; employe, Post Office Dept., Wash., D.C.; m. Josephine Zook, 1946; children: Barbara, Gerald; U.S. Army, 1941-46; dep. comr., terr. veterans affairs, Anchorage, and gen. mgr., Reeve Aleutian Airways, Anchorage, 1946-49; comr., Veterans' Affairs, Juneau, 1949-53; gen. office and traffic mgr., Alaska Coastal Airlines, Juneau, 1953-59; comr. of adm., 1959-66; left Alaska, early 1966; joined U.S. Postal Service, Seattle, then San Francisco, where living in Dec. 1973. Mem., Rotary, Juneau C. of C. (past pres.), Nat. Assn. State Retirement Adm. (reg. v.p., 1963). Democrat.

GUESS, Walter Eugene (Gene), lawyer. B. in Tutwiler, Miss.; s. Thomas L. and Ralda G.; gr. and h. sc., Alexandria, Va.; B.A., Coll. of William and Mary, 1955; LL.B., U. Va., 1959; m. Carolyn Bailey Suber, 1957; children: Carl Thomas, John Bailey, Philip Mosby, Gretchen Jean; asst. to solicitor, BLM, Anchorage, 1959-61; admitted to Alaska bar, 1960; pvt. prac., Ely, Rudd and Havelock law firm, 1961; discharged from U.S. Army with rank of capt., 1963; state H.R., 1965-73, minority whip, 1967-68, floor leader and chmn., legislative council, 1969-70, speaker, 1971-72; cand., U.S. Sen., 1974; died in Juneau hotel room, Mar. 13, 1975. Mem., Anchorage Dem. Club (pres., 1963-64), Anchorage Boys' Club (bd. dirs.), Development Council, AMU. Protestant, Democrat.

GUNDERSON, Amelia Schafer, nurse. B. in Vandalia, Ill., June 5, 1893; moved to Tex., 1893; grad., music, U. Tex.; Boston Conservatory, directed own all-girl orchestra, 2 yrs.; nurse's training, St. Mary's Hosp., Detroit, Mich.; m. Andrew W. Gunderson of Ketchikan, in Reno, Nev., 1930; U.S. Army Nurse's Corps, Denver, Colo., WWI, discharged, 1926; U.S. Army nurse, San Francisco area, WWII; terr. H.R., 1949-51; died of cancer, Ketchikan, Aug. 11, 1951. Mem., Am. Leg., VFW, Pioneers Aux., Women of the Moose. Catholic, Democrat.

GUNDERSON, Andrew W., fisherman, cannery operator. B. in Kristiansand, Norway, Sept. 4, 1887; m. Amelia Shafer, Reno, Nev., 1930; went to sea as boy; landed in San Francisco, Calif., 1901, where

father was port capt. for Southern Pacific R.R. ferries; cont. in sailing ships, including 2 seasons in Bristol Bay salmon fishery, until 1908; piledriver, fisherman for halibut, salmon and herring, Ketchikan; cannery supt., New England Fish Co., Chatham, 1929-40; terr. H.R., 1943-45, Sen., 1945-47; died in Ketchikan, Nov. 23, 1954. Mem., Elks, Moose, Pioneers, Scottish Rite Masons. Democrat.

GUNNISON, Royal Arch, lawyer. B. in Binghampton, N.Y., June 23, 1873; s. Christopher B. and Juliette T. G.; LL.D., Cornell Coll., 1896; m. Helena Cobb, Elmira, N.Y., 1900; s. Royal Arch, Jr.; reporter, Binghampton REPUBLICAN, 1893-96; admitted to N.Y. bar, 1897; referee in bankruptcy for northern N.Y., hdqrs., Elmira, 1898-1904; U.S. dist. judge, 1st jud. div., Juneau, 1904-09; pvt. law prac., Juneau, 1909-18; pres., Alaska Bd. for Promotion of Uniform Laws, 1913; Fed. Food Adm. for Alaska, 1917-18; died of heart attack in his home, June 15, 1918; buried in Juneau. Mem., Alaska Bar Assn. (pres., 1st div., 1917), Am. Bar Assn., 1914-18, Legal Adv. Bd., Masons (33d degree). Christian Scientist, Republican.

H

HAAG, Henry Lloyd, businessman. B. in Black Diamond, Wash., Apr. 4, 1895; s. Andrew H.; m. Dorothy English, Seattle, Wash., Feb. 18, 1928; U.S. Army, WWI; res., Seattle, until 1936; moved to Portland, Ore.; estab. trucking line between Portland and Depoe Bay; estab. taxi service, Kodiak, 1941-65; state H.R., 1959-61; moved to Hillsboro, Ore., 1965; died there, Nov. 28, 1969. Mem., Elks, Masons. Democrat.

HAAS, Michael J., miner, businessman. B. in Belleville, Ill., Jan. 5, 1902; s. Michael and Mamie (Wright) H.; grad., U. Southern Calif.; m. Mrs. Mary Griffith Ditman, Nov. 7, 1932 (div. 1965); step-s. Robert I. Ditman; coal and gold miner, baseball player, health inspector, labor conciliator, Valdez, Juneau, Anchorage, 1930-; sales mgr., wholesale grocery firm, Anchorage; comr. of labor, 1941-42; special rep., U.S. Dept. Labor, Juneau, 1943-47; dep. co. clerk and co. nurse, Belleville, Ill.; real estate salesman, Juneau, 1949-52; area rent dir. for Alaska, hdqrs., Juneau, 1952-; pres., Dem. Fed. of Ill.; died in Ill., Jan. 14, 1974; survived by widow, the former Mrs. Harriet E. Hughes, nee Houston. Mem., Rotary, Moose (1st pres., Alaska Moose Assn.), Nat. Fed. of Fed. Employees. Democrat.

HAGGLAND, Dr. Paul Burns, physician, surgeon. B. in Port Blakely, Wash., Apr. 25, 1900; s. O.A. and Louise (Lindquist) H.; B.A., U. Wash.; M.D., U. Va., 1933; internship, Va. Mason clinic, Seattle, Wash., 1933-34; res. orthopedist, U. Va. hosp., 1934-36; res. orthopedic surgeon, N.C. hosp. and Shriners' hosp., San Francisco, Calif., 1936-38; m. Margaret Calder, 1928; children: John, Paul, Peter; m. 2d, 1939; assoc. with Med. & Surgical Clinic, Fairbanks, 1939-; city councilman, chmn., utilities bd., mayor, Fairbanks, 1950s; terr. state Sen., 1957-59, 1967-71. Mem., terr. med. assn. (pres., 1946-54), Rotary (past pres.), Am. Coll. of Surgeons (fellow, 1958), Am. Med. Assn., Phi Beta Pi, Alpha Omega Alpha, Fairbanks Golf & Country, Wash. Athletic Club (Seattle). Presbyterian, Republican. Address: 502 Kellum, Fairbanks 99701.

HALL, John Barbee (Dixie), law clerk. B. in Marshal, Mo., Nov. 4, 1891; s. Robert Lee and Sue (Hayes) H.; grad., h. sc., prep. sc., 2 yrs.; m. Esther Clara Oliver in Anchorage, May 6, 1922; children: John Barbee, Jr., Robert Lee; youth in Colo.; moved to Anchorage, 1915; prospector-miner-trapper, Talkeetna area; employe, Alaska R.R.; U.S. Army, Camp Lewis, Wash., 1917-18; miner and time-keeper, Evan Jones coal mines, Chickaloon and Eska, 1918-23; agent, Northern Commercial Co., Nenana, 1923-28, Bethel, 1928-33; chief dep. U.S. marshal, Fairbanks, 1933-36; sec., sc. bd., Fairbanks, 1935-40s; clerk, dist. ct., 4th jud. div., Fairbanks, 1936-60 (Feb.); joined state ct. system, ret., June 30, 1960; res., Circle Hot Springs, 1960-67; state Sen., 1963-67; died in West Sacramento, Calif., while visiting son, May 15, 1967. Mem., Red Cross War Fund (chmn., 1941-46), Am. Leg. (past comdr.), Pioneers, Lions, Elks. Presbyterian, Democrat.

HALL, Robert A. (Bert), minister. B. in Lowell, Mass., Sept. 19, 1933; Lowell h. sc.; B.S., Lowell Technological Inst., 1955; B.D., Berkeley Baptist Divinity Sc., 1960; m. Helen Trice of Anchorage, 1957; children: Robert, Jr., Mark, Sheryl, David; U.S. Army, Ft. Richardson, 1955-57; pastor, Community Baptist Church, Cordova, 1960-65; exec. dir., Greater Anchorage Community Chest, 1965-69; dep. comr., health and welfare, 1969-70, comr., 1970-71; special asst., Fed. Dept. Health, Education & Welfare, Anchorage, 1971-. Elected Outstanding Young Man of Year, Capt. Cook Jaycees, 1966. Mem., Community Action Agency (exec. bd.), Anchorage, Greater Anchorage, Inc. (bd. dir.), Rotary. Baptist, Republican.

HAMMOND, Jay Sterner, fisherman, big game guide, aviator. B. in Troy, N.Y., July 21, 1922; s. Rev. Morris A. and Edna Brown (Sterner) H.; gr. and h. sc., Scotia, N.Y., 1928-40; family moved to southern Vt.; stud., Pa. State U.; B.S., biological sciences, UA, 1948; m. Bella Gardiner in Palmer, Sept. 25, 1952; children: Heidi, Dana; U.S. Marine Air Corps, fighter pilot, 1942-46; apprentice guide, fisherman, hunter, trapper, Rainy Pass, 1946-49; U.S. Fish & Wildlife Service, 1949-56; estab. air taxi service, registered game guide, built sportsmen's lodge on Lake Clark and fishing lodge on Wood River lakes, commercial fisherman during summers,

1957-; state H.R. (elected Ind., 1958, Rep. thereafter), 1959-65; state Sen., 1967-73, majority leader, 1970, pres., 1971-72; mgr., Bristol Bay Borough, 1965-66, mayor, 1973-74; Alaska Gov., 1974-. Mem., VFW, Alaska Airmen's Assn. Methodist, Republican. Address: Box 128, Naknek 99633.

HANFORD, Fred G., oil company agent. B. in Sparta, Mich., Feb. 28, 1879; s. James S. and Lois (Bloomer) H.; gr. and h. sc. (1 yr.), Sparta; m. Veva Mathews; children: James Brooks, Fred G., Jr.; U.S. Army, Philippines, Seattle, Wash., 1898-1901; mining camp cook, Hyder, 1910; res., Ketchikan, 1914-24; agent, Union Oil Co., Wrangell, 1924-47; terr. H.R., 1945-47; OPA dir. for Alaska, Juneau, 1951-53; cont. to make his home at Baranof hotel, Juneau; in retirement, rep., Pacific Northern Timber Co. in Alaska, which built a sawmill near Wrangell; city councilman, 4 yrs., mayor, 4 yrs., Wrangell; died in Wrangell, July 17, 1962. Mem., Masons, Elks (past dist. dep. grand exalted ruler), Redman. Democrat.

HANSEN, Harold Z. (Red), fisherman, labor union official. B. in Portland, Ore., 1910; fisherman, southeast Alaska, 1920s; trolled from Ketchikan, 1940-41; purchased seiner; crab fisherman, mailboat and tugboat operator, Kodiak; moved to Cordova; U.S. Navy, 7th Amphibious fleet, WWII; exec. sec.-treas., Copper River and Prince William Sound cannery workers, Cordova Dist. Fisheries Union, Cordova Aquatic Market Assn., Cordova Labor Hall Assn., Culinary Workers, Bartenders Union; chmn., Cordova Fish & Game Adv. Bd.; state H.R., 1959-63; state Sen., 1963-67; dir., Internat. Fisheries, Office of Gov., Juneau, 1971-74. Mem., Cordova Charter com., VFW. Democrat.

HANSON, James Arnold, lawyer, aviator. B. in Northwood, N. Dak., Aug. 19, 1934; s. Arnold S. and Jennie A. (Running) H.; gr. and h. sc., Fargo, N. Dak.; B.S., B.A., 1959, LL.B., 1962, J.D., 1969, U. N. Dak.; m. Judith Ann Jarrett, Winnipeg, Man., Can., Nov. 1959; children: Charlene Rae, Laura Jean, Robert James; m. 2d, Mary S. Glotfelty, Anchorage, May 1974; U.S. Navy Reserve, 1952-60; law clerk, Juneau, 1962-63; dist. magistrate, Anchorage, 1963-66, presiding, 1964-66; admitted to Alaska bar, 1966; master and ct. trustee, superior ct., 3d jud. dist., 1966-67; presiding dist. judge, Anchorage, 1967-69; pvt. prac., Anchorage, 1969-70, also instructor, criminal law, Kenai Community Coll.; superior ct. judge, Kenai, 1970-. Mem., Sigma Alpha Epsilon (pres.), McKinley Lions (bd. dir.), Western Alaska Boy Scouts Council (bd. dir.), Family Counseling Services, N. Dak., Alaska and Am. Bar Assns., Jud. Council Com. on Jud. Discipline and Removal. Lutheran.

HANSEN, Mildred Meiers, journalist, author. B. in Toledo, Ia., Nov. 19, 1903; d. Charles George and Florence (Boynton) M.; h. sc., 2 yrs.; m. Chris Hansen (div); m. 2d, Edward E. Wells, Juneau, June 5, 1965; Women's Army Corps, WWII; went to Nome, 1948; asst. sec., terr. legislature, wrote sen. journal, Juneau, 1949, 1951; wrote broadcasts covering activities of 1953 legislature session; legal sec., Anchorage and Fairbanks; res., Juneau, 1959-; pub.,

Legislative Reporting Service, 1948-; owner and pub., Alaska Reporting Service, reporting Alaska development after statehood; first woman cand., Alaska gov., 1966. Author: "Thesaurus of Humor," "Let the Record Speak," "Handbook for the Freshman Legislator or How Not to be Politically Naive." Mem., Anchorage Dem. Women's Club (pres., 1954), Juneau Emblem Club No. 90. Address: Box 1082, Juneau 99801. Democrat.

HARDCASTLE, Richard Egbert, businessman. B. in Newark, N.J., Dec. 29, 1878; s. Richard Egbert and Emma Catherine (Miller) H.; h. sc., bus. coll.; m. Ethel A. Minkler, Dec. 10, 1910; children: Richard M., Catherine Kiester, Edith McTague, Ann Wilson; mercantile clerk, 1893-1901; salmon cannery bookkeeper, 1902-06; insur. bus., 1906-16; fish packer, Ketchikan, 1916-22; estab. Ketchikan Bus Service, 1933; mem., unemployment compensation com., 1937-41; terr. H.R., 1943-45; ret. to Calif., 1946; died in Newport Beach, Calif., Feb. 1969; buried at Costa Mesta, Calif. Episcopalian, Democrat.

HARDING, Justin Woodward, judge. B. in Franklin, O., Dec. 19, 1888; s. Clarence H. and Lilly (Woodward) H.; grad., Phillips Exeter Acad., 1908; stud., U.S. Military Acad., West Point, 1909-10, Colo. Sc. Mines, 1910-11; LL.B., U. Mich., 1914; m. May Gaynor, Sept. 4, 1912; children: Mary Campbell, Justin W.; pvt. law prac., Warren Co., O.; Ohio H.R., 1921-27; U.S. Army, WWI, WWII, staff judge advocate, Alaskan Command, 1941-44; U.S. dist. atty., 1st jud. div., Juneau, 1927-29; U.S. dist. judge, 1st jud. div., Juneau, 1929-33; asst. atty. gen., O., 1934-37; judge advocate, Panama Canal dept., and Caribbean Defense Command, 1945-46; judge advocate, 4th Army, 1946, discharged, Dec. 31, 1946; assoc. judge, U.S. Military Govt. Ct. of Appeals, 1948-49; judge, U.S. Military Tribunals, Nuremberg, Germany, 1949-51; died in his home, Franklin, O., Aug. 31, 1972. Mem., Kappa Sigma, Masons. Republican.

HARDY, Nathan O., engineer. B. in Tacoma, Wash., Nov. 28, 1888; stud., electrical and steam engineering; m. Hilda Nystrom in Seattle, Wash., Nov. 1929; chief engr., Union Lumber Co., Lacy, Wash.; engr., Northern Pacific R.R. tunnel, Tacoma; chief engr., Home Power Co., Skagway, 1912-16; engr., Alaska Corp., Porcupine, 1916-17; dep. U.S. Marshal, 1st jud. div., Juneau, 1917-23; asst. cashier and cashier, 1st Nat. Bk., Juneau, 1923-27; U.S. Bur. of Fisheries, 1927-34; dep. U.S. Marshal, Ketchikan, 1934-47, res. due to ill health, Jan. 1947; died in Seattle, Wash., Dec. 11, 1947. Democrat.

HARLAN, Nathan V., lawyer. B. in Neb., 1841; children: Edwin V. (dec., Valdez, 1907), Mrs. Gertrude Boyer; U.S. dist. atty., 3d jud. div., Valdez, 1901-08; ret. to Neb.; died in his home, York, Neb., Sept. 1911.

HARMON, Henry Alois, government administrator. Gr. sc., Eau Galle, Wis., h. sc., Durand, Wis.; B.S., Stout State Coll., Menominee, Wis.; grad. stud., 1939, 1942; m. Genevieve Frances Schlumpf,

Juneau, Aug. 1936; children: James John, Joseph Henry, Patrick Henry; sc. teacher, industrial arts and vocational training, Juneau, 1935-49; dir., dept. public welfare, 1949-58; dep. comr., dept. health & welfare, 1959-66; community development specialist, BIA, 1967-68; management service officer, dept. health & welfare, 1968-69; state coordinator, office of aging, 1969-72. Mem., Pioneers, Boy Scouts of Am. (Silver Beaver), Rotary, Terr. Sportsmen, Elks, Moose, Terr. Guard, 1942-47. (co. comdr., 3 yrs.). Catholic.

HARRAIS, Martin Luther, miner. B. in Riga, Latvia, Russia, of Viking ancestry, Jan. 2, 1865; went to sea, 1874; moved to San Pedro, Calif., 1883; worked in shipyards during day and attended night sc.; B.A., U. Wash., 1897; joined gold stampede to Dawson, 1898; m. Margaret Keenan in Seward, 1921; moved to Chena, 1904, operated sawmill; coal miner, Nenana dist.; cand., del. in Cong., 1912; gold and copper prospector, McCarthy-Chitina dist.; res., McCarthy, Cordova, Valdez, 1920-34; cand., terr. treas., 1934; U.S. Comr., Valdez, 1934-36; mem., bd. regents, UA, Sept.-Dec. 1936; died of cancer, Seward hosp., Dec. 25, 1936. Mem., Pioneers (past pres., Valdez Igloo). Democrat.

HARRIGAN, Mrs. Alice, Democratic National Committeewoman, Sitka, 1963-72.

HARRIS, Arthur J., rancher. B. in Corvallis, Ore., 1898; s. Ben W. and Ida (Johnson) H.; Portland U. prep sc.; stud., Ore. State Coll.; m.; s. Dale; m. 2d, Rhoda Gordon, May 29, 1945; d. Patricia Kathleen; Ore. ranger; moved to Aleutian I., 1934; owner-operator, Harris Aleutian Livestock Co., Umnak I.; home near Aleut village, Nikolski; state H.R., 1961-65; mem., Nat. Adv. Bd. for Public Lands, 1962. Democrat.

HARRIS, Donald, construction contractor, aviator. B. in San Diego, Calif., Jan. 16, 1926; s. Richard Joseph and Maude Josephine (Docksteader) H.; pub. sc., Park City, Mont.; stud., Mont. State Coll., 2 yrs.; m. Alice Parent, Aug. 7, 1954; d. Josephine Anise; m. 2d, Donalene; children: Donalene Patricia, John Benjamin; U.S. Army service; constr. work and contracting, mining (2 summers), 1948-; state H.R., 1959-63; mem., state bd. fish and game, 1967-71; chmn., McGrath sc. bd., 1969; comr., public works, 1974-. Republican. Address: McGrath 99627.

HARRIS, Frank W., businessman. B. in Seattle, Wash., Mar. 13, 1920; St. John's gr. and h. sc., Milwaukie, Ore.; m. Mona M. Ward, Apr. 1946; d. Judith Marie; adopted Korean children, 1961: Jerry, Mathew, and 2 others; went to Alaska with U.S. Army Signal Corps from Seattle, 1946; owner-operator, Alaska Cleaners; owner, Central Bldg. (offices and shops); city councilman, Anchorage, 1957-60; chmn., Rep. state centennial com., 1963-65; state Sen., 1967-69; mem., state parole bd., 1967-73. Mem., Lions, Elks, Izaak Walton League, Anchorage Rep. Club. Catholic, Republican. Address: 1805 Scenic Way, Anchorage.

HARRIS, Jesse James (Jess), electrician. B. in Roganville, Tex., Oct. 4, 1930; s. Cecil C. and Iva H.; grad., Barstow Union h. sc., 1949; m. Georgia Diaz, Mar. 1953; children: Jessie Lee, Jenny Mae, Joann Margaret; U.S. Army, 1949-50, med. discharge; moved to Anchorage, 1956; employe, Alaska R.R., until 1960; electrician, Modern Electric, Inc. (foreman); employe, J. Ray McDermott Barge Co.; self-employed electrical contractor; state H.R., 1967-73, Sen., 1973-75. Mem., Internat. Brotherhood of Electrical Workers, Local No. 1547. Baptist, Republican. Address: 1016 W. 11th, Anchorage 99501.

HARRIS, Thomas C., electronics engineer. B. in Okla., 1926; m.; went to Valdez, 1950; pres., Communications Engineering, Inc., 1954; del., const. conv., 1955-56; pres., Trans-Alaska Telephone Co., Anchorage, 1961-63; pres., Consolidated Communications, Inc.; local rep., Allied Radio Shack Internat., Anchorage, 1970s. Mem., Toastmasters Clubs of Alaska (dist. gov.). Address: 529 C St., Anchorage 99501.

HARRISON, David C., fisherman, businessman, aviator. B. in Waynesville, N.C.; placed in orphanage, Ashville, N.C., at age 9 mos.; B.S., business and economics, Bob Jones U., 1955; U.S. Air Force, Japan, 1950-52; engineering aide, Dist. Corps of Engrs., Elmendorf AFB, 1952; chief expediter, Western Electric, Pt. Barrow, summer 1955; sc. teacher, Marshal, 1955-56; res., Dillingham, 1956-; commercial fisherman, hotel prop., sc. teacher and principal; del., NEA conv., 1956. Democrat.

HARRISON, William Frederick, lawyer. B. in San Francisco, Calif., Dec. 26, 1869; s. William Frederick and Annie I. (Robinson) H.; h. sc., bus. coll.; law stud., Dawson, Can.; unm.; prospector-miner, Dawson, 1898-1901; chief clerk, office of crown prosecutor, Dawson, 1902-11; prac. law, Ruby, 1911-; U.S. dist. atty., 2d jud. div., Nome, 1921-29, res. due to ill health; died in Juneau hosp., en route to Pioneers' Home, Sitka, July 12, 1929. Mem., Pioneers, Eagles, Moose. Protestant, Republican.

HART, Julius H., lawyer. Pvt. law prac., Juneau; asst. U.S. atty., Juneau; U.S. dist. atty., 2d jud. div., Nome, 1929-31, res. when not confirmed by U.S. Senate.

HARTIG, Robert Lee, geologist, lawyer. B. in Marysville, Kan., Oct. 3, 1928; s. Henry W. and Bernice May (Commel) H.; B.S., 1953, M.S., 1955, geology, Kan. State U.; J.D., Duquesne U., 1963; m. Alice Rae Davis, Aug. 6, 1950; children: Alan Robert, Lawrence Lee, Glenn Stuart; U.S. Navy, 1946-48, 1951-52; senior geologist, Mobil Oil Co., Casper, Wyo., 1954-67; asst. atty. gen., chief natural resources sec., Juneau, 1967-70, Anchorage, 1970-71; estab. Cole, Hartig, Nunley, Rhodes & Norman law firm, 1971-; state H.R., 1973-74. Mem., Public Land Law Review Com., state com. on conf. on law of sea, Anchorage C. of C. (dir.), Am. Assn. Petroleum Geologists, Rotary, Elks, Navy League. Presbyterian, Republican. Address: 711 H St., Anchorage 99501.

HARTMAN, Clifford Richard, educator. B. in Big Springs, Kan., Mar. 28, 1920; s. Gus and Ethel (Wilson) H.; B.A., York (Neb.) Coll., 1944; M.A., 1955, Ed.D., 1966, U. Neb.; post-grad., Stanford U., 1960, UA, 1960-61; m. Margaret Jane Hirschfeld, Apr. 23, 1944; children: Richard James, David Hirschfeld; teacher and sc. adm., Loup City, Neb., 1944-48; teacher and h. sc. principal, Anchorage, 1948-67; state comr. education, Juneau, 1967-71; asst. supt., instructional services, Anchorage Borough sc. dist., 1971-; chmn., official bd., First Methodist Church, Anchorage; del., World Confederation Organizations of the Teaching Profession, Rio de Janeiro, Brazil, 1963. Mem., Rotary, Methodist, Republican. Address: 1433 W. 13th, Anchorage 99501.

HASKETT, Edward W., lawyer. U.S. dist. atty. for Alaska, Sitka, 1884-85. Republican.

HATCH, Edwin T., collector of customs. M.; 6 children; Ore. Sen., from Polk Co.; collector of customs, Sitka, 1891-93; appt. dep. collector of customs, St. Michael, 1898. Republican.

HATCHER, Cornelia Templeton, magazine editor, lobbyist. Ed., "The Union Signal," nat. organ of WCTU, Chicago, Ill.; went to Alaska with tour party of newspaper writers, 1909; m. Robert Lee Hatcher, Willow Cr. gold miner; lived in Knik; traveled throughout the terr. organizing WCTU chapters; key promoter of Alaska bone-dry prohibition bill; lobbyist for prohibition, U.S. Cong., Feb. 1917.

HAUGEN, Ernest J., fisherman, businessman. B. in Silverdale, Wash., Sept. 29, 1916; grad., h. sc., Poulsbo, Wash., 1934; stud., Pacific Lutheran Coll., Tacoma, Wash.; m. Ruby, 1950; children: Edward, Lawrence, Julie; crew mem., halibut schooners from Seattle, Wash., 1934-36; res., Petersburg, 1936-, cont. work on halibut boats; U.S. Navy, Aleutians, Solomons, Philippines, 1942-45; ret. to Petersburg and fished one yr.; prop., Pastime restaurant, 15 yrs., sold bus., 1961; meat market and frozen food bus., commercial fisherman, 1961-; city councilman, 1951-55, mayor, 1955-59, Petersburg; mem., terr. highway com., 1954-58; state H.R., 1965-75. Mem., Masons, Scottish Rite, VFW, Elks, Sons of Norway, Pioneers, state C. of C. (dir., 1965). Republican. Address: Box 248, Petersburg 99833.

HAVELOCK, John E., lawyer. B. in Toronto, Can., July 30, 1932; s. Eric A. and Ellen H.; Phillips Acad., Andover; B.A., 1956, LL.B., 1959, Harvard U.; m. 2d, Judith Anne Luginbuhl, May 1969; children: Bruce Geoffrey, Eric, Brian, Scott, Jennifer Mary Ellen; U.S. Army police corps, 1953-54; estab. residence in Alaska, 1959; asst. atty. gen. and dep. atty. gen., 1960-63, res.; partner, Ely, Guess, Rudd & Havelock, law firm, 1963-70; White House Fellow, sp. asst. to Sec. Agriculture, 1967-68; state atty. gen., 1970-73; cand., U.S. H.R., 1974. Presbyterian, Democrat.

HAWKINS, James E., educator, fisherman. B. in Buenos Aires, Argentina, of Am. parents, 1922; B.A., M.A., U. Pa.; m. Mary; children: Charles, Richard; U.S. Army, 1943-45; BIA sc. principal, Ninilchik, 1950-53; sc. principal, Dillingham, 1954-56; homesteaded near Clam Gulch; exec. dir., Alaska Rural Development Bd., Juneau, 1956-58; area dir., BIA, 1958-61; BIA area dir., Minn., Wis., Mich., hdqrs., Minneapolis, 1962-.

HAWLEY, William H., lawyer. State dist. atty., 1st jud. div., Ketchikan, 1969-71. Republican.

HAYDEN, Henry E., surveyor, poet. Surveyor-gen. and ex-officio Sec. of Alaska, Sitka, 1887-90; clerk, district ct.; compiled 1st Alaska (ct.) *Reports*, pub. 1888. Author with J.S. Bugbee and O.T. Porter, "Poems on Alaska," 1891. Democrat.

HAYES, George Nicholas, lawyer. B. in Alliance, O., Sept. 30, 1928; s. Nicholas J. and Mary (Fanaday) H.; B.A., U. Akron, 1950; M.A., 1952, LL.B., 1955, Western Reserve U.; unm.; admitted to O. bar, 1955, Alaska bar, 1958; asst. prosecutor, Portage Co., Ravenna, O., 1955-57; prosecutor, city of Ravenna, 1955-57; atty., village of Mantua, O., 1956-57; asst. U.S. atty., Fairbanks, 1957-58, Anchorage, 1958-59; asst. atty. gen., Juneau, 1959-60; state dist. atty., 3d jud. dist., Anchorage, 1960-62; state atty. gen., Juneau, 1962-64; pvt. law prac., Anchorage, 1964-; del., Am. Bar Assn. conv., 1968. Democrat. Address: 360 K St., Anchorage 99501.

HAYMAN, Dr. Charles R., physician. Res. Md.; dep. comr. of health, Juneau, 1954-56, comr., 1956-57; U.S. Public Health Service, Wash., D.C., 1957-.

HAZELET, George Cheever, miner, businessman. B. in O., 1863; moved to Ia., 1870; public sc., Ia.; m. Harriet S. Potter in O'Neil, Neb., 1888 (dec. 1912); children: Calvin, Craig; teacher, Ia. and Neb., 1880-86; built first factory for processing chicory in O'Neil, 1892, later moved it to Omaha; gold prospector-miner, Valdez, 1898; copper prospector, rep., Guggenheim Bros.; moved family to Valdez, 1903; assisted in organizing Copper River & Northwestern Ry., 1905; mapped original townsite, trustee, placed lots on sale, 1908, 1st mayor, organizer-owner, city water works, light plant and telephone system, pres., C. of C., Cordova, 1908-26; mgr., Chilcat Oil Co., Katalla; active in developing Bering River coal fields; rep., Rep. central com., 3d div.; del., Rep. Nat. Conv., 1920; cand., Alaska gov., 1921; died in Cordova, Aug. 5, 1926. Republican.

HECKMAN, James Robert (Bob), businessman. B. in Colchester Co., Nova Scotia, Can., Oct. 17, 1865; public sc., Ferndale, Calif., 1875-; m. Miss Marie C. Capp, Mar. 1893 (dec. 1937); m. 2d, Gladys, 1938; gill net fisherman, Cook Inlet, 1886-87; machinist helper, Arctic Fish Packing Co. (later absorbed by Alaska Packers' Assn.), Loring, supt., 1889-1918; inventor of floating fish trap; terr. H.R., 1915-17, Sen., 1917-21; owner, gen. mercantile store, mortuary, several mines, pres., Miners & Merchants Bk. (1920-39), Ketchikan, 1889-1939; died in Ketch-

ikan, Aug. 22, 1939. Mem., Terr. Fish Com. (chmn.), 1917-25, Elks, K.P., A.B., Redmen, Eagles. Episcopalian, Republican.

HEID, John Godlove, miner, lawyer. B. in Wapakoneta, O., Dec. 14, 1852; m. Henrietta Claudina Jensen in Juneau, July 24, 1888; children: Henrietta (Mrs. Victor H. Dupuy), Gertrude (Mrs. Charles H. Sugden), Elizabeth (Mrs. W.H. Eberly); went to Denver, Colo., 1872, to engage in mining; drifted to various mining camps; arr. Juneau, Apr. 11, 1885; estab. law office, 1st lawyer in Juneau; engaged in mining enterprises; mem., Rep. Nat. Com., 1900-08; del., Rep. Nat. Conv., 1900, 1904; terr. H.R., 1915-17; died in San Francisco, Calif., Jan. 24, 1917. Mem., Masons, Pioneers (Grand Pres., 1916-17), Elks. Republican.

HEINTZLEMAN, (Benjamin) Franklin, forester. B. in Fayetteville, Pa., Dec. 3, 1888; s. Andrew J.H.; B.F., Pa. State Forest Sc.; M.F., Yale U., 1910; unm.; Pacific Northwest reg., USFS, Portland and Eugene, Ore., 1910-18; logging engr. and asst. reg. forester, Ketchikan, 1918-35; dep. asst., Nat. Recovery Adm., 1935-37; Alaskan rep., Fed. Power Com., 1937; reg. forester for Alaska, 1937-53; Comr., U.S. Dept. Agriculture, 1941-53; Alaska Gov., 1953-57, res.; mem., bd. regents, UA, 1957-59; adviser, Alaska Rail & Highway Com., 1960; died in Juneau, June 24, 1963; buried in Fayetteville, Pa. Awards: superior service award from U.S. Dept. of Agriculture, 1952; Fellow, Society of Am. Foresters, 1957; Sir William Schlich medal (highest professional honor), Soc. of Am. Foresters, 1958; Juneau's Man of the Year, Rotary Club, 1959; Outstanding Alaskan of the Year, state C. of C. Mem., Pacific Northwest Trade Assn., Rotary, Soc. of Am. Foresters, adv. bd., Yale U., Cosmos, Wash., D.C., Explorers, N.Y.C. Presbyterian, Republican.

HEISEL, Walter B., government administrator. B. in Cincinnati, O., Nov. 26, 1890; joined U.S. Land Office, Little Rock, Ark., 1909; U.S. Land Office, Anchorage, 1918-23; U.S. Customs Service, Juneau, 1923, head of office, 1955-61; ret. to Santa Barbara, Calif., 1962.

HELLAN, Walter G., U.S. Marshal, 1st jud. div., Juneau, Sept. 1950-Dec. 1951, acting. Democrat.

HELLENTHAL, John Albertus (Jack), lawyer. B. in Holland, Mich., Sept. 17, 1874; s. Albertus and Reimka (Sluiter) H.; stud., Hope Coll., Holland; LL.B., U. Mich.; m. Bertha Linsley, Feb. 12, 1900; law prac., Wyo. and Ut.; moved to Juneau, 1900; assoc. with Alaska-Juneau and Alaska-Treadwell mining cos., 1910-; mem., Dem. Nat. Com., 1935-40; ret. to Lake Co., Calif.; purchased ranch; died in Swedish hosp., Seattle, Wash., May 25, 1945; buried in Holland, near parents and grandparents. Author: "Alaska Melodrama." Democrat.

HELLENTHAL, John Simon, lawyer. B. in Juneau, Feb. 20, 1915; s. Simon and Katherine Josephine (Cunningham) H.; h. sc., Juneau; B.A., U. Mich.; stud., Santa Clara U., Calif.; LL.B., Notre Dame U., 1940; admitted to Alaska bar, 1940; m. Mary

Wildes in Anchorage, July 22, 1941; m. 2d, Larue Geiger at Mission Inn, Riverside, Calif., June 10, 1945; children: Catherine Lee (Mrs. Gregory Braund); Steve, Marc Edwin; U.S. Army, 1942-46; law prac. with Ralph Cottis, Anchorage, 1946; city atty., Anchorage, 1948-52; del., const. conv., 1955-56; state H.R., 1959-63; chmn., Dem. central com., 1960-61; mem., Legislative Council, which compiled first state code, 1963; mem., WICHE, 1964. Mem., Elks, Pioneers, Am. Leg., VFW. Democrat.

HELLENTHAL, Simon, lawyer. B. in Allegan Co., Mich., July 18, 1877; s. Albertus and Reimka (Sluiter) H.; stud., Hope Coll., Holland, Mich.; LL.B., U. Mich., 1909; m. Katherine Josephine Cunningham in St. Paul, Minn., Oct. 3, 1911 (dec. 1943); children: John Simon, Mary Claire (Mrs. Fred Ayer); m. 2d, Doris Jardine Swanson in Juneau, Sept. 10, 1947; mercantile bus., Mich., 1903-09; admitted to Alaska bar, Sept. 2, 1909; joined bro., Jack, in law prac., Juneau; custodian of Enemy Alien Property in Alaska, 1918; U.S. dist. judge, 3d jud. div., Valdez and Anchorage, 1935-45; ret. to Juneau; died there, Mar. 31, 1955. Mem., Pioneers, Elks. Democrat.

HELLERICH, George, mining engineer. B. in N.Y.C., c. 1895; m. Ruth Brightman of Sitka, in Nome; mining operator, Seward Peninsula, 1910-50s; wintered in San Francisco, Calif.; terr. H.R., 1931-35; died 1969. Republican.

HENDERSON, Lester Dale, educator. B. in Lenox, Ia., Apr. 13, 1886; s. Leander and Elizabeth (Hamilton) H.; B.A., Tarkio Coll., Mo., 1911; post-grad. stud., U. Calif.; m. 1916 (dec. 1918); m. 2d, Blanche Rae Mashin, 1920; 2 daughters; teacher, Ia., 1906, Emmett, Ida., 1911-12, Coeur d'Alene, Ida., 1912-14; supt. sc., Juneau, 1914-17; 1st comr. education, Alaska, 1917-29; supt. scs., Burlingame, Calif., 1929-45; died in Burlingame, Oct. 1945. Author: "Alaska: Its Scenic Features, Geography, History and Government."

HENDRICKSON, Waino Edward, businessman. B. in Juneau, June 18, 1896; s. Henry and Maria (Hannila) H.; h. sc., Juneau; m. Marion Kingsworth Jones, Aug. 12, 1924; d. Dorothea (Mrs. Linn Forrest, Jr.); U.S. Army, 1917-19; employe, Alaska-Juneau Gold Mining Co., 1919-24; asst. wharfinger, city dock, 1924-27; part-owner and operator, Alaska Laundry, 1927-45; mayor, Juneau, 1946-53; terr. H.R., 1951-55; salesman, Am. Wholesale Grocery, 1945-53; Sec. of Alaska, 1953-59; chmn., Alaska Field Com., Dept. of Interior, 1959-61; mgr., BLM, Juneau, 1961-65; ret. to Anchorage with daughter. Mem., Pioneers (past grand pres., 1965), Am. Leg. (past comdr.), Rotary. Episcopalian, Republican.

HENNINGS, Chris, fisherman, labor union official. B. in Denmark, 1899; s. Chris and Karen Marie H.; gr. sc., Clarion, Ia.; unm.; farmer, lumberjack, towboat operator, miner, longshoreman, prospector, fisherman; U.S. Army, 1917-18; moved to Alaska, 1928; terr. H.R., 1945-47; Alaska rep., CIO, Jan. 1945-; died in Fla., Apr. 23, 1971. Mem., Am. Leg., Moose. Democrat.

HENRI, Joseph Ross, lawyer. B. in Utica, N.Y., July 28, 1933; s. Chester C.H.; B.A., Niagara U., 1955; LL.D., Georgetown U., 1963; m. Aletha Joan Walker, 1962; 3 children; teacher, Skagway, 1956; U.S. Army, counter intelligence, Ft. Richardson and Ft. Wainwright, 1957-60; research asst., U.S. Sen. Gruening, Wash., D.C., 1960-63; state dist. judge, Fairbanks, 1963-64; city atty., Juneau, 1964-68, res.; acting city mgr., Juneau, 1968-69; pvt. law prac., 1969-70; state comr. of adm., 1971-74; pvt. law prac., Juneau, 1974-. Mem., Kiwanis, Elks. Address: Juneau 99801.

HENSLEY, William L., lobbyist. B. in Kotzebue, June 17, 1941; gr. sc., Kotzebue; h. sc., Harrison Chilbowee Acad., Knoxville, Tenn.; stud., UA, 2 yrs.; B.A., George Wash. U., 1966; post-grad stud., law, U. N. Mex., 1 yr.; exchange stud., Eastern Europe; m. April Quisenberry in Juneau, June 29, 1968 (div.); s. Baker; m. 2d, Abigail Ryan in Anchorage, Jan. 10, 1974; d. Priscilla; state H.R., 1967-71, majority leader, 1969; state Sen., 1971-75, minority whip, 1973; pres., Alaska Village Electric Cooperative, Anchorage, 1967-69; exec. dir., AFN, Anchorage, 1969-72, pres., 1972-73; chmn., Dem. state central com., 1970 (Apr.-Sept.); cand., U.S. H.R., 1974; del., Cong. on Arctic Development and Future of Eskimo Soc., Le Havre, France, Nov. 1969; del., Nat. Council on Indian Opportunity, Wash., D.C., Jan. 1970; organizer-past exec. dir., Northwest Native Assn. Democrat.

HEPP, Everett Warne, lawyer. B. in Milwaukie, Ore., Aug. 26, 1915; s. Louis O. and Louise (Pfaff) H.; public sc., Ore. and Calif.; privately tutored in academic and legal studies, Berkeley, Calif.; LL.B., U. Calif., 1941; m. Dorothy L. Paulicheck, Nov. 10, 1945; lived in Juneau, Sitka, Fairbanks, 1942; U.S. Army, 1943-47; admitted to Alaska bar, 1948, U.S. Supreme Ct., 1951; asst. U.S. dist. atty., Fairbanks, 1947-49; U.S. dist. atty., 4th jud. div., Fairbanks, 1950-52; pvt. law prac., Fairbanks, 1952-59; superior ct. judge, Fairbanks, 1959-75. Mem., Kiwanis, Adventurers (N.Y.C.). Democrat. Address: State Bldg., Fairbanks 99701.

HERBERT, Charles Francis (Chuck), mining engineer. B. in Cincinnati, O., Feb. 17, 1910; s. Joseph Charles and Maude (Johnson) H.; B.S., UA, 1934; m. Sarah Ann Stephens, Dec. 24, 1935 (div.); children: Stephen, Paul; m. 2d, Roberta Roberts, Oct. 31, 1953; miner, Interior Alaska, 1928-37; supervising engr., mining div., RFC, 1937-40; terr. H.R., 1941-42; U.S. Navy, 1942-46; miner and consult., Fairbanks and Anchorage, 1946-61; chmn., Alaska Public Service Com., 1961-63; state dep. comr., dept. natural resources, 1963-67; pvt. consulting office, Anchorage, 1967-70; state comr., dept. natural resources, Juneau, 1970-74. Mem., Am. Inst. Mining Engrs., Elks, Rotary, Wash. Athletic Club (Seattle). Democrat.

HERMANN, Mildred Robinson, educator, lawyer. B. in Ind., Feb. 28, 1891; d. William M. and Lucretia (Cassity) R.; gr. and h. sc., Ind.; stud., U. Ind., U. Wash.; LL.B., LaSalle U. correspondence course (began law studies in office of James Wickersham); admitted to Alaska bar, 1934; m. Russell

Royden Hermann, pharmacist, in Valdez, May 27, 1920 (dec. 1944); children: Barbara Ann (Mrs. Thomas R. Marshall), Russell Royden, Jr.; teacher, Yakima, Wash., 1910-19, Valdez, 1919-34; law prac., Juneau; dir., OPA, for Alaska, 1942-46; pres., AFWC, 1938-41; dir., Gen. Fed. Women's Clubs, 1941-44; legislative chmn., AFWC, 24 yrs.; reported legislative activities through radio broadcasts and newspaper columns; ed., annual special edition of ALASKA PRESS, analyzing legislature; sec., Alaska Statehood Com., 1949-59; mem., Alaska Employment Security Com., 1940s; del., const. conv., 1955-56; died in Juneau, Mar. 16, 1964. Mem., Soroptimist, Toastmistress, Eastern Star, Beta Sigma Phi (hon. mem.), Nat. Assn. Women Lawyers, Am. Assn. Press Women, Am. Leg. Aux., Am. Cancer Soc. (comdr., Alaska div.), Alaska Tuberculosis Assn. (bd. mem., 18 yrs.). Church of Christ, Republican.

HERMANN, Russell Royden (Chee), lawyer. B. in Seattle, Wash., May 18, 1924; s. Russell Royden and Mildred (Robinson) H.; gr. and h. sc., Juneau; B.A., Wash. State Coll., 1949; J.D., George Wash. U., 1952; m. Elizabeth M. (Susie) Winn, 1953; children: Mark Henry, Jay Winn; U.S. Army, WWII, with ski troops in Italy, awarded Purple Heart; U.S. dist. atty., 2d jud. div., Nome, 1953-59; pvt. law prac., LaCanada, Calif., 1964. Mem., Am. Leg., VFW. Protestant.

HERRING, Paul Clinton, machinist, butcher. B. in Phoenix City, Ala., Sept. 24, 1902; s. town's sheriff; public sc., East Lake, Ala., Columbus, St. Simons I., Ga.; m. Sadie; d. Arlene; U.S. Coast Guard (temporarily in Cordova), 1917-22; machinist, Copper River & Northwestern Ry., Cordova, 1924-34; butcher, Arctic Piggly Wiggly store, Cordova, mgr., 1934-39; butcher, ARRC, Palmer, 1 yr.; dep. U.S. Marshal, Valdez, Kodiak (10 yrs.); appt. U.S. Marshal, 3d jud. div., Anchorage, 1949; died of cancer in Anchorage hosp., Dec. 28, 1950. Hobby: Russian history and icons on Kodiak I.

HESS, Harriet Belle, school teacher, civic leader. B. in Winfield, Ia., 1881; d. Isaac Boggs and Lillian Mary (Hunt) Trimmer; h. sc., Minneapolis, Minn.; B.A. and teacher's certificate, U. Minn., 1902; m. Luther Constantine Hess in Dawson, Y.T., Can., Sept. 11, 1911; teacher, Lake Crystal and Windom, Minn., 1898-1900; h. sc. principal, Juneau, 1902-07, Fairbanks, 1907-10; mem., bd. regents, UA, 1917-51; Dem. Nat. Com., 1944-48; died in Seattle, Wash., Mar. 31, 1951. Mem., terr. bd. children's guardians, 1913-35. Girls' dormitory, UA, named in her honor, 1939; dining commons, UA, dedicated to Harriet and Luther Hess, May 2, 1971.

HESS, Luther Constantine, lawyer, miner, businessman. B. in Milton, Ill., Dec. 28, 1865; s. William and Nancy Minerva (Smith) H.; country dist. sc. and h. sc. (1 yr.), Perry, Ill.; stud., Whipple Acad.; B.A., Ill. Coll., Jacksonville, Ill., 1891; hon. degree, Ill. Coll., 1941; studied law in lawyer's office, Pittsfield, Ill.; m. Harriet Belle Trimmer in Dawson, Y.T., Can., Sept. 11, 1911; teacher and sc. principal, Ill., 1886-93; admitted before supreme ct., Ill., May 7, 1897; joined Klondike stampede to Dawson via Dyea

trail, 1898; licensed to prac. law, Alaska, June 3, 1901; asst. U.S. dist. atty., Fairbanks, 1902-05; organizer, employe, dir., 1st Nat. Bk. of Fairbanks, 1905-50s; terr. H.R., 1917-19, speaker, 1917, Sen., 1919-23, 1929-37, pres., 1931, 1935; chmn., Selective Service bd., WWI; dir., ARRC, 1937-42; mem., Alaska Planning Council, 1937; died in Seattle hosp., July 3, 1954. Mem., Pioneers, Rotary, Masons, Alaska Miners' Assn. (pres., 1939-). Democrat.

HESSE, William H., mining and civil engineer. B. Menasha, Wis., Nov. 2, 1860; s. William and Clara (Vehring) H.; public sc., Neenah, Wis.; stud., U. Notre Dame, Ind.; m. Flora May Dunham, 1887; d. Monica A.; hotel bus. with father, Neenah, 1881-93; mayor, Neenah, 1891-93; estab. water filter factory (Badger Quartz Mill), Wausau, Wis., 1893-; went to Nome area, 1903; res., Cordova, 1919; went to British Guiana, 1924, to investigate diamond mine; ret. to Alaska, 1925; went to Chandalar area for mining co.; terr. highway engr., 1930-44; mem., Nome sc. bd., many yrs.; died in his home, Los Angeles, Calif., June 5, 1954. Democrat.

HIATT, Dr. Robert Worth, educator. B. in San Jose, Calif., Dec. 23, 1913; s. Elwood B. and Bernice (Bane) H.; B.A., San Jose State Coll., 1936; Ph.D., U. Calif., Berkeley, 1941; m. Elizabeth A. Matthews, July 18, 1938; children: Judith L., Gerald A., William R.; teaching asst., U. Calif., 1936-41; asst. prof., Mont. State Coll., 1941-43; prof., U. Hawaii, 1943-63; v.p., U. Hawaii, 1963-69, ret.; exec. dir., U. Hawaii Research Corp., 1969; counselor for scientific affairs, Am. Embassy, Tokyo, Japan, 1970-73; pres., UA, 1973-. Mem., AAAS (Fellow); Oceanographical Soc. of Japan; Ecological Soc. of Am.; Am. Soc. of Zoologists; Am. Inst. Biological Sciences; Com. on Internat. Relations; Adv. Com., Nat. Science Foundation, 1960-70; chmn., Internat. Conf. Marine Biology Laboratories, Rome, 1955; Chinese Assn. for Advancement Science, 1966-73; Panel of Experts, Fisheries Div., FAO and UNESCO, 1962-73.

HICKEL, Walter Joseph, businessman. B. in Ellinwood, Kan., Aug. 18, 1919; s. Robert A. and Emma (Zecha) H.; public sc., Claflin, Kan.; m. Janice Cannon, Sept. 22, 1941 (dec. 1943); s. Theodore Jeffrey; m. 2d, Ermalee Strutz, Nov. 22, 1945; children: Robert, Walter Joseph, Jr., John Edward, Joseph William, William Karl; ended formal education at age 16; carpenter, Calif., 1935-40; bartender, Alaska R.R. employe, constr. worker, Anchorage, 1940-; builder-developer, homes, rental units, residential areas, hotels; founded Hickel Constr. Co., 1947-; built Travelers' Inn, Anchorage, 1953, Travelers' Inn, Fairbanks, 1955, Captain Cook Hotel, Anchorage, 1964; Rep. Nat. Com., 1954-64; Alaska Gov., 1966-69; Sec. of Interior, 1969-70; ret. to Anchorage; builder-developer, University Center supermarket and Capt. Cook Hotel addition; cand., Alaska Gov., 1974. Author, "Who Owns America?" 1971. Mem., Elks, K.C., Knights of Malta (1970). Catholic, Republican. Address: 935 W. 3d Ave., Anchorage 99501.

HICKEY, Daniel W., lawyer. State dist. atty., 1st jud. dist., Juneau, 1973-. Democrat.

HIEBERT, August G., electrical engineer. B. in Trinidad, Wash., Dec. 4, 1916; s. Peter and Josephine H.; h. sc., Quincy, Wash.; stud., technical sc., Los Angeles; hon. D.LL., UA, 1973; m. Patricia Ann Sadler in Wenatchee, Wash., Mar. 17, 1947; children: Margaret "Peggy" (Mrs. Dan Larson), Robin Ann (Mrs. Robert S. Chlupach), Catherine, Terry; asst. engr., KFAR-AM radio station, Fairbanks, 1939-47; technical dir., designer-builder, KENI-AM, Anchorage, 1947, station mgr., 1949; estab. Northern Television, Inc., 1953; estab. Alaska's 1st television station, KTVA-TV, Anchorage, Dec. 11, 1953; estab. Alaska's 1st FM station, KNIK-FM, Anchorage, 1959; acquired KBYR-AM, Anchorage, KFRB-AM, Fairbanks, 1965; founder, pres., Alaska Broadcasting System (9 Alaskan radio stations, affiliated with CBS nat. network), 1964. Received Am. Leg. Aux. "Golden Mike" award, 1961; Anchorage C. of C. Gold Pan award, 1970; Alaska Press Club's 49er Hall of Fame, 1970. Mem., Alaska Festival of Music (bd. dir., pres., 1959-); CBS-TV Network Affiliates Assn. (dir.); Alaska chapter, Assn. of U.S. Army (pres.); Alaska Educational Broadcasting Com., 1970-; Civil Air Patrol (hon.). Catholic, Republican.

HILL, Edward Coke, prospector, lawyer. B. in McMinnville, Ore., Jan. 18, 1866; s. William Lair and Julia Hall (Chandler) H.; stud., Wasco Ind. Acad., The Dalles, Ore., Sackett's Sc. for Boys, Oakland, Calif.; B. Litt., U. Calif.; studied law with father; law degree, U. Calif., 1892; m. Ella Martha Wilson in Ruby, July 4, 1920; prac. law, Seattle, Oakland, San Francisco; gold prospector-lawyer, Nome, 1900-; asst. U.S. atty., Nome, 1903-05, 1907-11; cont. law prac. and prospecting at various mining camps, Yukon Valley; asst. U.S. atty., Fairbanks, 1914-18, Ruby, 1918-24; U.S. Comr., Ruby; govt. contractor for mail delivery between Nenana and Flat by dogsled, 1916-24; pvt. law prac., San Francisco, 1924-27; U.S. dist. judge, 3d and 4th jud. div., Valdez and Fairbanks, 1927-35; law prac., San Francisco, 1935-52; moved to Oakland, 1952; died in Oakland, Calif., Mar. 31, 1961. Mem., A.B., Pioneers, Zeta Psi, Masons, Eagles, Commonwealth Club (San Francisco). Republican.

HILLSTRAND, Earl D., businessman. B. in Seattle, Wash., Aug. 20, 1913; s. Sigfried Eric and Hattie Adelia H.; B.A., Coll. Puget Sound, Tacoma, Wash.; LL.B., George Wash. U., Wash., D.C.; m. Marry Jane Lloyd, 1935; children: Gail C. (Mrs. Paul C. Johnson, dec. 1972), Mary Joanne, John Wesley, Mary Margaret; civilian atty., U.S. Army, Ft. Richardson, 1944-46; asst. U.S. dist. atty., Anchorage, 1946-; homesteaded, operated mink ranch, fished commercially near Homer, estab. real estate and insur. bus.; built fishermen's summer resort, "Land's End", Homer; Alaska H.R., 1957-60, 1963-67, 1969-74; died of cancer in Anchorage hosp., Jan. 22, 1974. Mem., Elks, Sportsman's Club, Anchorage C. of C., Omega & Alpha Soc. Democrat.

HILLYER, Munson Curtis, U.S. Marshal for Alaska, Sitka, 1884-85. Republican.

HILSCHER, Herbert Henry, author, public relations consultant. B. in Seattle, Wash., Apr. 1902; s. John F. and Leah (Zehnder) H.; B.B.A., U. Wash., 1924; m. 2d, Miriam Warner in Seattle, June 5, 1943; d. Hilary; ad mgr., Dollar SS line, San Francisco, Calif., 1926-33; foreign correspondent in Orient, *Christian Science Monitor*, 1934-38; free lance writer and ed., ALASKA LIFE magazine, Seattle, 1938-42; Office Special Services, U.S. Army, Bremerton, Wash., 1943-45; public relations consult., Fairbanks, 1945-52, Anchorage, 1952-; del., const. conv., 1955-56. Author: "Alaska Now," 1948; co-author with wife, "Alaska, U.S.A.," 1959. Mem., terr. development bd., Salvation Army (adv. bd., chmn., 1961), Pioneers, Lions, Fellowship of Royal Geographical Soc., Pan Xenia, Beta Gamma Sigma, Sigma Phi Epsilon, Explorers Club, N.Y.C. Episcopalian, Independent. Address: 2224 Foraker Dr., Anchorage 99503.

HINCKEL, Jack, civil engineer. B. in Worcester, Mass., Sept. 6, 1901; stud., Gates Lane sc., Worcester, Leicester Acad., Worcester Polytechnic Inst.; m. Justine H. Fiskin, 1930; d. Mrs. Peter Ramaglia; lived in N.Y.C.; mining engr., Alaska, 1922; ret. to west coast, associated with major oil cos., 1923; engr., Kaiser Corp., Vancouver shipyards, WWII; ret. to Kodiak, 1945; owner, Kodiak Oil Sales, Union Oil Co. consignee; city councilman, 1946-53, mayor, 1953, Kodiak; del., const. conv., 1955-56; moved to Borrego Springs, Calif., Sept. 1963. Mem., Rotary, Elks. Congregationalist.

HITCHCOCK, Ethan Allen, merchant. B. in Mobile, Ala., Sept. 19, 1835; s. Henry and Anne (Erwin) H.; pvt. sc., Nashville, Tenn.; grad., military acad., New Haven, Conn.; LL.D., U. Mo., 1902, Harvard U., 1906, Wash U., St. Louis, 1907; m. Margaret D. Collier, Mar. 22, 1869; mercantile bus., St. Louis, until 1860; entered com. house of Olyphant & Co., China, partner, 1866, ret., 1872; spent 2 yrs. in Europe; U.S. Minister to Russia, 1897-98; Sec. of Interior, 1899-1907; pres., several mfg., mining and ry. cos., 1874-97; died in Wash., D.C., Apr. 9, 1909. Mem., bd. trustees, Carnegie Inst., Wash. Republican.

HOBART, Clarence L., collector of customs, Juneau, 1905-08. Republican.

HODGE, Walter Hartman, lawyer. B. in Auburn, Ind., Aug. 29, 1896; h. sc., Seattle, Wash.; B.A., LL.B. (1919), U. Wash.; m. Alice Moberg in Seattle, 1924 (dec. 1929); children: Alice Patricia Johnson, Margaret Loraine Nordfors; m. 2d, Elizabeth Little, 1946; dep. prosecuting atty., Skagit Co., Wash., 1920-24; asst. U.S. atty., Cordova, 1925-29; pvt. law prac., Seattle, 1929-35; pvt. prac., city atty., Cordova, 1936-54; U.S. dist. judge, 2d jud. div., Nome, 1954-59; assoc. justice, supreme ct. of Alaska, 1960 (Feb.-Mar.); 1st U.S. dist. judge for Alaska state, Anchorage, 1960-66, ret.; moved to Santa Rosa, Calif., serving part-time fed. judge, Ninth Circuit Ct. district. Mem., Masons, Elks, Pioneers, Rotary. Presbyterian, Republican.

HODGES, H. Jay, lawyer. B. in 1938; LL.B., U. Colo., 1964; law clerk, chief justice, Alaska supreme ct., Anchorage, 1964-65; asst. dist. atty., Anchorage, 1965-66; state dist. atty., 4th jud. div., Fairbanks, 1967-68. Republican.

HOFFMAN, James, aviator. B. in Napamute, *c.* 1928; Indian-Eskimo extraction; orphaned at age 6 yrs.; pub. sc., Napamute; m. Dorothy Marsh, 1947; 9 children; mem., ground service crew, Northern Consolidated Airlines, Napamute, 1942-44; U.S. Army, 1944-46; pilot, Al Jones Airways, Bethel, 1948-49, Northern Consolidated Airlines, Bethel, 1949-; state H.R., from Bethel, 1959-61; pilot on F-27s, Wien Consolidated, Anchorage, 1970s. Address: Anchorage.

HOFMAN, Joseph S., hotel proprietor. B. in Austria of German-Jewish parents, May 14, 1873; emigrated to U.S., 1893; moved to Seattle, Wash., 1898; m.; res., Seward, 1905-; builder-operator, Belmont hotel; employe, Alaska Central Ry., Alaska Northern Ry., Alaska R.R., also longshoreman, fire chief, city councilman, Seward, 1924-29; dep. U.S. Marshal, Dillingham, Anchorage, Matanuska, 1930s; terr. H.R., from Seward, 1933-37, Sen., 1939; died of heart attack in hotel room, Seward, Mar. 29, 1939. Democrat.

HOGGATT, Wilford Bacon, naval officer, lawyer, mine operator. B. in Paoli, Ind., Sept. 11, 1865; s. William M. and Isabelle (Bacon) H.; grad., U.S. Naval Academy, Annapolis, June 1884; grad., Columbia U. law sc., June 1893; stud., Columbia sc. of mines, 1898-99; m. Marie Hayden, Wash., D.C., Jan. 12, 1893 (d. 1900); m. Clarissa Millard, Utica, N.Y., Feb. 25, 1908; 1 d. (b. Mar. 7, 1909); served in Spanish-Am. war, appt. Naval Bd. of Strategy by Pres. McKinley, 1898; res. Navy, Aug. 1, 1898; mgr. Jualin mines, Berner's Bay, 1899-1906; Gov. of Alaska, Apr. 30, 1906 - Oct. 1, 1909; pres., Keyes Products Co., New London, Conn., 1923; died at U.S. Veterans' hospital, N.Y. City, Feb. 26, 1938. Republican.

HOHMAN, George Harold, Jr., school teacher. B. in St. Louis, Mo., June 2, 1932; s. George Harold and Margaret (Church) H.; B.A., Mich. State U., 1959; m. Nancy Lou Mead, Mar. 29, 1953; children: Margaret Carrie, Laura Marie, Sally Anne, Catherine Ann, George Harold, III; U.S. Army, 1952-55, stationed in Alaska, 1955; BIA teacher, Emmonak, Nanapitchuk, Kwigillingok, state teacher, Bethel, 1962-; state H.R., 1967-73, Sen., 1973-76. Mem., Kuskokwim Native Assn., Alaska Education Assn. Address: Box 233, Bethel 99559.

HOLDSWORTH, Philip Ross, mining engineer. B. in Grants Pass, Ore., Aug. 21, 1910; s. Philip H. and Florence H. (Ross) H.; B.S., mining engr. and geology, U. Wash., 1937; m. Violet Opal Welsh in Fairbanks, Dec. 22, 1936; children: David, Phyllis, Bruce; went to Alaska with father, who built and operated lode mill at Skein-Lickner property near Moose Pass; mucker, miner, assayer, timberman, gold miner, B.C., Can., 1926-31; mill supt., Nabesna Mining Corp., Chitina, 1931-36; mill supt., Mindanao Mother Lode mines, P.I., 1937-41; U.S.

Army, taken prisoner by Japanese, 1941-45; cyanide plant foreman, Chelan, Wash., 1945-46; gen. mgr., Independence mine, Wasilla, 1946-47; project engr., Birch-Johnson-Lytle contractors, Ft. Richardson, 1947-49; gen. supt. and mining engr., Snowbird Mining Co., Anchorage, 1949-50; constr. engr., Corps of Engrs., Anchorage, 1950-52; terr. comr. mines, Juneau, 1952-59; state comr., natural resources, 1959-67; Alaska mgr., Internat. Nuclear Corp. of Denver, Juneau, 1968-. Received Outstanding Alaska Award from state C. of C. and elected Chamber pres., 1971. Mem., Am. Inst. Mining & Metallurgical Engrs. (since 1933), Elks, VFW, Am. Leg., Pioneers. Address: Juneau 99801.

HOLLAND, Thomas Henry, civil engineer. B. in Calwood, Mo., Apr. 10, 1876; unm.; started west at age 21; learned to be civil engr. by working with survey crews; engr., Copper River & Northwestern Ry.; built first log cabin and staked first homestead, Chitina; terr. H.R., 1915-17; dep. U.S. Marshal, Chitina, 1940. Mem., A.B., Odd Fellows. Democrat.

HOLM, Edith, merchant. B. in Takoma Park, Md., Jan. 30, 1921; d. Henry Le Roy and Hannah Howarth Transtrom; m. John Holm, June 10, 1941; children: Stuart, James; clerk-typist, dept. public examiner, Minn., 1 yr.; laboratory asst. to doctor, Calif., 1 yr.; sec., Tanana Valley Fair, 1 yr.; adm. asst. to comr. agriculture, Alaska, ed., "Alaska Farmer," 2 yrs.; sec. to mgr. and ad mgr., Northern Commercial Co., Fairbanks, 2 yrs.; moved to Fairbanks from southern Calif., 1946; homesteaded and farmed on Chena Hot Springs road, 13 yrs., sold farm and moved to Fairbanks; husband-wife realtor. landscaping, contracting and garden supplies bus., 1959-; pres., Alaska Fed. Rep. Women, 1968-70; Rep. Nat. Committeewoman for Alaska, 1970-. Mem., Fairbanks Garden Club (pres.), Alaska Fed. Garden Clubs (v.p.), Fairbanks Frontier chapter, Sweet Adelines (charter mem.), United Good Neighbors (bd. mem., 3 yrs.), Alaska Legislative Wives' Club (pres., 2 yrs.), Quota Internat., Fairbanks Urban Beautification Com. (chmn.), Fairbanks Drama Assn., Fairbanks-U. Symphony Orchestra Assn. Address: Box 682, Fairbanks 99707.

HOLM, John, farmer, businessman. B. in Roseau, Minn., Aug. 8, 1920; s. Mike and Bessie (Christenson) H.; pre-med. stud., La Sierra Coll., Arlington, Calif., 2 yrs.; pattern, tool and die-making stud., U. Minn., 2 yrs.; stud., plant breeding and grad., sc. of agriculture, U. Minn., 2 yrs.; stud., Pepperdine Coll., Calif.; m. Edith Transtrom, June 10, 1941; children: Stuart, James; worked in trades including carpentry, 9 yrs.; moved to Fairbanks area, 1946, and homesteaded at Chena Hot Springs road; farmer, 13 yrs., largest producer of cabbages and potatoes in Tanana Valley; sold farm and moved to Fairbanks; estab. landscaping, contracting and garden supplies bus.; dir., U.S. census in Alaska, 1960; state H.R., 1963-65, 1967-73. Mem., Kiwanis, Fairbanks C. of C., Golden Valley Electric Assn. (dir., treas.). Republican. Address: Box 1196, Fairbanks 99707.

HOLT, Edgar Luther, businessman. B. in Me., Jan. 18, 1870; prospector-miner, Mont., Ida., Wash., B.C., 1888-; hotel and grocery bus.; m. Martha; longshoreman and teamster, Nome, 1900-10; built Miners hotel; prop., Holt hardware store, 1910-25; mayor, Nome, 1919; terr. H.R., 1921-23; died in Nome, Sept. 26, 1925; buried at Belmont Point cemetery. Mem., Pioneers, A.B., Eagles, Odd Fellows, Nome Mine Workers Union (pres., 1905). Republican.

HOLZHEIMER, Georgina Nesbit, housewife. B. in Wilkes-Barre, Pa., 1876; m. William Andrew Holzheimer in Salt Lake City, Ut., June 17, 1900; d. Mary Catherine (Mrs. Samuel Gregory, dec.); lived in Ut., Ida., Wash.; arr. Juneau, 1915; mem., Dem. Nat. Com., 1928-40; died in Juneau, Oct. 25, 1942. Mem., LWV (pres.), Juneau. Episcopalian, Democrat.

HOLZHEIMER, William Andrew, lawyer. B. in Saginaw, Mich., Sept. 29, 1870; s. Christofer Frederick and Mary Louise (Cornell) H.; public sc., Saginaw; LL.B., U. Mich., 1898; m. Georgina McCall Nesbit, June 17, 1900; d. Mary Catherine (Mrs. Samuel Gregory, dec.); pvt. law prac., Eureka, Ut., 1898-1901; asst. prosecuting atty., Juab Co., Ut., 1899-1900; pvt. prac., Pocatello, Ida., 1901-05, Seattle, Wash., 1905-15; arr. Juneau, May 22, 1915; appt. asst. U.S. dist. atty., 1st jud. div., Ketchikan, Dec. 16, 1916; U.S. dist. judge, 2d jud. div., Nome, 1917-21; pvt. prac., Ketchikan, 1921-33; U.S. dist. atty., 1st jud. div., Juneau, 1933-44, res. because of eye trouble; city magistrate, Juneau, 1946-48; died in Juneau, Dec. 5, 1948; buried there. Mem., A.B., Masons, Elks, K.P., Eagles. Democrat.

HOOPES, Robert, mechanic, businessman. B. in Globe, Ariz., Feb. 17, 1903; s. William Calib and Mary Isabelle (Wilde) H.; h. sc., San Diego, Calif.; stud., auto sc., Los Angeles, Calif., 1920; m. Mary Josephine King in Fairbanks, Jan. 20, 1934 (div. 1942); s. Robert (b. Aug. 22, 1938); m. 2d, Rae Stevens in Fairbanks, Nov, 25, 1942; shop foreman, Hazard Constr. Co., San Diego, Calif., 1920-27; employe, mechanical dept., Fairbanks Exploration Co., 1928-36; machinist, Samson Hardware Co., 1936-38; owner, Fairbanks Garage, 1938-41; mechanic foreman and master mechanic, U.S. Army Corps of Engrs., Ladd Field, 1941-45; owner, Hoopes Auto Service, garage and service station, 1945-; terr. H.R., 1945-49; city councilman, 1949-50, mayor, 1950-52, Fairbanks. Mem., Masons (past master), Elks, Lions, C. of C., Moose, Dem. Club (4th div., past pres.). Mormon, Democrat.

HOPE, Andrew P., boat builder, fisherman. B. in Sitka, Apr. 9, 1896; s. Klondike gold-stampeder and maiden of Kha-won-ton clan, Tlingit tribe; stud., Sheldon Jackson Training Sc., Sitka; stud., carpentry, Cushman Trade Sc., Tacoma, Wash.; completed Chicago "Am. Correspondence Sc." course, equivalent to h. sc. certificate; m. Tillie Howard, 1912; children: Richard Lunde, Al Willard, John, Percy, Herbert, Fred, Mrs. Robert Petro, Mrs. Roger Lang; an organizer of ANB and Sisterhood, and pres., Grand Camp of the Brotherhood, several terms; built boats during winter and fished commer-

cially during summer; captain, Sheldon Jackson Sc. cruiser; terr. H.R., 1945-53, 1957-63; died in Mt. Edgecumbe hosp., Sitka, Apr. 12, 1968. Elected hon. grad., Sheldon Jackson Sc.; "Citizen of the Year," Sitka. Mem., Nat. Cong. Am. Indians, Salvation Army, Sitka (dir., 30 yrs.), Tlingit-Haida Assn. (pres., 1940-66); Sitka Camp, ANB (charter mem.). Democrat.

HOPPIN, Marshall C., businessman, aviator. B. in 1895; m. Margot; U.S. Army Air Corps, 1917-31, ret. reserve col., 1945; aviation div., U.S. Dept. of Commerce, 1931-39; 1st reg. adm., CAA, Anchorage, 1939-45; pres., Alaska Airlines, Anchorage, 1945-57; insur. and real estate salesman, Anchorage, 1958-60; moved to Brookings, Ore., 1960; died in Coos Bay, Ore., Feb. 11, 1973; interment in Willamette Nat. Cemetery, Portland, Ore. Mem., Rotary, WWI Vets, U.S. Reserve Officers Assn., Air Force Assn. Episcopalian, Republican.

HOPSON, Eben, heavy equipment operator. B. in Pt. Barrow, Nov. 7, 1922; s. Alfred and Maggie H.; gr. sc., Pt. Barrow; m. Rebecca Panigeo of Barrow; 12 children: Charles, Eben Jr., Flossie, Margaret, Catherine, David, Pauline, Patrick, *et al.*; terr. H.R., 1957-59; state Sen., 1959-67 (elected chmn. of "Ice Bloc" by colleagues of northwest and arctic sections); stud., Nat. Guard Officers' leadership sc., Ft. Benning, Ga., 5 wks.; commissioned in Nat. Guard, 1952, rose to rank of capt.; mem., Barrow village council, 1948, pres., 1956-66; exec. dir., Arctic Slope Native Assn., 1966-70; exec. dir., AFN, Anchorage, 1970 (Apr.-Dec.); special asst. to Gov. Egan, Juneau, 1970-72; mayor, North Slope Borough, 1972-; cand., Alaska gov. Mem., Omega and Alpha. Democrat. Address: Pt. Barrow.

HOWARD, Bartley, construction contractor, miner. B. in Fordsville, Ky., Mar. 1, 1878; stud., Lockyear Bus. Coll., Evansville, Ind.; m. Emma; d. Ophelia (Mrs. Harold Sogn); employe, Southern Pacific R.R., Tucson, Ariz., 1901-03; constr. work and mining, Eagle, 1903-04; prospector, Nome, summer 1904; constr. work, Fordsville, 1904-06; mill bus., Egramont, Miss., 1906-09; constr. work, Cordova, 1909-20, Anchorage, 1920-22; supt., bldgs. and bridges, Alaska R.R., Anchorage, 1922-24; coal mine operator, Moose Creek, Alaska-Matanuska Coal Co., 1924-33; terr. Sen., 1925-29; mem., terr. bd. of education, 1925-26; sales rep., Juneau Lumber Co., Ketchikan Lumber Co., Anchorage, 1933-40; died in Anchorage, Apr. 7, 1941; pvt. Masonic funeral. Mem., Masons, Scottish Rite, K.T., Shrine, Elks. Republican.

HOYT, Henry Martyn, lawyer. S. Henry Martyn Hoyt, Sr., who was U.S. Solicitor Gen., 1903-09; U.S. dist. atty., 2d jud. div., Nome, 1904-07; Dept. of Justice office, Seattle, Wash., May-Dec. 1907; atty. gen., Puerto Rico, 1907-10, res.; counselor, U.S. State Dept., Wash., D.C.; died in Wash., D.C., Nov. 1910.

HUBBARD, Oliver Perry, lawyer. B. in Wabash, Ind., Nov. 7, 1857; stud., Butler U.; law degree, Georgetown U.; m. Alice Freeman of Ia. City, Ia., 1886; d. Della Katherine (Mrs. DeWhite B. Libbey);

clerk for Ind. legislature, 1879-82; official reporter, superior ct., Henry Co., Ind., 1882-89; pvt. sec. to U.S. Atty. Gen., Wash., D.C., 1889-95; asst. atty., Dept. of Justice, Wash., D.C.; pvt. law prac., Chicago, 1896-98; went to Alaska, 1898, as promoter of R.R. from Unalakleet to Kaltag; diverted by Nome gold rush and R.R. plans never materialized; prac. law, Nome, 1899-1901, Valdez, devoting major attention to promoting constr. of Alaska R.R.; terr. Sen., 1915-19; cand., terr. atty. gen., Apr. 1920; active aspirant for Alaskan judgeship, 1921; legal counsel, Dept. of Interior; died in West Hartford, Conn., Oct. 1948.

HUBER, John, electronics engineer. B. in Schoolcraft Co., Mich., Mar. 26, 1924; s. C. Russell and Margaret H.; h. sc. grad.; technical training in electronics and radio; m. Frances; 6 children; U.S. Air Force, WWII, 2 yrs.; pvt. pilot and amateur radio operator; mem., Fairbanks city council and North Star Borough Assembly, 1965-; vice chmn., Gov.'s Com. on Adm. of Justice; state H.R., 1971-77; Mem., Fairbanks Lions (charter mem.). Democrat. Address: Box 2591, Fairbanks.

HULEN, Allen D., government administrator, aviator. B. in Lathrop, Mo., 1905; m. Freida (Fritzie); s. Douglas; radio operator, U.S. Navy, 1924-30; radio operator, CAA, Salt Lake City, Ut., Reno, Nev., Rock Springs, Wyo., Seattle, Wash., 1930-39; communications supervisor, controller, dep. reg. adm., CAA, Anchorage, 1939-55, reg. adm., 1955, asst. adm. for Alaskan reg., 1961-63; dep. asst. adm., Europe-Africa-Middle East reg., hdqrs., London, Brussels, 1963-69, ret.; moved to Anchorage; moved to Sun City, Ariz., 1971; died of cancer, Sun City, Apr. 23, 1973. Received meritorious service award by FAA, 1964. Mem., Lions, Anchorage C. of C. Presbyterian.

HUNT, Forest J., merchant, educator. B. in Newaygo Co., Mich., Jan. 15, 1858; public sc., Mich., Neb.; grad., Gibbon Acad., Neb., 1876; m. Harriett E. Frost, Pierce Co., Wash., 1880; children: Elmer Mason, Dale Ward, Amy (Mrs. Lee Craft), Bertha (Mrs. G.M. Wells), Elaine (Mrs. J.A. Talbot, Mrs. Johnson); moved to Pierce Co., Wash., 1876; teacher, merchant, postmaster, justice of peace, Hillhurst, Wash., 1881-94; assessor, Pierce Co., 1895-96; merchant, Wrangell, 1898-1900; operated grocery-meat market, estab. Hunt's News & Novelties, pioneered in shipment of fresh salmon, Ketchikan, 1900-47; city councilman, 1903-06, mayor, 1906-08, Ketchikan; del., Alaska Conv., Seattle, Wash., 1905; terr. Sen., 1921-29; died in Ketchikan, July 8, 1947. Mem., Masons, Elks, Pioneers. Republican.

HUNT, Harriet E. Frost, photographer, housewife. M. Forest J. Hunt, Pierce Co., Wash., 1880; children: Elmer Mason, Dale Ward, Amy (Mrs. Lee Craft), Bertha (Mrs. G.M. Wells), Elaine (Mrs. J.A. Talbot, Mrs. Johnson); res., Ketchikan, 1900-34; Alaska's 1st Rep. Nat. Committeewoman, 1928-32; died in Ketchikan, June 14, 1934. Republican.

HUNTER, Earle L., collector of customs, mariner. B. in Mondovi, Wis., c. 1871; m. Lulu; s. Earle L., Jr.; dep. customs collector, Wrangell, 1898-1904; various

salmon fishing and canning bus.; postmaster, Juneau, 1912-16; boat skipper, including vessels of Bur. of Fisheries, 1925-35; terr. H.R., 1921-23; died in Seattle, Wash., Sept. 1, 1935. Republican.

HUNTLEY, Walter Elliott, carpenter, farmer. B. in Rudyard, Mich., Mar. 4, 1897; s. George and Sarah Jane (Penfold) H.; gr. sc., Rudyard; h. sc., Sault Ste. Marie, Mich., stud., briefly at U. Mich.; m. Beatrice Hoag, Nov. 29, 1923; children: Beatric Jane Hulvey, Margie Lee Carlson, Duanne F., Laddie Penfold; U.S. Navy, 1917-19; mgr., Algoma Steel Corp. store, Fiborn Quarry, Mich., 1919-21, Union Carbide, Sault Ste. Marie, 1921-25; carpenter and brake inspector, R.R. terminal yards, Duluth, Minn., 1925-35; colonist, Matanuska Valley Colonization project, 1935; developed grade A dairy farm; U.S. Comr., Palmer, 1936-48; terr. H.R., 1945-49, Sen., 1949-53; U.S. Marshal, 3d jud. div., Anchorage, Am. Leg., Moose, K.P., United Protestant Church (charter, elder), Matanuska Valley Farmers' Cooperative Assn. (bd. dir., 1st pres., 1938), active in Boy Scout work, 20 yrs. Protestant, Democrat.

HURLEY, James J., businessman. B. in Oakland, Calif., Feb. 3, 1915; grad., h. sc., San Leandro, Calif., 1932; B.S., U. Calif., 1948; m. Dorothy Dow, Oct. 22, 1938 (div.); children: Judy, Joan, Kathy, Michael; m. 2d, Mrs. Katherine T. Alexander, July 1960; children: Susan, Mary; chemist, Shell Oil Co.; U.S. govt. employe in agriculture; moved from Weiser, Ida. to Alaska with family, June 15, 1948; soil conservation service, Palmer, 1948-49; gen. mgr., ARRC, 1949-63; mgr., Alaska Hardwoods sawmill, Wasilla, 1963-64; v.p., Matanuska Valley Bk., Palmer, 1964-69; owner-operator, Alaska Title Guaranty Co., Palmer, 1969-; mem., Joint Fed.-State Land Use Planning Com., 1970-. Mem., Elks, Grange, Kiwanis, Naval Reserve. Democrat.

HURLEY, Julien A., lawyer. B. in Fayette, Ore., Apr. 1, 1885; s. Andrew M. and Mary Almira (Smith) H.; stud., Ore. State Normal Sc., U. Ore.; admitted to Ore. bar, 1908; m. Fay Clark, Eugene, Ore., 1919; prac. law, Vale, Ore., 1908-22; state Sen., Ore., 1917-19; asst. U.S. atty., Anchorage, 1922-24; U.S. atty., 4th jud. div., Fairbanks, 1924-33; terr. H.R., 1953-55; died in Fairbanks, Jan. 25, 1962. Mem., K.P. (chancellor), Masons, Elks. Congregationalist, Republican.

I

ICKES, Harold L., lawyer, author. B. in Frankstown township, Blair Co., Pa., Mar. 15, 1874; s. Jesse Boone Williams and Martha Ann (McEwen) I.; B.A., 1897, J.D. (cum laude), 1907, U. Chicago; LL.D., Wash. and Jefferson Coll. and Lake Forest Coll., 1933, Berea, Pa., Military and Tufts colls. and Northwestern U., 1934, U. Ala., 1935, U. N. Mex., 1939; m. Anna Wilmarth Thompson, 1911 (dec. 1935); step-s. Raymond Wilmarth Thompson; m. 2d, Jane Dahlman in Dublin, Ireland, May 24, 1938; children: Harold McEwen, Elizabeth Jane; reporter, Chicago newspapers, 1897-1900; pvt. law prac., Chicago, 1907-; U.S. Army, 1918-19; Ind. Rep. cand., U.S. Sen., 1926; Sec. of Interior, 1933-46; adm. of public works, 1933-39; oil adm. under Nat. Recovery Act.; chmn., bd. trustees, Roosevelt Coll., Chicago, 1948-50; died in Wash., D.C., Feb. 3, 1952. Awarded Louis D. Brandeis medal for service to humanity, 1940; Cornelius Amory Pugsley gold medal for distinguished park service in U.S., 1941. Mem., Am. Bar Assn., SAR, Swedish Colonial Soc. (hon.), Chicago Press Veterans Assn., Am. Philatelic Soc., Phi Delta Theta, Phi Delta Phi, Pi Gamma Mu (hon.), Nat. Press Club, Saints and Sinners, N.Y.C. Author: "The New Democracy," 1934; "Back to Work," 1935; "America's House of Lords," 1939; "The Third Term Bugaboo," 1940; "Not Guilty," 1940; "Autobiography of a Curmudgeon," 1943; "Fightin' Oil," 1943; "My Twelve Years With F.D.R.," 1948.

INGERSOLL, Charles E., lawyer, businessman. B. in Gloucester, Mass., Oct. 22, 1866; public sc., Gloucester; stud., Harvard U., 1 yr.; m.; 1 s.; went to Wrangell, 1898, Ketchikan, 1899; hotel bus. and law stud.; city atty., Ketchikan, 1905-06; when fire destroyed his Revilla hotel, he rebuilt it, calling it Ingersoll; terr. H.R., on non-partisan ticket, 1913-15; moved to Tacoma, Wash., 1926; died in Tacoma, July 24, 1943.

INGRAM, Hunter B., businessman. B. in Belfort, Pa., Apr. 27, 1862; public sc., Phila., Pa.; m.; d. Marion; ranch hand on stock farm, Kan., 1878-, Tex., 1890; apprentice machinist, 1883-87; worked in sawmill, Portland, Ore., 1888-1900; cigar and tobacco bus., retail and wholesale, starting at Portland and moving to Valdez, 1906; terr. H.R., 1913-15; ret. to Portland, 1915; assoc. with wholesale grocery firms, Portland, making annual sales trips to Alaska; died of heart attack, Portland, Ore., Mar. 17, 1928; funeral services by Masonic lodge; interment in Lincoln Memorial Park mausoleum, Portland.

IPALOOK, Percy, clergyman. B. in Pt. Barrow, Apr. 2, 1906; s. Epalook and Elizabeth (Sooksralook) I.; stud., Sheldon Jackson Jr. Coll., U. Dubuque, Ia.,

1930-34, 1940-41; ordained, 1941; m. Esther Berryman, July 14, 1935; children: Elmer Clyde, Thomas Berryman, Percy, Helen Jane, Gerald Wayne, Edward Neil, Milton Joseph, Frederick Thornton, Joan Elizabeth, Molly Kathleen; terr. H.R., 1949-51, Sen., 1951-55, from Wales; appt. 1st Eskimo chaplain, U.S. Army Reserves, Alaska, rank of capt., 1st Alaskan Scout battalion, Nome, 1950; missionary, Wales, Wainwright, St. Lawrence I., Kotzebue. Presbyterian, Republican. Address: Kotzebue.

IRVING, George R., lawyer. B. in Mich., 1869; law degree, U. Mich.; prac. law, Port Huron, Mich.; asst. prosecuting atty., St. Clair Co., Mich.; went to Alaska, 1897; traveled in North, 2 yrs.; moved to Ketchikan, 1899; pvt. law prac., mining, interests in several local mining operations; mayor, Ketchikan, 1902-03, 1905-06; asst. U.S. atty., 1st jud. div., Ketchikan, 1906-12; law prac., Juneau, 1915-; chmn., Rep. central com., 1900-12, 1916-20; estab. Irving Packing Co., 1912; built cannery at Karheen, near Ketchikan; sold interest and moved to Seattle, Wash., c. 1920.

ISBELL, Brig. Gen. James H., career military officer. B. in Union City, Tenn., June 3, 1914; grad., U.S. Military Acad., West Point, N.Y., 1938, Nat. War Coll.; m. Virginia Fleming, Dec. 23, 1938; children: Reed Whitson (Mrs. John M. Meek), James H., Thomas; bomber pilot, 1939-53; planning staff, Pentagon, 1953-58; vice comdr., Alaska Air Command, Elmendorf AFB, 1958-62; chief of staff, hdqrs., Continental Air Command, 1963-64; comdr., 1st Air Force Reserve reg., Andrews AFB, Wash., D.C., 1964-67, ret.; state dir., disaster office, Anchorage, 1967-71; field rep., Dept. Interior, Anchorage, 1972-73.

IVEY, Capt. Joseph W., collector of customs, Alaska, 1897-1902; former res., Portland, Ore.

J

JACKSON, Barry W., lawyer. B. in Long Branch, N.J., Jan. 27, 1930; h. sc., Encenitas, Calif.; B.A., 1952, LL.B., 1958, Stanford U.; m. Susan; 4 children (2 eldest named Stacy Ann, Sydney Elise); 2d lt., Navy ROTC, Marine Corps, 1952-55; law clerk, U.S. dist. judge, Fairbanks, 1958-59; city atty., 1959-63; pvt. prac., 1963-; state H.R., 1965-67, 1969-71. Mem., Tanana Valley Bar Assn. (pres., 1961-63), Am. Civil Liberties Union, Kiwanis. Episcopalian, Democrat. Address: 500 Lincoln St., Fairbanks 99701.

JACKSON, Sheldon, missionary. B. in Minaville, N.Y., May 13, 1834; grad., Union Coll., N.Y., 1855; post-grad. stud., Princeton Theological Seminary, 1857; m. Mary Voorhees, 1857; 2 daughters; worked in hospitals, Ala. and Tenn., Civil War; assigned to mission work, Rocky Mt. dist., 1865; went to Alaska, 1877; founded missions at Wrangell, Sitka (Sheldon Jackson Jr. Coll.), Haines, Prince of Wales I.; lobbied, lectured throughout U.S., wrote magazine articles, in favor of Harrison Act of 1884 creating civil govt. for Alaska; Gen. Agent of Education for Alaska, with an office in Wash., D.C.; persuaded U.S. Cong. to support importation of reindeer from Siberia for starving Eskimos; ret. 1908; died in Wash., D.C., 1909. Author: "Alaska"; ed.-pub., "Rocky Mountain Presbyterian" magazine, 10 yrs.; pub., annual reports on reindeer industry, 1899-1906. Presbyterian.

JARVELA, Gilbert A., aviator. B. in Cloquet, Minn., Aug. 1, 1919; s. Charles Seigfreid and Selma (Koppenen) G.; h. sc., Butte, Mont.; m. Bonnie E. Parks, Tempe, Ariz., Aug. 7, 1943; children: Dawn L. (Mrs. Jay Prince), Andrea, Stephen, Dell Kathryn (Mrs. Alvin Eli Amason), Gwen A.; employed as cosmetologist; U.S. Air Force, 1943-44; went to Seward, 1947, Kodiak, 1948; chief pilot, Kodiak Airways, 1949-; mem., Kodiak sc. bd., 1952-60; state H.R., 1961-65. Mem., Kodiak Electric Assn. (bd. dir.), Elks. Democrat. Address: Box 537, Kodiak 99615.

JARVIS, David Henry, collector of customs, Revenue Cutter Service officer, businessman. B. in Berlin, Md., Aug. 24, 1862; grad., cadet sc., U.S. Revenue Cutter Service, 1883; m. Ethel Taber, Apr. 2, 1896; children: Anna, David, Jr., William; Alaska duty, 1888-1905; received U.S. Cong. gold medals for rescuing 275 stranded whalers, Pt. Barrow, 1897, and taking charge of smallpox epidemic, Nome, 1900; collector of customs, 1902-05; rejected Alaska gov. offer by Pres. Roosevelt, 1906; res. govt. service to head Morgan-Guggenheim operations, Alaska, including Northwestern SS Co., Northwestern Fisheries, 1905-11; interested in Chichagof mine, Sitka, Cliff mine, Valdez; committed suicide in Arctic Club, Seattle, Wash., June 23, 1911.

JENNE, Crystal Snow, businesswoman. B. in Sonora, Calif., 1884; d. George T. and Anna Edes (Rablen) S.; gr. and h. sc., Juneau; stud., Spencerian Commercial sc., Cleveland, O.; teacher's certificate, U. Calif.; m. Dr. Charles P. Jenne, dentist, July 6, 1916 (dec. 1938); children: Corinne (Mrs. D.F. Kenway), Charles J., Phyllis (Mrs. E.M. McClellan, dec.); arr. Alaska, Apr. 18, 1887; she and bro. Montgomery (Monte) were first white children to cross Chilkoot Pass, 1894, actor parents going to gold camps, Circle City, Fortymile, Dawson, 1894-98; teacher, secretary, Skagway, Sitka, Mendenhall, Juneau, 1906-19; prop., Forget-Me-Not Flower Shop, Juneau, 1940-43; terr. H.R., 1941-45; postmaster, Juneau, 1944-45; died in Sitka, June 5, 1968. Mem., Trinity Cathedral choir, Juneau (dir., 1918-38), Alaska-Yukon Pioneers (dep. grand pres.), Ladies of the Golden North, BPW. Episcopalian, Democrat.

JENNINGS, Robert William, lawyer. B. in Brooklyn, N.Y., Nov. 10, 1864; B.A., Vanderbilt U., 1882; LL.D., Harvard U., 1884; admitted to bar, Wash., D.C., 1888; m. Ada Pugh, 1897; d. Cordelia; co. atty. in several Puget Sound cos., including Port Townsend, Jefferson Co., 1891-95; prac. law, Wrangell, 1898-99; res., Skagway, 1899-1905, Juneau, 1905-12; maintained legal affiliations in Fairbanks and Seattle; cand., del. to Cong., 1912; U.S. dist. judge, 1st jud. div., Juneau, 1913-21; moved to San Francisco, Calif., Sept. 16, 1921; died at home, San Francisco, July 12, 1937. Democrat.

JENSEN, Marcus Frederick, businessman, big game guide. B. in Westhope, N. Dak., Aug. 8, 1908; s. John Frederick and Neva (Stephens) J.; gr. and h. sc., Minneapolis, Minn.; university stud., 2 yrs., civil engr. trade sc., 2 yrs.; m. Mamie Johana Feusi, Dec. 5, 1933; s. John Marcus; employe, public roads adm., Juneau, 1928-34; mgr., hardware and grocery store, Douglas, 1935-; pres., Douglas Canning Co., Feusi and Jensen, Inc.; mem. H.R., 1949-51, 1961-63, Sen., 1953-57; cand., Sec. of State, Rep. ticket, 1966; city councilman, 1935, mayor, 1945-47, Douglas. Mem., Gastineau Channel sports as baseball pitcher, 1928-46, basketball, 1933-45 (Southeastern all-star team), Masons, Eagles. Methodist, Democrat and Republican.

JENSEN, Thomas D., miner, businessman. B. in Buffalo, N. Dak., *c.* 1881; m. Mayme Brewster in Nome, June 19, 1929 (dec. 1938); m. 2d, 1949; joined bro. Andrew, who struck it rich on No. 5, Anvil Creek, Nome area, 1918; mem., Alaska Game Com., 1925; terr. H.R., 1925-27, Sen., 1927, res.; clerk, U.S. dist. ct., Nome, 1927-33; moved to Flat; assoc. with Donnelly & Sheppard and Miners & Merchants Bk.; ret. to Milwaukee, Wis., 1950; died June 28, 1953. Republican.

JESSEN, Ernest Forrest, newspaper editor-publisher. B. in Seattle, Wash., June 11, 1890; s. John M. and Ann (Larson) J.; public sc., Seattle; m. Catherine Mary Jones, Feb. 22, 1910; children: Lois (Mrs. Edwin Sandbeck), Ernestine (Mrs. Howard (Mickey) Peterson); visited bro. in Fairbanks, 1905; estab. delivery service bus.; ret. to Seattle, cont. schooling; went to Cordova to enter crab bus., but financial problems turned him into a reporter, Cordova

TIMES, 1910-19; reporter, Anchorage TIMES and cartoonist, PATHFINDER magazine, Anchorage, 1919-23; ed. and gen. mgr., Anchorage ALASKAN, 1923-24; estab. advertising agency, Anchorage, 1924-25; owner-operator, Seward GATEWAY, 1925-38; ed., Fairbanks NEWS-MINER'S weekly, Alaska WEEKLY MINER, 1938-42; estab. and pub., JESSEN'S WEEKLY, 1942-61, daily, 1961-68; estab. ALL-ALASKA WEEKLY, 1970-71; died in Fairbanks, Mar. 26, 1971. Elected to Alaska Press Club's Hall of Fame. Mem., Alaska Unemployment Compensation Com. (chmn.), Pioneers, Republican Club, Golf and Country Club (trustee). Republican.

JOHNSON, Arthur D., aviator. B. in Alaska, 1920; m. Grace O'Connor in Fairbanks, Oct. 25, 1946; 4 children; mechanic, Wien Alaska Airlines, Fairbanks; moved to Nome; estab. flying service, Unalakleet, 1949-51; pilot, Alaska Airlines, flying between Unalakleet and Bethel, 1951-60; moved to Nome; pilot, Wien Airlines, 1960-61; state H.R.', 1961; killed in plane crash, Dec. 8, 1961. Democrat.

JOHNSON, Axel C., mechanic, fisherman, trapper. B. in St. Michael; gr. sc., St. Michael; m. Pearly in Kwiguk, 1935; 5 children; moved to Emmonak when Yukon river banks caved in at Kwiguk; terr. Nat. Guard, WWII; mechanic, fisherman, trapper (mostly mink), pilot, active in Chemo Therapy (tuberculosis treatment program); both he and wife served as mid-wives; state H.R., from Kwiguk, 1959-61, 1963-67. Democrat. Address: Lower Yukon River, Emmonak 99581.

JOHNSON, Bjorn Gilbert, carpenter, lawyer. B. in Spokane, Wash., 1920; s. Gilbert and Selma (Gjefle) J.; B.A., 1954, J.D., 1967, Gonzaga U.; m. Sondra Powell, Juneau, Dec. 9, 1964; children: Sondra, JohnSona, Kjell; constr. foreman, Fairbanks, 1955-57; constr. worker, Seattle; attended law sc.; chief dep., state dept. labor, 1959-60, comr., 1960-66; pvt. law prac., Anchorage, 1967-. Mem., Carpenters' Union, Elks. Lutheran, Democrat. Address: 1200 Airport Heights Rd., Suite 500, Anchorage 99504.

JOHNSON, Charles Sumner, lawyer. B. in Jones Co., Ia., Aug. 31, 1854; public sc., Clarinda, Ia.; printer's apprentice, 1869; B.A., Ia. State Coll.; LL.B., U. Ia., 1877; m. Mary Davis, Wahoo, Neb., Sept. 18, 1879; s. Francis D. (dec. 1918); city atty., Wahoo, Neb., 1877-79; H.R., Neb., 1883-85; co. prosecuting atty., Nelson, Neb., 1885-89; U.S. dist. atty. for Alaska, Sitka, 1889-94; pvt. prac., Juneau, 1894-97; U.S. dist. judge for Alaska, Sitka, 1897-1900, res.; law prac., representing mining corp., Nome, 1900-06; del., Rep. Nat. Conv., 1884, 1888, 1896; died of Bright's disease in Los Gatos, Calif., Mar. 1, 1906. Mem., A.B. Republican.

JOHNSON, Frank Glonnee, labor union official, fisherman. B. in Rocky Pass, Kupreanoff I., Dec. 15, 1894; gr. sc., Shakan, 1906-10; stud., Sheldon Jackson training sc., Sitka, Indian Service sc., Chemawa, Ore.; h. sc., Salem, Ore., 1910-17; B.S., U. Ore., 1927; m. Mrs. Louise S. Mason, 1946; adopted d., Phyllis E.; teacher and commercial fisherman, Klawock and Kake, 1928-42; mechanic, Boeing Aircraft factory, Seattle, Wash., 1942-46; teacher, fisherman,

Kake, 1946-; terr. H.R., 1947-55, 1957, res.; U.S. Comr., Kake, 1957; city councilman, several yrs., mayor, 1947, Kake; organizer and sec.-treas., Alaska Purse Seiners Union; sec.-treas., Alaska Marine Workers Union; mem., exec. bd., ANB, 1930-, Grand Pres. twice; living in Ketchikan, 1974. Republican.

JOHNSON, Frank L., mechanic. B. in Council, 1904; grad., h. sc., Salem, Ore.; m.; 6 children; mayor, White Mountain; terr. H.R., from Nome, 1949-51. Mem., ANB. Swedish Covenant Church, Republican.

JOHNSON, Grace, housewife. B. at Salmon Lake, 1924; d. E.B. O'Connor of Nome; grad., h. sc., Nome, 1943; stud., UA; teacher training, Minneapolis, Minn.; m. Arthur D. (died in plane crash, Dec. 8, 1961, while state legislator); teacher, Haycock and Council, 1 yr. each, 1943-47; res., Nome, 1947-49, Unalakleet, 1949-60, Nome, 1960-, husband working as commercial pilot; state H.R., 1961-63. Democrat.

JOHNSON, John Earl, businessman. B. in Avon, Wis., Aug. 31, 1889; s. Ellick and Hannah (Hanson) J.; m. Agnes Hanson, Aug. 2, 1911; d. Mary (Mrs. C.E. Reid); grad., Whitewater (Wis.) State Teachers Coll.; B.A., U. Wash., 1917; teacher, Castle Rock, Wash., 1908-10; principal, Vader, Wash., 1911, Mosier, Ore., 1912-13, Brickelton, Wash., 1914-17; supt. sc., Kalama, Wash., 1917-20, Ketchikan, 1920-23; city clerk, Ketchikan, 1923-27; helped estab. (John H.) Davies & Johnson, real estate and insurance bus., 1927, pres., 1927-60; mayor, Ketchikan, 1926; terr. H.R., 1931-33; ret. to Tucson, Ariz., 1960. Mem., Rotary, Masons, Elks, Eagles, Odd Fellows, Redmen. Lutheran, Republican.

JOHNSON, John Patrick, railroad executive. B. Jan. 1, 1902; m. Roma; employe, Santa Fe R.R., 1917; U.S. Army Corps Engrs., Iran, India, China, South Pacific, Philippines; asst. gen. mgr., Alaska R.R., Nov. 1945-Jan. 1, 1946; in charge of building R.R., Madigan-Hyland South Am. Co., Bogota, Colombia; owner-operator, banana plantation and cattle ranch, with home in Barranquilla, Colombia, 1953-68; died in Topeka, Kan., Aug. 14, 1968; interment in Ark. City, Kan.

JOHNSON, Kenneth Charles, miner, businessman. B. in Seattle, Wash., May 9, 1914; gr. and h. sc., Seattle; stud., mining, UA, 3-1/2 yrs., 1935-; m. Louise Muriel Burget Thompson, May 30, 1940; d. Louise Muriel; mining and prospecting on his own and U.S. Smelting, Refining & Mining Co., Dome Cr., and Kuskokwim and Noatak areas; U.S. Army Corps Engrs., Seward, 1944-46; cand., comr. labor, 1946; estab. gen. insur. agency, Anchorage, 1946-58; terr. H.R., 1955-58, chmn., ways and means com., 2 sessions; died of cancer in Anchorage, June 4, 1958. Mem., Lions, Masons, Shrine, Elks. Presbyterian (trustee), Democrat.

JOHNSON, Lars L. (Larry), aviator, fisherman, miner. B. in Kloten, N. Dak., Jan. 5, 1918; h. sc., Kloten; m. Doris Wells in Hendersonville, N.C., June 30, 1946; children: Lars, Jr., Jonna, Jennifer; went to Alaska, 1938; commercial fisherman, Bristol Bay, summers, and gold-miner, Independence Mine, near Anchorage, until 1941; U.S. Army Air Corps, 1941-46; dep. tax collector, dept. taxation, Anchorage, 1950-51; adjt. gen., Nat. Guard, Juneau, 1951-53; comdr., Air Nat. Guard., 1953-55; station mgr., Alaska Airlines, McGrath airways traffic control specialist, FAA, Bethel, Unalakleet, Yakutat, 1958-61; state div. aviation, 1961-71, exec. asst., 1961-63, dir., 1963-67, chief operations, 1967-71, dir., 1971-.

JOHNSON, Maurice Theodore, lawyer. B. in Brainard, Minn., Nov. 18, 1901; s. William M. and Olgi I. (Carlson) J.; gr. and h. sc., Minot, N. Dak.; stud., U. N. Dak., LL.B., John Marshall law sc., Chicago, 1919-27; m. Marie Ann Lysing, July 25, 1927; children: M. Quentin, Reynold T., Virginia Marie; pvt. prac., Chicago and Woodstock, Ill., 1927-37; admitted to Alaska bar; employe, Alaska-Juneau mine; pvt. law prac., Juneau, 1937-40, Fairbanks, 1940-72; terr. H.R., 1945-49; del., const. conv., 1955-56; mayor, Fairbanks, 1949-50; mem., terr. bd. road comrs., 1953-57; died in Fairbanks, June 17, 1972. Mem., Masons, Shrine, Lions (past pres.), Moose, Elks, C. of C. (past pres.), Am. and Tanana Valley Bar Assns., Phi Delta Theta, Phi Delta Phi. Presbyterian (ruling elder), Republican.

JOHNSON, Sam E., civil engineer. B. in 1902; res., Ida.; dist. highway engr., Nome, 1960-61; state highway location engr. and asst. state constr. engr., Anchorage, 1961-62; 1st dir. and later comr. highways, Juneau, Jan.-Apr. 1962; head of maintenance div., dept. highways, Apr. 1962-; died in Boise, Ida., Jan. 21, 1965. Democrat.

JOHNSTON, Fred B., miner, mechanic. B. in Negaunee, Mich., Aug. 8, 1892; gr. and h. sc., Fairbanks; stud., UA; m. Eva Tripp of Juneau, 1936; d. Eva Janet; went to Dawson with parents, 1898; moved to Stewart R., where father was miner and roadhouse prop.; family moved to Fairbanks; employe, agriculture experiment farm, UA; U.S. Navy, 1917-18; estab. garage bus. and automobile sales agency, Fairbanks; cont. part-time mining, dragline operations in Circle dist.; terr. H.R., 1923-25, 1927-29, 1931-33; died in Seattle, Wash., Aug. 13, 1965; buried in Fairbanks. Mem., Am. Leg. (1st vice comdr., 1925). Republican.

JOHNSTON, Walker S., railroad executive. B. in Mo., 1917; coll. stud., St. Joseph, Mo.; m. Margaret; children: John Walker, Margaret Ann (Mrs. Mervin Wetherly); rodman, Chicago, Burlington & Quincy R.R., St. Joseph, trainmaster, asst. supt., supt., prior to merger with Northern Pacific R.R., Feb. 1970; operations mgr., asst. to v.p. of operations, Omaha, Neb.; gen. mgr., Alaska R.R., 1972-.

JONES, Charles Davenport, miner, laborer. B. in Zanesville, O., Apr. 26, 1875; s. Charles Hammond and Katherine Orrick (Davenport) J.; h. sc., 2 yrs.; m. Loretta Mary Sands Sexton, Oct. 1922; children: Mrs. Juanita Carrol, Jane (Mrs. Larry Galvin), Daniel A.; ranch-hand R.R. section-hand, bank clerk, circulation dept. employe, Chicago TRIBUNE, 1891-1900; moved to Nome, June 12, 1900; long-

shoreman, Seward Peninsula Ry. employe, prospector, miner, ARC foreman (8 yrs.); terr. H.R., 1913-15, state H.R., 1959-61; terr. Sen., 1947-51, 1953-57, pres., 1953; U.S. Marshal, 2d jud. div., 1925-33; tourist guide, Wien Alaska Airlines, summer mos.; died in Pioneers' Home, Sitka, May 17, 1963. Mem., Pioneers Igloo No. 1, Nome (founding mem.). One of 3 to cast Alaska's first electoral ballots for U.S. Pres., Dec. 1960. Episcopalian, Republican.

JONES, Charles M., State H.R., from Craig, 1959-61. Democrat.

JORDAN, Emmett Robert, miner. B. in Wis., 1869; m.; res., Nome, summers, Seattle, winters; U.S. Marshal, Nome, 2d jud. div., 1913-21; ret. to Seattle, 1923; traveling rep., Seattle Fur Exchange; died in street car, Seattle, Wash., Apr. 1, 1931. Democrat.

JOSEPHSON, Joseph Paul, lawyer. B. in Trenton, N.J., June 3, 1933; s. David Samuel and Jennie (Randelman) J.; public sc., Trenton; B.A., U. Chicago, 1953; J.D., Catholic U. Am., 1961; m. Karla Zander, May 29, 1960; children: Peter Ben, Andrew Lewis, Sara; U.S. Army, military police, 1955-57; legislative asst., U.S. Sen. E.L. Bartlett, Wash., D.C., 1957-60; admitted to Alaska bar, pvt. law prac., Anchorage, 1961-; Anchorage city councilman, 1966-68, mayor pro tempore, 1967-68; state H.R., 1963-67, Sen., 1969-72, minority leader, 1971-72; state co-chmn., Joint State-Fed. Land Use Planning Com., 1972-. Jewish, Democrat. Address: 1526 F St., Anchorage.

JOY, Louis F., farmer, electrician. B. in Clark Mills, N.Y., Apr. 25, 1890; gr. sc., Skagway; h. sc., Clinton, N.Y., 1909; m. Gladys Clark, May 26, 1914; children: William, Ruth (Mrs. William E. Reed), Lois (Mrs. Charles B. Hall), Robert; family moved to North, 1898; lived in Atlin, B.C., Can., 1 yr.; moved to Skagway; father killed in hunting accident, 1904; mother returned to Clinton, N.Y., 1906; apprentice electrician, Syracuse Rapid Transit R.R., Little Falls, N.Y., 1909-12; employe, Internat. Harvester Co., Auburn, N.Y., 1912-14; farmer, homestead near Fairbanks, 1914-21; supt. utility distribution, Northern Commercial Co., cont. in same capacity when system sold to city, 1922-57; experimented with crops and livestock, 156-acre farm on Badger road; terr. H.R., 1947-49; mem., Fairbanks sc. bd., 1932-57, pres., several yrs.; died Jan. 1972. Mem., Lions (charter mem., past pres.), Pioneers (past pres.), Tanana Valley Sportmen's Assn. (life mem.), Tanana Lodge No. 162, Masons (grand high priest, grand chapter). Republican.

JUDSON, Thomas B., miner. B. in Brant, N.Y., Apr. 10, 1882; m.; children: Evelyn (Mrs. H.M. Hollman, Mrs. Kenyon McLean), Thomas, Jr., Arthur, Charles Everett; employe, Treadwell mining complex, 1903-17; miner, Prince William Sound, Alaska-Juneau mines, Juneau; city councilman, 1923-26, mayor, Juneau, 1926-32, 1937-38; terr. H.R., 1933-35; died in Juneau, Mar. 31, 1938. Democrat.

JULIEN, Victor A., miner. B. in Stockholm, Sweden, c. 1867; m.; 3 children; miner, Nome dist., 1902-20s; owner-operator, Julien Dredge Co. on Osborne Creek; spent winters in Edmonds, Wash.; terr. H.R., 1921-23, elected to fill vacancy left by death of Edward W. Burroughs. Republican.

K

KADOW, Kenneth W., banker. B. in Urbana, Ill., Oct. 16, 1934; s. Kenneth J. and Dallas K.; B.A., Wash. State U.; m. Charity Allin Bowers, Oct. 16, 1957; children: Kenneth, Valerie, Lisa, Erin, Andrea Carol; U.S. Air Force reserve, jet pilot, 1957-64; pres., Spenard Utilities, Inc., Anchorage, 1964-65; mgr., real estate development project, Ozarks and Ore., 1965-67; v.p., First Fed. Savings & Loan Assn., Anchorage, 1967-70; state comr. commerce, 1970-73, res.; exec., Alaska Fed. Savings & Loan Assn., Juneau, 1973-. Mem., Beta Theta Pi (fraternity), Elks, Air Force Assn. Catholic, Democrat.

KALAMARIDES, Peter J., lawyer. B. in Waterbury, Conn., June 4, 1916; h. sc., Brooklyn, N.Y.; B.A., 1938, M.A., 1942, J.D., 1948, U. Ida.; m. Elizabeth; children: Joseph Alan, Peter, George; security guard, Brooklyn; police officer, Moscow, Ida., attending U. Ida. by day and police work by night, 1934-42; U.S. Army, 1942-44; lived in Juneau briefly, then Anchorage, 1944; police officer, chief of police, Anchorage, res. 1 yr. later to return to U. Ida. law sc.; ret. to Anchorage, 1948; pvt. law prac., Anchorage, 25 yrs.; state superior ct. judge, 3d jud. dist., Anchorage, 1973-. Mem., Alaska Bar Assn. (exec. sec., 1955-56); Legislative Council (chmn., 1960-); dir., Chugach Electric Assn. (pres., 1957-65, v.p., 1965-); Alaska Mutual Savings Bk. (bd. trustees, 1969-); Local Boundary Com. (chmn., 1966-67); Southcentral dist. Dem. com. (chmn.); Northwest Public Power Assn. (v.p., 1964-73, pres., 1973-); Alaska Rural Electric Cooperative Assn. (pres., 1969-70); Violent Crimes Compensation Bd., 1972-; Elks, Kiwanis. Democrat. Address: 3151 Lakeside Dr., Anchorage.

KALBAUGH, Frank E., railroad executive. Married; 1 d.; employe, Southern Pacific R.R., Bakersfield, Calif., 1919, supt., Salt Lake div., until 1953; gen. mgr., Alaska R.R., 1953-55; gen. mgr., Southern Pacific Pipe Lines Corp., 1955-, asst. v.p., 1962-64; ret. to Los Angeles, Calif.

KARNES, Anthony Edmund, educator. B. in Vinland, Kan., 1888; s. Loammi F. and Cora Alma (Nichols) K.; h. sc., Overbrook, Kan.; B.A., Washburn Coll., Topeka, Kan., 1911; M.Ed., U. Calif., 1924; LL.D., Washburn Coll., 1940; m. Helen G. Wilkins, May 27, 1930; children: Carol Jean, Jacqueline Ann, Nancy Lou; education adm., Kan., 1911-17; U.S. Army, 1917-18; principal, h. sc.,

Ponca City, Okla., 1919-20; supervising principal, Boise, Ida., 1920-21; principal, h. sc., Twin Falls, Ida., 1921-23; teacher, h. sc., Piedmont, Calif., 1923-25; principal, h. sc., Tomales, Calif., 1925-27; supt. scs., Ketchikan, 1927-33; comr. of education, 1933-40; dir., Selective Service for Alaska, 1940-41; U.S. Army Air Corps, 1941-44; mgr., reg. office, Veterans' Adm., Juneau, 1944-46; vocational rehabilitation, Veterans' Adm., Portland, Ore., 1946-47; supt. scs., Elsinore, Calif., 1947-54; died in Corona, Calif., 1970. Mem., Am. Leg., VFW, Disabled Army Vets, Officers' Reserve Corps, Rotary, Phi Delta Kappa, Masons, Elks. Presbyterian, Democrat.

KAY, Wendell Palmer, lawyer. B. in Watseka, Ill., Aug. 17, 1913; pub. sc., Watseka; B.A., DePauw U., 1935; J.D., Northwestern U., magna cum laude, 1938; m. Marget F. Reese, Oct. 7, 1943 (div. 1961); children: George R., Bronwen, Margaret Susannah, Wendy Kathleen, Edward James; m. 2d, Agnes Avery Fountain, Dec. 27, 1963; atty., Nat. Labor Relations Bd., Wash., D.C., 1938-40; pvt. law prac., Centralia, Ill., city atty., 1940-42; U.S. Army, 1942-45; reg. atty., BLM, Portland, Ore., 1945-47; exec. dir., ASHA, 1947-48; pvt. law prac., Anchorage; terr. H.R., 1951-57, state, 1969-71; chmn., Dem. state central com., 1961-62; cand., Alaska gov., 1966, U.S. Sen., 1970. Mem., Delta Kappa Epsilon (social), Phi Delta Phi (law), Order of Coif, Masons, Elks, VFW, Am. Leg., Amvets, Am. and Anchorage Bar Assns. Methodist, Democrat. Address: 425 G St., Anchorage 99501.

KEATING, Clarence, salesman. B. in Marshfield, Ore., c. 1915; grad., Coll. Puget Sound, 1938; m. Laura; children: Kathryn, Josephine, Sandra, Janis, Peter; U.S. Army, 1937-39; went to Seward, 1940; employe, Standard Oil, Alaska R.R., Army Transport Service; sales mgr., Alaska Airlines, 1949; city councilman, 1945-47, mayor, 1947-48, Seward; terr. H.R., 1949-51; census dir. for Alaska, Juneau, 1949-51; cand., del., const. conv., 1955; insur. salesman, Anchorage, 1952-58; moved to Seattle, Wash., 1958. Mem., Seward C. of C. (pres., 1951-52); Dem. Club, Anchorage (pres., 1954). Democrat.

KEATLEY, John H., lawyer, journalist. Married; 1 s.; served in Union Army, Civil War; ed., Council Bluffs (Ia.) GLOBE; mem., Sen., 21st Ia. Gen. Assembly; Wash., D.C., correspondent for GLOBE, 1 yr.; U.S. dist. judge for Alaska, Sitka, 1888-89. Democrat.

KEHOE, Joseph W., lawyer, artist. B. in Portland, Ore., July 19, 1890; s. Joseph and Josephine (Thomas) K.; gr. sc., St. Francis Acad., Portland, h. sc., Columbia U., Portland; B.A., LL.B., U. Ore.; m. Katherine L. Southard, Portland, Feb. 9, 1916; prac. law, Rainier, Ore. and Portland, 1915-17; U.S. Army, 1917-19; pvt. law prac., Haines, Juneau, 1919-24; U.S. Comr., Ketchikan, 1924-29; pvt. law prac., Ketchikan, 1929-33; terr. H.R., 1933-34, 1943-45; U.S. dist. atty., 3d jud. div., Valdez and Anchorage, 1934-42; pvt. law prac., Seward, 1942-43; special liaison officer, representing U.S. Atty. Gen., Seward, 1943-44; U.S. dist. judge, 2d jud. div., Nome, 1944-51; Sec. of Alaska, 1951-52;

pvt. law prac., Seward, 1952-54; moved to Portland, 1954; died of heart attack, Neskowin, Ore., Apr. 10, 1959. Gained recognition as water color artist of Alaskan scenes. Mem., Am. Leg., Delta Theta Phi, Elks. Catholic, Democrat.

KELLER, William Kenneth, educator. B. in Redmond, Wash., Oct. 15, 1896; gr. sc., Redmond; h. sc., Kirkland, Wash.; B.A., 1921, M.A., Ed.D., Wash. State Coll.; stud., Columbia U., 1-1/2 yrs.; m. (div. 1938); s. William K., Jr.; m. 2d, Dorothy Freeman Billson, May 1, 1938; supt. sc., Fairbanks, 1921-23, Juneau, 1923-31; comr. of education, 1931-33; supt. sc., Anchorage, 1933-36, Fairbanks, 1936-53; head, dept. education, UA, 1953-60, ret.; moved to Puget Sound, 1960-. Mem., Phi Kappa Phi, Delta Sigma Rho, Phi Delta Kappa, Rotary, Lions, Pioneers, Alaska Education Assn. (pres., 4 terms). Presbyterian, Republican.

KELLY, Milo, miner. B. in Wasau, Wis., Jan. 5, 1866; pub. sc., Wasau; m. Katherine; interested in smelter, Nogales, Ariz., 1884-87; estab. coal mining operation, Wilkeson, Wash., 1887-95; mem., Wash. state H.R., 1893-95; prospector-miner, Juneau, 1896-1900; prospector for copper, Copper River dist., 1900-06; one of the first operators in Willow Creek dist., 1910-39; operated Eska Cr. Coal Co., Matanuska Valley, 1916; terr. H.R., from Knik, 1913-15; died in Seattle, Wash., Sept. 9, 1943. Mem., Masons. Republican.

KELLY, Raymond John, lawyer. B. in Otsego, Mich., 1894; B.A., Notre Dame U., 1914; LL.B., U. Detroit, 1915; m. Nora Margaret Evans, Apr. 27, 1918; 6 children; U.S. Army, 1917-18; pvt. law prac., Detroit, 1918-30; gen. counsel, Detroit street railroads, 1930-33; corp. counsel, city of Detroit, 1933-39; reg. dir., office of civilian defense, 1940-42; U.S. Army, 1942-46; cand., Mich. gov., 1950; chmn., R.R. retirement bd., Chicago, 1953-56; U.S. dist. judge, 1st jud. div., Juneau, 1956-60; ret. to former home, Detroit; jud. officer and chmn., bd. of contract appeals for U.S. Post Office, 1961. Mem., Am. Leg. (past state comdr.). Republican.

KELLY, Thomas E., geologist. B. in San Diego, Calif., Oct. 15, 1931; s. Thomas E. and Fay K.; B.S., 1953, M.S., 1955, Tex. A. & M. U.; m. Jane Moore; children: Mark, Brook, Adrienne Moore, Isla Michele; grad. teaching fellowship, geology, U. Tex., 1953-54; res. geologist and gen. mgr., Halbouty Alaska Oil Co., Anchorage, 1958-62; exec. v.p., Halbouty Oil Co., Houston, Tex., 1962-67; state comr. of natural resources, 1967-70; estab. consult. firm in earth sciences, Anchorage, 1970-. Mem., Am. Assn. & Am. Inst., Petroleum Geologists; Am. Inst., Mining, Metallurgical & Petroleum Engrs.; Alaska Geological Soc.; Anchorage and Juneau C. of C. (dir.); Anchorage sc. bd., 1972-76; Southeast Council, Boy Scouts (pres., 1970-71). Episcopalian, Republican. Address: 700 H St., Anchorage 99501.

KENDALL, Bruce Biers, hotel owner-operator. B. in Martinsburg, Neb., Feb. 28, 1919; s. Leslie B. and Bernice (Roberts) K.; pub. sc., Sioux City, Ia.; m. LaVerne Peters, Sioux City, 1938 (div.); children: Brucella (Mrs. Charles Miser), Sherian (Mrs. Donald

M. Candey), Marsha (Mrs. Robert Bannon); m. 2d, Mae Bernadine McCabe, Seattle, Wash., Sept. 1, 1946; children: Bruce Biers, Jr., Lea Gilda; employe, Martin and Jackson Hotels, Sioux City, 1930-39; fireman, Yukon riverboat "Alice", summer 1939; desk clerk, Anchorage Hotel, 1939-40; timekeeper, Quartermaster Corps, U.S. Army, Ft. Richardson, 1940-41; prop., Lind-Dudley Hotel, Anchorage, 1941-43; interest in Yellow and Red Cab Cos.; U.S. Merchant Marine, 5 mos., 1942-43; sold Lind-Dudley Hotel and purchased Gastineau Hotel, Juneau, 1944-45; sold Gastineau Hotel to owners of Baranof Hotel, Juneau, Dec. 1945; prop., Fifth Ave. Hotel, Anchorage, 1948-49; part-owner-operator, Parsons Hotel, Anchorage, 1950-51; prop., Windsor Hotel, Cordova, Valdez Hotel, Valdez, 1951-59; state H.R., 1959-67, minority leader, 1959-63, speaker, 1963-64; owner-operator, hotel chain, including Roosevelt, Big Timber Motel, Woods Motel, Kobuk, North Star, Mush Inn Motel, Anchorage 1959-; Rep. cand., state gov., 1966; joined Dem. party. Mem., Masons, Shrine, Elks, Moose, Dem. Club. Methodist, Democrat. Address: 458 Aurora Dr., Anchorage.

KENNEDY, Daniel O'Connell, merchant. B. in Sitka, June 10, 1881; s. Daniel and Catherine (Kasnikoff) K.; pub. sc., Juneau; m. Mrs. Anna Maloney Sturgis, Anchorage, 1921 (dec. 1930); m. 2d, Gertrude Marie Watson, Anchorage, 1933; pack train freighter, Fairbanks dist. and Valdez Trail, 1904-16; prop., men's clothing store, Anchorage, 1916-44; operator, pack trains in McKinley Park, 1923-25; terr. H.R., 1937-39; died in Circle Hot Springs, July 8, 1944. Mem., Pioneers. Catholic, Democrat.

KENNEDY, James Charles, miner, merchant. B. in Cambridge, Mass., 1876; mined and operated gen. merchandise store, Nome and Candle, 1898-1926; mined on No. 5, Anvil Creek; terr. H.R., from Candle, 1913-15; U.S. Army, WWI; dep. U.S. Marshal and chief jailer, Nome, 1926-33; died in Nome, May 1, 1939. Mem., Am Leg. Catholic, Republican.

KERTTULA, Jalmar M. (Jay), farmer, businessman. B. in Milwaukee, Wis., Apr. 6, 1928; s. Oscar A. and Elvi K.; pub. sc., Palmer; stud., UA, 2 yrs., U Wash., 4 yrs.; m. Helen Joyce; children: Beth, Anna Marie; went to Matanuska Valley with parents, fed. colonization project, May 1935; dairy farmer, and mgr., Matanuska Co-operative, 1960-, and North Star Dairy, Anchorage; real estate developer, Matanuska Valley; state H.R., 1961-63, 1965-73, Sen., 1973-77; chmn., Dem. state central com., 1964-69. Mem., bd. trustees, Alaska Mutual Savings Bank, 1970-. Lutheran, Democrat. Address: Box Z, Palmer 99645.

KETTLESON, Theodore, miner, businessman. B. in Portage Co., Wis., June 15, 1874; gr. sc., Waupaca, Wis.; m. Mrs. Minnie Christiansen, Fairbanks, Oct. 4, 1908; m. 2d, Bessie V. White, Mar. 24, 1922 (dec. 1960); m. 3d, Claire; prospector, Rossland, B.C., Can., 1897-1905, Valdez and later, Goldstream, Tanana Valley, 1905-; postmaster, Chisana, 1913; steamer pilot on Tanana River; postmaster, Shushana; supt., Pioneers' Home, Sitka, 1921-33;

terr. H.R., from Livengood, 1921-23; real estate and cold storage bus., Sitka, 1933-; original dir., First Bk. of Sitka, 1939-, v.p., pres.; sec., Sitka public utilities; chmn., Sitka OPA bd., 4 yrs., ret. to San Diego, Calif., 1960; died there, Aug. 23, 1968. Theodore Kettleson Memorial Library, Sitka, dedicated to him, Oct. 1967. Mem., Elks, Pioneers. Lutheran, Republican.

KEYS, Edward M., miner. B. in Altoona, Pa., Mar. 14, 1860; gr. and h. sc., Altoona; m. (dec. 1922); children: Ralph, Edward, Jr., George; conductor, Northern Pacific R.R., Glendive to Missoula, Mont., 1885-95; miner, Circle City and Dawson, 1896-1904; miner, Fairbanks vicinity, remainder of his life; terr. H.R., from Healy Forks, 1923-25; mined with s. George on Moose Cr.; ret. to Fairbanks, 1946, after 2-1/2 yrs. in states; sold mining property, and moved to Pioneers' Home, Sitka; mining, June 1950; died in cabin near Ester Cr., Nov. 24, 1950. Mem., Pioneers, Order of Railway Conductors. Presbyterian, Republican.

KILCHER, Yule F., fisherman. B. in Laufen, Switzerland; s. Edwin and Lina K.; pub. sc., Switzerland; stud., U. Berne, Switzerland, Berlin, Germany, Grenoble, France; m. Ruth Helen Weber in Anchorage, July 1941 (div. 1970); children: Mairiis (Mrs. Arthur Lloyd Davidson, Jr.), Wurtila, Linda Fay (Mrs. Lurtis Lloyd Barber), Attila Kuno (Atz), Sunni (Sunrise), Diane I. (Mrs. Per Sjoberg), Edwin Otto, Stella Vera Septina (Bonnie), Catkin Melody; visited Alaska, 1936; ret. to Switzerland; ret. to Alaska, 1940; settled on homestead, Anchor Point, 1944; del., const. conv., Fairbanks, 1955-56; state Sen., 1963-67. Mem., Pioneers, Fox River Cattlemen's Assn. (founder and past pres.). Old Catholic, Democrat. Address: Box 353, Homer.

KING, Leonard H., businessman. B. in Mich., 1901; h. sc., Fairbanks; stud., UA and correspondence courses; went to Alaska, 1920; forest service foreman, WPA supervisor, mining foreman, CAA constr. foreman, logger, fisherman, businessman, licensed guide; city councilman, mayor, Haines, 1946; del., const. conv., Fairbanks, 1955-56. Democrat.

KING, Walter Bradley, lawyer. B. in San Francisco, Calif., Sept. 15, 1890; s. John Alden and Mary Huntington (Bradley) K.; m. Lillian Lucile Metz, San Francisco, Jan. 7, 1925; children: Walter Bradley, Harry Alden; went to Alaska, 1915; employe, various clerical jobs; U.S. Army, WWI; stud. law, Juneau, 1923-26; admitted to Alaska bar, 1926; asst. U.S. dist. atty., 1st jud. div., Ketchikan, 1929-33; referee in bankruptcy, 1934-36; pvt. prac., Ketchikan, 1936-50; died in Covina, Calif., Oct. 31, 1969. Mem., Am. Leg. (Alaska dept. comdr., nat. sec. com.).

KINKEAD, John Henry, businessman. B. in Smithfield (now Somerville), Pa., Dec. 10, 1826; s. James S. and Catherine (Bushey) K.; gr. sc., Zanesville, O.; h. sc., Lancaster, O.; m. Lizzie Fall in Marysville, Calif., Jan. 1, 1856; engaged in mercantile ventures, St. Louis, Salt Lake City, Marysville, Calif., N.Y.C., San Francisco, Carson City, Nev., 1844-67; Nev.'s first treas., 1862; mem., const. conv., Nev., 1864;

postmaster and trading post operator, Sitka, 1867-71; Gov., Nev., 1879-83; Gov., Alaska, 1884-85; died in Carson City, Aug. 15, 1904. Republican.

KIRKNESS, Walter, biologist. B. in Seattle, Wash., Aug. 9, 1920; grad., U. Wash. sc. of fisheries; m.; 2 children; U.S. Marine Corps, 1942-45; employe, Wash. state dept. fisheries, 1945-50; research section, Alaska fish & game dept., 1950-54, senior biologist, 1954-57; dir., commercial fisheries div., 1957-61; state comr. fish and game dept., 1961-67.

KNAPP, Lyman Enos, newspaper editor, lawyer. B. in Somerset, Vt., Nov. 5, 1837; s. Hiram K.; B.A., Middlebury Coll., 1862; M.A., LL.D., 1893, Whitman Coll.; m. Martha L. Severance, Jan. 23, 1865; children: George, Frances (Mrs. Everett R. Morgan); pvt. to lt. col., breveted by Pres. Lincoln, 1862-65; ed. and prop., Middlebury REGISTER, 1865-78; read law, admitted to bar, 1876; Vt. H.R., 1886-88; probate judge, Addison dist., Vt., 1879-89; Gov., Alaska, 1889-93; pvt. law prac., Seattle, Wash., 1893-1904; died in Seattle, Oct. 9, 1904. Founder and first pres., Anti-Saloon League of Wash. Republican.

KNIGHT, William Wellington, collector of customs. B. in London, England, 1889; s. Arthur S. and Amelia (Alderman) K.; gr. sc.; m. Marie C. Volt, 1923 (dec.); m. 2d, c. 1960; acct., Booth Fisheries, 1919-; partner with H.C. Bradshaw in Sitka Men's Store; U.S. Comr., Sitka, 1938-46; supt., Pioneers' Home, Sitka, 1946-53; del., const. conv., Fairbanks, 1955-56; dept. of revenue, Juneau, 1959-60; collector of customs, Juneau, 1961-65; died in Sitka, Mar. 30, 1971. Mem., Selective Service bd., Sitka, 1941-46 (chmn.), Elks, Pioneers. Episcopalian, Democrat.

KOSLOSKY, Janis Marvin, merchant. B. in Muskogee, Okla., July 17, 1909; s. Isaac and Lena (Schindelman) K.; pub. sc., Anchorage; stud., U. Wash., 1928-32; m. Alice Mae Phillips, Dec. 19, 1941 (div.); children: Janis Marvin, Jr., Susan Diane, Linda Ann; m. 2d, Isabelle; moved to Anchorage with parents, 1915; salesman, Koslosky's stores, Anchorage, 1932-35; estab. and operated Koslosky's gen. merchandise and grocery store, Palmer; U.S. Army, 1942-45; dir., mgr. and pres., Matanuska Valley Bk., 1950s; city councilman, Palmer, 1955-56; chmn., Matanuska-Susitna Borough, 1960-66; state Sen., 1967-73. Holder of Grand Slam North Am. Sheep trophies. Mem., Palmer Elks, 1842 (past exalted ruler), VFW, Am. Leg., Sigma Alpha Mu, Moose, Pioneers, Sportsman's Club, Polar Prop Busters' Club, Kiwanis. Jewish, Republican. Address: Box I, Palmer 99645.

KRAUCZUNAS, Kazis, lawyer. B. in Lithuania, Russia, 1872; emigrated to U.S., 1890; m. Lillie; children: Kazis Kay, Jr., Mrs. Julia Duncan, Mrs. Beth Seivers, Mrs. Alice Hilling, Mrs. Afie Reedy; head of U.S. Immigration Service, Alaska, Ketchikan, 1906; stud. law and admitted to bar, 1911; Socialist cand., del. in Cong., 1912; pvt. law prac., Ketchikan, 1912-13; moved to Seattle, Wash., 1913;

name officially changed to Kazis Kay, 1926; Superior Ct. judge, Seattle, 1931-38; died in Seattle, Sept. 16, 1938.

KRAUSE, Joseph Francis, fisherman. B. in St. Joseph, Minn., July 21, 1887; s. Joseph and Mary (Betzen) K.; m. May Atkinson, Jan. 10, 1920; m. 2d, Florence; automobile dealer, Minneapolis, Minn., 1911-12; traffic mgr., Glacier Nat. Park, 1913; owner, Puget Sound garage, Seattle, 1913-18, Anchorage garage, 1916-17; U.S. Army, 1917-18; co-owner, Krause & Bucey Motor Co., Ketchikan, 1920-25; halibut and salmon commercial fisherman, Ketchikan, 1930s-40s; terr. H.R., from Ketchikan, 1945-47; died in Gresham, Ore., March 6, 1970. Mem., A.B., Internat. Assn. Machinists (since 1906), Am. Automobile Assn. (since 1910), Alaska Sportsmen's Assn. (pres., 1937), Am. Leg., VFW, Disabled Am. Veterans, Pioneers. Democrat.

KRUG, Julius Albert, business executive. B. in Madison, Wis., Nov. 23, 1907; s. Julius John and Emma (Korfmacher) K.; B.A., 1929, M.A., 1930, U. Wis.; m. Margaret Catherine Dean, Mar. 22, 1926; children: Marilyn Ann, James Allan; research statistician, Wis. Telephone Co., 1930-31; chief, depreciation section, Wis. Public Service Com., 1932-35; public utilities expert, Fed. Communications Com., Wash., D.C., 1936-37; chief power engr., Tenn. Valley Authority, 1938-40, mgr. of power, 1940; chief power consult., O.P.M., 1941; dep. dir. gen. for priorities, War Production Bd., 1942; program vice-chmn. and dir., Office of War Utilities, 1943-44; chmn., War Production Bd., 1944-45; U.S. Navy Reserves, 1944; Sec. of Interior, 1946-49; chmn. bd., Brookside Mills, Inc., 1949-. Democrat.

KUBLEY, Walter Lawrence, businessman. B. in Ketchikan, Mar. 16, 1921; s. Lawrence Henry and Ellen Frances (Newcoman) K.; gr. and h. sc., Ketchikan; stud., Whitman Coll., 3 yrs.; m. Fern A. Bellamy; children: Larry, Karen, Donald; U.S. Coast Guard, 1942-46; operator-owner, gen. merchandise store and mgr., bus. investments, Ketchikan, 1947-67; city councilman, Ketchikan, 1957-60; state H.R., 1961-65; state dep. comr. commerce, 1967-68; legislative asst. to Gov. Keith Miller, 1968-69; state comr. commerce, 1969-70; Alaska rep., U.S. Dept. Agriculture, Anchorage, 1971-. Mem., Elks, Moose, VFW, Am. Leg. (Distinguished Citizen award, 1965), Little League baseball (5 yrs.). Methodist, Republican. Address: 2226 Susitna Dr., Anchorage 99503.

L

LABOYTEAUX, Charles H. (Alabam), miner. B. in Tuscaloosa, Ala., Apr. 15, 1880; public sc., Tuscaloosa; unm.; fought in Spanish-Am. War and Panama revolution, 1898-99; conductor, Panama R.R.; purser, "Porteus C. Weare" river steamer, St. Michael and Dawson, 1900; moved to Nome, 1901; drifted to gold camps, including Koyukuk (agent, N.A.T. & T. Co.), Iditarod and Ruby (traveling rep., E.W. Griffin Merchandise Co.), Kantishna, Marshall, Big Chena, Chisana; operated sawmill, freighting service, log-cabin hotel, gen. merchandise store, Livengood; postmaster, U.S. Comr., 1925-31, 1943-, Livengood; terr. Sen., 1939-43; died in Fairbanks, Oct. 31, 1951. Democrat.

LAIBLIN, George F., miner, fisherman. B. in Nome, c. 1903; s. Grant W. L.; m. Mrs. Annabelle Dennard Tibbitts of Sitka, 1937; m. 2d, Mrs. Katherine Hundley Nolte, Ketchikan, June 19, 1957; mined and operated charter flying service, Nome, 1930s; U.S. Navy, 1943-45; fisherman, Myers Chuck, near Ketchikan, 1956-57; terr. H.R., from Nome, 1937-39; moved to Petersburg, Va., 1957. Mem., Pioneers (pres., Igloo 1, Nome, 1937). Democrat.

LAKTONEN, Jacob, carpenter. B. in Karluk, Jan. 18, 1917; s. Jacob and Fedosia (Anakanak) L.; h. sc. grad.; m. Ruth Bennett, Larsen Bay, Mar. 4, 1962; employe, Alaska Packers' Assn., Karluk, 1931-56, Larsen Bay, 1956-; U.S. Army, 1943-46; state H.R., 1973-75. Mem., VFW, Am. Leg., Masons (Kodiak). Russian Orthodox, Republican. Address: Larsen Bay 99624.

LAMAR, Lucius Quintus Cincinnatus, jurist, educator. B. in Eatonton, Ga., Sept. 17, 1825; s. Lucius Q.C. and Sarah (Bird) L.; B.A., Emory Coll., Oxford, Ga., 1845; m. Virginia Longstreet, July 15, 1847; prof., U. Miss., 1849-53, 1866-67; mem., U.S. Cong., from Miss., 1857-60, 1873-77; mem., Miss. secession conv., 1861; col. in Civil War, judge advocate, 1864-65; Confederate comr. to Russia, 1862-64; mem., Miss. const. convs., 1865, 1868, 1875, 1877, 1881; U.S. Sen., 1877-85; Sec. of Interior, 1885-88; assoc. justice, U.S. Supreme Ct., 1888-93; died in Vineville, Ga., Jan. 23, 1893; buried in St. Peter's cemetery, Oxford, Miss. Democrat.

LANDER, Jesse Dewayne, miner, businessman. B. in Nipomo, Calif., Feb. 16, 1892; s. David Edward and Marcia (Davis) L.; m. Miss Jessie Reno, Anchorage, July 6, 1925; d. Elizabeth Wayne (Mrs. James Franklin Haynes); U.S. Army, 1917-20; operated barber shop, Anchorage, 1922-25; moved to Seward; operated barber shop-billiard hall, 1936-46, restaurant, 1946-, Fairbanks; terr. H.R., 1939-47, speaker,

1945; died in Seattle, Wash. hosp., Aug. 19, 1960. Mem., Dem. Club (pres., 1942-44, 4th div.), Elks, Pioneers, Eagles, VFW, Am. Leg., SAR. Catholic, Democrat.

LANDIS, Lee H., railroad executive. Employe, various railroads in U.S.; industrial agent, Western Pacific R.R.; gen. mgr., Alaska R.R., 1923-24.

LANE, Franklin Knight, lawyer, journalist. B. near Charlottetown, Prince Edward I., Can., July 15, 1864; s. Christopher S. and Caroline (Burns) L.; gr. sc., Napa, Calif. and pvt. sc., "Oak Mound," h. sc., Oakland, Calif.; B.A., U. Calif., 1886; LL.D., U. Calif., N.Y.U., Brown U., U. of N.C.; D.Sc., Trinity Coll., Conn.; admitted to bar, Calif., 1888; m. Anne Wintermute, Apr. 11, 1893; engaged in newspaper work early in life; reporter and later N.Y. correspondent for western papers; part-owner and ed., Tacoma DAILY NEWS; prac. law, San Francisco, 1889-1902; cand., gov. of Calif., 1902; mem., Interstate Commerce Com., 1905-13; Sec. of Interior, 1913-20; mem., Permanent Internat. R.R. Com.; mem., Am.-Mexican High Com., 1916; v.p., Pan-Am. Petroleum & Transport Co., N.Y.; died in Rochester, Minn. hosp., May 18, 1921. Democrat.

LATHROP, Austin Eugene (Cap), businessman. B. in Lapeer, Mich., Oct. 5, 1865; s. Eugene and Maria (Parson) L.; gr. and h. sc. (1 yr.), Harrisville, Mich.; m. Mrs. Lillian McDowell, Valdez, Feb. 18, 1901 (dec. 1910); constr. contractor, Puget Sound area, 1889-96; freighting and transfer bus., Cook Inlet, 1896-1907; cont. transfer bus., also building theatres and apartment houses, Cordova, Anchorage, Fairbanks, 1907-23; mem., Anchorage Adv. Council, 1918; pres., Alaska Moving Picture Corp., which filmed full length movie "Cheechakos," 1923, in Anchorage area; purchased Healy River coal mine, Fairbanks DAILY NEWS-MINER, First Bk. of Cordova, radio and TV stations, 1923-50; terr. H.R., 1921-23; pres., First Bk. of Cordova, 1933; Rep. Nat. Com., 1928-32, 1949-50; mem., Fisheries Adv. Com., 1935; mem., bd. regents, UA, 1932-50; dir., Olympia Brewing Co., Olympia, Wash., 1935-50; killed in train accident, Healy River coal mine, July 26, 1950; interment, Forest Lawn cemetery, Seattle, Wash. Mem., Pioneers, Rotary, Elks. Republican.

LAWS, William W., fireman, policeman. B. in Clark Co., Wash., Jan. 23, 1882; h. sc., Camas, Wash.; m.; s. William; professional baseball, 1911-17; bugler, drum and bugle corps, U.S. Army, Vancouver, Wash., 1917-20; policeman, sheriff, fireman, Vancouver, 1920-35; went to Nome to reorganize fire dept., remained to become both police and fire chief, 1935-46; terr. H.R., 1947-49, 1951-53; del., const. conv., Fairbanks, 1955-56; gold-miner, 1963-65; died in Maynard Memorial Methodist hosp., Nome, July 10, 1967. Republican.

LEE, Eldor R., commercial fisherman. B. in Petersburg, 1920; public sc., Petersburg; m.; del., const. conv., Fairbanks, 1955-56. Democrat.

Le FEVRE, Dr. Walter Howard, optometrist, registered game guide. B. in Marion, N.C., Mar. 27, 1918; s. Walter William and Mary Lou (Swann) L.;

stud., Marsh Hill Jr. Coll., N.C., 2-1/2 yrs.; grad., Southern Coll. of Optometry, Memphis, Tenn., 1951; m. 2d, Dr. Nancy Downs, Holly Springs, Miss., 1951; U.S. Army, 1940-45; optometrist, Newton, N.C., 1952-53, Fairbanks, 1953-67; city councilman, Fairbanks; state H.R., 1965-67; died Oct. 11, 1967. Mem., Elks, Moose, VFW, Tanana Valley Kennel Club, Amaranth, Shrine, Order of Eastern Star, White Shrine, Kiwanis (pres. and lt. gov.), state bd. of examiners optometry (pres., 3 yrs.), Alaska Optometrist Assn. (pres., 3 yrs.). Democrat.

LEONARD, Bennie L., real estate broker, tour bus operator. B. in Spokane, Wash., Dec. 25, 1915; gr. sc., Donner and Sacramento, Calif.; h. sc., Olympia and Puyallup, Wash.; stud., St. Martins' Coll., Lacy, Wash.; B.S., Wash. State Coll.; m. Mary Patricia Park, 1941; children: Lewis, Margaret Anne; engaged in food canneries and employe, S.H. Kress & Co., Puyallup, Wash.; moved to Anchorage, 1941; estab. Leonard's Variety store; U.S. Army, ACS, 1943-46; real estate broker and tour bus operator, Anchorage, since 1950s; state H.R., 1961-65; city councilman, Anchorage, 1959-62, 1967-74; borough assemblyman, Anchorage, 1967-74. Mem., Anchorage fire dept. volunteers (28 yrs.), Elks, Am. Leg., Kiwanis, Toastmasters, Am. Red Cross (dir.), King's Lake Camp (dir.), C. of C. (dir.), Real Estate Exchange Club (past pres.), Anchorage Bd. of Realtors (dir.). Episcopalian, Republican.

LEWIS, Andrew T., missionary, lawyer. Married Miss Margaret Dauphin, Sitka, Nov. 28, 1885; went to Alaska as missionary, early 1880s; surveyor-gen. and ex-officio Sec. of Alaska, Sitka, 1884-87; administered oath to first dist. ct. jury, Alaska; moved to Portland, Ore., 1887; senior mem., Lewis, Lewis & Finnegan law firm, Portland, 1926 (then past 80 yrs. of age). Republican.

LEWIS, Clyde R. (C.R.), mechanical contractor. B. in Lewiston, Mont., Nov. 12, 1916; s. J.F. and Inez (Trotter) L.; public sc., Mont.; licensed marine engr. and certified welder; m. Patricia Ann Drumm in Anchorage, Apr. 11, 1959; children: Russell, Rebecca, Deborah, Robert Ross, Michael, Cindy; went to Alaska, 1939, as merchant seaman; U.S. Merchant Marine, 1942-46; moved to Anchorage, 1947; estab. mechanical contracting firm, 1948; state Sen., 1967-75; cand., U.S. Sen., 1974. Received contractor of the year award, 1967; Civil Air Patrol (comdr., 1959-63) meritorious service award, 1972. Mem., state plumbing contractors assn. (past pres.), Anchorage C. of C. (past dir.), Boys' Clubs of Am. (dir.), Elks. Methodist, Republican. Address: 1922 Logan St., Anchorage 99501.

LEWIS, Eben Herbert, lawyer. B. in Boothbay Harbor, Me., Nov. 15, 1918; s. Benjamin West and Beatrice (Tucker) L.; gr. sc., Boothbay; h. sc., Hebron Acad., Hebron, Me.; B.A., Bowdoin Coll., 1941; J.D., cum laude, Syracuse U., 1948; m. Shirley Jewett Trussell, 1945; children: Cynthia Boyndon, Eben Thaddeus, Charles William Tucker; U.S. Navy, 1941-45; pvt. law prac., Portland, Me., also employe, Consumers Water Utility Co., 1950-52; staff mem., office of solicitor, Dept. of Interior, 1952-59, atty.-advisor, Wash., D.C., 1952-54, field and asst. solicitor, 1954-59, Juneau; city atty., Anchorage, 1959-60; pvt. law prac., Anchorage, 1960-67; superior ct. judge, 3d jud. dist., Anchorage, 1967-; Alaska Bar Assn. del., World Conf. on Peace Through Law, Geneva, Switzerland, 1967. Mem., Gov.'s adv. com. on mental retardation; southcentral dist. Rep. (chmn., 1965-66), Anchorage Symphony Assn. (pres., 1967-69), Alaska Airmen's Assn., Anchorage Ski Club, Petroleum Club, Elks. Presbyterian, Republican. Address: 2073 Arlington Dr. N., Anchorage 99503.

LHAMON, William Lloyd (Dan), mechanical engineer, salesman. B. in Minneapolis, Minn., May 27, 1892; s. William Jefferson and Clara Ellen L.; gr. and h. sc., Columbia, Mo.; m. Luella Wolff in Seattle, Dec. 29, 1929; children: William Lloyd, Jr., Donna Lou; marine engr., Ketchikan, 1930-31; stationary engr., Cleary Hill Mines Co., Fairbanks, 1931-34; power plant, and later mgr., heavy equipment sales and service, Northern Commercial Co., 1934-47; Ford motor dealership, 1947-54, ret.; terr. Sen., 1951-55. Awarded Silver Beaver for outstanding service to Boy Scout movement. Mem., Rotary, Fairbanks Golf & Country Club, Elks (past exalted ruler), Alaska Scout Council (vice pres.). Christian Church, Republican.

LICHTENBERG, John, miner, merchant. B. in Germany, c. 1866; m.; d. Mrs. Gladys Solvin; went to Chignik, 1889, Klondike, 1898, Nome, Treadwell; employe, Treadwell mines; ret. to Nome; miner, Candle, until 1915; lived in Kotzebue, 3 yrs.; partner, Wright Hardware Co., Nome, 1918; terr. H.R., 1937-39; died in San Francisco, Calif., June 20, 1947; left trust fund of $10,000, to be distributed each Christmas for 10 yrs. to residents of Pioneers' Home, Sitka. Democrat.

LINCK, Alaska Stewart, airline traffic agent. B. in Seattle, Wash., Dec. 2, 1910; d. James A. and Christia (Robinson) Stewart; gr. sc., Wasilla and Seward; h. sc., Fairbanks; stud., UA, 2 yrs.; m. James Edson Moody in Fairbanks, 1932; s. James Edson; m. 2d, L.E. "Jack" Linck in Juneau, Feb. 8, 1941; postmaster, Berry, Alaska, 1934-35; reservations supervisor, Pan-Am. Airlines, Fairbanks, 1935-; terr. H.R., 1943-47; reporter of 1947 legislature session, Fairbanks NEWS-MINER and Juneau EMPIRE. Mem., Pioneers' Aux. No. 6 (past pres.), Soroptimist (past pres.), Eastern Star. Democrat. Address: Fairbanks 99701.

LIND, Marshall Lee, educator. B. in Appleton, Wis., June 1, 1936; s. Darwin and Elsie (Blohn) L.; B.A., U. Wis., 1958; M.A., U. Mont., 1965; Ph.D., Northwestern U., 1969; m. Lois Zimmerman, Appleton, Wis., Nov. 22, 1958; children: Elizabeth, Peter, Jeffry; teacher, Bonduel, Wis., 1959-61, Kwigillingok, 1961-62, Goodnews Bay, 1962-66, Emmonok, 1966-67; adm. asst., Northwestern U., 1967-69; supt., Kodiak I. borough sc. dist., 1969-71; state comr. of education, 1971-. Mem., Am. Assn. Sc. Adm., NEA, Alaska Education Broadcasting Com., Phi Delta Kappa (life), Rotary. Methodist.

LINGO, George Archibald, miner, businessman. B. in Anaconda, Mont., 1901; s. Archibald and Dora (Robinson) L.; h. sc., Anchorage, 1918-; grad., Lincoln h. sc., Seattle, 1921; stud., U. Wash., 1921-23; B.S., UA, 1927; m. Dorothy Troy Morgan in Juneau, May 15, 1935; step-d. Joan Morgan; asst. mgr., Mt. McKinley Tourist & Transportation Co., McKinley Park and pres., Grayline Bus Co., Juneau, 1927-35; employe, mining cos., Salt Chuck, Latouche, Kennecott, Chickaloon, quartz miner, Copper River dist., 1927-35; registrar, U.S. General Land Office, Anchorage, 1935-41, 1946-52; U.S. Navy, 1941-46; terr. H.R., 1933-37; mem., bd. regents, UA, 1933-40; ret. to Wickerberg, Ariz., later to Palm Desert, Calif., 1952-. Mem., Elks, Moose. Protestant, Democrat.

LLORENTE, Fr. Segundo, Jesuit priest. B. in Leon, Spain, 1906; entered Jesuit order in Spain, 1922; stud., Gonzaga U., 1930-31, St. Mary's Coll., Kan., 1931-34, ordained; stud., Santa Clara U., Calif., 1 yr.; missionary, Kuskokwim area, Bethel, McGrath, 1935-38, Kotzebue, 1938-41, Alakanuk, Kwiguk, Sheldon's Pt., 1941-64; state H.R., from Alakanuk, 1961-63; St. Joseph's parish, Nome, 1964-66; Immaculate Conception parish, Fairbanks, 1966-67; Cordova, 1967-70; Holy Family parish, Anchorage, 1970-. Author of 10 books, written in Spanish, about his experiences in Alaska. Catholic, Democrat.

LLOYD, John H., Jr., railroad executive. B. in Havre, Mont., 1917; B.S., U. Pa., 1941; m.; children: Edith L., John H., III, Robert, Joseph; brakeman, Great Northern R.R., 1936, master mechanic, traveling car inspector, trainmaster, 1950; U.S. Navy, 1942-45; asst. gen. mgr., Chicago, Rock I. & Pacific R.R., El Reno, Okla., 1951-56; gen. mgr., Alaska R.R., 1956-58; exec., Rock I. R.R., Chicago, 1958-61; v.p. in charge of operations, Missouri-Pacific R.R., 1961-64. Mem., Masons, Shrine. Episcopalian, Republican.

LOCKEN, Edward, banker. B. in Hudorp, Norway, 1886; s. Johannes and Gertrude (Haugen) L.; grad. h. sc.; m. Sibyl DeSpain, July 20, 1918; went to U.S.,1907; worked on farms, Minn. and N. Dak., in sawmills, Wash.; U.S. citizen, 1914; operated sawmill, Petersburg, 1919-20; cashier-mgr., pres., principal stockholder, Bk. of Petersburg, 1920-; mayor, Petersburg, 14 terms; terr. H.R., 1951-57; died in Petersburg, May 8, 1967. Mem., Rotary (pres.), All-Alaska C. of C. (dir.), Am. Leg., Sons of Norway, Masons. Lutheran, Republican.

LOGAN, Balfour John (Bob), marine engineer, surveyor. B. in Cotati, Calif., June 24, 1906; s. Hugh B. and Madelin (Ferguson) L.; h. sc. education; m. in Calif.; children: Mrs. Dorothy Morey, Mrs. Madeline Magin; m. 2d, Mrs. Marie Rosswog Nester in Cordova; fisherman, Alaska Packers' Assn., 1923-34; ship capt., deep-sea diver, salvage master and rep., Am. Inst. Marine Underwriters, Lloyds' Insur. Co. of London, since late 1930s; res., Cordova, until 1960s; moved to Anchorage; U.S. Navy, 1941-46; mem., Anchorage Port Com., 1971-74; died following heart attack at Beekman hosp., N.Y.C., Jan. 26, 1974; interment, Catholic Gardens of Angeles Memorial Park, Anchorage. Honored as Knight of the Order of Malta (highest layman's award). Mem., Alaska Internat. Development Com., Cordova city council, Cordova C. of C. (pres., 1957), Rotary, Elks, Moose, Am. Leg., VFW, Pioneers. Catholic, Democrat.

LOMEN, Alfred Julian, miner, businessman. B. in St. Paul, Minn., Oct. 31, 1888; s. Gudbrand J. and Julie (Joys) L.; h. sc., St. Paul; m. Mildred Lehman, July 6, 1917; children: Alfred J., Lucile, Jean (Mrs. LeConie Stiles), Ann, Marian; moved to Nome, 1903; mem., Nome basketball team, which toured 19 states and B.C., Can., and won championship, winter 1906-07; mgr., Nome DAILY GOLD DIGGER, 1907-08; partner with father and bros., photographic studio, drug store, men's furnishing store, all estab. in 1908; U.S. Army, 1917-18; city councilman, Nome, 1923-24; terr. H.R., 1929-31, Sen., 1931-35; field mgr., Lomen interests, including lighterage service, merchandise stores, reindeer packing bus., 1935-40s; died in Seattle, Wash., May 17, 1950. Mem., Pioneers (grand pres., 1933), Masons. Congregationalist, Republican.

LOMEN, Gudbrand, J., lawyer. B. in Decorah, Ia., Jan. 28, 1854; s. Jorgen G. and Elizabeth (Brandt) L.; stud., Lutheran Coll., Decorah; LL.B., Ia. State U., 1875; m. Julie Joys in Caledonia, Minn., May 27, 1878; children: Carl Joys, Harry, George, Ralph, Alfred Julian, Helen (Mrs. F. Clinton Austin); law prac., Caledonia, 1875-, clerk of dist. ct., 1878-85; mem., Minn. H.R., 1891-92; went to Nome, 1900; estab. bus. with 5 sons, including raising and processing reindeer meat commercially; mayor, Nome, 1917-19; U.S. dist. atty., 2d jud. div., Nome, 1918-19; U.S. dist. judge, 2d jud. div., Nome, 1921-32, res.; Norwegian consul, 1919-29; died in Seattle, Wash., June 13, 1934. Received Order of St. Olaf from King Haakon of Norway, 1923, in recognition of assistance to explorer Roald Amundsen in polar expeditions. Mem., Pioneers. Lutheran, Republican.

LOMEN, Ralph, miner, businessman. B. in St. Paul, Minn., 1887; s. Gudbrand J. and Julie (Joys) L.; h. sc., St. Paul; m. Vella Weaver, May 8, 1919; children: Rosemary (Mrs. Warren Loomis David), Francis J.; partner with father and bro. in various bus., Nome; v.p., Lomen Commercial Co., Nome and Seattle; went to Alaska, 1903; city councilman, Nome, 1915; terr. H.R., 1927-29; living in Seattle, Wash., 1974. Mem., Masons, Pioneers. Lutheran, Republican.

LONDBORG, Rev. Maynard D., missionary. B. in Lynch, Neb., May 11, 1921; s. Peter Alfred and Amanda Elizabeth (Lantz) L.; h. sc., Bristow, Neb.; stud., North Park Coll., 1941, North Park Seminary, Chicago, 1946; ordained, Evangelical Covenant Church of America; B.S., Neb. Wesleyan U., 1963; post-grad., UA, under Nat. Science Found., summers, 1960-62, Mankato State Coll., Minn., summer, 1973; m. Loraine Lundstedt, Red Oak, Ia., Mar. 12, 1945; children: Linda (Mrs. Charles Hungerford), Peter, John, Elizabeth (Mrs. Michael Nelson); missionary, Evangelical Covenant Church, Yakutat, Marshall, Unalakleet, 1946-66; supt., Covenant Children's Home, Unalakleet, 1947-50; U.S. Comr., Wade-Hapton precinct, Nome dist.,

1953-54; principal and teacher, Covenant h. sc., Unalakleet, 1954-66; del., const. conv., Fairbanks, 1955-56; chaplain-teacher, Minnehaha Acad., Minneapolis, Minn., 1966-. Address: 3548 46th Ave., S. Minneapolis, Minn. 55406.

LONGWORTH, John E., fisherman. B. in Prescott, Wis., Dec. 10, 1910; s. Edward and Anna Belle (Cooney) L.; gr. and h. sc., Prescott; stud., Washington State Coll.; m. Mary Alice Foster in Wrangell, July 7, 1942; children: Anna Sue Martinsen, Bonnie Kay, John Richard, Mary Lou; went to Alaska, Dec. 1940, to work for Game Commission on MV Brown Bear; military service; employe, Petersburg Fisheries; city councilman, Petersburg; state H.R., 1959-65; commercial fisherman and mgr., Vessel Owners' Assn. Mem., Fishermen's Union Ind. (sec.), Elks, Pioneers, Lambda Chi Alpha, Am. Leg. Catholic, Republican.

LOPP, William Thomas, educator. B. in Valley City, Ind., June 21, 1864; B.A., 1888, M.A., 1911, LL.D., 1925, Hanover (Ind.) Coll.; m. Ellen Louise Kittredge, Aug. 22, 1892; children: Lucy Alaska, Dwight Thomas, Sara Louise, Katherine Kittredge, Weyana, Irena Frances, Mary, Alice Marguerite; principal, various Indian schools, 1884-90; missionary teacher, Cape Prince of Wales, 1890-92; supt., Teller Reindeer Station, 1893-94; missionary teacher and reindeer supt., Cape Prince of Wales, 1894-95, 1896-1902; supt. scs. and reindeer, North dist. of Alaska, 1904-09; chief, Alaska Div., U.S. Bur. Education, 1910-23; supt. education of Alaska Natives, 1923-25; reindeer expert for Hudson's Bay Co., 1925-27, covering Baffin Land and Norway; made survey of Eskimo reindeer industry, Alaska, 1936, for Indian Rights Assn.; in charge of reindeer herd, Barrow Relief Expedition, 1897-98; died in Seattle, Wash., Apr. 10, 1939. Author: "White Sox, a Story of Domestication of Reindeer."

LOTTSFELDT, Carl Fredrik, merchant. B. in San Francisco, Calif., May 28, 1898; s. John Fredrik and Signe (Kinander) L.; grad., Franklin h. sc., Seattle, Wash.; m. Sophia Anderson of Douglas, in Juneau, Mar. 11, 1929; children: Frances Marie Leon, Carl Fredrik, Jr.; U.S. Army, 1917-18; went to Alaska, 1919; worked in Juneau gold mine; clerk, later supt., ARC, Takotna, Skagway, Anchorage, Mt. McKinley Nat. Park, Fairbanks, 22 yrs.; prop., Ophir trading post, 1940s; operated heavy equipment rental and sales firm until retirement, Anchorage, 1947-70, ret.; state H.R., from Anchorage, 1963-67; he and wife reigned as king and queen regents, 1968 Fur Rendezvous festivities. Mem., Nat. Baseball Cong. (state comr., 1961-65), Pioneers (past grand pres., 1960), Masons, Shrine, Elks, Am. Leg., Vets WWI. Lutheran, Democrat. Address: 3000 DeBarr Ave., Anchorage.

LOVE, Henry K., U.S. Marshal. B. in Ia., Oct. 1864; s. Judge James Love; m. in Manila, Philippine I., 1902; 2 daughters, Bonnie and Madison, 1 s.; following formal education, moved to S. Dak., then to Okla. terr.; enlisted in Teddy Roosevelt's "Rough Riders" and fought in Cuba, 1898-99; civil gov., Guam, 1899-1900; govt. official, Manila, 1900-03; U.S. Land Office, Ore., 1903-04; special timber agent for Alaska, Juneau, 1904-08; U.S. Marshal, Valdez, 3d jud. div., 1908-09, Fairbanks, 4th jud. div., 1909-13; U.S. Army, quartermaster corps, 1917-20. Republican.

LOWELL, Donald, electronics engineer. B. in Hoquiam, Wash., 1929; m. Phyllis; mgr., KIBH radio station, Seward, 1950-; mgr., Gen. Telephone Co. exchange, Seward branch, 1956-61; state dir., civil defense (disaster office), Anchorage, 1961-67; chief appraiser for loans, SBA, and mgr., disaster office, Fairbanks, 1967-71; state dir., disaster office, Anchorage, 1971-.

LYNG, Howard, miner. B. in Sand Point, May 8, 1891; s. Rasmus Thorolf and Rebecca (Thorsen) L.; B.A., Santa Clara Coll., 1909; unm.; res., Nome, 1900-55; placer miner, Seward Peninsula; staff mem., Matanuska Valley colonization project, Palmer, 1935-36; chmn., Dem. central com., 1940-44; Dem. Nat. Com., 1944-52; terr. H.R., 1935-37, 1939-43, Sen., 1945-47, state Sen., 1959-65; unopposed cand., del. const. conv., 1955; died of head injuries sustained in fall from hosp. window, Seattle, Wash., Sept. 20, 1955. Mem., Pioneer, Elks. Democrat.

LYONS, Thomas R., lawyer. B. in Bendigo, Australia, Mar. 19, 1867; moved to Walla Walla, Wash., 1870; grad., Whitman Coll.; stud., Ottawa Coll., Ottawa, Can.; LL.D., U. Mich.; m. Rose Dovell of Walla Walla, 1906; left Heppner, Ore. for Juneau; comr., BLM, Juneau; original trustee for townsite entries, 1898-1900; asst. U.S. atty., Juneau, 1900-04; U.S. dist. atty., 1st jud. div., interim appt. by ct., Dec. 1902-Apr. 1903; pvt. law prac., 1904-09; U.S. dist. judge, 1st jud. div., Juneau, 1909-13; moved to Seattle, Wash. to prac. law, 1913; died there, Jan. 4, 1941. Republican.

M

MacCLANAHAN, George R., civil engineer. B. in 1926; civil engr. degree, UA; mgr., Burgess Constr. Co., Fairbanks, 1963-67; state comr. public works, 1967-68; pres., Burgess Constr. Co., Fairbanks, 1968-69. Mem., Assoc. Gen. Contractors, Alaska chapter (bd. dir.). Republican.

MacKENZIE, Roderick M., dentist. B. in Saanichton, B.C., Can., Dec. 8, 1902; m. Dorothy; children: Carol (Keleske), Margo (Miller), Heather (Meyers), Sheila (Page); m. 2d, Jean; went to Ketchikan, c. 1924; prac. dentistry; terr. Sen., 1949-51, res.; dental dir., ANS, 1951-; ret. to Victoria, B.C., Can., 1960; died in Sydney, B.C., Jan. 22, 1972. Democrat.

MacKINNON, James Simpson, businessman. B. in Juneau, Mar. 1897; s. Lockie and Martha (Lokke) MacK.; grad., h. sc., Juneau, U.S. Naval Acad., Annapolis, 1921; m. Hazel Jaeger, Dec. 5, 1923; s. James Simpson, Jr.; U.S. Navy, 1921-26, res.; laundry and dry cleaning bus., Juneau; city councilman, Juneau, 1939-40; terr. H.R., 1951-53; U.S. Naval Reserves (active), 1939-46. Mem., Am. Leg., Pioneers, Masons, Elks. Presbyterian, Republican.

MacSPADDEN, Morrell Lewis (Molly), businessman. B. in Garrison, Mont., Jan. 24, 1903; h. sc., Missoula, Mont.; stud., U. Mont., 1921-22; m. Janice Lowe in Juneau, 1928; children: Sheila (Mrs. Richard Zagars), Molly Jo (Mrs. Bushfort); laborer, miner, contractor, cost and payroll acct., Alaska-Juneau Gold Mining Co., 1923-32; marine salesman, warehouseman, Union Oil Co., Juneau, 1934-43; agent, Fish & Wildlife Service, 1943-46; plant foreman, Juneau Cold Storage Co., 1946-51; self-employed contractor, 1951-56; terr. H.R., 1953-55; mayor, Juneau, 1955-58; died in Juneau, Nov. 2, 1961. Mem., Masons (past master), Elks, Pioneers. Republican.

MADSEN, George P., businessman. B. in Seattle, Wash., c. 1914; went to Alaska, c. 1935; city councilman, Nome, 1938; terr. H.R., from Nome, 1951-53. Democrat.

MAHONEY, William Thomas, businessman. B. in Blue Lake, Calif., July 24, 1886; s. Daniel and Annie E. (Mahan) M.; stud., Kildale's Prep. Sc., Eureka, Calif., Eureka Bus. Coll.; m. Lillian A. Anderson in San Francisco, 1911; s. Daniel W.; acct., Sulzer Mining Co., Sulzer, 1909-11; prop., Ketchikan Drug Co., 1911-13; U.S. Comr. and dep. clerk, dist. ct., Ketchikan, 1913-21; owner, Ketchikan Soda Bottling

Works, 1921-34; U.S. Marshal, Juneau, 1st jud. dist., 1934-50; died of heart attack in his home, July 9, 1950; buried in family plot, Arcata, Calif. Mem., Pioneers, Sierra Club, Woodman of the World, Elks, Eagles, K.C., Nat. Fed. of Fed. Employees. Catholic, Democrat.

MALLOTT, Byron I., fisherman. B. in Yakutat, Apr. 6, 1943; Sheldon Jackson h. sc.; stud., Western Wash. State Coll., Bellingham; m. Antoinette; 2 children; mayor, 1965, city councilman, 1967-68, Yakutat; local govt. specialist, gov.'s office, 1966; special asst. to U.S. Sen. Mike Gravel, Wash., D.C., 1969; exec. dir., Rural Alaska Community Action Program, 1970; dir., local affairs agency, gov.'s office, 1971; comr. community & reg. affairs, 1972-74. Mem., AFN (bd. dir.), state rural affairs com. Democrat.

MALONE, J. Hugh. B. in Catskill, N.Y., Jan. 22, 1944; h. sc. grad.; m. Christine; 2 children; res., Alaska, 1958-; city councilman, borough assemblyman, Kenai; chmn., local boundary com.; state H.R., from Kenai, 1973-77. Democrat. Address: Box 9, Kenai 99611.

MALONEY, William R., miner, government mine inspector. B. in Mt. Jackson, Va., 1869; m. Mrs. Belle Campbell of Fairbanks; children: Ethel Campbell (step-d.), William J.; arrived in Nome, 1900, from Colo.; miner, Seward Peninsula, 12 yrs.; first terr. mine inspector, 1913-18; cand., del. in Cong., 1918; moved to San Francisco; employe, Union Constr. Co.; supt., Kelsey Mine, Placerville, Calif., 1923; pres., Eldorado-Alpine Mine, Georgetown, Calif.; died in San Francisco, June 27, 1937. Democrat.

MANDERS, John Edgar, lawyer. B. in Denver, Colo., Feb. 3, 1895; s. Robert Francis and Letha Clementine (Barnes) M.; public sc., San Francisco, Los Angeles, Berkeley, Calif.; prep. sc., Menlo Park; stud., San Francisco Law Sc., 1912-18; admitted to Calif. bar, 1918; m. Henrietta Bertolas, June 6, 1914; children: Jeanne (Mrs. Willard Treadwell (div.), Mrs. Day), Jack M., Letha (Mrs. Arthur G. Woodley (div.), Mrs. Green); law prac., San Francisco, 1918-41; law prac., Anchorage, 1941-; cand., del. in Cong., 1944; mayor, Anchorage, 1945-46; cand., U.S. Sen., 1958; died in Anchorage hosp., Feb. 18, 1973. Mem., Am., Alaska and Anchorage Bar Assns.; Anchorage Utility Bd., 1949-54; Masons, K.T., Scottish Rite, Shrine, Elks. Episcopalian, Republican.

MANLEY, John E., railroad executive. B. in Fort McLeod, Alta., Can., May 28, 1913; h. sc. and jr. coll., Pasadena, Calif.; m. Lenore Pauline "Sunny" Obremski (dec. 1970); children: Lynn Mary, Richard William; moved from Can. to Calif., 1917; employe, tool and die shop, Detroit, Mich.; moved to Alaska, 1937; laborer, Alaska R.R., Seward; fireman, locomotive engr., road foreman of engines, supt. of operations, asst. mgr., 1949-62, gen. mgr., 1962-71, Alaska R.R., ret., Dec. 31, 1971. Mem., Rotary, Elks. Address: 1522 W. 15th, Anchorage 99501.

MARQUAM, Thomas A., lawyer. B. in Portland, Ore., Jan. 29, 1874; s. Circuit Judge T.A. Marquam, Multnomah Co., Ore.; m. Mrs. Iowa V. Allman, Sept. 23, 1910 (dec. 1917); step-s. Jack; m. 2d, Miss Ray Alderman, 1920; asst. to Joseph W. Ivey, Collector of Customs, Alaska, 1897-; in charge of revenue launch at Sitka; pvt. law prac., Skagway and Haines, 1898-1906; nominated Rep. Nat. Com., Juneau, but refused recognition by Nat. Com., 1903-06; pvt. law prac., Fairbanks; ed., Fairbanks TIMES, 1908; nominated for 4th div. judgeship by Fairbanks Rep. Club, but failed to get presidential nomination, 1921; mayor, Fairbanks, 1920-25; attended Rep. Nat. Conv., 1924; mem., bd. regents, UA, 1925-31; cand., del. in Cong., on Ind. ticket, 1926; moved to N.Y.C., 1929; died there, Nov. 23, 1931; cremated and ashes sent to Portland, Ore. for interment. Republican.

MARSHALL, John B., lawyer. B. in 1872; m. Mrs. Martha S. Osborne in Juneau, Apr. 21, 1912; children: Roy Osborne (step-s.), Elizabeth; stenographer, Royal A. Gunnison, Juneau, 1911-; admitted to bar, 1912; formed law partnership with Gunnison, later pvt. law prac.; city councilman, Juneau, 1912-13; U.S. Comr., Juneau, 1914-; Alaska's first Dep. Prohibition Adm., 1921-; transferred to legal dept., Prohibition Enforcement Bur., Wash., D.C., several yrs.; ret. to pvt. law prac., Juneau, also engaged in fur farming, 1928-30; died of influenza complications, Apr. 2, 1930.

MARSTON, Marvin R. (Muktuk), businessman. B. in Tyler, Wash., Jan. 5, 1890; s. Martin and Cassandra M.; gr. and h. sc., Seattle; stud., Seattle Pacific Coll.; Ph.B., Greenville Coll., Greenville, Ill., 1913; m. Pauline H. Brooke (dec. 1962); children: Bonnie (Mrs. Robert Cuthell, later Mrs. Robert Marshall), Billie Mae (Mrs. Ben J. Atkinson, dec. 1955), Brooke; U.S. Army, transportation service, 1917-18; insur. and bond salesman, East Coast; salesman, realtor, homebuilder, oil operator, Long Beach, Calif., 1920s; gold miner and airline exec., subarctic area of Hudson Bay, Quebec, Can., 1930s; U.S. Army, Elmendorf AFB, with rank of maj., later lt. col., military aide to Gov. Gruening, 1941-46; organized Eskimo Scouts for Terr. Guard, known as "Gruening's Guerrillas"; developed Turnagain-by-the-Sea, Anchorage residential subdiv., 1950-; del., const. conv., 1955-56; gov. appt. Alaska's goodwill ambassador, 1963. Received distinguished alumnus award, Greenville Coll., 1968; hon. brig. gen., Alaska Nat. Guard, 1973; outstanding civilian service medal, U.S. Army, 1973. Author: "Men of the Tundra," 1969. Mem., Anch. Nat. Guard Armory (bd., 1961), Cook Inlet Hist. Soc., Cook Inlet Native Assn. (lifetime), VFW, Yukon Pioneers. Address: 1110 W. 6th Ave., Anchorage 99501.

MARTIN, Garnet W., mechanic, businessman. B. in Liverpool, England, Mar. 1, 1895 (mother was visiting her home); parents resided in Juneau, 1887-1909; m. Miss Jennie Patterson, Anchorage, 1917; children: George, Thomas; res., Nome, 1909-64; master mechanic, Hammon Consolidated Gold Fields and U.S. Smelting, Refining & Mining Co., Nome; game comr., Nome area; operated North Pole Baker,

1942-50; moved to Fairbanks; switchboard engr., Ft. Wainwright; terr. H.R., 1935-37, 1939-41; ret. to states, 1964; died autumn, 1966. Democrat.

MARTIN, Verne O., lawyer. B. in Corona, Calif., Apr. 21, 1916; h. sc., Great Falls, Mont.; grad., bus. sc., Billings, Mont., 1934; B.A., LL.B., U. Denver, 1950; m. Carolyn Clark, 1935; children: Mona (Mrs. David Swinehart), Eric, John, Mrs. Janet Guinn, Vikki, April; civil service employe, Provo Ordnance depot, S. Dak., 1936-42; U.S. Navy, flight engr., med. discharge, 1942-44; office adm., Ft. Peck, Mont., 1944-46; stud., U. Denver and Westminster law sc., 1946-50; pvt. law prac. and dep. dist. atty., Kremmling, Colo., 1950-52; moved to Anchorage, 1952; pvt. law prac., referee in bankruptcy (3 yrs.); cand., gov. of Alaska. Republican. Address: 3014 Madison, Anchorage 99502.

MASON, John D., lawyer. B. in Detroit, Mich., Oct. 5, 1934; s. Harold R. and Lela May (Hodges) M.; B.A., Mich. State U., 1957; LL.B., U. Mich., 1963; m. Ruth S. Davidson in Anchorage, 1964; children: Michael James, David Roy, Kristina Sue; commissioned officer, U.S. Navy, 1958-61; pvt. law prac., Me., 1963-64; dist. atty., 2d jud. div., Nome, 1964-65; employe, dept. of highways, Anchorage, few mos.; magistrate, Kodiak, 1965-70; dist. judge, Anchorage, 1970-. Address: 941 Fourth Ave., Anchorage 99501.

MATTHEWS, Howard A., educator. B. in 1921; B.A., Southern Ida. U.; M.A., U. Ida., 1952; journeyman's electrician license, Ida.; U.S. Army, 1943-45; sc. teacher, Rupert and Mountain Home, Ida.; elementary sc. teacher, Anchorage, 1953-54; principal, Woodland Park Sc., Anchorage, 1954-55; supervisor, h. sc. and vocational education, terr. dept. education, 1955-57; dep. comr., dept. education, 1957-59, acting comr., Apr.-Oct. 1959, res. as dep. comr., Dec. 31, 1959; manpower utilization officer, U.S. Dept. Education, Wash., D.C., 1960-.

MAYNARD, Russell G., newspaperman. B. in Nome, c. 1907; s. George F. and Mary (Shafer) M.; mgr., Nome NUGGET, 1930s; dir., dept. public welfare, Juneau, 1941-49; staff mem., Alaska DAILY EMPIRE, Juneau, 1950-. Democrat.

McALLISTER, (Samuel) Ward, Jr., lawyer, judge. U.S. dist. judge, Sitka, July 5, 1884-Aug. 28, 1885; held only one ct. session in Sitka, fall 1884, leaving terr. immediately thereafter; summarily suspended, July 21, 1885; vacated office, Aug. 28, 1885; sued U.S. govt. for salary due until expiration of appointment, Sept. 6, 1886; U.S. Supreme Ct. disallowed claim (*McAllister vs U.S.*, 141 U.S., 174, 23 Stat. 24, chapter 58); family originally from Savannah, Ga.; estab. law firm, San Francisco, Calif.; died following appendectomy, San Rafael, Calif., Apr. 1, 1908. Republican.

McBRIDE, John C. (Jack), collector of customs, mine assayer, businessman. B. in Mono Co., Calif., 1873; public sc., San Francisco, Calif.; bus. course, Stockton, Calif.; m. Cynthia; d. Miriam; assayer, Virginia City, Nev.; asst. assayer, purchase agent, Utica Mining Co., Angels Camp, Calif.; went to Alaska, 1897; asst. supt., Sumdum Mining Co., 5 yrs.; prospector, 3 yrs.; moved to Juneau, 1904; pres. and gen. mgr., C.W. Young Hardware Co., 1906-22; Alaska comr. to Alaska-Yukon-Pacific Exposition, Seattle, 1908-09; Rep. Nat. Com., 1920-24; collector of customs, 1922-33; died in Berkeley, Calif., Nov. 20, 1933. Mem., Masons, Elks. Republican.

McCAIN, Harry Golden, minister, lawyer. B. in Brownsville, Ore., 1886; s. James N. and Alice (Hausman) McC.; B.D., Willamette U.; B.A., Northwestern U.; post-grad. stud., U. Chicago; m. Roxanna Cleveland Cox, July 20, 1904; d. Ruth Elere (dec.); Methodist minister and temperance lecturer, hdqrs., Topeka, Kan., Kan. City, Mo., 1914-17; v.p., Intercollegiate Prohibition Assn.; joined parents, minister for Congregational Church, Anchorage, 1917-; asst. U.S. atty., 3d jud. div., Anchorage, 1921-26; cand., del. in Cong., 1926; pvt. law prac., Ketchikan; city councilman, 8 yrs., mayor, 3 yrs., Ketchikan; died in Ketchikan, Oct. 20, 1948. Mem., Alaska Bar Assn., Pioneers, Lions, Eagles (past worthy pres.), Elks, Moose. Methodist, Republican.

McCAIN, James N., miner. B. near Sheridan, Ore., July 7, 1865; s. Rev. John S. and Sarah McC.; m. Alice Hausman, 1885; s. Harry Golden; m. 2d, Frances Spicer, 1914; gold prospector, Kotzebue Sound, 1898; Nome, 1899; Candle, 1903-06, Fairbanks, 1906, Iditarod, 1910-13, Ruby, 1914; homesteaded in Anchorage, 1915, operating fox farm for awhile; mem., adv. council, 1918, sc. bd., 1919, Anchorage; terr. H.R., 1929-31; died in Ketchikan, Sept. 4, 1946. Mem., Western Alaska Fur Breeders Assn. (pres., 1926), Odd Fellows, Pioneers. Republican.

McCARREY, James Lewis, Jr., lawyer. B. in Logan, Ut., Jan. 30, 1906; s. James Lewis and Alice Maiben (Squires) McC.; gr. and h. sc., Richmond, Ut.; stud., Brigham Young Coll., 1924-25; LL.B., U. Ut., 1939; m. Cora Broadbent, Apr. 3, 1939; children: Cora Alice, David Broadbent, Margaret Anne, James Lewis, III; Mormon missionary, Germany and Austria, 1926-29; salesman, Ut. Woolen Mills, in Alaska, 1939-42; U.S. Army Signal Corps, 1943-45; pvt. law prac., Anchorage, 1945-63; U.S. dist. judge, 3d jud. div., Anchorage, 1953-60; pvt. prac., Anchorage, 1960-. Mem., Delta Theta Phi (legal), Delta Phi (soc., past pres.). Mormon, Republican. Address: 117 W. 4th Ave., Anchorage 99501.

McCOMBE, Robert S., miner, teamster, lodge operator. B. in England, 1902; grad., UA; m. Muriel "Mollie" Birchmore in Fortymile, Sept. 26, 1940; no children; went to Alaska, 1918; worked from Ketchikan to Nome; operated lodge, part-time mining and freighting, Chicken; state H.R., 1959-61, 1963-67. Mem., Masons, Elks, Alaska Order of Pioneers, Yukon Order of Pioneers. Democrat.

McCORMICK, John, government administrator, miner. B. in Douglas, July 25, 1896; s. Richard and Nora (Connors) McC.; public sc., Douglas and Oakland, Calif.; m.; d. Irene Mavis (Mrs. Everett

Schafer); m. 2d, Betty P. Stiles, June 3, 1931; stock clerk, ARC, 1912-; U.S. Army, 1917-18; employe, Treadwell Mining Co. and Alaska-Juneau Gold Mining Co., 14 yrs.; employe, Del Monte Properties Co., Pacific Grove, Calif., late 1920s; dock foreman, Alaska Gastineau Mining Co., Thane, 3-1/2 yrs.; dep. U.S. Marshal, Juneau, 1934-37; city councilman, Juneau, 1938-39, res.; city policeman, Juneau; terr. H.R., 1939-41, res.; dir., Selective Service, 1941-late 1950s; died in Seal Beach, Calif., Sept. 9, 1966. Mem., Am. Leg., Pioneers, Lions, Elks. Democrat.

McCORMACK, Peter Constantine, lumberjack, businessman. B. in Monticello, Prince Edwards I., Nov. 11, 1861; U.S. citizen in Bellingham, Wash., 1892; common sc. education; worked as farm hand and studying at nights, until 1883; m.; children: Peter C., Jr., Mrs. Robert Murphy; lumberjack, Pa., until 1887; worked in logging camps near Mt. Vernon, Wash. Terr., railway and bridge work, Seattle & Eastern Ry., near Snoqualmie Falls; gen. contracting bus., Fairhaven, Wash. (now Bellingham), 1889-96; mining and constr. work, Kootenai, B.C., during Stikine River goldrush, estab. mercantile firm, St. Michael Trading Co., Wrangell; real estate, logging bus. and owned Wrangell dock; mayor, Wrangell, 5 terms; terr. H.R., 1917-19, 1929-31; mem., sc. bd.; died in Wrangell, July 29, 1944. Republican.

McCUTCHEON, Herbert Hazard, railroad foreman. B. in Bayside, Calif., July 31, 1876; gr. sc., Yreka, Calif.; m. Clara Kreuger in Chitina, 1910; children: Stephan Douglas, Stanley, Jerome "Jerry"; seaman, 1891-1900; miner, Exploration Co., Golovin Bay, 1900-03; prop., roadhouse and gen. store, Golovin, 1903-08; participated in Bristol Bay gold stampede, 1908-09; employe, Copper River & Northwestern Ry., 1909-11; res., Vancouver, B.C., 1911-15; yard foreman, Alaska R.R., Anchorage, 1915-38; city councilman, Anchorage, 1929-30; terr. H.R., 1931-43, speaker, 1941, Sen., 1943-45; died in Anchorage, Nov. 14, 1945. Mem., Pioneers (pres.), Elks. Democrat.

McCUTCHEON, Stanley, lawyer. B. in Anchorage, Sept. 1917; s. Herbert H. and Clara (Kreuger) McC.; h. sc., Anchorage; "read law" in lawyer's office, Anchorage, admitted to Alaska bar, 1939; m. Evelyn; children: Cheryl Scotte (Mrs. Stuart Ramstad, Mrs. Charles Erkel), Shelley; pvt. law prac., Anchorage, 1939-; terr. H.R., 1943-47, 1949-53, 1955-57, speaker, 1949; pres., Alaska Airlines, 1949-; Dem. Nat. Com., 1952-53; sec., dir., Union Bk., Palmer, until 1952; mem., adv. council for UN, 1959; bd. govs., Alaska Bar Assn., 1960-63; Statehood Com., 1949-59. Mem., Elks, Pioneers. Democrat. Address: 213 W. 6th Ave., Anchorage 99501.

McCUTCHEON, Stephan Douglas, commercial photographer. B. in Cordova, Aug. 30, 1911; s. Herbert H. and Clara (Krueger) Mc.; gr. and h. sc., Anchorage; m. 1930; d. Diane; m. 2d, Phyllis Schuyler Malcolm, Mar. 1944 (div. 1966); m. 3d, Delores Roguska, 1966 (div. 1972); m. 4th, Gloria Britt, Feb. 12, 1972; employe, Alaska R.R., An-

chorage, 1928-40; dep. U.S. Marshal, Valdez, 1940-41; asst. comr. labor, 1941-42; dist. mgr., 4th jud. div., Fairbanks, OPA, 1942-44; U.S. Army Signal Corps, 1944-46; estab. Mac's Foto Service, Anchorage, 1946-66; res., Ketchikan, 1966-67, Anchorage, 1967-; terr. H.R., 1947-49, Sen., special session, 1946-, 1949-53; del., const. conv., 1955-56; chmn., southcentral dist. Dem. com., 1959-. Received "Gold Pan" service award from Anchorage C. of C., for documentary film "Spotlight Anchorage". Regular contributor of articles and pictures to magazines and encyclopedias, U.S. and Europe. Mem., Elks, VFW, Pioneers. Democrat. Address: 3363 Lakeside Dr., Anchorage.

McDONALD, Joseph A., U.S. Marshal, miner, merchant. B. in Waltham, Mass., May 15, 1876; s. Donald and Mary (McEachern) McD.; St. Andrew's Prep Sc., Nova Scotia, Can.; stud., Coll. of St. Francis Xavier, Antigonish, Nova Scotia, Can.; m. Katherine Regan in Fairbanks, Jan. 22, 1913; moved to Seattle, 1889; joined gold rush to Dawson, 1898, Nome, 1900; ret. to Dawson, 1901; prospector, Fairbanks, dist., 1905-11; estab. gen. merchandise store at Ester Cr., cont. part-time mining, until 1929; terr. H.R., 1929-35, speaker, 1933; U.S. Marshal, 4th jud. dist., Fairbanks, 1933-46; ret. to Seattle, Wash.; died in Fairbanks while on visit, July 20, 1950. Mem., Pioneers, Elks. Catholic, Democrat.

McDONALD, J. Scott, government administrator. B. in Tex., Dec. 1926; m. Molly Joe; children: Molly Melinda, Carol Annette; U.S. Navy, 1943-46; credit mgr., paymaster, truck dispatcher, Morrison Milling Co., Denton, Tex., 1949-51; office clerk, Pan-Am. Petroleum Corp., Hobbs and Farmington, N. Mex., and Can., 1951-62, Anchorage, 1962-66; asst. comr. of adm., Juneau, 1966-67; dep. comr. health and welfare, 1967-68, comr., 1968-69. Republican.

McGANN, Thomas F., miner. B. in Can., near N.Y. state, Sept. 27, 1868; reared in Buffalo, N.Y.; left home at age 15; unm.; rancher-miner, Stockton, Calif., storekeeper, Los Angeles, Calif., 1883-98; joined Klondike gold rush to Dawson, 1898-99; res., Rampart, 1899-1900, Nome, 1900-21; terr. Sen., 1915-17; clerk of dist. ct., Nome, 1917-21; moved near Bellevue, Wash., 1921. Mem., Pioneers (Nome Igloo No. 1), Nome Miners' Union. Democrat.

McGILL, Joseph E., fisherman, construction worker. B. in Kinsman, O., Jan. 13, 1924; h. sc., Kinsman; m. Katherine Mulkaeit in Dillingham, 1951; children: Karla, David; U.S. Marine Corps, 1942-45, twice awarded Purple Heart, med. discharged as disabled veteran; arr. Sitka, 1946; fisherman, constr. worker, longshoreman, Juneau, Valdez, Seward, Anchorage, 1946-49; res., Dillingham, 1949-; mem., sc. bd., 2 terms; mayor, Dillingham, 3 terms; state H.R., 1965-76. Democrat. Address: Box 218, Dillingham 99576.

McGINN, John L., lawyer. B. in Portland, Ore., Feb. 26, 1871; s. Charles and Anna M. (Hill) McG.; public sc., Portland; LL.B., U. Ore., 1893; m. Elsa Searing in Nome, Apr. 20, 1904; children: Laura

Edith (Mrs. Thomas Reily Smith), John W.; estab. law partnership with bro., Henry, U.S. Sen. from Calif., 1893-98; U.S. Army, Spanish-Am. War, Philippines, 1898-1900; gold prospector-lawyer, Nome; asst. U.S. atty., Oct. 1900; U.S. dist. atty., 2d jud. dist., Nome, 1901-02; moved to Fairbanks, 1905, spending summers there and winters in San Mateo, Calif.; oil interests in Bakersfield area; died in San Mateo, Calif., Nov. 3, 1959. Mem., Pioneers, VFW, Elks. Republican.

McGINNIS, Frederick P., minister, educator. B. in Atlanta, Ga., Jan. 9, 1921; B.A., Asbury Coll., Ky.; B.D., Asbury Theological Seminary, 1948; D.D., U. Puget Sound, Tacoma, 1960; Dr. Humane Letters, UA, 1967; m. Harriet Riggs, Minneapolis, Minn., June 1948; children: Brian Timothy, Mary Ann; minister, Quincy, O., 1948-50, First Methodist Church, Juneau, 1950-54, First Methodist Church, Anchorage, 1954-57; field supt., Methodist Church, Alaska, 1955-59; pres., AMU, 1959-71; state comr. health and social services, 1971-; U.S. Internat. North Pacific Fisheries Com., 1962-69; Rhodes Scholarship Com., Alaska, 1960-64. Elected to Alaska Hall of Fame, 1968. Mem., Alaska Council of Churches (pres., 1959-61), Rotary. Methodist, Democrat. Address: 2413 Capt. Cook Dr., Anchorage 99503.

McKANNA, Robert J. (Mickey), transportation agent. B. in Douglas, May 21, 1889; s. Michael J. and Katherine Alice McK.; public sc., Douglas; m. Theo in Seward, 1923; transfer bus., Juneau, with older bros.; later took over all waterfront shipping on Gastineau Channel, consisting of 15 docks; U.S. Army Corps Engrs., France, 1917-19; employe, Alaska SS Co., Douglas, part-time freight clerk and purser, SS *Alameda;* moved to Fairbanks, 1929; agent, Alaska SS Co., Pacific-Alaska Airways (later Pan-Am. Airways); operated Golden Heart taxi service, and Model Liquor store; sold bus. interests, 1948; moved to homesite near Fairbanks; Rep. Nat. Com., 1952-54; died in Fairbanks, Nov. 24, 1958. Mem., Pioneers. Catholic, Republican.

McKAY, Douglas, businessman. B. in Portland, Ore., June 24,1893; s. E.D. and Minnie A. (Musgrove) McK.; B.S., Ore. State Coll., 1917; m. Mabel Hill, Mar. 31, 1917; children: Douglas (dec.), Shirley (Mrs. Wayne Hadley), Mary Lou (Mrs. Lester D. Green); U.S. Army, WWI, WWII, decorated with Order of Purple Heart; automobile salesman and sales mgr., Portland, 1920-27; estab. auto bus., dealer for Chevrolet and Cadillac, Salem, Ore., 1927-59; mayor, Salem, 1933-34; state Sen., 1935-49; Ore. Gov., 1949-53; Sec. of Interior, 1953-56; cand., U.S. Sen., 1956; died in Salem, July 22, 1959. Mem., Masons, Shrine, K.T., Am. Leg. (comdr.), VFW, SAR, Phi Delta Theta, Eagles, Elks. Presbyterian, Republican.

McKENZIE, Alexander, central figure in Nome political scandals, 1900-01; no formal educ.; went to N. Dak. from Minn. as section hand, Northern Pacific R.R.; land agent, later receiver, Northern Pacific R.R.; pres., gen. mgr., Alaska Gold Mining Co., 1900; arr. Nome with Judge Arthur H. Noyes, July 1900; appt. receiver for many rich mining

properties; sentenced to prison for contempt of ct., Circuit Ct. of Appeals, San Francisco, Feb. 1901; pardoned by Pres. McKinley after 3 months incarceration, on a plea of ill health; ret. to Bismarck, N. Dak.; Rep. Nat. Com.; chief lobbyist in Cong. for Northern Pacific R.R. and others; living in retirement, Chicago, fall 1908, reputedly a multi-millionaire. Republican.

McKINLEY, Lee Lawrence, dentist, farmer. B. in DeQueen, Ark., Aug. 22, 1906; s. Joseph Golden and Georgia Ann McK.; gr. and h. sc., Fayetteville, Ark.; D.D.S., Kan. City Western Dental Coll.; post-grad., Internat. Sc. of Orthodontia, 1941; m. Doris M. Blakely, Oct. 15, 1933; children: Ira Blakely, Lee Lawrence (Larry), Judith Lorraine (Mrs. Nathan Dale Bagley), William David, Rodger Dean, Karen Lu, Steven Charles; prac. dentistry, Detroit, Mich., 1935-46; purchased 80-acre farm, Matanuska Valley (Bodenburg Butte area) and opened dental office, Anchorage, commuting in own airplane, 1946-; known as the "flying dentist" because he flew in bush areas to provide dental care for residents; terr. H.R., 1953-55; cand., U.S. Sen., 1960, 1966. Received outstanding community service award from VFW, dept. Alaska, 1959. Mem., Mt. McKinley Lions (charter), Masons, Elks, Alaska Dental Soc. (pres., southcentral dist., 1966). Presbyterian, Republican. Address: 429 D St., Anchorage 99501.

McKINNON, Donald A., civil engineer. B. in Sioux Falls, S. Dak., Oct. 7, 1895; Wash. h. sc., Sioux Falls; B.S., U. S.Dak., 1919; m. Barbara; children: Barbara (Mrs. William Dye), Christine (Mrs. Dennis Carlson), Katherine, Linda; U.S. Army, 1917-19; S. Dak. highway dept., 1919-27; Larson Engr. Co., Sioux Falls, 1927-33; state engr., PWA, Helena, Mont., 1933-41; project engr., Peter Kiewit Sons Co., Kan. Ordnance Plant, Parsons, Kan. and LaHunta (Colo.) Air Base, 1941-43; U.S. Army Corps Engrs., Missouri River div., 1943-46; estab. constr. co., Helena, 1946-56; sold bus. and estab. consult.'s office, Kalispell, Mont., 1956-62; comr. highways, Juneau, 1962-66; partner, McKinnon Bros. constr. co., Los Angeles, Calif., 1968-70; died in Calif., Oct. 17, 1970. Mem., Am. Soc. Engrs., Am. Military Engrs., Am. Leg., VFW, Vets of WWI, Elks.

McLAUGHLIN, George M., lawyer. B. in Hempstead, N.Y., Dec. 19, 1914; B.A., St. Peter's Coll., Jersey City, N.J.; grad., magna cum laude, Fordham U. Sc. of Law, 1938; m. Ruth Becker; children: Frances Jo, Michael Sean; ed., Fordham *Law Review*, 1936-38; U.S. Army, WWII, and mem., Foreign Claims Com., 1943-49; pvt. law prac., Anchorage, 1949-58; city magistrate, 1952-55; del., const. conv., 1955-56; died of heart attack at home, June 23, 1958; interment in Ft. Richardson cemetery; Anchorage youth center for delinquents named as memorial to him, 1959. Mem., Cook Inlet Hist. Soc. (bd. dir., 1955-58); Alaska Igloo of the Friendly Sons of St. Patrick (founder); Alaska Nat. Guard (one of the founders of 207th Infantry battalion, lt. col. at time of death); Greek vice consul; Family Counseling Service (charter); terr. bd. juvenile institutions. Catholic, Democrat.

McLEAN, Joseph Alexander, lawyer, insurance broker. B. in Juneau, Apr. 16, 1917; s. Hector and Elsie (Peterson) McL.; B.A., U. Wash., 1939; law clerk, Juneau, 1939-40, Anchorage, 1940-41; admitted to bar, 1947; m. Isabel Parsons, San Francisco, Jan. 23, 1945; children: Alexandra, Neil, Heather, Duncan; U.S. Army, WWII; mem., Alaska Nat. Guard, 1941-46; entered bus. with father, McLean Insurance Agency, Juneau, 1946-68; terr. H.R., 1955-57; pvt. law prac., Juneau, 1968-. Mem., Pioneers, Lions, Juneau C. of C. (pres., 1948). Republican. Address: 401 Angus Way, Juneau 99801.

McNABB, George Brinkworth, Jr., lawyer. B. in Indianapolis, Ind., July 28, 1919; s. Dr. George B. and Vera McN.; h. sc., Carthage, Ind., 1937; Kentucky Military Inst., 1938; B.A., 1942, LL.B., 1948, Ind. U.; m. Colleen Joyce Porter, Aug. 1953; s. George B., III; m. 2d, Suzanne; U.S. Army, 1942-46; law prac., Bloomington, Ind., 6 mos.; went to Fairbanks, Nov. 1948; estab. law prac.; terr. H.R., 1955-59; state Sen., 1959-63. Mem., Sigma Chi (soc.), Phi Delta Phi (legal), Delta Sigma Pi (internat. bus.), Masons, Am. Leg. (1st vice comdr., dept. Alaska), C. of C. Methodist, Democrat.

McNEALY, Robert James, lawyer. B. in Louisville, Neb., Feb. 23, 1907; gr. and h. sc., Louisville; "read law" in lawyer's office, Omaha, Neb.; admitted to Neb. bar, 1929; m. Mary; children: Maureen (Mrs. Kenneth Rice), Patricia (Mrs. Richard D. Clark), James J., Kathleen, Michael; moved to Alaska; civilian employe, Kodiak Naval base, 1940-46; opened law office in Seldovia; U.S. Comr. and city atty., 1946-49; pvt. prac., Fairbanks, 1949-52; U.S. atty., 4th jud. dist., 1952-53; ret. to pvt. prac.; terr. H.R., 1955-57; del., const. conv., 1955-56; state Sen., 1959-67, majority leader, 1961-65, pres., 1965-67; Alaska Gov., 1966; moved to Anchorage, 1967. Mem., Am. and Alaska Bar Assns., Alaska Airlines (bd. dir.), Elks. Catholic, Democrat. Address: 1133 N St., Anchorage 99501.

McNEES, John A., meteorologist, businessman. B. May 26, 1917; grad., Willamette U.; m.; s. Roger; res., Nome, 1944-; meteorologist, U.S. Weather Bur., 1944-49; pvt. transportation bus., 1949-; del., const. conv., 1955-56; Alaska Sen., 1957-63. Democrat.

McROBERTS, Theodore R., U.S. Marshal, miner. Unm.; res., Nampa, Ida.; moved to Anchorage, 1935; employe, Alaska R.R. at Matanuska Colony, 1935-36; owner-publisher, KUSKO TIMES, A WEEKLY, Takotna, with Alaska Egan, 1936-38; sold newspaper; agent, Northern Commercial Co., Takotna, 1938-39; operated freighter between McGrath and Takotna, also trucking service to mines at Ophir, miner with bro. on Ganes Cr., 1939-42; dep. U.S. Marshal, Bethel, 1942-50; U.S. Marshal, Fairbanks, 4th jud. dist., Dec. 1950-Mar. 1951, Aug.-Nov. 1951, Feb. 1953-Mar. 1954; chief dep. U.S. Marshal, Fairbanks, 1954-59; pres., 11th reg., Assn. U.S. dep. Marshals, Jan. 1958.

McSMITH, Blanche Preston, businesswoman, social worker. B. in Marshall, Tex., May 5, 1920; d. William A. and Obelia Myrtle Preston; B.A., Wiley Coll., Marshal, Tex., 1941; post-grad., UCLA, 1944; hon. LL.D., Wiley Coll., 1960; m. William McSmith, 1949 (div. 1962); children: Kimberly Blanche; social worker, Am. Red Cross, Los Angeles, Calif., 1945-49; joined husband in Kodiak, 1949-50; estab. McSmith-Enterprises (electrical appliances sales and service, real estate), Anchorage; state H.R., 1959-61; dir., social services, Project Head Start, Anchorage, 1968-72; state dir., Public Employment Program, Juneau, 1972-; Whittier city library dedicated to her, 1973. Mem., NAACP (pres., 1959-71); Order of Eastern Star; Alpha Kappa Alpha; Anchorage TB Assn. (pres., 1957-58); Toastmistress Club; LWV (bd. dir.); Anchorage Woman's Club; AAUW; Cook Inlet Hist. Soc. (charter). Baptist, Democrat.

McVEIGH, Richard Laurence, lawyer. B. in Spalding, Neb., June 12, 1933; s. Arthur and Alberta McV. (later Mrs. Philip Clarke); gr. and h. sc., Fairbanks; stud., UA; B.A., Notre Dame U., 1955; LL.B., J.D., Georgetown U., 1962; m. Carolyn Best; children: David Lawrence, Katherine Lewis, Steven Lawrence; moved with parents to Anchorage, 1939, Fairbanks, 1946; jet fighter pilot, U.S. Air Force, 1955-59; legislative asst., U.S. Sen. E.L. Bartlett, 1961-62; asst. atty. gen., Juneau, 1962-63; asst. dist. atty., Anchorage, 1963-64; pvt. prac., Anchorage, Jan.-Oct. 1964; U.S. Atty. for Alaska, Anchorage, 1964-68; pvt. prac., Anchorage, 1968-; state H.R., 1969-75. Mem., Elks, Alaska Bar Assn., Anchorage chapter, Fed. Bar Assn. (pres.). Catholic, Democrat. Address: 4809 Nottingham Way, Anchorage 99503.

MEARS, Col. Frederick, civil engineer. B. in Ft. Omaha, Neb., May 25, 1878; s. Col. Frederick and Elizabeth (McFarland) M.; gr. and h. sc., N.Y. and Wash.; grad., Shattuck Military Acad., Faribault, Minn., 1897; m. Jennie Wainwright, Ft. Clarke, Tex., Apr. 6, 1907; children: Josephine (Mrs. John P. McVay), Elizabeth McFarland (Mrs. Henry Meiggs), Frederick, Jr., Helen Rogers (dec. 1929); employe, Great Northern R.R., Ida., 1897-99; enlisted as private, U.S. Army, Oct. 1899, Co. K, 3d Infantry, 2d lt., 1901, 1st lt., 1906; served with 5th Cavalry, Philippine I.; ret. to U.S., 1903; asst. engr., Panama Canal Com., chief engr., gen. supt., Panama R.R. & S S Line, 1906-14; mem., AEC, 1914-17; 31st Regiment of Engrs., U.S. Army, France, gen. mgr., R.R. Dept. Transportation Corps; chmn., AEC, gen. mgr., Alaska R.R., Anchorage, 1919-23; ret. from active service with rank of col.; chief engr., St. Paul Union Depot Co., in charge constr. of St. Paul Union Depot, 1923-25; asst. chief engr., Great Northern R.R., in charge constr. of tunnel through Cascade Mts., 1925-39; died in Seattle, Wash., Jan. 11, 1939. Awarded Distinguished Service Medal, French Legion of Honor. Mem., Soc. Military Engrs. (dir.), Am. Soc. Civil Engrs., Rainier Club, Wash. Athletic Club, Seattle. Episcopalian, Republican.

MEATH, Lawrence William, banker. B. in Tacoma, Wash., Jan. 10, 1909; gr. and h. sc., Tacoma; m. Lucile Lavery, June 15, 1938; children: Robert,

Marian, Larry, Jr.; bank employe, Tacoma, 1926-33; employe in sawmill, co. treas.'s office and disbursing office, state welfare dept., Tacoma, 1933-36; teller, First Nat. Bk., Fairbanks, 1936-45; owner-mgr., Fairbanks Cigar Store, 1945-55; terr. H.R.,1947-49; city councilman, Fairbanks, 1941-; mgr., Alaska Nat. Bk., Fairbanks, 1956-; dir., Alaska Development Corp., dep. comr. commerce, 1973-. Mem., Masons, Elks, Lions. Republican.

MEEKINS, Edward R. (Russ), salesman. Married Adele; children: Edward R. "Russ", Jr., Susan Carol (Mrs. Timothy M. Sullivan, div. 1974); moved to Anchorage, 1945; salesman, new and used automobiles; state H.R., 1959-61. Democrat. Address: 1540 K St., Anchorage 99501.

MEEKINS, Edward R., Jr. (Russ), businessman. B. in Anchorage, June 29, 1949; s. Edward R. and Adele M.; grad. h. sc., Anchorage; stud., Ore. State U., U. Ore.; m. and div.; s. Rodney; v.p., Alaska Water Refining Co.; state H.R., 1973-75. Mem., Ad Hoc Organizing Com., Young Dem., Anchorage, 1972. Democrat. Address: 522 E. 10th Ave., Anchorage.

MELAND , H.D. (Pete), businessman. B. in Postville, Ia., Mar. 21, 1919; s. Peter and Mabel (Meyer) M.; h. sc., Postville; m. Lorraine Flaskerud, Nov. 28, 1940; s. David John; employe, Siems-Drake-Puget Sound Co., naval base constr., Sitka, 1940-43; asst. chief, air transportation unit, CAA, Sitka, 1943-48; self-employed businessman, Sitka, 1947-; city councilman, Sitka; state H.R., 1971, Sen., 1972-76. Mem., state jud. council (6 yrs.), Elks, Moose, C. of C. Democrat. Address: Box 53, Sitka 99835.

MELLEN, Henry W., lawyer. B. in Booneville, Ind., June 23, 1864; farmer, blacksmith and employe, woodworking shops, while attending sc., until 1881; h. sc., Booneville; stud., U. Ind., 2 yrs.; law prac. with Mellen & Fuller firm, until 1893; U.S. Comr., Juneau, 1894-97; law partnership with Arthur K. Delaney, Juneau, 1897-1905; operated copper smelter, Prince of Wales I., 1905-; cand., del. in Cong., 1906; stock rancher near Sumner, Wash., 1925-. Democrat.

MERBS, James C., lawyer. B. in 1924; B.A., U. Colo., LL.B., U. Denver, LL.B., Westminster Coll., Denver; admitted to Colo. bar, 1950; m. Carol Yvonne Marsh in Boulder, Colo., Apr. 7, 1948; children: Daniel, David, Douglas, Denise; U.S. Army, 1943-45; chief prosecutor, 17th jud. dist., Denver, until 1961; chief trial asst., dist. atty.'s office, Anchorage, 1961-62; state dist. atty., 3d jud. div., 1962-63, res.; pvt. law prac., Anchorage. Democrat. Address: 1026 W. 4th Ave., Anchorage 99501.

MERDES, Edward A., lawyer. B. in Leetsdale, Pa., Jan. 12, 1926; stud., U. Pittsburgh, 1946; B.S., 1949, LL.B., 1951, Cornell U.; m. Norma Jane Wardle, 1950; children: Mark Edward, Theresa Diane, Beth Andrea, Robert Arthur, Marlene Ellen, Ward Matthew; U.S. Army Air Corps, 1944-45; law clerk, Judge Folta's office, Juneau, 1951-52; asst. U.S. atty., Juneau, 1952-53; asst. atty. gen., Juneau, 1953-57; city atty. and acting city mgr.,

Fairbanks, 1958-59; state Sen., 1969-73; city councilman, Douglas and Fairbanks; dir., Alaska State Bk., Fairbanks, dir., Nat. Bk. of Alaska, 1972-; dir., Alaska Airlines, 1962-66. Mem., Boy Scouts (master, 20 yrs.), Eagle Scouts, Jaycees (Alaska pres., 1957, U.S. v.p., 1958, Internat. pres., 1965), Alaska Nat. Guard Officers' Assn. (pres., 1956), Goldpanners (dir.), Elks, Eagles, Sigma Chi (soc.), Phi Delta Phi (legal), Fairbanks C. of C., K.C. (grand knight), Am. Leg., Am. and Alaska Bar Assns. Catholic, Democrat. Address: Fairbanks.

METCALF, Frank A., civil engineer. B. in Bardolf, Ill., July 22, 1882; B.S., 1910, C.E., 1912, Cornell U.; m. Ruth Grefe in Ida.; d. Mary (Mrs. E.S. Turley); employe, Bunker Hill & Sullivan mine, Ida.; engr., Alaska-Juneau Gold Mining Co., 1913-; estab. pvt. engring. firm, Juneau; city engr., Juneau and Sitka; U.S. Army Corps Engrs., WWI; civilian engr., U.S. Army, Adak, WWII; terr. highway engr., 1947-53, 1957-60; coordinator, state dept. public works, 1961, ret.; moved to Alameda, Calif., 1961; died there, Apr. 2, 1969. Mem., Elks (exalted ruler, Sitka), terr. liquor bd., Pioneers. Democrat.

METCALFE, Irwin Logan, U.S. Marshal, grocer. B. in Hartline, Wash., May 2, 1908; s. John Henry and Stella M.; h. sc., Ephrata, Wash.; B.A., U. Wash., 1932; m. May Kennedy (Mrs. James) in Palmer, 1940; no children; went to Ketchikan as seaman, U.S. Merchant Marine, 1927; employe, Alaska R.R., Fish and Wildlife Service; moved to Kodiak, 1934; sc. teacher, Kodiak, Palmer, 1936-39; dep. U.S. Marshal, Seward, 1939-51, U.S. Marshal, 1951-54 (court appt., 3d jud. div., Anchorage, June-Sept. 1951, thereafter dep. in Seward); prop., grocery store near Seward, 1939-72; del., const. conv., 1955-56; terr. H.R., 1957-59, state, 1965-71; state Sen., 1959-63; mem., Kenai Peninsula Borough Assembly; died following long illness in Seward hospital, Dec. 30, 1973; interment, Evergreen cemetery, Wenatchee, Wash. Mem., Masons (master, Seward, no. 219), Scottish Rite (32d degree), Order of Eastern Star (patron), Pioneers, Elks (trustee), Am. Assn. Retired People, Kenai. Democrat.

METCALFE, Vernon M., businessman. B. in Wenatchee, Wash., Mar. 12, 1923; gr. and h. sc., Wenatchee; m. Patricia McAlister of Skagway, June 28, 1947; children: Vernon M., Kimberly Lynn, Peter McAlister, Patricia Margaret, Kathleen Ann; employe, Rice & Ahlers Plumbing & Heating Co., 1941-42; U.S. Army, 1942-46; estab. Metcalfe Sheet Metal firm, in partnership with father, Juneau, 1946-; sports announcer, KINY, 1950s; terr. H.R., 1951-53, 1955-57; state civil defense dir., 1959-61; publicity agent for legislative Dems., 1961-; employe, state dept. education, 1971-. Protestant, Democrat.

MILLARD, Benjamin Franklin, civil engineer, miner. B. in Baraboo, Wis., May 5, 1850; left home, 1865; worked in lumber camps, foreman, 1870; employe, Weyerhaeuser Miss. Logging & Timbering Co., 10 yrs.; stud., land surveying and civil engring.; estab. timber brokerage, 1884, making and losing fortune; city councilman, 5 yrs., mayor, 1 term, Chippewa Falls, Wis.; Wis. state H.R.,

1889-90; sergeant-at-arms, Wis. state Sen., 1891; m., dec. 1912; children: Ray and Ida Mae (Mrs. R.S. Packard, later Mrs. Sloan Danenhower); 2d m.; went to Valdez, 1898, Nome, 1900; ret. to Copper River area; acquired interest in Bonanza copper mine and Cliff gold mine, from which he took $250,000 in gold in one yr.; lost gold fortune in Calif. oil ventures; one-time pres. of 5 Alaska mining cos.; terr. H.R., from Valdez, 1913-17; moved to Seattle, Wash., 1920; died there, Jan. 27, 1926. Mem., Elks, Masons (32d degree), Shrine, K.T., A.B., Odd Fellows, Pioneers. Republican.

MILLER, Alex, businessman. B. in Juneau; s. Charles Bertaloni; h. sc., Juneau; stud., UA, 2 yrs., bus. coll., Seattle; m. Doris Anne Driscoll, Fairbanks, 1948; U.S. Army, 1943-45; Dem. Nat. Com., 1956-62; adm. asst., Gov. Egan, 1970-73; dir., govt. affairs, Alaska Internat. Air, Inc., Fairbanks, 1973-. Mem., VFW (dept. comdr., 1954). Catholic, Democrat.

MILLER, Eugene Vernon, lawyer. B. in Mo., 1915; reared in Okla.; m. Francis Louise McMillen; children: Kathy Marie, Debra Louise, Lindsey Emily, William Frank, Norman Sidney, Charles Eugene; res., Fairbanks, 1950-; city atty., 1958-60; pvt. law prac., 1960-; state H.R., 1969-71; chmn., state bd. of fish and game, 7 yrs. Mem., VFW, Elks (exalted ruler), Rotary, Shrine, Moose (gov.), Tanana Valley Bar Assn., Campfire Girls (bd. dir.), Methodist church (pres., bd. trustees). Methodist, Democrat. Address: 700 10th St., Fairbanks 99701.

MILLER, JoAnn, businesswoman. B. in Benton, Ark., Sept. 20, 1932; d. Mrs. Otto C. Hall; h. sc., Odessa, Tex.; stud., Tulsa U., Anchorage Community Coll.; m. Robert Miller (div.); children: Dennis Lee, Steven C., Theresa Ann; moved to Alaska, 1959; homesteaded in Potter area; reg. management position, finance and adm. div., J.C. Penney Co., Anchorage, 1965-; state H.R., 1973-75; cand., state lt. gov., 1974. Mem., Anchorage C. of C. (bd. dir.). Republican.

MILLER, Keith Harvey, businessman. B. in Seattle, Wash., Mar. 1, 1925; s. Keith M., Sr.; h. sc., Bothell, Wash.; stud., U. Ida.; B.S., U. Wash., 1952; m. Diana Mary Doyle in Seattle, Dec. 26, 1953; no children; U.S. Army Air Corps, 1943-45; owner-operator, holly farm, Olympia, Wash., 1946-53; sold farm, estab. bill collection agency, Seattle, 1953-57; agent, IRS, Anchorage, 1957-59; homestead at Talkeetna, 1959-61; credit mgr., bill collector, city of Anchorage, and insur. salesman, 1961-64; state H.R., 1962-64; employe, Consolidated Freightways, Fairbanks, 1964-66; state Lt. Gov., 1966-69; Alaska Gov., 1969-71; pres., Alaska Local Development Corp. and mobile home park owner, Anchorage, 1971-; state Sen., 1972-76. Mem., Am. Leg., Elks, Moose, Lions, Explorers'. Republican. Address: 836 M St., No. 202, Anchorage 99501.

MILLER, Mrs. Louise, Democratic National Committeewoman, Ketchikan, 1952-53.

MILLER, Mortimer Michael (Mike), author. B. in Trinidad, Colo., July 17, 1929; s. L. Hoy and Juanita (Risk) M.; B.A., U. Wichita (Kan.); m. Marilyn Jean Bills, Wichita, Kan., June 15, 1951; children: Gail, Kevin, Shelley; ed., COLEMAN SPOT-LITE (employee house magazine, Coleman Co., Inc.), Wichita, 1951-54; sales rep., Pacific Northern Airlines and commercial mgr., Ketchikan Public Utilities, Ketchikan, 1954-60; publicity dir., Alaska Travel Div., 1960-70; mem., Greater Juneau Borough Assembly, Assembly of the Unified City, Borough of Juneau, 1966-70; state H.R., 1971-75. Author: "Soapy," 1970; "Camping and Trailering in Alaska, Anchorage, Aug.-Dec. 1969; owner-operator, Miller & Associates Management Consultants, Anchorage, 1970-.

MILLER, Norman Dale, law enforcement officer. B. in 1923; m. Virginia; dep. U.S. Marshal, Wrangell, Juneau, Ketchikan, 1955-64; chief dep. U.S. Marshal, Anchorage, 1964-69; U.S. Marshal for Alaska, Anchorage, Aug.-Dec., 1969; owner-operator, Miller & Associates Management Consultants, Anchorage, 1970-.

MILLER, Terry, businessman. B. in San Francisco, Calif., Nov. 10, 1942; s. Con and Nellie M., owners, Santa Claus House at North Pole; gr. and h. sc., North Pole; B.A., UA, 1965; grad. stud., Cornell U. Law Sc., 1967-68; m. Terry Lucille Niemann in Palmer, July 20, 1963; d. Jennifer; mem., North Pole city council and North Star Borough Assembly, 1963-66, presiding officer, 1964-66; military duty, Ft. Ord, Calif., Apr.-Sept. 1966; state H.R., 1967-69, Sen., 1969-77, majority leader, 1971-72, pres., 1973-74; cand., U.S. Sen., 1974. Mem., Kappa Alpha Psi (frat.). Protestant, Republican. Address: (North Pole) Fairbanks 99705.

MILLSAP, Claude, Jr., businessman. B. in Los Angeles, Calif., 1920; B.A.A., UCLA; m. Gloria; 2 daughters; m. 2d, Pamela (div. 1972); U.S. Coast Guard, Ketchikan, 1944-46; employe, several firms, including Juneau Sawmill, pres., Lumber & Sawmill Workers, Juneau, 1946-48; res., Los Angeles, 1948-60; owner-gen. mgr., Juneau Credit Service Co. and Credit Assn., 1960-63; chmn. (mayor), Greater Juneau Borough, Alaska's first 1st-class borough, 1963-67; exec. dir., Alaska Alcoholic Beverage Control, 1967-70; dir., housing and urban development, FHA, for Alaska, Anchorage, 1970-72; res. Sept. 1, 1972. Mem., Elks, Am. Leg., Alaska Municipal League, Anchorage and Alaska C. of C., State Community Action Program (bd. dir.). Republican.

MISCOVICH, George J., miner. B. in Flat, c. 1916; s. Peter and Stana (Bagoy); h. sc., Fairbanks; m.; U.S. Army Air Corps, WWII; placer miner, Poorman and Flat, during summers, Fairbanks res., during winters; employe, Burgess Constr. Co.; terr. H.R., 1949-55. Catholic, Republican.

MOODY, George Clifford, machinist. B. in Napa, Calif., Nov. 28, 1871; m. Bertha C. Heegler in Napa, June 29, 1892; children: Mrs. Reed Harris, Clifford H., George B., James Edson; learned machinist trade at age 16; went to Dawson, 1899,

Fairbanks, 1904; shop foreman, Brumbaugh, Hamilton & Kellogg, Northern Chemical Co., Fairbanks Exploration Co.; terr. H.R., 1925-27; died in Fairbanks, Sept. 28, 1935. Mem., Eagles (pres.), Pioneers (grand sec., 1925, sec., Igloo 4, Fairbanks, 10 yrs.).

MOODY, Ralph E., lawyer, judge. B. in Vance, Ala., Nov. 23, 1915; s. Charles F. and Harriet R. M.; gr. sc., Citronelle, Ala., Murphy h. sc., Mobile, Ala.; B.A., LL.B., 1940, U. Ala.; m. Carolyn Rose Krebs, May 9, 1942; no children; U.S. Army, Signal Corps, 1940-46; atty. for U.S. Corps of Engrs., Elmendorf AFB, 1946-47; asst. U.S. atty., 3d jud. div., Anchorage, 1947-51; city atty., Anchorage, 1951-54; pvt. law prac., Anchorage, 1954-60; Alaska Sen., 1957-60, majority leader, 1959-60, res.; state atty. gen., Juneau, 1960-62; state superior ct. judge, 3d jud. dist., 1962-, presiding judge, 1964; chmn., legislative council, 1957-59; chmn., state com. on judicial qualifications, 1970-. Mem., Kiwanis (pres.), Elks, Salvation Army Adv. Bd., Greater Anchorage Planning Bd. Democrat. Address: 1032 Cordova, Anchorage 99501.

MOORE, Alfred Stibbs, lawyer. B. in Beaver, Pa., Sept. 13, 1846; s. Alfred R. and Jane (Small) M.; Beaver Acad., Wash. & Jefferson Coll.; B.A., 1867, M.A., 1869, Jefferson Coll.; R.R. employe between St. Louis and Ill., 1865-68, rising from baggage man to conductor; stud. law in pvt. office, Beaver; admitted to bar, 1871; m. Celia J. Richardson, 1883; m. 2d, Florinda M. Knox, Beaver, July 21, 1902; 2 children; pvt. prac., Tidioute, Butler, Beaver, Pa., 1871-1902; dist. atty., Beaver Co., 1880-; U.S. dist. judge, 2d jud. div., Nome, 1902-10; pvt. law prac., Beaver, Dec. 1910-; died in Spartanburg, S.C., Jan. 21, 1920; last rites performed at Beaver. Mem., bd. trustees, Beaver Coll., 20 yrs.; First Natl. Bk. (dir.), Beaver; Alaska Acad. of Sciences (1st pres.); Alaska Geographic Soc. (v.p.). Methodist, Republican.

MOORE, Benjamin P., collector of customs. B. in N.Y.C., 1861; s. J.S. Moore; m. Estelle Meyer in N.Y., Jan. 11, 1894; Indian Agent for Wash. Terr., 1885; collector of customs, Dist. of Alaska, Sitka, 1893-97; promoted gold mining ventures, 1897-1903; left Sitka, 1903. Democrat.

MOORE, Martin B., businessman. B. in Emmonak; son-in-law of Axel Johnson, former state legislator; m.; 3 children; owner, pool hall and grocery store, Emmonak; state H.R., 1971-73; chmn., Kuskokwim Yukon Economic Development & Planning Bd.; v.p., Yukon Delta Fish Marketing Corp. Democrat. Address: Emmonak 99581.

MOORE, Mortimer M., businessman. B. in Mich., June 22, 1913; gr. sc., Puerto Rico; h. sc., Mich.; stud., Bible Coll., Denver, Colo.; m. Marian, 1937; children: Sara Ann, Michael; test driver and inspector, Oldsmobile Co., Lansing, Mich., 1930s-46; homesteaded near Anchorage; employe, city police dept. and instructor, Jack Carr flying service, commerical fishing, 1946-50; employe, dept. taxation, Anchorage, 1950-59; registered guide, 1952; motor vehicle adm., Juneau, 1959-62; insur. salesman and

later employe, Alaska Title Insur. & Trust Co., 1962-67; mgr., Capt. Cook hotel athletic club, 1967-; state H.R., 1967-69. Republican.

MOORE, Neil F., auditor. B. in Mason City, Ia., Feb. 29, 1912; gr. sc., Eatonville, Wash.; h. sc., North Bend, Wash.; m. Rita Lynch, June 30, 1930; children: Michael, Thomas, Deloris, Jean, Earl; employe, Alaska-Juneau mine, 1936-39; clerk, 1939-43, dep. auditor, 1943-50, auditor, 1950-57, terr. auditor's office; employe, Wells, Fargo & Co., San Francisco, Calif., 1957-. Democrat.

MOORE, Dr. Terris, educator, scientist, mountaineer, aviator. B. in Haddonfield, N.J., Apr. 11, 1908; s. Robert Thomas and Selma Helena (Muller) M.; grad., Storm King Sc., Cornwall, N.Y.; B.A., Williams Coll., 1929; M.B.A., 1933, Dr. Commercial Sciences, 1937, Harvard U.; D. Litt., UA, 1967; m. Katrina Eaton Hinks, June 17, 1933; children: Katrina, Henry Winslow; treas.-dir., William R. McAdams, Inc., Boston, 1940-49; instructor, finance, U. Calif., 1937-39; pres., Boston Museum of Science, 1945-48; pres., UA, 1949-53; dir., Mt. Wrangell Research Observatory, 1953; dir., industrial cooperatives, U. Me., 1954-55; prof., bus. adm., Colby Coll., 1955-; scientific and education consult., Cambridge, Mass., 1960s-70s. Author: "Mt. McKinley, The Pioneer Climbs." Mem., Adv. Bd. Geophysical Inst., Am. Geographical Soc. council, Harvard Bd. Overseers Com. for dept. biology & Bussey Inst., Fellow Royal Geographical Soc., Explorers, N.Y.C., St. Botolph, Boston.

MOORE, Thomas James, carpenter. B. in Ballyna, Ireland, Dec. 10, 1917; s. Richard and Catherine (Sadelier) M.; m. (dec.); s. Richard; m. 2d, Mrs. Irene Yeada, Juneau, May 1947; children: Patrick, Irene Faye (Mrs. Christian Warncke), Henry; m. 3d, Mrs. Joan Farleigh, Dec. 23, 1968; res., Ketchikan, 1936-47, Juneau, 1947-51; legislative rep., terr. Fed. of Labor and Fishermen's Union, 1945-49; moved to Anchorage, 1951; cand., terr. comr. labor, 1958; employe, Alaska Industry Bd., 3 yrs.; mediator for labor disputes, terr. dept. labor; technical dir., Anchorage Sand & Gravel Co., 1960s; state comr. labor, 1967-70. Mem., Anchorage Dem. Club (exec. bd.); Mt. View Dem. Club (pres.); Young Dem. of Anchorage (pres.); Anchorage Council PTA (pres.); Anchorage Mental Health Assn. (pres.); Carpenters Local No. 128 (pres., 1953-60); Central Labor Council, Ketchikan (pres., 1946); Alaska Terr. Fed. Labor (pres., 1946-47), Elks, Eagles, Moose, Alaska Statehood Assn. Democrat. Address: 1319 H St., Anchorage 99501.

MORAN, Martin Franklin, miner, banker. B. in Shenandoah, Pa., June 28, 1872; left sc., Kan., and went to sea, 1886; m.; went to southeastern Alaska, 1891; moved to 3d div. and later to Nome, 1900; remained in 2d div.; gold and copper miner; owned copper mine near Shungnak; terr. H.R., from Shungnak, 1915-17; U.S. Comr., Kobuk dist., 8 yrs., Fortuna Lodge, 1917; postmaster, Kiwalik, 1902-05; left Alaska, c. 1920; employe, State Bk., Nekonia, Kan., 1924; bank employe, Hays, Kan., 1927. Mem., Pioneers. Democrat.

MORAN, William J., lawyer. B. in Parkersburg, W. Va., 1917; J.D., U. of W. Va., 1940; m. Sieglinde in Munich, Germany, 1954; s. Liam; special agent, FBI, W. Va., 1941-45; U.S. Army, OSS counterintelligence unit; in charge of de-Nazification with military govt., Munich; in charge of police throughout Bavaria; transferred to Foreign Service Office, U.S. State Dept., Bavaria; consul gen., Frankfurt, 1945-54; worked for terr. legislature, Juneau, 1955; U.S. Comr., Anchorage, 1956-; admitted to bar, 1957, pvt. law prac.; atty., Chugach Electric Assn., 1956-; state H.R., 1965-69, 1971-73; German consul for Alaska, 1962-. Address: 610 C St., Anchorage 99501.

MORISON, James Henderson Stuart, lawyer. B. in Cumberland Gap, Tenn., Dec. 12, 1864; s. Dr. James H.S. and Amanda (Jones) M.; B.A., 1887, M.A., 1889, U. Tenn.; LL.M., Nat. U., Wash., D.C., 1890; LL.D., Lincoln Memorial U., Cumberland Gap, 1930; m. Victoria Morgan of Ewing, Va., May 3, 1899; children: James H.S. (dec.), Edith Morgan (Mrs. William B. Powell); co. judge, Claiborne Co., Tenn., 1910-18; v.p., Lincoln Memorial Coll.; U.S. dist. judge, 2d jud. div., Nome, 1934-44; ret. to Cumberland Gap; died there, Sept. 30, 1952. Author: "Pleadings and Practice" (considered a standard law textbook in Tenn.). Mem., Royal Arch Masons. Disciples of Christ Church, Democrat.

MORKEN, Owen D., engineer, government administrator. B. in Brainerd, Minn., 1912; B.A., Bemidji State Teachers Coll., 1934; asst. camp supt., Net Lake Indian reservation, BIA, Minn., 1939-; worked with Sioux, Hopi, Navajo, on various engring. and adm. jobs; asst. area dir. for economic development, BIA, Aberdeen, S. Dak., 1962-65; area dir., BIA, Juneau, 1965-68; special asst. for Alaskan affairs, Wash., D.C. for a few mos.; area dir., BIA, Minn., Wis., Mich., hdqrs., Minneapolis, Minn., 1968-.

MORRIS, William Gouverneur, collector of customs, lawyer. B. in Morrisania, N.Y., Dec. 25, 1832; father was Army officer; collector of customs, Key West, Fla., 1849; B.A., Georgetown Coll.; LL.B., Harvard U.; clerk, Calif. Supreme Ct., 1857-; fought in Civil War; U.S. Marshal, Calif., 1865-74; special agent, U.S. Treas. Dept., 1875-; made 2 trips to Alaska; collector of customs for Alaska, Sitka, 1881-84; died in Sitka, Jan. 31, 1884; buried in Nat. Cemetery, Sitka. Mem., Masons, Loyal Leg., GAR. Republican.

MORRISON, George A., accountant. B. in Spokane, Wash., 1927; B.A., bus. adm. and secondary teacher's certificate, Gonzaga U., 1945; m.; 3 children; U.S. Army, 1945-46, 1953-55; sc. teacher, Spokane, 3 yrs.; agent, IRS, Southeast Alaska, 1955-57; acct., Ketchikan, 1957-58; IRS, San Francisco, Calif., 1958-59; cost acct., Gen. Telephone, Spokane, 1959-60; exec. dir., Legislative Audit com., Juneau, 1960-67; dep. comr. revenue, July-Nov. 1967, comr., 1967-70; comptroller, Alaska ct. system, 1970-73; internal auditor, Alaska Mutual Savings Bk., Anchorage, 1973-. Republican. Address: 3423 Knik Ave., Anchorage 99503.

MORTON, Rogers Clark Ballard, businessman. B. in Louisville, Ky., Sept. 19, 1914; s. David Cummings and Mary Harris (Ballard) M.; B.A., Yale U., 1937; m. Anne Jones, May 27, 1939; children: David C., Anne McCance; U.S. Army, 1941-45; v.p., Ballard & Ballard, flour miller and food mfr., Louisville, 1946-47, pres., 1947-51 (co. merged with Pillsbury Co., 1951), v.p., Pillsbury, 1951-53, dir., 1953-71; mem., U.S. Cong., 1st dist. Md., 1963-71; Sec. of Interior, 1971-. Mem., Soc. Cincinnati, Minneapolis Club, Chesapeake Bay Yacht Club. Republican.

MOSELEY, Homer W., mechanical engineer, businessman. B. in Okla. City, Okla., Apr. 20, 1907; coll. stud., Okla. City, 2 yrs.; m. Ruth Jones, 1928; children: Wilma Ruth (Mrs. Larry Carr, dec.), Paul L. (dec.); mechanical engr., U.S. Dept. Justice, Okla., 1930-42; U.S. Army Engrs. and Merchant Marine, 1942-46; plumbing and steamfitting bus., Ketchikan, 1946-47; operated commercial ice plant, Anchorage, 1947-49, Homer's Refrigeration Service, Anchorage, 1949-56, coin-operated laundries and cleaning establishments, rental units (owner), Anchorage, 1956-61; state H.R., 1963-66, res.; dir., State Alcoholic Beverage Control Bd., 1966-68. Mem., plumbers & steamfitters union, Masons, Shrine, Aircraft Owners & Pilots Assn., southcentral Dem. dist. com. (chmn.). Democrat. Address: 1510 W. 13th Ave., Anchorage 99501.

MOSES, Carl E., merchant, fisherman. B. in Santa Cruz, Calif., July 16, 1929; ret. to Aleutian I. with mother, 1933; gr. sc., Sanak; h. sc., Seattle, Wash.; stud., U. Wash.; m. Christine; children: Lewis, Arline; U.S. Army, Elmendorf AFB, 1951-53; commercial fisherman for yrs.; estab. gen. store, Carl's Commercial, King Cove, 1960; purchased Northern Commercial Co. interest in Unalaska and sold King Cove holdings, 1966; owner, king crab boat; city councilman, King Cove, 1961; state H.R., 1965-73. Republican. Address: Unalaska 99685.

MOZEE, Benjamin B., U.S. Marshal, prospector. B. in Geneva, Neb., 1886; s. Benjamin Brandon and Lydia (Rankin) M.; h. sc., Geneva; stud., Cotner U., 1 yr.; B.A., Wash. State Coll.; post-grad. stud., Coll. City of N.Y., Cornell U., Columbia U.; m. Jessie Harper, 1916; children: Bonnie Eloise, Jeanne Carolyn, Yvonne Natalie; m. 2d, Narene Elliott, 1928 (dec. 1941); s. Elliott; m. 3d, Margaret Stockton, Nov. 22, 1942; employe, auditor office, Burlington R.R., 1903; moved to Alaska, 1909; mayor, Tanana, 2 terms; dist. supt., Alaska reindeer, medical and sc. service, 1920-28; gen. reindeer supt. of Alaska, 1929-33; clerk, U.S. atty.'s office and ARC, Nome, 1933-34; chief dep. U.S. Marshal, Nome, 1934-37; U.S. Marshal, 2d jud. div., Nome, 1937-53; living in Albuquerque, N. Mex., 1974. Mem., Pioneers, Masons. Democrat.

MULALLEY, James J., lawyer, miner, businessman. B. in Ireland, c. 1879; family moved to Wash. state, then to Ida.; grad., U. Ida., U. Mich.; admitted to Ida. and Alaska bars; m. Miss Augusta Gunderson in Fairbanks, July 28, 1913; 2 sons, eldest named James Marion Hughes; served in Spanish-Am. War; went to Fairbanks, July 1907; elected to first terr.

leg., Nov. 5, 1912, refused to serve because of ill
health, res.; employe, Waechter Bros. & Gardner
and Pacific Cold Storage Co.; estab. store at Fox;
moved to Concrete, Wash., 1913; mercantile bus.,
1913-19; automobile bus., Centralia, Wash.,
1919-29; moved to Calif.; died in Santa Rosa,
Calif., July 1933.

MUNDY, G.M., lawyer. U.S. dist. atty., 2d jud.
div., Nome, 1917-18. Democrat.

MUNLEY, William A., lawyer, journalist. B. in
Carbondale, Pa.; public sc., Carbondale; m.; 4
sons; h. sc. principal, Oliphant, Pa.; moved to Ore.,
1883; city ed., daily newspaper, Portland, 1884-87;
pvt. sec. to Ore. gov., law stud., 1887-95; law
prac., Portland, interested with bros. in mining
property near Wrangell and on Prince of Wales I.,
operated first cannery in Cross Sound, 1899-1902;
asst. U.S. atty., 3d jud. div., Valdez, 1915-16, Anchorage, 1916-17; U.S. dist. atty., 3d jud. div.,
Valdez, 1917-21; ret. to Portland, Ore., 1921; died
there, Apr. 1940. Catholic, Democrat.

MUNSON, Theodore, lawyer. Grad., Cornell U.;
m.; 3 children; law clerk and legal consult., U.S.
dist. ct., Juneau, 1953-54; dist. atty., 1st jud. div.,
Juneau, 1954-56, res.; asst. U.S. atty., northern
N.Y., hdqrs., Syracuse, N.Y., 1956-.

MUNZ, William S., merchant, aviator. B. in Port-
land, Ore., July 12, 1909; s. Victor Emanuel and
Louise (Orchi) M.; h. sc., Portland; m. Wilhelmina
Bernhardt, July 20, 1944; m. 2d, Edith; children:
Donald, Richard, Allison; bush pilot, northern
Alaska, 1934-42; owner-operator, Munz Air Service,
Nome, 1942-55; terr. Sen., from Nome, 1947-51;
ret. to states; res., Congress, Ariz., 1970s, where he
manufactured jade jewelry from his jade mine in
Kobuk. Awarded Air Medal for role in rescue of
bomber crew, crashed Dec. 23, 1947. Republican.

MURANE, Cornelius D., lawyer, miner. B. in Free-
born Co., Minn., Feb. 6, 1867; public sc., Austin,
Minn.; stud., bus. coll.; grad., Northern Ind.
Normal Sc. law dept., 1890; m. Lydia E. Millard,
1892; children: Millard C., Edward Elmer, Ralph;
law prac., Valparaiso, Ind., Austin, Minn.,
1890-92; res., Yakima, Wash., 1892-98; miner,
Dawson, 1898-99; miner-lawyer, Nome, 1899-1909;
municipal judge, Nome, 1904-; cand., del. in
Cong., 1906; U.S. dist. atty., 3d jud. div., Valdez,
1909-10; U.S. dist. judge, 2d jud. div., Nome,
1910-13; prac. law, Seattle, 1914-15; miner-lawyer,
Juneau, 1915-20; Rep. Nat. Com., 1916-20; moved
to Casper, Wyo. Mem., Masons, Odd Fellows,
Eagles. Republican.

MURKOWSKI, Frank Hughes, banker. B. in
Seattle, Wash., Mar. 28, 1933; s. Frank Michael and
Helen Ellen (Hughes) M.; h. sc., Ketchikan; stud.,
Santa Clara U., San Jose Coll.; B.A., Seattle U.,
1955; m. Nancy Rena Gore, 1955; children: Carol
Victoria, Lisa Ann, Michael Francis, Eileen Marie,
Mary Catherine, Brian Patrick; U.S. Coast Guard,
1955-58; employe, Pacific Nat. Bk., Seattle,
1958-59, Nat. Bk. Alaska, 1959-66, asst. cashier, An-
chorage, 1959-62, mgr., Wrangell branch, 1962-66,

v.p. in charge of bus. development, Anchorage,
1966-; state comr. economic development, 1966-70;
cand., U.S. Cong., 1970; pres., Alaska Bk. of North,
Fairbanks and Anchorage, 1971-; moved from Fairbanks to Anchorage, 1973. Mem., Wrangell C. of C.
(pres., 1963-65); Anchorage C. of C. (dir.); state C.
of C. (dir.); Alaska Bankers Assn. (pres.); Elks,
Lions, Jaycees, Alaska Nippon Kae. Catholic, Republican. Address: 4th & E, Anchorage 99501.

MURPHY, Jeremiah C. (Jerry), miner, lawyer. B. in
Wellsville, N.Y., Mar. 26, 1875; gr. and h. sc.,
Minot, N. Dak.; grad., St. John's U., Collegeville,
Minn.; sc. teacher, near Minot; law stud., admitted
to bar, law prac., 1890s; went to Alaska to prospect
for gold; dep. U.S. Marshal, Hot Springs, Fair-
banks, Ft. Gibbon, Iditarod, Ruby, Koyukuk and
Kuskokwim districts, Cordova, 1905-15; moved
from Knik to Anchorage, estab. law office, 1915;
asst. dist. atty., 3d jud. div.; atty. gen., 1919-20,
Juneau; pvt. law prac., Anchorage, 1920-25; died
Mar. 25, 1925. Catholic, Democrat.

MURRAY, Charles J., miner. B. in Co. Donegal,
Ireland, Aug. 14, 1887; mined with bro., Nome,
1908-18; U.S. Army, 1918; ret. to Nome, miner,
until 1921; estab. chain of trading posts, Siberia,
mining, freighting, trading, 1921-26; engaged in
dredging operations between Circle and Eagle,
1926-; fisherman, Cordova, pres., local fishermen's
union, early 1930s; employe, Cliff mine near
Valdez, 1934-; terr. H.R., from Valdez, 1935-37;
miner, Fortymile dist.; sold 34 mining claims, 1947,
ret. to states. Democrat.

MURRAY, Joseph H., lawyer, miner. B. in Albany,
N.Y., June 30, 1877; stud., Sacred Heart Acad.,
Westchester Co., St. Mary's Inst., Amsterdam,
N.Y.; law stud., admitted to N.Y. bar, 1900; unm.;
law prac., N.Y.C., 1900-03; miner-lawyer, between
Valdez and Calamity Gulch (35 mi. from
McCarthy), 1903-26; city magistrate, Valdez,
1907-11; pvt. law prac., Cordova, 1926-44; terr.
H.R., 1917-19, 1921-33; died in Cordova, June 20,
1944. Catholic, Republican.

N

NAUGHTON, Edward F., baker. B. in Cordova, June 14, 1930; h. sc., Kodiak; U.S. Army, 2 yrs., 1950s; postal clerk and coordinator, mental health center, Kodiak; owner-operator, bakery bus., Kodiak; state H.R., 1971-75. Mem., Kodiak Native Assn. (pres.), C. of C. (pres.). Democrat. Address: Box 765, Kodiak 99615.

NECRASON, Conrad F. (Nick), military officer. B. in Cooperstown, N.Y., 1915; grad., U.S. Military Acad., West Point, 1936, Air War Coll., 1949, management sc., George Wash. U.; m. 2d, Myrle Cafee; children: Sandra Anne (Mrs. Arthur F. Kelly, Jr.), Virginia Leigh "Ginger"; command pilot, WWII, Europe, Far East, Philippines, S.W. Pacific; vice comdr., Korean Bomber Command, Korean War; asst. chief of staff for operations, Elmendorf AFB and comdr., 11th Air Div., Ladd AFB, 1957-58; comdr., Alaska Air Command, Elmendorf, 1958-61; comdr., 28th Air Div. and 28th North Am. Air Defense Command, Hamilton AFB, San Francisco, Calif. area, 1961-65; ret. to Novato, Calif., 1965-67; adjt. gen., Nat. Guard, Anchorage, 1967-71; state dir., Selective Service, 1968-71; labor relations exec., Bechtel, Inc., supercontractor, trans-Alaska oil pipeline constr., Fairbanks and Anchorage, Mar.-Dec. 1974; comr. of military affairs, 1974 (Dec.). Legion of Merit medal with oak leaf cluster; Silver Star with oak leaf cluster; Distinguished Flying Cross with oak leaf cluster; Air Medal with 2 oak leaf clusters; Purple Heart; 4 Air Medals; 4 Pres. citations; Bene Merenti Papal medal, 1961. Catholic, Republican.

NELSON, Urban C. (Pete), biologist, forester. B. in Minneapolis, Minn., Jan. 10, 1912; grad., wildlife and forestry, U. Minn., 1935; m. Ruth; d. Anne; agent, Bur. Plant Industry and Soil Conservation Service, USFS, Minn. and Mo., 1935-48; U.S. Bur. of Sports Fisheries & Wildlife, Juneau, 1948-59, reg. dir., Juneau, 1959-62; asst. reg. dir., Minneapolis, 1962-67; asst. reg. dir., Portland, Ore. 1966-67, ret.; state comr., Fish and Game, Juneau, 1967-68; dep. comr., Sport Fish and Game, Feb.-May 1968. Republican. Address: Juneau 99801.

NERLAND, Andrew, merchant. B. in Molda, Norway, Apr. 18, 1870; emigrated to U.S., settling in Minneapolis, Minn., 1885; h. sc., Minneapolis, Minn.; moved to Seattle, Wash., 1889; stud., bus. coll. and night sc., painting and wallpapering trades; hon. LL.D., UA, 1952; m. Annie Paulson in Seattle, Oct. 16, 1899; s. Arthur Leslie; estab. paint and wallpaper contracting bus., Dawson, 1898, Fairbanks, 1904, branches in Nenana, Iditarod, Anchorage; gradually shifted to furniture bus.; estab. residency, Fairbanks, 1929; city councilman, 1914, mayor, 1915, Fairbanks; terr. H.R., 1917-19, 1921-23, 1931-39; terr. Sen., 1945-51, pres., 1947; died of heart attack in his Fairbanks store, Feb. 6, 1956. Mem., bd. trustees, UA, 1929-56 (pres., 1934-56); Pioneers (grand pres. grand igloo, 1934); Masons (33d degree); Alaska Statehood Com., 1949-56. Presbyterian, Republican.

NERLAND, Arthur Leslie, merchant. B. in Dawson, Y.T., Mar. 11, 1902; s. Andrew and Annie (Paulson) N.; gr. and h. sc., Seattle, Wash.; B.B.A., U. Wash., 1924; m. Mildred J. Kildall, Jan. 16, 1926; children: Stuart Gerald (Jerry), Ronald, Milesse N. (Mrs. Woleben); salesman, streetcar advertising co., Seattle, 1925-27; salesman, Frigidaire Sales Corp., Seattle, 1927-29; partner with father in furniture bus., hdqrs., Fairbanks, 1930-; city councilman, 1932-38, mayor, 1938-40, Fairbanks; chmn., Fairbanks War Finance Com., 1941-45; mem., Alaska Development Bd., 1945-47; del., const. conv., 1955-56; mem., bd. dir., Alaska Nat. Bk. of Fairbanks (pres. and chmn. bd., 1953-). Mem., Pioneers, Lambda Chi Alpha, Alpha Delta Sigma, Masons, Shrine, Rotary. Presbyterian, Republican.

NESBETT, Buell A., lawyer, judge. B. in Estancia, N. Mex., June 2, 1910; stud., electrical and radio engring., U. N. Mex., Stanford U.; LL.B., U. San Francisco, 1940; m. Barbara; children: Raymond, Marianne (Mrs. Tyron Wieland), Barbara (Mrs. Stephen M. Clark), Linda, Walter, Elizabeth; probation and parole officer, San Francisco, 1938-40; U.S. Navy, rank of comdr., won bronze star medal, 1940-45; pvt. law prac., Anchorage, 1945-59; city magistrate, Anchorage, 1946-47, 1948-52; referee in bankruptcy for Alaska; chief justice, state supreme ct., Anchorage, 1959-70, ret. due to eye injury suffered in pvt. plane accident, 1969; moved to Solana Beach, Calif., 1972. Mem., Calif., Alaska, Anchorage, Am. Bar Assns., Anchorage Charter Com., Am. Judicature Soc., Elks, Scottish Rite. Protestant, Democrat.

NEWELL, Harry F., businessman. B. in Ketchikan, July 20, 1923; s. Harry V. and Mary T. (Snyder) N.; grad., Ketchikan h. sc., 1941; m. Florence Lorine Schahuber, Jan. 17, 1944; children: Steven Anthony, Carole Lorine, Douglas B., Sharon L.; U.S. Army Air Corps, 1942-45; partner with father, owner-operator, Ketchikan Wholesale Grocery Co., 1945-; terr. H.R., 1947-49. Mem., Ketchikan C. of C., Am. Leg., VFW, Elks. Catholic, Democrat.

NEWMARKER, John Paul, steamboat inspector, marine engineer. B. in Clarion, Pa., Sept. 26, 1875; m. Virginia; s. Jack; family moved to Olympia, Wash., when child; orphaned, 1891; oiler on tugs, later on ships to Alaska during goldrush and to Orient; U.S. Army, WWI, U.S. Coast Guard, 1943-45; U.S. SS Inspection Service, Dept. Commerce, Alaska dist., 1919-; pvt. marine surveying, 1945-49; moved to Wash. state, 1949; died in Woodburn, Ore., June 1965.

NICHOLS, Stanley Joseph, U.S. Marshal, businessman. B. in San Francisco, Calif., Feb. 21, 1897; s. Walter Ryan and Minnie Susan (McGratton) N.; stud., bus. coll., San Francisco; m. Marguerite Lyman in Anchorage, Oct. 26, 1942; U.S. Army field infantry, 1917-18; went to Alaska immediately after WWI; dep. U.S. Marshal, 3d jud. dist., Takotna, McGrath, Nenana, Anchorage, 1928-42; prop., trading posts, Ruby, Galena, McGrath, 1942-46; del., Dem. Nat. Conv., 1944; U.S. Marshal, 4th jud. div., Fairbanks, 1946-51; died in Key West, Fla., found unconscious in motor court, Feb. 11, 1951; interment in Nat. Cemetery, San Francisco. Mem., Am. Leg. (dept. comdr., 1937-38), Fairbanks Golf & Country Club, C. of C., Elks, Lions. Catholic, Democrat.

NIEMI, William J., civil engineer. B. in Calumet, Mich., 1904; gr. sc., Douglas; h. sc., Anchorage; B.S., Colo. Sc. of Mines, 1926; m. Bernice Kingsbury, 1929; children: Miriam Anne, Celia Beth; lived in Gastineau Channel area, 1910-18, Anchorage, 1919-21; constr. engr., Alaska R.R., 1926-28; chief of surveys, U.S. Smelting & Refining, Fairbanks, 1929-30; constr. engr., ARC, Chitina, Cordova, Anchorage, Palmer, 1930-41; U.S. Army Corps Engrs., rising from capt. to col., 1941-45; engr., Bur. Reclamation, Pasco, Wash., 1946-49; dist. engr., ARC, Anchorage, 1949-50; chief of operation div., ARC, Juneau, 1950-51, chief engr., 1951-56; asst. div. engr., BPR, 1956-59, reg. engr., 1959-62; reg. adm., Fed. Highway Adm., 1962-67; ret. to Ore. Awarded meritorious service silver medal by U.S. Dept. Commerce, 1965; elected to Alaska Press Club's 49er Hall of Fame, 1967.

NOBLE, John Willock, lawyer. B. in Lancaster, O., Oct. 26, 1831; s. John and Catherine (McDill) N.; stud., Miami Coll., 3 yrs.; B.A., honors, Yale U., 1851; LL.B., Cincinnati Law Sc., 1852; m. Lisabeth Halsted, Feb. 8, 1864; law prac., Keokuk, Ia., 1856-61; fought in Civil War, breveted brig. gen.; U.S. dist. atty., St. Louis, Mo., 1867-70; pvt. prac., St. Louis, 1870-89; Sec. of Interior, 1889-93; died in St. Louis, Mar. 22, 1912. Mem., GAR, Sons of Veterans. Presbyterian, Republican.

NOERENBERG, Wallace H., biologist. B. in Longview, Wash., 1924; mem., Fisheries Research Inst., U. Wash., stationed in Bristol Bay, Chignik, Kodiak, Prince William Sound, Cook Inlet, Southeastern, 1949-60; researcher, State of Alaska, stationed at Cordova to make life hist. studies of salmon, 1960; state dir., biological research, Juneau, 1964-67; dep. comr., commercial fish and game, 1968-69; comr., fish and game, 1969-72, res.; moved to Longview, Wash.; part-time fisheries consult. Received award from Gov. for outstanding service to Alaska.

NOLAN, James, businessman. B. in Boston, Mass., June 23, 1901; s. John J. and Mary (Ringrose) N.; h. sc., Boston; m. Elsie Sylvester in Wrangell, July 19, 1925; lithographer, Am. Can Co., Boston, 1917-20; went to Wrangell; misc. jobs, including Vt. Marble Co., Prince of Wales I., 1920-24; ice cream and confectionary bus. with short-order lunch room; commercial fisherman during summer mos.; dep. U.S. Marshal, 1924-, 1934-45; purchased Wrangell Drug Co., 1941, and combined both businesses; city councilman, Wrangell, 3 terms; terr. H.R., 1947-51, speaker, 1949 special session; terr. Sen., pres., 1955;

del., const. conv., 1955-56; chmn., Selective Service bd., 1944-46. Mem., Elks, Redmen, Wrangell C. of C. (pres.). Catholic, Democrat.

NOON, John, miner, businessman. B. in Red Bluff, Calif., Aug. 10, 1859; m. Clara in Salidas, Calif., 1889 (div. 1904); m. 2d, Martha E. Kepfe in Valdez, 1908; s. John Henry; worked in various Calif. gold mining camps; hotel prop., Redding, Calif., and in Mohave country, 1880s; went to Juneau, 1895, Cook Inlet area, 1896, Dawson, 1897, Nome, 1899, Circle City, 1900, Nome and Koyukuk, Seward, 1903; bus. with Cal M. Brosius, operating planing mill, hardware store, fish cannery and constr. contracting firm; operated wayside inn on Valdez Glacier; terr. H.R., from Seward, 1915-17, 1919-20; left Alaska, 1920, due to ill health; died of diabetes in Portland, Ore., July 26, 1923; cremated and ashes scattered in Resurrection Bay. Mem., Masons, Elks, Moose, Odd Fellows, Pioneers. Democrat.

NORBY, Theo (Theophilus) J., educator. B. in Bellingham, Wash., 1908; public sc., Bellingham; B.A., M.A. (1936), U. Ore.; Ed.D., Stanford U.; m. 2d, 1958; 4 children; teacher, Glenoma, Wash., 1928-29; principal, Mossyrock, Wash., Stayton, Ore., Milwaukie, Ore., Vancouver, Wash., 1929-; supt. sc., Ashland, Ore., 1937-38, San Leandro, Calif., 6 yrs., Inglewood, Calif. unified sc. dist., 6 yrs.; asst. supt., San Diego, Calif.; asst. supt., Marin Co., San Rafael, Calif., 1959 (2 mos.); state comr. of education, 1959-62, res. Mem., Rotary, Boy Scouts of Am. (comr.), Ore. Supts.' Assn. (past pres.).

NORDALE, Alfeld Hjalmar, journalist, hotel proprietor. B. in Seattle, Wash., June 19, 1894; s. Anton Johann and Anna Mathilda (Anderson) N.; gr. and h. sc., Fairbanks; stud., Stanford U.; m. LaDessa Hall in Fairbanks, June 9, 1926; s. Anthony John; commercial photographer, 1913-15; game warden, 4th jud. div., 1916-17; U.S. Army, 1918-19; reporter and managing ed., Fairbanks NEWS-MINER, 1919-30; acct., Am. Airways, Alaska div., Fairbanks, 1930-32; traffic dept., Pacific-Alaska Airways (later Pan-Am. Airways), 1932-44; mgr., Nordale Hotel, 1940s; city councilman and mayor, Fairbanks, 3 terms each, 1942-48; terr. Sen., 1941-45; died of heart attack in his home, Jan. 7, 1952. Mem., Am. Leg., Pioneers, Masons. Democrat.

NORDALE, Alton Gerald, miner. B. in Dawson, Y.T., May 28, 1900; s. Anton Johann and Anna Mathilda (Anderson) N.; public sc., Fairbanks, 3 yrs.; stud., U. Wash.; m. Katherine Driscoll in Spokane, Wash., Feb. 21, 1930; children: Mary Anita, James Driscoll; moved to Fairbanks with parents, 1908; employe, ARC, 3 yrs.; mgr., Nordale Hotel; terr. H.R., 1933-35; appt. dep. clerk of dist. ct., July 1935; killed in airplane crash, Aug. 19, 1935. Democrat.

NORDALE, Anton Johann, hotel proprietor. B. in Goteborg, Sweden, Sept. 10, 1869; m. Anna Mathilda Anderson, 1893; children: Alfeld Hjalmar, Arnold M., Alton G., Anita Marie (Mrs. Willard Cox), Adler Jennings, Alice Dolores (Mrs. L.

Couey); emigrated to U.S., settling in Omaha, Neb., 1886; prop., restaurants, San Francisco, Calif., Seattle, Wash., 1887-96; res., Juneau, 1896-97; estab. hotel and restaurant bus., Dawson, 1897-1904; estab. hotel at Cleary City, 1904-08, Fairbanks, 1908-30; terr. H.R., 1919-21; city councilman and mayor, Fairbanks; died in Swedish hospital, Seattle, Sept. 9, 1930. Democrat.

NORDALE, Katherine Driscoll, school teacher, secretary. B. in Reardan, Wash.; d. James Cornelius and Mary (Berrigan) Driscoll; B.A., Wash. State U., 1925; m. Alton Gerald Nordale, Feb. 21, 1930 (dec. Aug. 19, 1935); children: James Driscoll, Mary Anita; h. sc. teacher, Fairbanks, 1925-27, Grandview, Wash., 1928-29; dep. clerk of ct., 4th jud. div., Fairbanks, 1935-43; dep. adm., War Finance Com. for Alaska, in charge of war bonds and stamp sales, 1943-47; head of Fed. Security Agency, 1947-51; U.S. Collector of Customs, 1951-53; employe, terr. treasury office, 1953-59; Dem. Nat. Com., 1954-56; del., const. conv., 1955-56; exec. asst., state dept. commerce, 1959-60; election supervisor, 1960; staff mem., Legislative Council, 1961-63; postmaster, Juneau, 1964-71. Mem., Pioneers' Aux. Catholic, Democrat.

NORENE, James E., realtor. B. in Portland, Ore., Aug. 30, 1905; h. sc. extension courses; m. Vivian Edith Erickson, 1928 (div.); children: Robert James, Joan Vee (Mrs. Larry Anderson); lived in Juneau and Kodiak, 1939; moved to Anchorage, 1940; employe, U.S. Dist. Engrs.; prop., grocery store, Mt. View, Anchorage suburb, 1944-47; estab. Norene Realty, 1947; paint contractor, 1952; Alaska H.R., 1957-61; mem., Anchorage sc. bd., 4 yrs.; Anchorage City Planning Com., many yrs. Mem., Lions. Democrat. Address: 717 Irwin St., Anchorage.

NOTTI, Emil Reynold, electronics engineer. B. in Koyukuk, Mar. 11, 1933; s. Joseph and Madeline Pitka (Pavalov) N.; gr. sc., Eklutna boarding sc.; grad., Mt. Edgecumbe h. sc., 1951; A.A., Marshall Coll., Huntington, W. Va.; B.S.E.E., Northrup Inst. Technology, Inglewood, Calif., 1961; postgrad., engring., UCLA; hon. Dr. Humane Letters, AMU, 1969; m. Lenora Peterson in Anchorage, 1964; children: John, Cynthia, Joseph; U.S. Navy, electronic technician's sc., 1952-56; design engr., FAA, Alaska, 1963-65; pres., Cook Inlet Native Assn., hdqrs., Anchorage, 1962-67; field rep., State Human Rights Com., 1966-67; southcentral reg. coordinator, State Community Action Program, Jan.-Apr., 1967; mem., Greater Anchorage Ind. Sc. Bd., 1967-68; owner-operator, electronic bus., Sitka, 1969-72; exec. dir., Alaska Native Found., Anchorage, 1972-; cand., sec. of state, 1970, U.S. Cong., 1973; chmn., Dem. state central com., 1972-73; dep. comr., health and welfare, Juneau, 1971-72; mem., state rural affairs com. (chmn., 1971); bd. dir., Nat. Bk. Alaska, 1973-. Address: 1905 W. 47th Ave., Anchorage.

NOYES, Arthur H., lawyer. B. in Baraboo, Wis., 1854; grad., Baraboo h. sc., 1872, Wis. State U., 1876; LL.B., U. Wis., 1878; pvt. law prac., Grand Forks, N. Dak., 1878-85, Minneapolis, Minn., 1886-

1900; cand., dist. judge, Hennepin Co., Minn., 1900; dist. judge, 2d jud. div., Nome, 1900-02. Mem., A.B. Republican.

NOYES, John R., civil engineer. B. in Kenwood, near Oneida, N.Y., Apr. 5, 1902; s. Charles R. and Gertrude (Hayes) N.; grad., U.S. Military Acad., West Point, 1923; civil engr. degree, Cornell U., 1926; m. Eunice Zimmerman in Juneau, 1928 (dec. 1952); children: John Zimmerman, Daniel H.; m. 2d, Lily Erickson in Juneau, Mar. 4, 1955; s. Eric; engr., ARC, 1926-; U.S. Army Corps Engrs., Alaska, 1932-34; transportation officer, 6th Army Group, France and Germany, decorated twice, made Chevalier of Legion of Honor by French govt., 1942-46; comr. of roads, 1948-51; ret. from Army, July 31, 1953; adjt. gen., Nat. Guard, 1953-56; died in Nome hospital from injuries sustained in plane crash 4 days earlier on Nat. Guard inspection tour, Jan. 31, 1956; Noyes Mt. in Mentasta Mts., 50 mi. south of Tok, named in his honor. Mem., Am. Leg., VFW, Elks, Explorers, N.Y.C., Am. Soc. Civil Engrs., Soc. Am. Military Engrs., Nat. Defense Transportation Assn., Arctic Inst. North Am., Nat. Guard Assn., Army & Navy Club, Wash., D.C.

NUSUNGINYA, John, carpenter, businessman. B. in Barrow, 1928; m. Vera Bolt (dec. 1961); 7 children; delivery service bus., Barrow; mayor and civil defense dir., Barrow; state H.R., 1959-63. Democrat.

NYLEN, Andrew, miner. B. in Sweden, 1862; m. Miss Mabel Nigh Ranum in Juneau, May 23, 1932; went to Nome, 1900, engaged in mining operations; terr. H.R., from Nome, 1925-27, 1929-31, from Solomon, 1931-33; moved to North Bonneville, Wash., 1958; died there, Jan. 13, 1958. Mem., Alaska-Yukon Pioneers, Masons. Independent.

O

OCCHIPINTI, C.J. (Connie), lawyer, judge. B. in N.Y.C., Mar. 23, 1922; s. Giovanni C.O.; stud., N.Y.C. Coll., 1940-42, Ariz. State U., 1949-50, Whittier Coll., 1951-52; J.D., Gonzaga U., 1962; m. and div.; m. 2d, Anita Sue Menath, June 1961; children: Carl, Lori; U.S. Army, 1942-46 (stationed in Ft. Richardson, 1945-46); employe, Alaska R.R., accounting dept., 1946-51, IRS, Anchorage, 1952-58, Social Security Adm., Spokane, Wash., 1958-62; asst. atty. gen., Anchorage, 1962-63; pvt. law prac., Anchorage, 1963-68; superior ct. judge, 3d jud. dist., Anchorage, 1968- (presiding, 1972-). Mem., Elks, Am. Leg. Catholic, Republican. Address: 2946 Madison Way, Anchorage 99502.

O'CONNELL, John W., plumber. B. c. 1910; m. Claudia; children: Mrs. Donald Peterson, Charles Lewis; family moved to Alaska, 1942; U.S. Navy, 1943-45; moved to Fairbanks; estab. plumbing and heating bus., Sitka, 1950s; state H.R., 1965-67; mayor, Sitka, 1963-67; sales rep., Alaska Airlines, 1970; died in Sitka, Feb. 14, 1971; bridge between Japonski I. and Sitka named in his honor, 1972. Mem., Am. Leg., VFW, Elks, ANB. Democrat.

OHLSON, Otto Frederick, railroad executive. B. in Halmstadt, Sweden, June 6, 1870; s. Otto and Cecelia (Swenson) O.; grad., Electric Technique, Stockholm, 1890; m. Marie E. Richetts, Sept. 1897 (dec. 1930s); electrician in South Africa and India; seaman on English sailing ship, received honorable discharge when ship docked at N.Y.C., 1893; employe, Pa. R.R., 1893-1901; U.S. citizen, Franklin Co., O., Mar. 10, 1899; U.S. Army, 1917-19; telegraph operator, station agent, train dispatcher, train master, asst. to gen. supt., directing supt., Northern Pacific R.R., 1901-28; gen. mgr., Alaska R.R., 1928-45; appt. receiver for sawmill, Wrangell, 1945-46; lived in Seattle, Wash. for several yrs.; made a world tour before entering veterans' hospital; died in hospital, Hampton, Va., June 19, 1956. Lutheran, Republican.

OLIVER, Robert W., U.S. Marshal, 2d jud. div., Nome, 1955-60. Republican.

O'CONNOR, William, lawyer, editor. Admitted to Alaska bar, fall 1909; ed., MINERS' UNION BULLETIN, Fairbanks; cand., del. in Cong., on Labor ticket, 1910; blacksmith in Fairbanks mines. Mem., Western Fed. Miners.

OLSEN, Lloyd Clarence, travel agent. B. in Rice Lake, Wis., June 26, 1905; s. Emil and Louise (Hanson) O.; stud., St. Olaf Coll., Northfield, Minn.; grad., Am. Inst. of Banking, Minneapolis, Minn., 1934; unm.; bk. examiner, Minneapolis; fiscal agent, Matanuska Valley Farmers Cooperative, Palmer, 1939-42; U.S. Army, Ft. Richardson, 1942-45; dir., Tours to Alaska, 1946-47; part-owner-operator, Anchorage Travel Bur., 1947-; terr. H.R., 1953-55; moved to Minneapolis, 1957; moved to Franklin, Tenn.; died there, Aug. 21, 1971. Lutheran, Republican.

OLSEN, William Holman, lawyer. B. in Loring, Aug. 11, 1920; s. John and Louise (Holman) O.; gr. and h. sc., Ketchikan; LL.B., U. LaSalle; m. Hazel Burr, Dec. 6, 1942; 5 sons, 1 d.; U.S. Army, 1941-46; admitted to bar, Juneau, Dec. 30, 1944; pvt. law prac. and 1st city magistrate, Anchorage, 1946-54; dir., BIA, Juneau, 1954-58, res.; special agent as life underwriter, Prudential Insur. Co., Seattle, Wash., 1958-. Mem., Anchorage Rep. Club (pres.), U.S. C. of C. (dir.), WWII Veterans Com. for Alaska, Elks, VFW, Odd Fellows, Kiwanis. Republican.

OLSON, Oscar G., accountant, banker. B. in Newfolden, Minn., Jan. 23, 1891; s. Hans and Hansine (Samuelson) O.; public sc. and bus. coll.; m. Aileene T. Cohen; children: Claire Ella, Carol Ann; m. 2d, Ethel Egan; U.S. Army, Ft. Gibbon, Alaska, 1914-18, Camp Dodge, Ia., 1918-19; clerk, agent, cashier, Copper River & Northwestern Ry., Cordova, 1920-35; terr. treas., 1935-49; organizer and 1st pres., Bk. of Fairbanks, sold to A.E. Lathrop, 1940-41; Dem. Nat. Com., 1940-44; died in Air Force hospital, Anchorage, Nov. 1963. Mem., Am. Leg., Sons of Norway, Elks. Democrat.

OLSON, Robert D., U.S. Marshal. B. in 1934; m.; reserve dep. sheriff for King Co., Wash., 1956-63; state trooper, with rank of corporal, Fairbanks and Tok, 1963-69; U.S. Marshal for Dist. of Alaska, 1969 (Dec.)-78 (reconfirmed, Mar. 1974, for another 4-yr. term). Mem., Anchorage chapter (pres.) and state Peace Officers' Assn. Republican.

O'NEIL, Hugh, lawyer, journalist. B. in Bodie, Calif., June 25, 1882; h. sc., Virginia City, Nev.; B.A., LL.B., U. Calif.; m. Lily Theoline Ingwaldson in Nome, 1913; law prac. in San Francisco, Valdez, Ft. Gibbon (1911-12); res., Nome, 1912-39; pub., THE NOME DEMOCRAT, weekly newspaper, 1912-14; U.S. Comr., 1917-20; special asst. to U.S. atty., 1920-21; asst. U.S. atty., 1921-25; city atty., 1925-33; U.S. dist. atty., 2d jud. div., Nome, 1933-39; died of heart attack, Jan. 24, 1939. Democrat.

OPLAND, Robert N., lawyer. B. in Minot, N. Dak., 1928; h. sc., Anchorage; stud., UA; B.A., 1952, J.D., 1954, U. N. Dak.; m.; 4 children; moved to Alaska, 1938, with parents who were BIA teachers at Igloo, Teller, Dillingham, Kanakanak, Cordova, Fairbanks; law prac., Fairbanks, Cordova, Anchorage; dep. U.S. Comr., Anchorage, 1957; dist. magistrate; joined Alaska's dept. of law, Sept. 15, 1960; asst. dist. atty., Fairbanks, Jan.-June, 1961, Anchorage, 1961-67; state dist. atty., 3d jud. div., Anchorage, June-Sept., 1967; pvt. law prac., Anchorage, 1967-.

ORBECK, Edmund N., labor union official. B. in West Union, Minn., Sept. 16, 1915; stud., Winona (Minn.) Teacher's Coll., Columbia Coll., Ia., Knox Coll., Ill.; m. Sherry; children: Sharon Lynn (Mrs. Hersey L. Wright), John; professional football player with various teams, including Milwaukee Chiefs; shipyard supt., Consolidated Steel at Terminal I. shipyard, Los Angeles, Calif., 1943-45; constr. foreman, M-K Co., Fairbanks, and football coach, UA, 1949-50; professional football, L.A. Bulldogs and Hollywood Rangers, 1950-51; agent, Laborers' Union, Fairbanks; state H.R., 1959 (appt.), 1965-73; state Sen., 1960-61 (appt.); city councilman, Fairbanks, 1957-59; state comr. labor, 1975-. Mem., Elks, Eagles, Kiwanis, Tanana Valley Grange, YMCA bd., Laborers' Union Local No. 942 (pres.), Boy Scouts (exec. bd.), C. of C. (bd. dir.). Methodist, Democrat. Address: 1033 Lathrop St., Fairbanks.

ORR, Edward S., teamster. B. in 1854; m.; s. Thorold; mayor, Tacoma, Wash.; operated tramway across Chilkoot Pass for T.B. & Hugh C. Wallace, Tacoma capitalists, 1898-1900; stage coach freighting bus., Dawson, 1900-04; moved to Fairbanks; estab. first stage coach line over Valdez-Fairbanks Road (later Richardson Highway); mayor, Fairbanks; cand., del. in Cong., 1910; lumber bus., Chehalis, Wash.; died there, June 29, 1926. Mem., Masons. Republican.

ORSINI, Joseph L., professor, engineer. B. on Staten I., N.Y., May 18, 1939; B.S., Princeton U.; B.A., Sacramento State, 1970; M.S., UA; m. Janice V.; U.S. Army, Ft. Richardson, 1961-64; employe, U.S. Army Corps Engrs., 1964-; prof., engring. management, UA, Anchorage, 1969-; state H.R., 1973-75; engr., Tryck, Nyman & Hayes, Anchorage, 1974-. Mem., Am. Soc. Engring. Education; Faculty Assn. of UA, Anch. (pres.). Republican. Address: 2912 Alder Dr., Anchorage 99504.

OSE, Alfred O., farmer, educator. B. in Brinsmade, N. Dak., Feb. 4, 1916; M.A., education; m. Buela; U.S. Army Air Corps in Alaska, 1941-46; ret. to Alaska, 1962; principal, Wasilla Jr.-Sr. h. sc., 1962-70; principal, Central Jr. h. sc., Palmer, 1970-73; state H.R., 1973-77. Democrat. Address: Box 832, Palmer 99645.

O'SHEA, John Joseph, mining assayer, insurance and real estate agent. B. in Fairbanks, Mar. 4, 1910; gr. sc., Fairbanks; h. sc., Enumclaw, Wash.; B.S., UA, 1939; m. Florence Mary Walker, Nov. 23, 1938; children: Mary Jane (Mrs. Robert C. Townsend), William John; gold-room foreman, Fairbanks Exploration Co., 1938-43; terr. H.R., 1943; U.S. Army, 1943-45; coal analyst, Alaska R.R., 1945-48; assayer, terr. dept. mines, Anchorage, 1948-51; agent, Equitable Life Assurance Soc., 1951-58; real estate agent, Anchorage, 1958-70; dir., div. of insur., dept. commerce, Juneau, 1970-; Anchorage sc. bd., 1953-58, pres., 1957; Greater Anchorage Health dist. bd., 1951-53; Alaska Insur. Com., 1955-58. Mem., Nat. Assn. of Life Underwriters, Am. Leg., 40 & 8, Lions, Elks. Catholic, Democrat.

OST, Ludvig Evald, missionary. B. in Grangarde, Sweden, Oct. 2, 1885; public sc., Triumph, Minn.; grad. as Swedish Covenant church missionary, North Park Coll., Chicago; m. Ruth Elim Hall in Ashland, Wis., July 15, 1910 (dec., Nome, 1953); children: Ruth Elizabeth, Lois, John, Nathan, Joseph, Lincoln, Dennis; missionary, Golovin, Elim, Council, Fortuna Ledge, 1910-1960s; freighting bus., Golovin and Council area; terr. H.R., 1947-49. Republican.

OVERFIELD, Peter D., lawyer, miner. B. in Auburn, Pa., 1875; s. Paul J. and Sarah (Roe) O.; stud., Mansfield State Normal Sc., Auburn; B.A., 1899, LL.B., 1901, U. Pa.; m. Virginia Beale Leckie of Wash., Apr. 28, 1906; fought in Puerto Rico, Spanish-Am. War, 1898; law prac., Pittsburg, Colo., Portland, Ore.; miner-lawyer, Nome, 1903-; U.S. dist. judge, 4th jud. div., Fairbanks, 1909-12, 3d jud. div., Valdez, 1912-13; estab. law office in Los Angeles, Calif., 1913; law prac., Oatman, Ariz., 1916, still maintaining L.A. office; head of Overfield Sheafe Motor Co., L.A., distributor of Stutz automobiles, 1924. Mem., Sigma Chi (frat.). Republican.

OWEN, Alfred Aaron, labor union official, fisherman. B. in Seattle, Wash., Mar. 7, 1910; B.A., U. Wash.; m. Hazel; 7 children; operated shingle mill, Kennydale, Wash., 1932-38; moved mill to Ketchikan, 1938-42; chief clerk, Post Engrs., Ft. Greely, also employe, War Manpower Com., Fairbanks, 1942-45; mgr., terr. employment service office, Kodiak, and fished commercially, 1945-50; dir., U.S. Dept. Labor apprenticeship training program; sec., United Fishermen of Cook Inlet, bus. agent, Internat. Longshoremen's Assn., Local No. 38171; public relations rep., Laborers' Local No. 341, Anchorage; terr. H.R., from Kodiak, 1949-51; Alaska Sen., from Anchorage, 1955-59, from Uganik Bay, 1959-67; cand., terr. comr. labor, 1950; operated sales agency for heavy duty equipment, Anchorage, 1957-59; estab. cannery at Uganik Bay, Kodiak I., 1959-. Mem., U.S. State Dept.'s Fishery Industry Adv. Com.; adv. com., Am. section, Internat. North Pacific Fisheries com. (chmn.); Anchorage port com., 6 yrs.; city council, Anchorage and Kodiak.

P

PALMER, Harry B., civil engineer. B. in Charleston, S.C., Mar. 6, 1914; s. Melville K. and Nellie Augusta (Holmes) P.; gr. sc., New Orleans, La.; h. sc., Petersburg, Fla.; B.S., UA; stud., San Francisco Law Sc., 1956-; m. Ruth E. Avey, Aug. 20, 1944; children: Delphine Ann, Arlene Kay; law clerk, N.Y.C.; employe, Alaska-Juneau mine, 1936-39; office mgr., Castleton & Keenan, Nome, 1939-41; surveyor, U.S.E.D., Ladd Field, 1941-42; field engr., CAA, 1942-43; U.S. Army Corps Engrs., 1943-45; chief, sales section, surplus property, RFC, 1945-; project engr., Haddock engrs., Anchorage, 1951-54; terr. H.R., 1955-56; project mgr., Ramstad Constr. Co., Anchorage, 1955-56; left Alaska to attend law sc., San Francisco, 1956. Mem., Am. Inst., Mining & Metallurgy Engrs., Elks, Am. Leg., VFW, Toastmaster Internat. Episcopalian, Republican.

PALMER, Walter I. (Bob), school teacher, fisherman, farmer, aircraft engineer. B. in Hutchinson, Kan., Aug. 7, 1926; h. sc., Hutchinson, 1944; B.S., Mich. State U., 1948; grad. stud., UA; m. Sue; children: David, Katherine, Steven, Cindy, Sandy, James, Earl; U.S. Navy aviation cadets, 1944-46; employe, Fairbanks Exploration Co., Fairbanks, and carpenter, Big Delta AFB, summer 1947; homesteaded at Ninilchik, working as sc. teacher, farmer, commercial fisherman, 1948-53, 1960-; farmer and engr., Douglas Aircraft Corp., Tulsa, Okla., 1953-60; state Sen., 1967-74; exec. asst. to gov., 1974-78; named conservative legislator of the year in Alaska by nat. organization, 1970; del., Internat. Law of Sea conf., Geneva, 1973; selected by Rutgers U. as outstanding legislator, 1968, to attend Eagleton Inst. of Politics seminar. Mem., Am. Leg., Alaska Conservation Soc., C. of C. Methodist, Republican.

PARKER, Walter B., community planner. B. in Spokane, Wash., Aug. 11, 1926; s. Bruce V. and Lucile K. P.; stud., UA, AMU, U. Wash., Syracuse U., George Wash. U., U. Puget Sound; m. Patricia I.; children: Sandra (Mrs. Roberts), Patrick B., Douglas S., Lisa M.; U.S. Navy, 1944-46; active reserve, U.S. Navy, 1946-54; went to Alaska, 1946; research assoc., UA, 1971-73; mem., Greater Anchorage Area Borough assembly, 1971-74; comr. of highways, 1974-. Mem., Arctic Inst., Alaska Conservation Soc., Nordic Ski Club, Am. Soc. for Public Adm., Alaska Center for the Environment. Address: 3724 Campbell Airstrip Rd., Anchorage.

PARKER, William K., ironworker, journalist. B. in Des Moines, Ia., Sept. 24, 1944; B.S., Immaculate Conception Seminary, Conception, Mo., St. Joseph's Seminary, Yonkers, N.Y.; m. Peggy; d. Mara; went to Anchorage, 1965; union ironworker, aux. fireman, cannery worker, counselor in regional h. sc. dormitory, Kodiak, newspaper sportswriter, Anchorage; employe, state economic opportunity office, Anchorage; state H.R., 1973-77. Mem., Ad Hoc Organizing Com. of Young Democrats, 1972. Catholic, Democrat. Address: 917 Cordova St., Anchorage 99501.

PARKS, George Alexander, cadastral engineer. B. in Denver, O., May 29, 1883; s. James and Mary Leach (Ferguson) P.; Denver h. sc.; E.M., Colo. Sc. of Mines, 1906; unm.; mining engr., Mexico, Can., western U.S.; went to Alaska, 1907; mineral examiner, U.S. Land Office, Alaska, 1908-17; U.S. Army Corps Engrs., 1918-19; chief, U.S. Land Office, Juneau, 1920-23; asst. supervisor of surveys, public lands for Alaska, Anchorage, 1924-26; Gov., Alaska, 1925-33; dist. cadastral engr. for Alaska, 1934-48, ret.; employed part-time, R.J. Sommers Constr. Co., Juneau, 1948-; v.p., First Nat. Bk. of Juneau, 1948-. Elected to 49er Hall of Fame, Alaska Press Club, Anchorage chapter, 1967. Mem., Masons, Shrine, Elks, Alaska Council Boy Scouts (treas.). Republican.

PARSONS, James C., clinical psychologist, professor. B. in N.Y.C., 1926; s. George P.; B.A., Pacific Union Coll., 1948; M.A., Columbia U.; unm.; instructor, Pacific Union Coll., 1946-48, Ozark Acad., Gentry, Ark., 1949-50; freshman counselor, U. Minn., 1950-51, while grad. stud.; clinical psychologist, Harding Sanitarium, Worthington, O., 1951-53; psychologist, state div. of mental health, Anchorage, 1953-56, 1958-60; professor, AMU, 1960-74; state H.R., 1961-65; pvt. prac., clinical psychologist, Anchorage, 1972-. Received distinguished service award, Anchorage Jaycees, 1959. Mem., Anchorage Ind. sc. bd., 1954-56; city parks & recreation adv. bd., chmn., 1963-; Anchorage Concert Assn. (pres.); Kiwanis (pres.); Anchorage Community Chorus; Alaska Mental Health Assn. (v.p.); del., Int. Cong. of Psychology, Moscow, 1966. Republican.

PATTERSON, James Henry, U.S. Marshal, machinist, blacksmith. B. in Cold Spring, N.Y., May 30, 1877; s. James and Minnie (Hawks) P.; gr. and h. sc.; m. Edna May Sackett, 1909 (dec. 1948); children: Ethel Louise (Mrs. Warren Silloway); went to Valdez, 1898; city councilman and mayor, Valdez; moved to several gold camps; settled in Valdez, 1902; terr. H.R., 1919-21, 1933-37, Sen., 1937-41; U.S. Marshal, 3d jud. div., 1939-48; died in Lakeside, Calif., March 17, 1951; buried in Seattle, Wash., beside wife. Mem., Odd Fellows, Pioneers, Eagles, Masons, Moose. Democrat.

PATTY, Dr. Ernest Newton, mining engineer, educator. B. in La Grande, Ore., Mar. 27, 1894; s. Thomas Franklin and Zora Euphemia (Beach) P.; B.S., 1919, E.M., 1925, U. Wash., D. Sc., UA, 1953; m. Kathryn B. Stanton, Dec. 28, 1918 (dec. 1961); children: Ernest N. (dec.), Stanton Hutchison, Dale Franklin; m. 2d, Mrs. Andrew Price, 1968; U.S. Army, 1918-19; mining engr., Wash. State Geological Survey, 1919-20; engr. in charge, Black Rock mine, Northport, Wash., 1921; prof., geology and mineralology, UA, 1922-25, dean of coll., head of sc. mines, 1925-35, pres., 1953-60; pres., gen. mgr., Gold Placers Ltd., Clear Cr. Placers, Ltd., near Dawson, Y.T., and Alluvial Golds, Inc., Fairbanks, 1935-53; ret. to Seattle, Wash., as mining and education consult., 1960-. Mem., Fellow Arctic Inst. North Am., AAAS, Am. Inst. Mining & Metallurgy Engrs., Am. Mining Cong., Canadian Metal Mining Assn., Alaska Miners Assn. (pres.), Explorers, N.Y.C., Rainier Club, Seattle.

PAUKAN, Moses, grocer. Married Agnes; appt. to state H.R., Feb. 1968, filling vacancy left by death of bro.-in-law, John L. Westdahl; state H.R., 1968-71; mayor, St. Mary's; pres., Village Council Presidents Assn. Democrat. Address: St. Mary's.

PAUL, William Louis, lawyer. B. in Port Simpson, B.C., Can., May 7, 1885; s. Louis Francis and Matilda "Tillie" (Kinnon) P.; Sheldon Jackson gr. sc., Sitka, Carlisle (Pa.) sc., 1902, Banks Bus. Coll., Phila., 1903; B.A., Whitworth Coll., 1909; grad. stud., Calif.; law. grad., LaSalle U. extension courses; m. Frances; children: William Louis, Jr., Frederick, Frances (Mrs. de Germaine); auditor and adjuster, Fidelity & Deposit Co., of Md.; Sitka, 1910-21; admitted to Alaska bar, 1921; prac. law, Wrangell, Ketchikan, Juneau; terr. H.R., 1925-29; field agent for Wheeler-Howard program, BIA, 1936-; moved to Seattle, Wash., 1957. Mem., ANB (pres.), Masons, Odd Fellows. Republican. Address (1974): 1521 16th Avenue East, Seattle, Wash. 98102.

PAYNE, John Barton, lawyer. B. in Pruntytown, Va., Jan. 26, 1855; s. Dr. Amos and Elizabeth Barton (Smith) P.; pvt. scs., Orleans, Fauquier Co., Va., 1860-70; LL.D., George Wash. U., 1919, U. Cincinnati, 1920, Coll. of William and Mary, Wash. and Lee U., 1926; admitted to Va. bar, 1876; m. Jennie Byrd, May 1, 1913 (dec. 1919); law prac., Kingwood, W. Va., 1877-82; special judge circuit ct., Tucker Co., W. Va., 1880; mayor, Kingwood, 1882; law prac., Chicago, Ill., 1883-93; superior ct. judge, Cook Co., Ill., 1893-98; pvt. law prac., Chicago, 1898-1918; gen. counsel, U.S. Shipping Bd., Wash., D.C., 1917-18; gen. counsel, U.S. R.R. adm., 1917-19; chmn., U.S. Shipping Bd., 1919-20; Sec. of Interior, 1920-21; chmn., Am. Red Cross, 1921-; died in Wash., Jan. 24, 1935. Democrat.

PEARSON, Grant Harold, park ranger. B. in Litchfield, Minn., 1900; s. Andrew F. and Dora Etta (Simmons) P.; gr. sc. and correspondence courses; m. Margaret Wolfe in Seward, Sept. 19, 1938 (dec. 1966); d. Shirley Margaret (Mrs. Fred Shipman, Mrs. Younger); worked in lumber camps, Mich., 1914-23, logging camps, Wash., Ore., 1923-25; went to Cordova, 1925; employe, ARC, summer 1925, Fairbanks Exploration Co. and Lucky Shot mine, winter 1925; park ranger, chief ranger and supt., Mt. McKinley Nat. Park, 1926, employe, Yosemite Nat. Park, 1939-42, Sitka and Glacier Bay Nat. Monument, 1947-49, Mt. McKinley Nat. Park, 1949-56; ret. from park service, 1956; moved to Los Altos, Calif.; ret. to his homesite within McKinley Park boundaries and later to Nenana; state H.R.,

from McKinley Park, 1959-61, Nenana, 1961-65; state Sen., 1965-67. Awarded Medal of Freedom by U.S. Army, 1947. Author: 2 pamphlets, "The Taming of Denali" and "The Seventy Mile Kid"; book "My Life of High Adventure," 1962. Mem., Am. Leg., Masons. Democrat.

PECKINPAUGH, Nicholas R., surveyor-general and ex-officio Secretary of Alaska, Sitka, 1890-93. Republican.

PENNINGTON, George Washington, sawmill operator. B. in Fredericktown, Md., Oct. 12, 1856; m. Molly Rittenhouse in Butte, Mont., 1889; children: 1 s., 2 daughters; left home in youth; traveling salesman; went to Dawson, 1897, losing outfit in Whitehorse Rapids; employe, NAT & T Co., agent, Fortymile, 1902; operated sawmill, Nenana, 1915-; terr. H.R., 1919-21; moved to Amarillo, Tex., 1919; died from injuries suffered in auto accident, Amarillo, Nov. 4, 1933. Mem., Pioneers (pres., Nenana Igloo). Democrat.

PEPPLER, Wayne M., miner, mechanic. B. in Rochester, Minn., Mar. 26, 1942; h. sc., Los Angeles, Calif.; stud., Pierce Agricultural Coll., 1 yr.; m. Linda Joan; s. Wayne Louis; owner-operator, Gold Dust mine, Denali-Susitna area, 1961, Eagle area, 1962-69, Fairbanks, 1969-; cand., lt. gov., on Alaskan Independence ticket, 1974.

PERATROVICH, Frank, fisherman, logger, cannery operator, merchant. B. in Klawock, Apr. 2, 1895; s. John and Mary (Skan); gr. sc., Klawock, Chemawa (Ore.) h. sc.; stud., Haskell Inst., Topeka, Kan., Capital Bus. Coll., Salem, Ore., Portland Bus. Coll.; hon. Dr. Public Service, UA, 1973; m. Harriet Smith, 1935; U.S. Navy, 1917-18; commercial fisherman, cannery operator, logger, estab. own gen. store, Klawock, 1930-; mayor, Klawock; Alaska H.R., 1945-47, 1969-73; Alaska Sen., 1947-51, 1957-67; del., const. conv. (vice chmn.), 1955-56; chmn., Dem. state central com., 1962-64. Elected to 49er Hall of Fame, Anchorage chapter, Alaska Press Club, 1972. Mem., Alaska Purse Seiners' Union (organizer, pres., 1939-46), Alaska Marine Workers (pres., 1946-47); Am. Leg., ANB (Pres.). Catholic, Democrat. Address: Box 366, Klawock.

PERKINS, Col. William T., lobbyist, lawyer. B. in Buffalo, N.Y., Nov. 2, 1858; s. Nathaniel and Annette (Hawkins) P.; public sc., Buffalo and Lockport, N.Y.; New Hampton Institution, N.H. prep. sc., 1877; B.A., Bates Coll., Me., 1881; LL.B., U. Mich., 1884; admitted to bar, Mich., N. Dak., Alaska; m. Katherine Laub, Denison, Ia., Dec. 16, 1884; law prac., Bismarck, N. Dak., 1884-96; col., N. Dak. Nat. Guard; v.p., 1st Nat. Bk., Bismarck, 1892-96; miner, Colo., 1896-98; mem., sc. bd., Bismarck, 12 yrs.; co. supt. of sc., Burleigh Co., N. Dak., 1889-98; gold prospector, Alaska, 1898-1900; gen. auditor, Northwestern Commercial Co., Nome, 1900-08; Alaskan del. to Rep. Nat. Conv., Chicago, 1904; cand., Alaska gov., 1904; chmn., Rep. conv., Juneau, Nov. 14-16, 1907; one of 3 Alaskan del. to spend winter in Wash., D.C. seeking legislation on Alaska's behalf, 1907-08; moved to Wash. state, 1908; organized banks, Roy,

Oakville, West Seattle, Kirkland; regent, U. Wash.; died in 1947. Mem., Masons, Shrine, Scottish Rite, K.T., A.B. (grand arctic chief, 1904). Episcopalian, Republican.

PERRINE, Mrs. Bertha, Democratic National Committeewoman, Palmer, 1940-44.

PERRY, George E., U.S. Marshal. B. in Ia., *c.* 1853; m.; U.S. Marshal, 3d jud. div., 1900-08; realtor, Seattle, Wash., 1909-; died in Dubuque, Ia., Nov. 10, 1915. Republican.

PERSONNETT, Melvin J., law enforcement officer. B. in Kan., 1928; grad., Keeler Polygraph Inst., Chicago, 1961; grad., FBI Nat. Acad., Wash., D.C., 1964; m. Shirley; children: Melvin J., Jr., Tami; dep. sheriff and detective, Kitsap Co., Wash., 1950-56; Ketchikan police dept., 1956-57; terr. police and state troopers, Fairbanks and Juneau, 1957-65; O'Neill pvt. investigating firm, Anchorage, 1965-67; comr., public safety, 1967-70; enforcement specialist, Nat. Highway Traffic Safety Adm., U.S. Dept. Transportation, Seattle, Wash., 1970-74; security mgr., Alyeska Pipeline Service Co., Anchorage, 1974-. Mem., Nat. Highway Safety Adv. Com., 1970, Western Assn. Gov.'s Highway Safety Reps. (v.p., 1970).

PETER, Richard L., lawyer, author, radio and television newscaster. B. in Canton, O., Feb. 17, 1916; s. Louis P.; LL.B., O. Northern U., 1972; m. Mary Scott of Taconite, Minn., 1945; children: Eric, Scott Leahy (dec. 1958); went to Alaska with U.S. Army, 1942; laboratory technician, U.S. Army, Juneau and Excursion Inlet; news dir., KINY, Juneau, 1945-68; state Sen., 1965-67; asst. atty. gen., Juneau, 1972-. Coined the Purchase Centennial slogan "North to the Future". Author of plays, poetry, prose, fiction. Democrat. Address: Juneau 99801.

PETERSON, Allan L., school teacher, merchant, fisherman, registered guide. B. in Tillamook, Ore., 1891; m. Jetret "Jetty" Stryker, 1920; d. Margaret Arness; went to Alaska, 1916; U.S. Army, 1917-18; dep. U.S. Marshal, Seldovia, Unga, Kenai, 20 yrs.; dep. U.S. Marshal and sc. teacher, Unga, WWII; moved to Kenai, 1946; state H.R., 1959-61. Mem., Pioneers. Democrat.

PETERSON, Almer J., lawyer. B. in Madison, Minn., June 11, 1890; s. Peter and Liva (Jacobson) P.; stud., sc. of pharmacy, 1914; LL.B., St. Paul Coll. of Law, St. Paul, Minn., 1915; m. Lila A. Phillips, May 17, 1916; children: Imogene E. (Mrs. Brown), Almer J., Jr., Shirley G. (Mrs. Carlos), Robert P. (dec. 1944); pharmacist, 10 yrs.; law prac., 1915-; moved to Anchorage, and admitted to Alaska bar, 1935; law prac., Anchorage, 1935-54, ret.; city atty., 2 yrs.; terr. H.R., 1941-43, 1945-47; cand., del. in Cong., 1946, 1950; moved to Juanita Beach, Wash. upon retirement; died following 2 yr. illness, Kirkland, Wash., July 16, 1962; funeral conducted by Masonic order of Knights Templar. Mem., Masons, Rotary, Eastern Star, Elks. Protestant, Republican.

PETERSON, Lawrence D., electronics technician. B. in Fort Yukon, Apr. 5, 1939; stud., coll., 1-1/2 yrs., electronics course, 18 mos.; employe, RCA and ITT, 1963-; state H.R., 1973-75. Mem., Ft. Yukon Native Assn. (pres.), city council, Tanana Chiefs (v.p.). Democrat. Address: Box 19, Ft. Yukon 99740.

PHILLIPS, Bradford E., travel and insurance agent, lawyer. B. in Lansing, Mich., Oct. 20, 1925; s. Wendell W. and Nathalie P.; stud., UA, Mich. State, U. Tenn.; B.A., U. Miami; M.A., Cornell U., 1951; LL.B., Calif. Western U., San Diego, 1974; m. Patricia Shanly, 1949 (dec. 1967); d. Sheila Toi; m. 2d, Helen Starr, June 23, 1971; U.S. Air Corps, 1943-46; went to Fairbanks, 1946, where parents operated travel agency; worked in family bus. in summers while attending coll.; helped organize Westours Co., 1948, Gray Lines Tours, early 1950s; city councilman, Anchorage, 1956-60; mgr., Arctic Travel Center, Anchorage, part-owner, 1958; operator, tour boat "Gypsy" between Whittier and Valdez, 1952-63; sales mgr., Alaska Airlines, Anchorage, 1963-64; cand., sec. of state, 1958, 1970; chmn., civil rights com., 1958-60; state Sen., 1961-71, minority leader, 1963-66, majority leader, 1967-68, pres., 1969-70; chmn., legislative council, 1967-; operated Brad Phillips Insur. Center, merged with Seattle-based insur. brokers, Dougan, Eader, Reynolds & Wheller, 1968, gen. mgr., 1966-71; operator, tour boat "Glacier Queen" between Whittier and Valdez, summer 1974. Received distinguished service award, Jaycees, 1958. Mem., Elks, Anchorage C. of C. (dir.), Anchorage Jaycees (dir.), Greater Anchorage, Inc. (dir.). Protestant, Republican.

PHILLIPS, Vance W., construction contractor, real estate developer. B. in Garfield, Ut., Dec. 28, 1915; s. George C. and Etta P.; gr. sc. and Juab h. sc., Nephi, Ut.; m. Gertrude M. Bertelsen in Haines, July 9, 1943; children: Vance, Jr., Cynthia Karen; res., Portland, Ore.; surveyor and heavy equipment operator, Kodiak, 1941; U.S. Army, Aleutians, southeastern and central Alaska, Ft. Richardson, 1944-46; owner, Mt. McKinley Excavating Co., co-owner, Phillips & Wilson constr. contractors, co-owner and pres., Caribou's dept. stores, 1954-64; real estate developer, Anchorage area; state Sen., 1961-65, 1967-71, mem., finance com., 1961-65, chmn., 1967-70. Mem., city parks and recreation bd., Lions (pres.), Elks, Anchorage C. of C., Alaska Big Game Trophy Club, Anchorage Roundtable. Mormon, Republican. Address: 2449 Glenwood, Anchorage.

PINKERTON, Lucille, accountant. Married James G. (mayor, Ketchikan; operator, Ketchikan Cold Storage Co.; sec. of state, 1966); acct., Ketchikan Cold Storage Co.; state H.R., from Ketchikan, 1965-67. Democrat.

PLETT, Walter P., electronics engineer. B. in Boston, Mass.; public sc., Boston; engring. degree, Northwestern U., 1927; m. Beatrice Stern; s. Paul Christopher; radio engr., Westinghouse Electric, 1927-33; radio engr., CAA, transcontinental airway, Billings, Mont. to Seattle, Wash., 1934-37; CAA hdqrs., Wash., D.C., 1937-39; asst. supt. of airways, CAA, 1939-41, supt., 1941-45, reg. adm., Anchorage, 1945-55; dep. reg. adm., Los Angeles, Calif., 1955-56, reg. adm., 1956-; died following abdominal surgery, Santa Monica, Calif., July 12, 1965. Mem., Kiwanis (pres., Anchorage, 1946). Catholic.

PLOTNICK, M. Daniel, merchant, land developer. B. in Richmond, Va., Mar. 1, 1921; s. David Joseph and Ann (Levi); B.A., UCLA, 1948; grad. stud., Georgetown U.; m. Sandra Jean Romick in Anchorage; children: Rochelle (Mrs. Neil MacKinnon), David, Sara Lynn, Barbara, Michael, Ann Lee, Allen; U.S. Air Force, Elmendorf AFB, 1949-53; exec. v.p., Fed. Distributing Co., gen. mgr., Romick's men's clothing stores and surplus store, Anchorage, 1954-66; state H.R., 1965-67; joined Abe Romick, father-in-law, in land development venture, Douglas, 1966-; lobbyist, Alaska State Employees Assn., Feb. and Mar., acting dep. comr. labor, July, dir., Gastineau Information & Opportunity Center, Community Action program, Aug. 1967; dep. state comr., labor, 1970-72. Mem., Elks, Am. Leg., VFW, Masons, Lions (pres., 1963), Congregationalist Beth Shalom (pres., 1961), Air Force Assn. (comdr.), Greater Anchorage Dem. Club (pres., 1962). Congregationalist, Democrat.

PLUMMER, Raymond Eugene, lawyer, judge. B. in Harlan, Ia., Mar. 27, 1913; s. Joseph Carl and Stella Mae (Keldgord) P.; B.A., 1937, LL.B., 1939, U. Neb.; m. Mary Marjorie Provost, Dec. 28, 1941; children: Raymond E., Jr., Marjorie Jane (Mrs. Robert Francis Lloyd Polley, Jr.); pvt. law prac., Lincoln, Neb., 1939-44; asst. U.S. dist. atty., 3d jud. div., Anchorage, 1944-46; U.S. dist. atty., 3d jud. div., Anchorage, 1946-49, res.; pvt. law prac., Anchorage, 1949-61; Dem. Nat. Com., 1953-56; terr. H.R., 1955-57; cand., U.S. Cong., 1958; U.S. dist. judge for Alaska, Fairbanks, 1961-63, Anchorage, 1963-73, ret., June 1, 1973 as chief judge; senior judge, serving part-time, 1973-. Mem., terr. bd. bar examiners; Boys Club of Alaska (pres., 1966-); Anchorage sc. bd., 1956-59; jud. council, 1959-61; Am. Bar Assn., Lions, Phi Alpha Delta, Elks. Catholic, Democrat. Address: 1729 W. 11th, Anchorage 99501.

PLUMMER, William T., lawyer. B. in Mason City, Ia., 1915; s. Joseph Carl and Stella Mae (Keldgord) P.; B.A., LL.B., U. Neb.; m. Helen Marie Vlach (dec. 1970); children: William T., Jr., Robert John, Timothy James, Patrice; U.S. Army, 1942-45, received bronze star for valor; pvt. law prac. and city atty., North Platte, Neb., 1946-51; pvt. prac. with bro. Raymond, staff mem., Arctic Adjusters insurance firm, Anchorage, 1951-53; U.S. dist. atty., 3d jud. div., Anchorage, 1953-60; U.S. atty. for new Dist. of Alaska (entire state), Feb.-June 1960, res.; pvt. law prac. Mem., VFW, Lions, Phi Delta Phi. Republican.

POLAND, Kathryn R., accountant. B. in Portland, Ore., Oct. 12, 1919; d. James and Mae Kennedy; stud., U. Wash.; m. William Merle Poland (div. 1973); children: Patrick Kennedy, Kathleen Ann, Shannon Elizabeth; res., Alaska, 1920-; chief clerk, treas., acct., Kodiak Fisheries and Columbia Wards Fisheries, 12 yrs.; state Sen., 1970-75. Mem., Pioneers Aux., Igloo 4, Anchorage, LWV, BPW, Kodiak C. of C. Democrat. Address: Box 45, Kodiak 99615.

POLAND, William Merle, registered guide, fisherman. B. in Artesia, N. Mex., July 7, 1912; s. William and Mary P.; stud., U. Kan.; m.; s. Bradley M.; m. 2d, Kathryn Kennedy (div. 1973); children: Patrick Kennedy, Kathleen Ann, Shannon Elizabeth; supt., fuel depot, Kodiak Naval Station, 1941-45; registered guide, 1947-57; city mgr., Kodiak, 1957-64; state H.R., 1965-67, Sen., 1967-70, res. following heart attack, Mar. 1970; wife appt. to vacant Sen. seat. Mem., Elks, C. of C. Democrat.

POLLARD, Clayton Armstrong, dentist. B. in Mexcio, Mo., Apr. 1, 1887; s. John and Martha Frances (Bradley) P.; gr. and h. sc., Jackson Co., Tex.; grad., Colo. Dental Coll., Denver, 1913; m. in Delta, Colo., 1919, wife died 1 mo. later; m. 2d, Lucy Mae Mattson in Kodiak, Oct. 31, 1923; children: Clayton James, George Robert; cattle rancher, Aztec, N. Mex., 1904-07; dentistry prac., Cedar Edge, Colo., 1913-17; U.S. Army, 1917-19; went to Seldovia, Seward, Anchorage, 1920; city councilman, Anchorage, 1926-29; dentistry prac., 1921-40, ret.; moved to farm, Kasilof, 1946; terr. H.R., from Anchorage, 1945-47, Kasilof, 1947-53; died in Kasilof, Mar. 19, 1960. Protestant, Democrat.

POLLEY, Ernest Milton, carpenter, bookkeeper. B. in Boston, Mass., June 9, 1887; h. sc., Winchester, Mass.; m. Edna Evelyn York; s. Clayton Leslie; carpenter, various mining cos., 1904-18; U.S. Army, 1918-19; employe, W.P. Mills Co., Sitka, 1920-21; tax clerk in terr. treas.'s office, then with USFS, Juneau; terr. H.R., 1923-25; died in Juneau, Feb. 26, 1942. Mem., Am. Leg., holding highest positions in terr. and serving on Nat. Com. Republican.

POLLOCK, Howard Wallace, lawyer. B. in Chicago, Ill., Apr. 11, 1920; h. sc., Perkinston, Miss., 1935-39; stud., Perkinston Jr. Coll., 1939-41, U. Santa Clara Sc. of Law, 1952-53; J.D., U. Houston Sc. of Law, 1955; M.S., Mass. Inst. Technology, 1960; m. Maryanne Passmore, July 5, 1942 (div. 1973); children: Ronald, Pamela, Randolph, Patricia, Rick; m. 2d, 1973; U.S. Navy, enlisted as seaman and ret. as lt. comdr., 1941-46; went to Fairbanks, 1948, Anchorage, 1949; asst. civilian personnel officer, USARAL, Ft. Richardson, 1949-52; asst. project mgr. and legal advisor, White Alice project, RCA, 1955-59; pvt. law prac., Anchorage, 1961-67; terr. H.R., 1953-55, state Sen., 1961-63, 1965-67; cand., Alaska gov., 1962, 1970; U.S. Cong., 1967-71; dep. adm., Nat. Oceanic & Atmospheric Adm., Wash., D.C., 1971-. Awards and honors: Outstanding American, U.S. Jaycees, 1955; nat. pres., Phi Theta Kappa, scholastic honor soc., 1940; nat. pres., Am. Law Stud. Assn., 1954; elected to Alaska Press Club's 49er Hall of Fame, 1970. Mem., K.C., Elks, Kiwanis, VFW, Am. Leg., ANB, Phi Delta Phi (leg.). Catholic, Republican.

PORTER, Orville, U.S. Marshal. B. in Albany, Ore., 1837; m. Carrie Delph, August 1890; U.S. Marshal for Alaska, Sitka, 1889-94; died in his home, Albany, Ore., Mar. 31, 1916. Republican.

PORTER, Wallace C., miner. B. in Redwood Co., Minn., Apr. 10, 1872; went to Rampart, 1898, Nome, 1900; m.; 3 children, all of whom preceded him in death; terr. H.R., from Haycock, 1939-41, 1943-47; operated dredge and store, Haycock, many yrs.; postmaster, Haycock, 1920-33; moved to Pioneers' Home, Sitka, 1952; died there, Oct. 5, 1957. Lutheran, Democrat.

POST, Alfred M., U.S. dist. atty., 3d jud. div., Eagle, 1900-01. Republican.

POULSON, Chris Peter, mine operator, real estate broker, businessman. B. in Denmark, 1904; s. Jens and Camilla Matilda (Anderson); education in Denmark; m.; children: Richard Lee, Nels Howard, Diana Kristina; res., Anchorage, 1933-64; buying and selling real estate, owned chain of theaters in Anchorage, Kodiak, Seward, Palmer; operated King Crab, Inc. cannery, Kodiak, Pioneer Mining Co. coal mine, Matanuska Valley; del., const. conv., 1955-56; moved to Seattle, Wash., 1964.

POWELL, Charles A. (Chuck), transportation operator. B. on Jan. 5, 1924; m.; 2 children; owner, transfer co.; state H.R., from Kodiak, 1967-69. Republican.

POWELL, Thomas Cader, U.S. Marshal, realtor. B. c. 1865; m. (div., 1903 and 1908); m. 3d, Miss Mildred Johannah Thorsk, Nome, Mar. 14, 1911; prospector-miner, Nome, summer 1900; in charge of real estate bus., Ladd & Co., Portland, Ore.; U.S. Marshal, 2d jud. div., Nome, 1905-13. Republican.

POWERS, John B., teamster, miner, merchant. B. in Memphis, Tenn., Mar. 2, 1870; moved as child with family to Minn.; worked from water boy to engr., various railroads, 11 yrs.; served in Spanish-Am. War; m.; res., Eagle, 1899-1944; mail contractor, Eagle to Chicken, using dog teams, 1908-38; freighter, miner, store prop.; U.S. Comr., U.S. Marshal, 1913-21, mayor, several terms, Eagle; del. to many Dem. Nat. Conv.; terr. H.R., 1935-39; died in Fairbanks, Feb. 14, 1944; survived by wife, who was in Ore. sanitarium. Mem., Pioneers. Catholic, Democrat.

PRACHT, Max, collector of customs, businessman. B. in Palatinate, Germany, 1846; m. Mary Winings in Cincinnati, c. 1868; children: William B., Lottie, Alexander Humboldt; emigrated to U.S., 1848 or 1852; res., Cincinnati; U.S. Navy, 1862, serving aboard Civil War gunboat LAFAYETTE; cabinet maker, telegraph operator, advertising mgr., O., Ind., Mo.; moved to San Francisco, 1878, Portland, Ore., 1881; an organizer and mgr., Alaska Salmon Packing & Fur Co. cannery, Loring, 1885-87; fruit rancher, Ashland, Ore., 1887-89; collector of customs, Sitka, 1889-91; special Treasury Agent for protection of Alaska salmon, Sitka, 1892-93; employe, Treasury Dept. and U.S. Land Office after leaving Alaska.

PRATT, Harry Emerson, lawyer. B. in Norton, Kan., Jan. 26, 1884; s. Louis Kossuth and Lyde (Donaldson) P.; North Side h. sc., Denver, Colo.; B.A., 1907, LL.B., 1909, U. Colo.; m. Katherine McKenzie in Boulder, Colo., Jan. 12, 1916; m. 2d, Helen Bernice Baker in Fairbanks, Aug. 16, 1927; children: Octavia Theron (Mrs. Edmund O. Hansen), Andrea L. (Mrs. David L. West); law prac., Pueblo, Colo., 1909-10; joined father in law firm, Fairbanks, 1910-11; ret. to Pueblo, 1911-16; asst. dist. atty., Fairbanks, 1919-22; ret. to Fairbanks; res. atty., for Fairbanks oil exploration, also in Mexico City with oil corp., 1919-22; ret. to Fairbanks; res. atty. for Fairbanks Exploration Co., 1922-35; terr. Sen., 1925-29; mem., terr. bd. education, 1926-30; U.S. dist. judge, 4th jud. dist., Fairbanks, 1935-54; moved to Tucson, Ariz., 1956; died there, Dec. 14, 1957. Democrat.

PRATT, Henry S., Jr., lobbyist, public relations consultant. B. in Tex., 1927; Jefferson h. sc., San Antonio, Tex.; stud., Tex. Western Coll.; m. Donna; children: Mark, Charlene (Mrs. John D. Carman); U.S. Air Force, Elemendorf AFB, 1951-56; dist. agent, Pacific Nat. Life Assurance Co.; state H.R., 1961-63; cand., U.S. Cong., 1962; public relations consult., 1963-; exec. asst., Gov. Keith Miller, 1969, special consult. on oil transportation, 1970. Mem., Anchorage Young Rep. Club (pres.). Presbyterian, Republican. Address: 2417 Hialeah Dr., Anchorage 99503.

PRICE, Frank D., fisherman, laborer. B. in Sitka, 1885; grad., Sheldon Jackson Sc., Sitka; m. Jessie F.; children: Frank J., James, Gertrude, Myrtle, Georgia; dep. U.S. Marshal, Juneau and Sitka, 1928-32; city councilman, Sitka, 1926-46; elected to terr. H.R., 1946, but died, Dec. 20, 1946, before session began. Mem., CIO Hod Carriers' local (pres.); United Trawlers' union (pres.); ANB (organizer and pres.). Presbyterian (elder, 1932-46), Republican.

PRICE, John Garland, lawyer, miner. B. in Guthrie Center, Ia., 1871; law degree, U. Ia.; law prac., Okla. Terr., 1893; chmn., first sen. conv. in Cherokee strip, 1894; law prac., Rice, Colo., 1895-97; Skagway, 1897-; elected provisional del. in Cong. at political conv., Juneau, Oct. 9, 1899; he was not seated, but permitted to appear before com.; miner-lawyer, Nome and Fairbanks; moved to Seattle, Wash., 1946; died in St. Vincent's Home for Aged, Seattle, where he had lived for 3 yrs., May 29, 1955.

PRICE, Robert E., lawyer, government administrator. B. in Chicago, Ill., Oct. 23, 1933; s. George and Kathryn (Gaughan) P.; B.A., 1955, J.D., 1957, DePaul U.; M.C.L., N.Y.U., 1961; m. Nadine Williams in Anchorage, 1972; pvt. law prac., Chicago, 1958-59; research atty., U. Wis. Sc. of Law, Madison, 1962-64; consult., Agency for Internat. Development, Brazil, 1965; asst. atty. gen., Juneau, 1967-71; reg. solicitor, Dept. Interior, Anchorage, 1971-. Independent. Address: P.O. Box 166, Anchorage 99510.

PRICE, Thomas C., plumber, lawyer. B. in Grizzly Gulch, Mont., Apr. 14, 1874; s. John W. and Orline E.P.; m. Lois Evans in Juneau, June 21, 1894; d.

Lois Ethel (Mrs. A.D. Haverstock); family moved to Portland, Ore., 1887; family prospected for gold in Portland Canal country, hdqrs., Loring; moved to Juneau, 1894, becoming one of the earliest settlers in that town; city councilman, Juneau; operated sheet metal bus.; estab. plumbing bus., Cordova and part-time law stud., 1909-15; city councilman, Cordova; moved to Anchorage, 1915; estab. plumbing bus., Price & Bennett and law prac.; U.S. Comr., 1935-44, coroner and recorder; terr. H.R., 1917-19, 1923-25, Sen., 1919-23; died Aug. 20, 1944. Mem., Pioneers (charter mem., Igloo 15); Elks (charter mem. and exalted ruler, Anchorage); Anchorage C. of C. (pres., 4 terms). Protestant, Democrat.

PRIOR, Dorothy Mary, accountant, real estate broker. B. in Yakima, Wash., Feb. 11, 1915; d. Archie M. and Martha (Beck) P.; gr. and h. sc., Yakima; B.A., Wash. State U.; unm.; service rep., Pacific Tel. & Tel., Seattle, Wash.; went to Anchorage, 1939; office mgr., McCarthy Bros. Constr. Co., 1939-40, moving with firm to Panama, 1941-43; supply and disbursing officer, WAVE, U.S. Navy, 1943-45; estab. public stenographic service, "Your Girl Friday", Anchorage, 1947-51; public acct., 1951-58; real estate broker, 1958-65; terr. H.R., 1953-55; sold real estate bus., moved to former ranch home, Yakima; took charge of Prior Land Co., developing property firm owned by family, 1966-. Mem., Quota Club (charter mem., pres., Anchorage Chapter, mem., nat. bd., elected 3d v.p. nat., 1961), AAUW, Pan Hellenic, Kappa Alpha Theta, LWV, BPW, Am. Leg., Pioneer Daughter of State of Wash. Presbyterian, Republican. Address (1974): 4015 W. Walnut St., Yakima, Wash. 98902.

PUGH, John Fraser (Jack), collector of customs. B. in Jefferson Co., Wash., Dec. 25, 1877; s. John E. and Cassie (Grant) P.; gr. and h. sc., Port Townsend, Wash.; grad., Willamette U., Salem, Ore.; m. Miss Venetia Lauretta Fehr in Oakland, Calif., Dec. 20, 1900; d. Venetia (Mrs. Karl A. Hahn); res., Skagway, 1900-02; U.S. Custom Service, Ketchikan, 1902-05, Skagway, 1905-08, Sulzer, 1908-09, Juneau, 1909-18, appt. in charge of all Alaska, Dec. 1913; died in wreck of SS Princess Sophia, Lynn Canal, Oct. 25, 1918; buried in Juneau, Oct. 31, 1918. Democrat.

R

RABINOWITZ, Jay Andrew, lawyer, judge. B. in Phila., Pa., Feb. 25, 1927; s. Milton and Rose R.; B.A., U. Syracuse, 1949; LL.B., Harvard U., 1952; m. Ann Marie Nesbit; d. Judith; U.S. Army Air Corps, 1945-46; pvt. law prac., N.Y., 1952-57; law clerk, U.S. dist. ct., Fairbanks, 1957-58; asst. U.S. atty., Fairbanks, 1958-59; dep. atty. gen., Juneau, 1959-60; superior ct. judge, 4th jud. dist., Fairbanks, 1960-65; assoc. justice, state supreme ct., Fairbanks, 1965-, chief justice, Sept. 1972-75. Mem., N.Y. and Alaska Bar Assns. Address: Box 109, Fairbanks 99701.

RACE, Harry Ronald, pharmacist. B. in Coupeville, Wash., Nov. 27, 1891; s. F. Puget and Hattie W. (Swift) R.; public sc., Coupeville; stud., Whidby Acad., U. Wash.; m. Violet Wood, Feb. 2, 1917 (div.); children: William H., Robert S., Mrs. James Crowdy; m. 2nd, Charlotte Sweaney in Coupeville, Jan. 15, 1951; druggist, 1913-40s, operating stores in Ketchikan and Juneau, 1916-40s; terr. H.R., 1937-39; fur farmer, Ketchikan, 1921-26; sold his stores, one in Ketchikan to s. Robert, also pharmacist; ret. to Coupeville; died there, Dec. 22, 1962. Congregationalist, Republican.

RADER, John Lafayette, lawyer. B. in Howard, Kan., Feb. 11, 1927; s. Ralph R. and Amy V. R.; gr. and h. sc., Howard; stud., U. Ore., Stanford U.; B.S., 1948, LL.B., 1951, Kan. U.; m. Carolyn Weigland, 1951; children: Timothy, Matthew, Janet; U.S. Navy, 1945-46; Industrial Relations Dept., Lago Oil & Transport, Netherlands West Indies, 1948-49; employe, Fairbanks Exploration Co., Fairbanks, summer 1949; ret. to Kans. for coll.; pvt. law prac., Anchorage, 1951-54; city atty., Anchorage, 1954-55; pvt. law prac., 1955-58; mgr., William Egan gubernatorial campaign, 1958; Alaska H.R., 1959, 1963-64; state atty. gen., 1959-60, res.; pvt. law prac., 1960-; cand., U.S. Cong., 1968; state Sen., 1969-78. Elected "Young Man of the Year," Anchorage Jaycees, 1960. Mem., Greater Anchorage Health dist. bd.; 1st Fed. Savings & Loan Assn. (chmn., 1962, bd. dir.). Presbyterian, Democrat. Address: 430 C St., Anchorage 99501.

RAELSON, Eric Richard, miner, businessman. B. in Stockholm, Sweden, May 16, 1868; m.; 2 children; public sc., Stockholm; stud., U. Stockholm; emigrated to Chicago; grocery store prop., traveling salesman; went to Wrangell, 1898, then into Cassiar; mining and mercantile bus., Nome, 1900-23; city councilman, Nome, 2 yrs.; terr. H.R., 1923; died in Nome, Sept. 8, 1923. Mem., Pioneers. Republican.

RANDOLPH, Richard (Dick), school teacher, insurance agent. B. in Salmon, Ida., Apr. 10, 1936; B.A., Ida. State U.; m. Janice; 3 children; teacher, Fairbanks, 1960-64; insur. agent, Fairbanks, 1964-; state H.R., 1971-75. Republican. Address: Box 123, Fairbanks 99701.

RASMUSON, Edward Anton, school teacher, missionary, lawyer, banker. B. in Copenhagen, Denmark, Apr. 5, 1882; gr. sc., Sweden; stud., Minnehaha Acad., Minneapolis, Minn., LaSalle U. extension services; law stud., Minneapolis, 1912-15; admitted to bar, Minn., 1914, Alaska, 1915; m. Jenny Olson in Yakutat, Apr. 28, 1905; children: Maude Evangeline (Mrs. Robert B. Atwood), Elmer Edwin; emigrated to U.S., settling in Minneapolis, 1901; sc. teacher, asst. missionary, missionary, postmaster, U.S. Comr., Yakutat, 1904-12; ret. to Juneau, 1915; U.S. Comr., Skagway, 1916-17; pres., Bk. of Alaska, hdqrs., Skagway, with branches in Wrangell, Cordova, Anchorage, Ketchikan (1924), 1917-43, chmn., bd. dir., 1918, ret. pres., 1943, remained chmn., bd. dir.; Swedish vice consul for Alaska, 1929-49 (knighted by King of Sweden, 1938); mayor, Skagway, 1921; Rep. Nat. Com., 1932-49; died in Minneapolis, Jan. 28, 1949; buried there in family plot. Mem., A.B. (Arctic Chief, Skagway), Elks, Masons, Shrine, Eastern Star, Pioneers. Presbyterian (elder), Republican.

RASMUSON, Elmer Edwin, accountant, banker. B. in Yakutat, Feb. 15, 1909; s. Edward Anton and Jenny (Olson) R.; gr. sc., Skagway; h. sc., Seattle; B.S., magna cum laude, 1930, M.A., 1935, Harvard U.; stud., U. Grenoble, 1930; LL.D., UA, 1970; m. Lile Vivian Bernard, Oct. 27, 1939 (dec. 1960); children: Edward Bernard, Lile Muchmore (Mrs. John Gibbons, Jr.), Judy Ann; m. 2d, Col. Mary Louise Milligan, Nov. 4, 1961; chief acct., Nat. Investors Corp., N.Y.C., 1933-35; acct., Arthur Anderson & Co., N.Y.C., 1935-43; pres., Nat. Bk. of Alaska, 1943-65, chmn., bd. dir., 1965-; mayor, Anchorage, 1964-67; cand., U.S. Sen., 1968; civilian aide to Sec. of Army, 1959-67; Swedish consul for Alaska, 1950- (knighted by King of Sweden, 1967); state sec., Rhodes Scholar Com., 1960-66; regent, UA, 1950-69; mem., Internat. North Pacific Fisheries Com., 1969-79. Awards: Outstanding Civilian Service medal, Outstanding Citizen, Alaska Press Club award, 1964; Silver Beaver award, Nat. Council of Boy Scouts of Am., 1968; Golden Plate award, Am. Acad. of Achievement, 1972; Outstanding Alaskan, state C. of C., 1974. Mem., Rotary (pres.); Phi Beta Kappa; Pioneers; Girl Scouts of Am. (nat. adv. bd.); Alaska Council of Boy Scouts (pres., 1953); sec.-treas., Loussac Found., Rasmuson Found. (chmn.); CPA, N.Y., Tex. and Alaska; Alaska Bankers Assn. (pres.); Elks, Masons, Harvard Club (N.Y.C., Boston), Explorers', Wash. Athletic Club, Rainier (Seattle), West Vancouver Yacht Club. Presbyterian, Republican.

RAY, Elbert E., miner, carpenter. B. in Jefferson, S.C., c. 1862; father reportedly a superior ct. judge, S.C.; mgr., hometown newspaper owned by relatives, 1880s; went to Dawson, 1898, Nome, 1901-07; bridge carpenter, Copper River & Northwestern Ry., Cordova; part-time fisherman and miner; terr. H.R., 1919-21; died of heart attack in Seattle, Wash., July 5, 1923. Mem., Masons, K.P. Democrat.

RAY, Leroy Vincent, lawyer. B. in Martha's Vineyard, Mass., May 14, 1875; s. Charles Macreading Vincent and Sarah Coffin (Smith); orphaned, adopted by Wallace W. Ray of Groveland, Mass., 1883, named L.V. Ray; grad., Mt. Hermon Acad., Northfield, Mass.; law stud. in atty.'s office; admitted to Mass. bar, 1900; m. Edna Hazel Sheldon in Valdez, 1908; children: Hazel Patricia (Mrs. Williams), Lee Vincent (dec. 1941); law clerk in atty.'s office, Seattle, Wash., 1903-06, admitted to Wash. bar; went to Seward, Jan. 1906; asst. dist. atty., 3d jud. div., transferred to Valdez, 1907-08; res., Seward, 1908-46; city atty., mayor, Seward; terr. Sen. (pres.), 1913-15; died of cerebral hemorrhage, Jan. 20, 1946. Mem., A.B., Elks, Odd Fellows, Moose. Republican.

RAY, William L., merchant, artist. B. in Anaconda, Mont., Apr. 6, 1922; s. Eli and Marchette R.; grad., h. sc., Kellogg, Ida., 1938; m. Jeanne Haas, Apr. 13, 1946; children: Terry (Mrs. Roger Shattuck), William L., Jr.; longshoreman, laborer, commercial fisherman, Juneau, 1938-42; radioman, U.S. Navy, 1942-46; ret. to Juneau, 1946; estab. retail liquor bus.; tourist charter boat bus., 7 yrs.; state H.R., 1965-71, Sen., 1971-79. Received distinguished honor award from Alaska Peace Officers' Assn. and certificate of distinguished achievement in public service, Am. Fed. of Police, 1973. Mem., Alcoholic Beverage Control Bd. (chmn., 1959-65); adv. bd., U.S. Fish & Game dept., 1957-58; VFW, Am. Leg., Elks, Toastmasters (pres.), Jaycees.

READER, Peter L. B. in N. Dak., 1913; went to Nome, 1934; del., const. conv., 1955-56.

REDMOND, William W., lawyer. B. in Marysville, Kan.; legal div., Dept. Interior, Wash., D.C., 1956; asst. solicitor, Fish & Game div., Wash., 1959-60; solicitor, Dept. Interior, Anchorage, 1960-65.

REED, Irving McKenny, highway engineer, mining engineer. B. in Seattle, Wash., July 13, 1889; s. Thomas M. and Ida (McKenny) R.; gr. sc., Nome; stud., Anderson Military Acad., Irvington, Calif.; B.S., U. Calif.; m. Eleanor Doris Stoy, Jan. 7, 1923; children: Irving Stoy, Anna Beatrice (Nancy, Mrs. Bauer), Cynthia Louise; U.S. mineral surveyor, 1911-43; assoc. terr. mining engr., 1928-38; moved from Nome to Fairbanks, 1924; gen. engring. and surveying bus.; chief locator, U.S. Dist. Engrs., 1942, asst. area engr., 1943; city councilman, Fairbanks, 8 yrs.; terr. game com., 13 yrs., res., 1940; terr. highway engr., 1953-57; ret. to home, Farmer's Loop Road, Fairbanks; died in 1968. Mem., Tanana Valley Sportsmen's Assn., Masons, Shrine, Scottish Rite. Episcopalian, Republican.

REED, Morgan W., businessman. State H.R., from Skagway, 1959-65, 1971-73. Democrat.

REED, Pauline Hovey, hotel proprietor. B. in Munson, O., Oct. 20, 1883; d. Sarah N. Boyton; m. Frank I. Reed in Nome, 1904; children: Paul, Frank, Metcalf; moved to Anchorage, 1915, where husband engaged in lumber bus.; mgr., Anchorage

Hotel, later owners; Rep. Nat. Com., 1932-34; died following operation, Seattle hospital, May 4, 1934. Mem., DAR. Republican.

REED, Thomas Milburne, lawyer, miner. B. in Old Shasta, Calif., Jan. 27, 1857; s. Thomas Milburne and Elizabeth (Finlay) R.; public sc., Wash.; family moved to Wash., 1859; B.A., 1878, LL.B., Princeton U.; m. Ida McKenny, 1880s; children: Constance Donna (Mrs. Theodore N. Haller, div. 1927), Irving McKenny; m. 2d, Mrs. John F. (Venetia) Pugh, Mar. 2, 1924; ret. to Wash., law prac. and employe, U.S. Land Office, several yrs.; superior ct. judge, Pierce Co.; mem., 1st state legislature, 1890-92; went to Dawson, 1898, in charge of 4 riverboats loaded with freight; left Dawson after a few mos.; mined near Dutch Harbor and discovered rich sulphur mine on Makushin volcano; estab. law office, Nome, 1900-21; U.S. Comr., 1901-06; clerk of dist. ct., 1912-13; clerk of terr. Sen., two terms, 1919-21; U.S. dist. judge, 1st jud. div., Juneau, 1921-28; died of heart attack in Juneau, Apr. 30, 1928. Mem., Masons, Elks. Presbyterian, Republican.

REETZ, August F. (Augie), businessman. B. in Hebron, N. Dak., July 10, 1931; h. sc., Billings, Mont.; stud., Eastern Mont. Coll. of Education, Billings Bus. Coll.; m. Eileen; children: Anthony, Albert, Holly, Joseph; bookkeeper, Jones and Anderson, accts., Anchorage, 1948-54; U.S. Marine Corps, 1951-53; bookkeeper, Yukon Office Supply, Anchorage, 1954, pres. and sole owner, 1962, with branches in Juneau, Fairbanks, Soldotna, Ketchikan; state comr., fish and game, 1968-69. Mem., Anchorage C. of C. (pres., 1973); Anchorage Businessmen's Assn.; Anchorage Human Relations Com.; state bd. fish and game (1967-68); adv. environmental quality control com. (1970); Rotary; Rep. state finance chmn., 1966. Catholic, Republican. Address: 935 Gambell St., Anchorage.

REEVE, Janice Beverly (Tillie), nee Morisette, bookkeeper. B. in Muscoda, Wis., Sept. 22, 1912; m. Robert Campbell Reeve in Fairbanks, July 22, 1936; children: Richard D., Roberta B. (Mrs. Don Sheldon), Janice Mae (Mrs. William E. Ogle), David C., Whitham D.; res., Stevens Point, Wis.; res., Valdez, 1934-42, Anchorage, 1942-; went to Valdez from Stevens Point, Wis., 1934; telephone switchboard operator until 1936; husband's bookkeeper, dispatcher and office mgr.; Rep. Nat. Com., 1958-64; vice chmn., Rep. state central com., 1964-66. Mem., Pioneers. Presbyterian, Republican.

REEVE, Robert Campbell, businessman, aviator. B. in Waunakee, Wis., Mar. 27, 1902; s. Hubert L. and May (Davenport) R.; gr. and h. sc., Waunakee; stud., U. Wis., 3 yrs.; hon. D.Sc., UA, 1963; m. Janice Beverly (Tillie) Morisette in Fairbanks, July 22, 1936; children: Richard D., Roberta B. (Mrs. Don Edward Sheldon), Janice Mae (Mrs. William E. Ogle), David C., Whitham D.; began flying as barnstormer, 1926-27; pilot, Scenic Airways, Phoenix, Ariz., 1928, Ford Motor Co. airplane div., 1928-29, Pan-Am. Airways and Pan-Am. Grace Airways, foreign mail routes in Central and South Am., 1929-32; estab. Reeve Airways (later certified as

Reeve Aleutian Airways), Valdez, 1932-42, hdqrs., Anchorage, 1942-; cand., del. in Cong., 1952. Awards: Order of Daedalians, 1969; Gold Pan Award, Anch. C. of C.; Outstanding Civilian Service, USARAL, 1971; Exceptional Service, U.S. Air Force, 1973; Alaskan of the Year, 1972; subject of book entitled "Glacier Pilot" by Beth Day, 1957. Mem., terr. bd. police comrs. (chmn.), Pioneers (trustee), Petroleum Club, Alaska Big Game Trophy Club, Explorers, Boone & Crockett, N.Y.C., Elks, Masons, Shrine, Am. Leg., Vets WWI (comdrs., 1969), Cook Inlet Hist. Soc. (pres., 1964), Anchorage C. of C., Wash. Athletic, Arctic and Rainier (Seattle), Adventurers, Conquistadores del Cielo, Quiet Birdmen, Kiwanis, Nat. Defense Transportation Assn. (life), Air Force Aid Soc. (life). Presbyterian, Republican. Address: 209 E. 11th Ave., Anchorage 99501.

REGER, Fred O., Adjutant General, National Guard, Apr.-July, 1964, acting.

REID, Eugene C., farmer, carpenter. B. in N. Dak., 1918; m. Emma Dell (dec. 1964); children: Emagene E. Clarke, Suellen M. Alger, Leonard B.; potato farmer, Bismark, N. Dak., Matanuska Valley, 1947-; carpenter, Alaska R.R., until 1953; full-time farmer; state H.R., 1963-65. Mem., Matanuska Valley C. of C. (pres.), Matanuska Telephone Assn. (pres.). Republican.

REID, Silas Hinkle, lawyer. B. in Duquoin, Ill., Sept. 1871; public sc., Duquoin; stud., state normal sc. and later Wellesley law coll., Bloomington; law stud. in father's office; m. Nellie Goodwin in Decatur, Ill., 1901; law prac., El Reno, Okla.; co. atty.; cand., state atty. gen.; endorsed for judgeships in Alaska and Puerto Rico; U.S. dist. judge, 3d jud. div., Valdez and Fairbanks, 1907-09, resignation requested; law prac., Chicago; died of Bright's disease in sister's home, St. Louis, Mo.; interment in Duquoin.

RENTSCHLER, Carl Thomas, school teacher, real estate broker. B. in Reading, Pa., Sept. 27, 1920; s. Frank and Della D. (Bucks) R.; B.S., Pa. State U.; m. Madelynne Layden, Aug. 31, 1946; children: Patricia D., Laron P.; teacher in pvt. sc., Pa.; U.S. Air Corps (transport pilot in Aleutians, 1944-), 1943-47; owner, Anchorage Realty Co.; terr. H.R.,1953-55. Mem., Masons, Elks, VFW, Am. Leg., Kiwanis, Alaska Jaycees (pres., 1948). Presbyterian, Republican.

RETTIG, Ron L., accountant, banker. B. in Filer, Ida., Apr. 23, 1912; s. Edward H. and Martha Ellen R.; h. sc., Seattle, Wash.; grad., Wash. Western Inst. Accountancy, 1936; m. Evelyn Shield, 1937; d. Judy (Mrs. Eric Benson, Mrs. Williams); acct., State of Wash., 1936-52; practicing CPA, estab. firm of Rettig, Scott & Co. (1953), Anchorage, 1952-60; cand., U.S. Cong., 1960; city councilman, Anchorage, 1961, 1965; organizer, pres. and chmn. bd., Alaska Mutual Savings Bk., Anchorage, 1961-; state comr., revenue, Feb.-Oct., 1967; state H.R., 1969-71, Sen., 1971-75. Mem., Pacific Marine Fisheries Com.; Greater Anchorage Borough assembly; state bd. fish and game, 1968-; Alaska Sport Fish &

Game Inst. (pres.); Anchorage C. of C. (bd. dir.); Alaska Soc., CPAs (charter mem. and pres.); Nat. Assn. Mutual Savings Bks. (dir.); Pacific Northwest Trade Assn.; Am. Inst. CPAs (council mem.); Alaska bd. public accountancy (pres., 1957-60); Rotary. Presbyterian, Republican. Address: 601 W. 5th Ave., Anchorage 99501.

RHODE, Clarence J., government administrator, aviator. B. in Sultan, Wash., Apr. 15, 1913; s. Charles J. R.; gr. and h. sc., Colville, Wash.; stud., Success bus. coll., Seattle; m. Gazil E. Burcham in Juneau, 1934 (dec. 1972); children: Jack, James B., Sally Jo (Mrs. Hunter); worked in game and forestry conservation, Colville; joined cousins, Leo and Cecil Rhode, in Alaska, 1934; agent, Alaska Wildlife, Juneau, Cordova, Fairbanks, Anchorage, Ketchikan, estab. aircraft operations of Fish and Wildlife Service as aircraft supervisor, 1935-44; pilot, Alaska Coastal Airways, Juneau, 1944-46, Peterson Air Service, Anchorage, 1946-48; reg. dir., U.S. Fish & Wildlife, Juneau, 1948-58; killed in plane crash, Brooks Range, Aug. 21, 1958, accompanied by s. Jack and another passenger. Memorial fund for scholarships, UA, estab. in his name; Kuskokwim Nat. Wildlife Refuge near Bethel renamed in his honor, 1960. Mem., Pioneers. Presbyterian.

RHODE, Leo, accountant. B. in Mohall, N. Dak., Aug. 31, 1908; s. Ernest E. and Nellie M. (Culver) R.; h. sc., Eureka, Kan.; B.B.A., UA, 1940; m. Floris K. Licht (dec. 1951); employe, USGS, Juneau, 1933-35, Anchorage, 1939-40; adm. officer, U.S. Fish & Wildlife Service, Juneau, 1941-43; cold storage bus., Anchorage, 1943-51; office mgr., acct., Homer Electric Assn., 1951-71; state H.R., from Homer, 1961-63, Sen., 1975-77. Mem., bd. regents, UA, 1948-55; Pioneers; Elks; Homer C. of C. (dir. and sec.); hospital adv. bd.; dir., Homer Electric Assn.; city council; adv. bd., Nat. Bk. of Alaska, 1961-73; bd. dir., Nat. Bk. of Alaska, 1973-. Methodist, Republican. Address: Box 406, Homer 99603.

RICHARDS, Frank H., U.S. Marshal, miner. B. in McHenry Co., Ill., March 21, 1858; stud., Columbia U. Law Sc.; admitted to bar but never practiced; m. Miss Bessie Wilke, Oct. 8, 1903; lived on farm until he moved to Puget Sound area, 1883; worked on first R.R. survey between B.C., Can., and Seattle, Wash.; one of the incorporators of Bellingham Bay & B.C. R.R. Co.; mem., Harbor Com., Wash state, 1890-93; Wash. state Sen., from Whatcom Co., 1891-95; prospector-miner, southeastern Alaska, late 1890s, Fortymile, 1899, Nome, 1900; U.S. Marshal, 2d jud. div., Nome, 1901-04; died of pneumonia in Carlsbad, N. Mex., Nov. 13, 1937; interment in Chicago, Ill. Mem., A.B. Republican.

RICHARDSON, Wilds Preston, military officer, civil engineer. B. in Tex., Mar. 20, 1861; grad., U.S. Military Acad., West Point, 1884; unm.; tactics instructor, West Point, 1892-97; assigned to Alaska duty in charge of constructing army posts, 1897-1904; pres., ARC, 1905-17; in charge of Am. forces in northern Russia, 1917-18; ret. at Ft. Lewis, Wash., 1920; died in Walter Reed hospital, Wash.,

D.C., May 20, 1929; buried at West Point. Richardson Highway between Valdez and Fairbanks named in his honor.

RICHMOND, Charles A., government administrator, educator. B. in Huntington, N.Y.; grad., West Tex. State Coll.; joined BIA as teacher, Unalakleet, 1954; supt., Bethel-Alaska Indian Agency, 1968; area dir., BIA, for Alaska, 1968-71.

RICKERT, Paul John, miner, farmer, businessman. B. in Minneapolis, Minn., Jan. 27, 1867; gr. and h. sc., Minneapolis; m.; 1 d.; m. 2d, Stacia in Chena, May 17, 1904; joined Klondike gold stampede, mined and worked for telephone co., Dawson and Chena, 1898-1904; moved to Fairbanks, mining and working for telephone co. and experimental farming bus., Fairbanks Gardens; ret. from telephone co., 1916; full-time farmer, 1904-38; terr. H.R., 1921-23; died in Fairbanks, Oct. 9, 1938. Mem., bd. regents, UA, 1918-23; C. of C. (pres., 1924-33); Pioneers (pres., Fairbanks Igloo, 1928, grand pres., 1929-30); Alaska-Internat. Highway Assn. (pres., 1929); organizer and pres., Tanana Valley Farmers Assn., Tanana Valley Fair Assn. Ice Carnival and Dog Derby; charter mem. and pres., Curling Club, Eagles. Republican.

RIGGS, Thomas Christmas, Jr., civil engineer. B. in Ilchester, Md., Oct. 17, 1873; s. Thomas and Catherine (Gilket) R.; stud., Emerson Inst., Wash., D.C.; B.S., Princeton U., 1894; m. Rene C. Coudert, Apr. 30, 1913; children: Elizabeth Catherine "Lisette" (Mrs. Isely), Thomas, III; family lived in Wash. Terr., 1893-97; newspaper reporter, Tacoma; joined gold rushes to Dawson, and Nome, 1897-1901; surveyor, Ut., Mont., Ida., 1901-03; surveyor, asst. engr., chief engr., Alaska-Can. Boundary Com., 1903-13; engr. in charge, Alaska R.R., northern terminus, AEC, 1914-18; Gov., Alaska, 1918-21; moved to N.Y., with home in Millbrook and office in N.Y.C., engaged in constr., mining and oil properties, 1921-35; comr., U.S. section, Internat. Am.-Can. Boundary Com., Wash., D.C., 1935-45; mem., Internat. Highways Com., 1938-45; died in his home, Wash., D.C., Jan. 16, 1945. Mem., Pioneers, A.B. Catholic, Democrat.

RILEY, Burke, lawyer. B. in Mont., Apr. 2, 1914; s. Edmund B. R.; LL.B., U. Wash., 1937; m. (div. 1953); children: Robin, Margen; m. 2d, Doris Ann Bartlett in Wash., D.C., Dec. 27, 1956 (div. 1968); children: Joseph, Katherine, Deirdre, Ann Christine (dec. 1961), Alan, Michael; m. 3d, 1970; employe, caterpillar dept., Northern Commercial Co., Fairbanks, 1938-39; law clerk, U.S. dist. atty.'s office and city assessor, Fairbanks, 1939-41; U.S. Army, 1942-45; dir., vocational rehabilitation, Juneau, 1946-47; adm. asst. to Gov. Gruening, 1947-52; Sec. of Alaska, 1952-53; pvt. law prac., Haines, 1953-57; terr. H.R., 1955-57; del., const. conv., 1955-56; employe, D.J. Belcher & Assoc., Ithaca, N.Y., 1957-59; exec. asst. to Gov. Egan, 1959-61; chmn., Alaska Field Com., Juneau, 1961-65; reg. coordinator for Alaska, U.S. Dept. Interior, 1965-69; exec., BLM, Wash., D.C., 1969-. Democrat.

RITCHIE, Elmer E., lawyer, newspaper publisher. B. in LaSalle Co., Ill., Dec. 3, 1861; grad., U. Kan., 1884; unm.; admitted to Kan. bar, 1886; law prac., Kan. and Salt Lake City, Ut., 1886-97; employe, Seattle newspapers, 1897-1905; pub., Seward GATEWAY, 1905-08; law prac. and pub., Valdez PROSPECTOR, mayor, Valdez, 1912-15; U.S. dist. judge, 3d jud. div., Valdez, 1921-27; lived in Seattle, Wash., 1930s; died in Seward, Mar. 28, 1941. Republican.

RIVERS, Ralph Julian, lawyer. B. in Seattle, Wash., May 23, 1903; s. Julian Guy and Louisa (Lavoy) R.; gr. sc., Flat; grad., Franklin h. sc., Seattle, Wash., 1921; B.A., LL.B., 1929, U. Wash.; m. Carol Caldwell, Dec. 17, 1928 (div.); children: Julian Ralph, Joyce Carol (Mrs. John T. Mansfield); m. 2d, Martha Wendling, c. 1950; went to Flat with parents, 1906; asst. postmaster and placer-miner during summer, Flat, 1921-23; pvt. law prac., Seattle, 1930-31, Fairbanks, 1931-56; U.S. dist. atty., 4th jud. div., Fairbanks, 1933-44, res.; terr. atty. gen., 1945-49; terr. Sen., 1955-56, res.; del., const. conv., 1955-56 (2d v.p.); Alaska-Tenn. Congressman, Wash., D.C., 1957-58; U.S. Cong., 1959-66; ret. to Fla., 1967; moved to Chehalis, Wash. Mem., terr. employment securities com., 1950-53 (chmn.); League of Alaska Cities (pres., 1954); Pioneers, SAR, Soc. of Mayflower Descendants, Sigma Chi, Phi Alpha Delta, Elks. Protestant, Democrat.

RIVERS, Victor Claudius, civil engineer. B. in King Co., Wash., Jan. 15, 1905; s. Julian Guy and Louisa (Lavoy) R.; gr. sc., Flat, Franklin h. sc., Seattle; stud., U. Wash., Northwestern U.; B.C.E., McKinley Coll. of Engring., 1930; m. Rosa Edna Johnstone, July 23, 1931 (div. 1951); s. Keith Victor; m. 2d, Elleighfare "Rusty" Amason, Apr. 8, 1955; went to Flat with parents, 1906; pvt. prac. engring., Fairbanks, 1930-37; mayor, Fairbanks, 1 term; constr. engr., NPS, McKinley Park, 1937-39; terr. Sen., from Fairbanks, 1937-41, from Anchorage, 1947-51, 1957-59; U.S. Army Corps Engrs., Anchorage, 1940-45; pvt. prac., consulting engr., Anchorage, 1945-59; del., const. conv., 1955-56; cand., Alaska gov., 1958; died of cancer in Anchorage, Sept. 25, 1959. Mem., Legislative Council; bd. examiners for engrs. and architects; Alaska C. of C. (pres., 1937-39); Statehood Com. (exec. bd.); Pioneers, Anchorage Sportsmen's Assn., Elks, Moose, Sigma Nu. Democrat.

ROADY, James Raymond, businessman. B. in Auburn, Ill., 1907; s. James R. and Sadie (Tucker) R.; gr. and h. sc., Yakima, Wash., 1926; m. Alberta Mae Reid, 1941; went to Alaska, 1923; owner-operator, truck transfer co., Ketchikan; pres., *Alaska Sportsman* magazine, 1935-58; dir., Investors in Alaska Co.; operated Ketchikan Meat Co., 1944-; dir., Recreation Inc., 1946-; state H.R., 1959-61; postmaster, Ketchikan, 1963-70; dir., Div. of Occupational Licensing, Dept. Commerce, 1971-. Mem., Elks, Lions. Methodist, Democrat.

ROBERTSON, Ralph Elliott (Bob), lawyer. B. in Sioux City, Ia., Oct. 18, 1885; s. Charles A. and Jessie F. (Elliott) R.; h. sc., Onawa, Ia., 1903;

stud., bus. coll., Omaha, Neb., Mich. Sc. Mines, U. Wash.; law stud. in atty. offices, Juneau; admitted to Alaska bar, 1911; m. Caroline Benning Green in Juneau, Mar. 26, 1913; children: Ralph Elliott, Jr., Duncan, Carol Benning (Mrs. Frederick O. Eastaugh); reporter, U.S. Comr.'s ct., Juneau, 1906-11; pvt. law prac. until retirement, 1960; law partner of Royal A. Gunnison, 1916, later Robertson, Monagle, Eastaugh & Annis; pvt. sec. to Judge Thomas R. Lyons, 1911-13; city councilman, mayor, 1920-23, chief dep. U.S. Marshal, dep. clerk, dist. ct., U.S. Comr., Juneau and Ketchikan; dep. clerk of ct., Valdez; ret. to Seattle, Wash., 1960; died there, Feb. 28, 1961; ashes buried in Elks plot, Evergreen cemetery, Juneau. Mem., sc. bd. (pres., 1924-47); C. of C. (pres., 1924, 1935); trustee, UA, 1925-33; Am. Bar Assn., House of Delegates; Masons; Elks (exalted ruler, life mem.); Shrine, Moose, Lions. Presbyterian (treas., 30 yrs.), Republican.

ROBISON, Paul F., lawyer. B. in Miltonvale, Kan., June 28, 1919; gr. and h. sc., Miltonvale; stud., Kan. State U., Miltonvale Wesleyan; B.A., LL.B., Washburn U.; post-grad. stud., George Wash. U. sc. of law, 1954; m. Roberta L. Shannon, Dec. 25, 1941; children: Pamela Ann (Mrs. John Berg Vantress), Paula Lee (Mrs. Larry G. Honchen); U.S. Army Quartermaster Corps, 1941-46, stationed at Ft. Richardson, 1942-45, awarded Legion of Merit; pvt. law prac., Anchorage, 1947-; terr. Sen., 1953-55; chmn., legislative council; special legislative counsel to Gov. Heintzleman, Jan.-March, 1955; cand., del. in Cong., 1958. Received Silver Beaver award, Boy Scouts of Am. Mem., Boy Scouts (pres., Western Alaska Council); Anchorage Gas Corp. (bd. dir.); Phi Alpha Delta, Delta Tau Delta, Phi Kappa Delta, Masons, Elks, Lions, Alaska Council, Anchorage C. of C. Presbyterian, Republican.

RODEN, Henry, lawyer, miner, businessman. B. in Basel, Switzerland, Aug. 1874; education in Germany and England; law stud., Chena; admitted to bar, 1906; m. Margaret (dec. 1961); joined Klondike gold stampeders, having bought transportation direct from London to Skagway with stopover in Juneau; prospector, miner, wood cutter for riverboats, Dawson, Rampart, Chena, Fairbanks, Ruby, Iditarod, 1897-1906; estab. law office, Fairbanks, asst. U.S. atty., Fairbanks and Iditarod, city atty., Iditarod, 1906-14; law prac. and bus. ventures, Juneau; lived awhile in Petersburg; co-founder of Pelican City, 1938-60; terr. Sen., 1913-15, 1935-41, pres., 1941; atty.-gen., 1941-45; cand., del. in Cong., 1944; terr. treas., 1949-55; moved to Seattle, Wash., 1960; died there, June 5, 1966; interment in Evergreen cemetery, Juneau. Author: "Alaska Mining Laws." Mem., Pioneers (grand pres., 1943-45); Pioneers Home (chmn., bd. trustees), Sitka; Pelican Cold Storage Co. (pres.). Democrat.

RODERICK, John Rochester (Jack), publisher, lawyer. B. in Seattle, Wash., Mar. 16, 1926; s. David Morgan and Mary Louise R.; Broadway h. sc., Seattle; B.A., Yale U., 1949; LL.B., U. Wash., 1959; m. Martha Martin; children: Sarah, Elizabeth; U.S. Navy Air Corps, 1945-46; moved to

Anchorage, 1954; estab. various oil-oriented publications, including *Alaska Industry* magazine, *Alaska Scouting Services*; estab. Petroleum Publications, Inc. and Alaska Title Guaranty Co.; pvt. law prac., 1959-63; dir.-pres., Alaska Exploration Corp., 1965-67; mgr., Wendell Kay's gubernatorial campaign, 1966; dep. dir., Peace Corps, New Delhi, India, 1967-68; dir., exec. v.p., Alaska Industrial Publications, 1968-70; govt. relations consult., Alyeska Pipeline Service Co., 1970-72; mayor, Greater Anchorage Area Borough, 1972-. Mem., YMCA (bd. dir.), Anchorage Community Theater, C. of C. Democrat. Address: 1620 Hidden Lane, Anchorage 99501.

RODEY, Bernard Shandon, lawyer. B. in Ireland, c. 1860; m. Minnie Coddington, 1886; s. Pearce Coddington and 1 d.; pvt. sec. to ry. mgr., N. Mex., 1881; law stud. and admitted to bar, N. Mex.; entirely a self-educated man, having but a few months district schooling in early yrs., Can.; spent early yrs. farming, clearing land and merchandising, coal mining (1882); ct. stenographer, 2d div., N. Mex.; prolific writer for local press upon political and terr. subjects; del. in Cong. from Terr. of N. Mex., 1901-05; U.S. dist. judge, Puerto Rico, 1906-10; U.S. dist. atty., 2d jud. div., Nome, 1910-13; his family remaining in N. Mex.; estab. law prac., Albuquerque, N. Mex., 1913, joined by s. Pearce, a Harvard U. law sc. grad., 1916. Republican.

ROGERS, Charles D., physician. Married; medicine prac., Sitka, 1890-94; clerk of U.S. dist. ct., surveyor-gen., ex-officio Sec. of Alaska, Sitka, 1894-97; medicine prac., Juneau; died in Denver, Colo., 1905. Democrat.

ROGERS, James G., government administrator, aviator. B. in St. Paul, Minn.; B.A., Macalester Coll.; bomber pilot, U.S. Army Air Corps, 1944-46; controller, air traffic control center, FAA, Anchorage, 1947-53; chief, air traffic control div., southern reg., FAA, Atlanta, Ga., 1961-63; reg. adm., FAA, Anchorage, 1963-65; dir., southern reg., FAA, Atlanta, Ga., 1965-.

ROGGE, Leo William, miner. B. in Davenport, Ia., Aug. 18, 1878; parents operated trading post, Yakutat Bay, early 1900s; gr. and h. sc., Davenport; m. Mrs. Elizabeth Murray Cohee in Seattle, Wash., Jan. 25, 1923; partner in butcher shop, Davenport, 1897-1900; joined father and brother in mining operations, Fortymile dist., 1900-12; miner, Pedro, Cleary, Goldstream and Fairbanks Creeks, Fairbanks area; sold claims to U.S. Smelting, Refining & Mining Co., 1924; supt. of distribution, U.S. Smelting, Refining & Mining Co., until retirement, 1945; terr. H.R., 1937-45, Sen., 1945-49; died in Seattle, Wash., Feb. 16, 1952. Mem., Dem. div. com. (chmn., 1944), Pioneers. Catholic, Democrat.

ROLOFF, H. Henry, journalist, government administrator. B. in Wis., 1919; stud., San Diego (Calif.) State Coll., Bryant & Stratton Coll., Ill.; m. Barbara Nieman, 1944; children: Lea Rene, Cathleen, John Henry "Jack", Seth, Rex, Kirk Carl "Casey"; U.S. Army Air Corps, 1943-46; reporter, Scripps-Howard newspapers, Los Angeles and San

Diego, 1937-43; dir., industrial development and public relations, San Diego C. of C., 1946-60; asst. port dir., San Diego, 1950-60; port dir., Anchorage, 1960-62; comr., economic development and planning, Juneau, 1962-64; dir., Pacific Coast Assn. of Port Directors, Los Angeles, 1964-; UN technical adviser, East African Harbors Corp., Dar-es-Salaam, Tanzania, 1973-.

ROMICK, A.H. (Abe), businessman. B. in Pittsburgh, Pa., Jan. 7, 1903; s. Sander and Rachael R.; gr. and h. sc., Pittsburgh and Chicago; m. Frances Towb, 1925; children: Sandra Jean (Mrs. Danny Plotnick), Gerald J.; U.S. Army, China Expeditionary Forces, 1919; estab. merchandising bus., 1925, in various parts of world; founder, Fed. Distributing Co., El Paso, Tex., 1948-49; owner, 3 retail clothing stores, Anchorage, 1949-59, ret.; state comr. commerce, 1959-65. Mem., Alaska Civil Rights Com., Alaska Family Counseling Services (pres.), Elks, Am. Leg., Beth Shalom Congregation (bd. mem.). Democrat.

RONAN, John (Jack), miner. B. in Kan. City, Kan., June 28, 1871; m. Margaret Kelly in Kan. City, Feb. 24, 1914; children: Mrs. Raymond L. Cote, Mrs. Irvin Bowman, Mrs. John McCabe; worked in logging camps, Wash.; miner, Atlin and Dawson, B.C., Circle City, Fairbanks, Nome, Iditarod, Seward, Juneau, Hyder, 1898-; cand., del. in Cong., 1908; del., Dem. Nat. Conv., St. Louis, Mo., 1916; terr. Sen., from Anchorage, 1917-21; mem., terr. bd. education, 1919-21; U.S. Comr. and dep. U.S. Marshal, Hyder, 1920s; appt. liquor license officer, 4th div., Fairbanks, 1935; moved to Seattle, Wash., 1947; died there, Dec. 18, 1955. Mem., Mine Owners' Assn. Democrat.

ROSE, Nissel A. (Mike), lawyer, school teacher. B. in Calais, France, Apr. 27, 1921; gr. sc., Dunkirk, France; h. sc., Paris, Lille and Libourne; B.A., U. Syracuse, 1950; LL.B., Catholic U. of Am. (Columbus), Wash., D.C., 1955; m. Beatrice K.; children: Samuel B., Nathaniel, Beth Elli; went to N.Y.C., 1940, engaged in retail bus., Endicott, N.Y. and Wash., D.C.; teacher, French language, Calif. and Wash., D.C., and law courses at Anchorage Community Coll.; U.S. Marine Corps, 1942-45, 1950-51; law prac., Wash., D.C., 1955-57; dist. counsel, U.S. Army Corps Engrs., Elmendorf AFB, Anchorage, 1957-64; pvt. law prac., Anchorage, 1964-67, 1969-; hearing officer, Alaska Transportation Com., 1967-69; state H.R., 1971-73. Mem., Am. Federation Fed. Employees, Anchorage chapter (pres.), Fed. Bar Assn., Anchorage chapter (pres., 1959), Alaska Trial Lawyers Acad., Alaska State Employes Assn. (bd. dir.), Am. Leg., Masons, Eagles, Anchorage and Alaska Bar Assns., Congregation Beth Shalom. Democrat. Address: 2263 Chilligan Dr., Anchorage 99503.

ROSS, Hosea H., businessman. B. in Almont, Mich., Aug. 13, 1876; public sc., Mich. and N. Dak.; h. sc., Ellendale, N. Dak.; m. Alma; children: Mrs. Harold Christenson, Mrs. Arthur (Thelma) Hering; joined gold rush to Dawson, 1898, Fairbanks, 1904; conducted the only mortuary, Fairbanks, and owned extensive real estate; div. road comr., 1915-19; terr.

H.R., 1921-29; bought insur. and real estate bus. from Harry Woodward, 1932; prop., Steel Creek roadhouse, 1936-45; chmn., Fairbanks Selective Service bd., 1942-45; charter mem., Fairbanks Commercial Club; moved to Kennewick, Wash., 1945; died there, July 9, 1956. Mem., Pioneers, Eagles, Masons. Republican.

ROSS, Robert A., salesman. B. in Red Bluff, Calif., June 24, 1922; grad., h. sc., Garden Grove, Calif., 1940; stud., Anchorage Community Coll., 1957-58; m. Nita Jane Gott, Dec. 24, 1945; 5 children; U.S. Army Signal Corps, 1942-45; farmer, Calif., 1945-49; mechanic and heavy equipment operator, 1949-50; arr. Wasilla, 1950, cleared farm land in Matanuska Valley; mechanic and equipment operator, ARC, 1950-56; moved to Anchorage; employe, U.S. Army, Ft. Richardson, 1956-59; estab. Ross auto and equipment repair shop, 1959-60; real estate salesman, Anchorage, 1960-63; Anchorage Planning Com., 1960-62; cand., sec. of state, 1962; estab. Bob Ross Insurance and Real Estate Co., Soldotna. Mem., Am. Leg., Izaak Walton League, Anchorage Rep. Club (pres., 1961-62). Republican.

ROSSWOG, John H., merchant. B. in Wash., 1904; s. Charles and Elizabeth R.; gr. and h. sc., Cordova; m.; children: Iris, Joseph; went to Douglas with parents, 1905; res., Cordova, 1909-, where family estab. stationery and drug store; del., const. conv., 1955-56; bd. dir., Pioneers Home, Sitka, 1957-; city councilman, Cordova, 5 yrs.; chmn., utility bd., 3 yrs.; pres., dir., First Bk. of Cordova. Mem., Pioneers, Elks (exalted ruler), Izaak Walton League, C. of C. (pres.).

ROTH, Rhinehart F., lawyer. B. in 1865; m.; children: Irma (dec. 1909), Dorothy (Mrs. Arthur Loftus), Florence Ada (Mrs. Charles O. Thompson); law prac., Fairbanks, 1906-26; del., Dem. conv., Skagway, 1914; mem., Dem. 4th div. com.; U.S. dist. atty., 4th jud. div., Fairbanks, 1914-18; pvt. law prac., Fairbanks; pvt. law prac., Los Angeles, Calif., 1926-; died in Los Angeles, Apr. 18, 1937. Democrat.

ROTHENBURG, Richard Carl, miner. B. in Berlin, Germany, Oct. 23, 1868; m. Mrs. Amelia White Struck, Fairbanks, Nov. 18, 1933; miner, Coeur d'Alene, Ida., 1897; went to Dawson via Chilkoot Pass, 1898, to Fortymile, Nome, Fairbanks, 1903; terr. H.R., 1929-31, speaker; re-appt. sc. tax collector, Fairbanks, 10th term, 1941; died in Fairbanks, June 4, 1949. Mem., Pioneers (grand pres., 1924). Republican.

ROUST, Christian A., miner, salesman. B. in Oakland, Calif., June 18, 1901; s. Abel and Margrethe (Markinson) R.; Berkeley h. sc., 3 yrs.; stud., Polytechnic Sc. Engring., 2 yrs.; m. Belva Williams, Nome, Aug. 26, 1942; s. Christian Thomas; engring. equipment salesman, 1916-20; hard rock miner, mill operator and electrician, 1920-30; placer miner, Seward Peninsula, 1932-41; Nome city councilman; terr. H.R., from Candle, 1943-45; dist. mgr., Glenn Carrington Co., Nome, Anchorage,

Fairbanks, 1941-55; res., Seattle, for health reasons, 1955-62; employe, Lyle's Hardware Store, Juneau, 1962-. Mem., Pioneers.

RUSSELL, Edward Crawford, Jr., newspaper editor-publisher, lecturer. Accompanied father to Dyea, Mar. 1898; father-son pub., THE DYEA PRESS, 1 yr.; father pub., (Haines) PORCUPINE QUILL; estab. ALASKA DAILY DISPATCH, Juneau (until 1919), Seattle, 1919-23; sold newspaper, new owners changing the name to ALASKA WEEKLY; m. and div., Juneau; m. 2d, Mrs. Josephine Stoel Stevens in Chicago, Feb. 15, 1914; publicity agent, Consolidated Vultee Corp., and ed., firm's monthly publication, until 1943; found dead in his car, apparently from heart attack, Whittier, Calif., Apr. 25, 1943. Author: book on game of bridge. Republican.

RUSTGARD, John, lawyer, author. B. in Norway, 1867; grad., prep. sc., Red Wing, Minn., 1886; LL.B., U. Minn., 1890; m., 1902 (dec. 1924); d. Mrs. Vivien Stevens; m. 2d, Mrs. Josephine Halvorsen in Seattle, June 24, 1926; left home, 1882; cabin-boy on clipper ship; sc. teacher, Minneapolis, Minn., 1890-92; law prac., Minneapolis, 1892-1900; pvt. law prac., mayor, 1903, city atty., 2 terms, Nome, 1900-09; U.S. dist. atty., 1st jud. div., Juneau, 1910-14; pvt. law prac., Juneau, 1914-20; terr. atty.-gen., 1920-33; cand., del. in Cong., 1930; lived in southern Italy, 1 yr.; res., Babson Park, Fla., his country estate named "Villa Sorgenfri," 1934-50; special consult., Am. Economic Found., N.Y.C., 1950; died in his home, Feb. 10, 1950. Author: THE PROBLEM OF POVERTY, SHARING THE WEALTH, BOTTOM SIDE UP, INTERNATIONAL VAGARIES, THE BANKRUPTCY OF LIBERALISM, several articles for *Saturday Evening Post*, including "Human Rights and Property Rights." Mem., Masons (life), Scottish Rite (life, since 1912).

RUTHERFORD, Bert C., merchant. B. in Leavenworth, Wash., 1914; grad., Wash. Technical Inst.; m. (div.); children: Catherine Jean, Jean Ann; m. 2d; went to Anchorage, 1938; owner-operator, Rutherford's 2 men's clothing shops, Finley's and Bootery shoe shops, Alaska Auto Co.; terr. H.R., 1953-55; left Anchorage, early 1960s. Republican.

RYAN, Irene E., geological engineer. B. in Boston, Mass., Sept. 10, 1909; B.S., N. Mex. Inst. of Mining & Technology, 1941; m. John E. Ryan, Feb. 19, 1938; children: Marcella Aurenea (Mrs. Patrick Lynn Sharrock), Patricia (Mrs. Roy L. Wright, Jr.); res., Tex.; visited Anchorage, 1931-32; ret. to N. Mex. for studies; res., Anchorage, 1941-; consulting bus., geological exploration and survey work for pvt. and public agencies; Alaska H.R., 1955-59, Sen., 1959-61; state comr., economic development and planning, 1970-74; exec. sec., Yukon Power for America (promoting Rampart dam), 1963-. Mem., Gov.'s Adv. Reapportionment Bd., 1961-; Am. Inst. Mining & Metallurgy Engrs.; Soc. Women Engrs.; Am. Soc. Civil Engrs.; Am. Soc. Advancement Science; Arctic Inst.; Nat. Assn. Geology Teachers; BPW. Catholic, Democrat. Address: Star Route A, Box 84, Anchorage 99502.

RYAN, James Cecil, educator. B. in Dickson, Tenn.,
Oct. 19, 1900; s. Dennis and Orpha (Howard) R.;
B.S., Northwestern Teachers Coll., Okla., 1925;
M.A., 1932, Ed.D., 1936, U. Okla.; m. Irice Anna
Butler, Aug. 8, 1928; s. James Dennis; teacher and
supt., Okla. scs., 1918-25; English teacher, Philip-
pines, 1925-27; sc. teacher, Tulsa, Okla., 1927-28;
prof., education, UA, 1928-41; terr. comr., educa-
tion, 1941-51; supt. scs., Fairbanks, 1951-66. Mem.,
Rotary, Elks, NEA.

RYAN, John Joseph (Jack), journalist. B. in Wash.,
1919; stud., U. Wash.; m. Patricia; children:
Stephen, Margaret Mary, Patti Ann, Jacqueline;
owner-skipper, salmon troller "Maggie Murphy",
southeastern waters, 1939-41; columnist, Ketchikan
DAILY NEWS, 1947-48; managing ed., Anchorage
DAILY NEWS, 1948-50; United Press mgr. for
Alaska, 1950-51; managing ed., Fairbanks NEWS-
MINER, 1951-57, news ed. and sports writer,
1959-60; lived aboard 40-ft. ketch, while free lance
writing, spent time in Hawaii, 1957-59; ret. to
Alaska; cand., U.S. Cong.; campaign mgr., GOP
central dist., Fairbanks, 1960; ed., Alaska DAILY
EMPIRE, Juneau, 1961-62; mgr., Mike Stepovich's
gubernatorial campaigns, 1962, 1966; coordinator,
William Egan's gubernatorial re-election campaign,
1966; ed. and sports writer, Tacoma NEWS
TRIBUNE, 1964-. Author: "Maggie Murphy," 1961.
Republican.

RYAN, Richard S., lobbyist, civil engineer. B. in Wa-
terford, Ireland, 1861; stud., Clinquowes Wood
Coll.; worked for father, who headed contracting
firm, John Ryan & Sons; emigrated to U.S., 1881;
ry. contracting bus., building in part: Elkhorn &
Missouri Valley R.R., Cheyenne & Northern R.R.,
Colo. & Western, Union Pacific, Denver & Gulf,
and many branch lines; estab. Blue Star Navigation
Co. for Alaska bus., 1897; joined Klondike
stampeders to Dawson, 1898, Nome, 1899; chmn.,
Anvil Township Com. to organize govt. for Nome;
elected mayor, Nome, refusing to serve; lobbyist in
Wash., D.C., on behalf of Nome, 1899-1907; cand.,
Rep. nomination for del. in Cong., 1906; often men-
tioned as potential nominee for gov., Alaska; pres.,
Controller Bay R.R. & Coal Co.; died in W. Va.,
Nov. 28, 1931; survived by wife. Republican.

RYDEEN, Almer, miner. B. in Stockholm, Sweden,
1877; m.; d. Mrs. Boris Glazounow; went to
Candle, 1902, to join bro., Robert, a founder of
Candle; postmaster, Kiwalik, 1905-07; terr. H.R.,
1919-21, 1927-29, 1949-51; mgr., Lomen Reindeer
Corp., Golovin, 1930-; mem., Nome sc. bd.,
1939-40; clerk of dist. ct., Nome, 1934-40; died in
Seattle, Wash., Aug. 16, 1964. Democrat.

S

SACKETT, John C., businessman. B. in Cutoff,
Alaska, June 3, 1944; s. Lucy (Vant) Lawrance (dec.
1968); Sheldon Jackson h. sc., Sitka, valedictorian,
1963; B.A., UA, 1968; unm.; state H.R., from
Huslia, 1967-71; state Sen., from Galena, 1973-77;
owner, Galena Yukon Lodge and shopping center.
Mem., Doyon Ltd. (Fairbanks-based native reg.
corp.), chmn., bd. dir., 1973-; Fairbanks Native
Assn.; Tanana Council of Chiefs (pres., 1967-69);
Remote Housing exec. com.; Rural Affairs Com.;
Kappa Alpha Psi; Pacific Northwest Reg. Adv.
Com., NPS, 1972-. Republican.

SANDERS, William Hobart, lawyer, author. B. in
Gurley, Ala., Oct. 5, 1920; B.S., 1942, LL.B., 1947,
J.D., 1969, U. Ala., Tuscaloosa; m. Margaret
Timbes; children: Skyla Ann, Marsland; U.S.
Army, counter-intelligence corps, 1943-46; went to
Alaska, 1938; pvt. law prac., Anchorage, 1951-63;
cand., atty. gen., 1956; state H.R, 1961-64;
superior ct. judge, 2d jud. div., Nome, 1964-.
Awarded: Kellogg Found. fellowships to sessions of
Nat. Coll. of State Trial Judges, 1965, 1973. Author:
articles on travels and Eskimo life in Alaska. Mem.,
Alaska and Am. Bar Assns.; Am. Leg. (No. 1 post
comdr.), Kiwanis, Moose, Elks, Odd Fellows, 40 &
8 (grand chef de gare, 1953), Alaska Nat. Guard (capt.
and exec. officer), VFW. Methodist, Republican.

SASSARA, Charles J., Jr. (Chuck), businessman. B.
in Detroit, Mich., Oct. 19, 1930; s. Charles J. and
Kathleen S.; B.S., UCLA, 1955; m. Ann Baaches,
1952; children: Charles J., III, Richard; prop.,
Yacht Club lodge, Big Lake, near Palmer, 1955-62;
moved to Anchorage, 1962; prop., auto sales
agency, 1962-; advertising mgr., Anchorage NEWS,
1966; charter boat operator, "Arctic Tern," Prince
William Sound, 1968-70; state H.R., 1965-70,
majority leader, 1970; cand., sec. of state, 1970; left
Alaska, 1971. Mem., Elks, Moose, Alaska Airmen's
Assn., Civil Air Patrol, Jr. C. of C., Anchorage Race
Car Drivers Assn., state adv. bd., SBA. Episcopalian, Democrat.

SAXTON, H.M., lawyer. B. in Ky., 1864; grad.,
Central Normal Sc., Danville, Ind.; m. Mary King
in Fla.; sc. teacher, 16 yrs.; supt., Danville city scs.,
and law stud.; admitted to bar; res., Fla., several
yrs.; law partnership with bro.-in-law, Will R.
King, Ontario, Ore.; partnership interrupted with
King's appointment to Ore. Supreme Ct., 1911; U.S.
dist. atty., 2d jud. div., Nome, 1913-17. Democrat.

SAYLORS, Aubrey M. (Bud), businessman. B. in
Greenville, S.C., Oct. 18, 1933; s. William E. and
Nina S.; h. sc., Greenville, 1952; stud., U. S.C.; m.

Sara, "Jerie" (div.); s. Durk; m. 2d, Patricia Ann Janout in Juneau, Apr. 21, 1974; U.S. Marine Corps, 1955-57; ret. to U. S.C., 1957-59; customer service agent, Northwest Airlines, Anchorage, 1959-60; personnel officer, RCA, Anchorage, 1961-63; exec. dir., Greater Anchorage Community Chest, 1963-65; adm. asst. to chmn., Greater Anchorage Borough, 1965-72; owner-operator, Roadrunner Rapid Print Shop, 1972-; state H.R., 1973-74; dir., adm. services, state dept. adm., 1974-. Mem., Greater Anchorage, Inc. (pres., 1971-73); Greater Anchorage Community Action Agency (mem., bd. trustees, 1965-, pres., 1969-); YMCA, (bd. pres.); Am. Assn. Public Adm.; Rotary. Methodist, Republican. Address: 630 W. 4th Ave., Anchorage 99501.

SCAVENIUS, Jack Frederick, lawyer, aviator. B. in Denmark, Mar. 5, 1904; s. Carl S. and Fredericka (Zytphen-Adler) S.; stud., U. Copenhagen, 2-1/2 yrs.; LL.B., U. Chicago, 1954; admitted to Alaska bar, 1955; m. Emogene Kale in Cordova, Mar. 5, 1942 (div.); d. Helen Marie; m. 2d, Irma R.; emigrated to U.S., 1927; bush pilot, Alaska, 1938-42; U.S. Army Air Corps, 1942-45; owner-operator, McKinley Airways, Inc., 1946-50; terr. H.R., 1951-53; city councilman, Anchorage, 1948-49; cand., mayor, 1955; probate master, 3d jud. dist., superior ct., 1959-61; vice consul for Denmark, 1957-60s; state dir., div. air commerce, 1961-62. Mem., Masons, Eastern Star, VFW, Am. Leg., NAACP, Rotary, Red Cross (chmn., bd. dir.), Civil Air Patrol (organizer and first commissioned officer, 1947-50), Anchorage, Alaska, Am. Bar Assns., Cook Inlet Hist. Soc. Presbyterian, Democrat.

SCHLEPPEGRELL, John D. (Jack), businessman. B. in Park Rapids, Minn., Feb. 15, 1926; gr. sc., Menahga, Minn.; h. sc. and jr. coll., Temple, Tex.; stud., Coll. of St. Thomas, St. Paul, Minn. and U. Minn.; m. Bonnie; 4 children; U.S. Army, 1944-46, awarded bronze star; constr. worker, Fairbanks, 1951-53; salesman-mgr., Bates Candy Co., Fairbanks, 1953-55; owner-operator, Steese Market and Beverage store, Fairbanks, 1955-66; chmn., Fairbanks North Star Borough, Fairbanks, 1964-66; cand., sec. of state, 1966; clerk-adm., village of Shoreview, Minn., 1967-; named dir., state rural development, 1966, but declined; Alaska mgr., Ellerbe Corp., architecture engrng. and planning firm, bases in St. Paul, Minn., Anchorage, 1972-. Mem., Rep. central com., 1962-67, Kiwanis, Hamilton Acres Public Utilities bd. (pres., 1961-64). Lutheran, Republican. Address: 6029 Doncaster Dr., Anchorage.

SCHOFIELD, George D., lawyer, miner. B. in Portland, Mich., Aug. 23, 1864; stud., Northwest U. and Normal Sc., Dixon, Ill.; m. Sarah E. Amidon of San Francisco, 1896; children: George D., Mary Gwendolin; operating hoisting engr., Butte, Mont., 1879-83; law stud.; admitted to bar, Wash. Terr., 1883-85; ct. reporter and dist. atty., Nebraska City, 1888-90; joined father's law firm, Montesano, Wash., 1890-92; prosecuting atty., Chehalis Co., Wash., 1892-94; Wash. state Sen., 1896-1900; miner-lawyer, Nome, 1900-30; city atty., Nome, 1907-10; U.S. Comr., 1910-14; hard rock and

placer miner; opened tin mines of Tin City; operator, hydraulic plants on Dahl Cr. and mined on Submarine beach near Nome; cand., terr. atty. gen., 1916; res., Seattle, Wash., 1930-32; ret. to Long Beach, Calif., 1932; died in his home, Long Beach, Feb. 5, 1937. Mem., Alaska C. of C., Alaska Bar Assn. (pres.). Republican.

SCHULZ, Thomas E., lawyer. B. in Spokane, Wash., Oct. 15, 1936; s. Ellsworth W. and Mary (Bain) S.; stud., UA, 1954-56, U. Ore., 1956-59, Willamette Coll. of Law, 1959-62; m. Mary Gale Sullivan, Nov. 24, 1960; children: Bryan, Kathryn, William; presiding dist. judge, Juneau, 1964-67; pvt. law prac., Juneau, 1967-73; superior ct. judge, Ketchikan, 1973-; chmn., Juneau Planning Com., 5 yrs. Mem., Alaska and Am. Bar Assns., Am. Trial Lawyers Assn. Democrat.

SCHWAMM, John Anthony, businessman. B. in Sitka, Aug. 25, 1943; s. George S. (Tony) and Kathryn (Schilstra) S.; stud., U. Ore., Santa Barbara City Coll.; B.A., AMU, 1967; m. Beverly Vance in Anchorage, June 28, 1968; s. John Anthony; office mgr., Tyonek Indian Corp., 1967-; state H.R., 1969-71. Democrat. Address: 540 L St., Anchorage 99501.

SCOTT, Nell, legal secretary. B. in Marengo, Mich., c. 1901; public sc., Seattle, Wash.; legal sec., Anchorage, 1923-34; m. Mr. Richard; moved to Seldovia when husband appt. dep. U.S. Marshal, 1934-; first woman legislator in Alaska, terr. H.R., 1937-39. Mem., Anchorage Woman's Club, Alaska Fed. of Women's Clubs (chmn.), Am. Citizenship Com. Democrat.

SCOTT, Thomas S., accountant, banker. B. in York, Neb., Sept. 15, 1883; grad., U. Wash.; m. Arline Hanson in Seattle, Wash., 1909; children: Mary, Jane, Ann, Robert; went to Valdez where father was asst. dist. atty.; employe, Valdez Bk. & Mercantile Co., dep. clerk of ct., Valdez, 1907-14; cashier, First Bk. of Cordova, 1914-20; v.p., Bk. of Alaska, Cordova, pres., Cordova Packing Co., 1920-31; died in hotel room, Ontario, Calif., determined suicide, July 24, 1931. Mem., Masons (master), Shrine, Elks, Cordova C. of C. (pres.). Republican.

SCOTT, Tolbert Paton, miner. B. in Morganton, N.C., May 6, 1880; s. Thomas and Margaret (Alexandra) S.; m. Vallie Wilson, Apr. 2, 1914; children: Tolbert Paton, Jr., Margaret, Robert, Charlotte Jane (Mrs. Perkins); lived on farm; went to Seattle, Wash., via St. Louis, Mo., 1901; worked in lumber camps, Wash., 1901-06; went to Nome, 1906; miner, Nome area, 2 decades, part-time for Lomen Bros.; lived in Solomon until children reached school age, then moved to Nome; terr. H.R., 1933-39, 1943-45, Sen., 1945-49; died in Pioneers Home, Sitka, Feb. 17, 1961; buried in Nome. Mem., Masons. Methodist, Democrat.

SEATON, Frederick Andrew, newspaper publisher. B. in Wash., Dec. 11, 1909; s. Fay Noble and Dorothea Elizabeth (Schmidt) S.; stud., Kan. State Coll., 1927-31, LL.D., 1955; Dr. Humanities, Maryville Coll., 1956; LL.D., UA, 1958; m. Gladys

Hope Dowd, Jan. 23, 1931; children: Johanna Christine (dec.), Donald Richard, Johanna Christine, Monica Margaret, Alfred Noble; dir., sports publicity, Kan. State Coll., 1927-31; radio sports announcer, KSAC, WIBW, 1929-37; assoc. ed., Seaton Pub., Manhattan, Kan., 1933-37; pres., KHAS-TV, Hastings, Neb., pres., Sheridan (Wyo.) Newspapers, Inc., Seaton Pub. Co., Lead, S. Dak., Winfield (Kan.) Pub. Co., Inc., Seaton Pub. Co., Hastings, Neb., Alliance (Neb.) Pub. Co., Neb. Broadcasting Co., Hastings; asst. Sec. Defense, 1953-55; adm. asst. to U.S. Pres., 1955; Sec. Interior, 1956-61; pub., Hastings DAILY TRIBUNE, 1961-74; died in Hastings, Jan. 17, 1974. Mem., Elks, Masons, Rotary, Sigma Delta Chi, Pi Kappa Delta, Beta Theta Pi. Methodist, Republican.

SEE, Frank, fisherman, registered guide, lodge proprietor. B. at Excursion Inlet, June 9, 1915; gr. and h. sc., Hoonah and Juneau; m. Hilda Greenewald, 1952; children: 5 by previous m., Katherine Jean, Franklin, et al.; worked winters for USFS and fished summers; security guard, Mt. Edgecumbe naval station, 1942-46; police officer, Hoonah, 1946-52; stream guard supervisor, U.S. Fish & Wildlife; prop., Thunderbird Lodge, Chichagof I., in summer, prop., Greenewald Mercantile gen. store, Hoonah; perpetual mayor, Hoonah, 1958- ; state H.R., 1965-69. Mem., sc. bd., ANB, grand pres. and exec. com., Fish & Game bd., 1961-65. Democrat.

SEXTON, George, farmer, miner, hotel proprietor. B. in Mantoir, Ind., c. 1862; wife from Topeka, Kan.; children: Sylvia, Neil; went to Skagway, 1898; employe, White Pass & Yukon Ry.; farmer, Sitka experiment station, Sunrise, Moose Pass; dep. U.S. Marshal, Moose Pass and Seward, 1902- ; participated in gold rush at Sunrise and prospected on Kenai Peninsula; prop., Sexton Hotel, Seward; Rep. Nat. Com. for Alaska, 1924-28; died in Seward, Feb. 28, 1936. Mem., Modern Woodman of World, Odd Fellows, Pioneers (charter mem., Seward Igloo). Republican.

SHACKLEFORD, Lewis P., lawyer. Pvt. law prac., Juneau, early 1900s; del., Rep. Nat. Conv., Chicago, 1908, 1912; Rep. Nat. Com., 1908-12; chmn., Rep. terr. com., 1909-12; moved to Tacoma, Wash., where family lived; associated with bro. in law prac. Republican.

SHARPE, Walter P., accountant. B. in Nome, 1906; s. Walter B. and Sara (Connors) S.; gr. and h. sc., Ketchikan; stud., U. Portland, Ore., 2 yrs., bus. coll., 1 yr.; m. Mary MacKenzie, 1930 (dec.); children: Sharon Sarah, Julia Elizabeth; acct., Ketchikan Cold Storage, 1929-37; terr. tax collector, 1935-37; exec. dir., terr. unemployment compensation com., Juneau, 1937-41; dir., social security agency, 1941-42; terr. comr. labor, 1942-46; asst. mgr., Alaska Salmon Industry, Inc., Seattle, Wash., auditor, office mgr., 1947-60; tax consult., 1960- ; res., Chehalis, Wash., 1974. Mem., Pioneers. Catholic, Democrat.

SHARROCK, George, businessman. B. in Zanesville, O., 1910; stud., electrical engring., U. Detroit, 1928-30; m. Pauline Livesay, Jan. 15, 1938; chil-

dren: Patrick, Dianne (Smith, div.); employe, Motor States Products, Ypsilanti, Mich., asst. supt., 1930-47; dist. sales mgr., Pacific Northern Airlines, 1947-66; mayor, Anchorage, 1961-64; state comr. commerce, 1966-69; chmn., Fed. Field Com. for Development Planning in Alaska, Anchorage, 1969-71, ret.; mobile home travel in states. Received Gold Pan award, Anchorage C. of C., 1959. Mem., adv. bd., U.S. Conference of Mayors, 1963; AMU (founding trustee); YMCA (bd. mgrs.); Anch. C. of C. (pres.); Alaska C. of C.; Greater Anchorage Inc.; Anchorage Development Corp., Lions, Moose, Anchorage Ski Club. Republican.

SHATTUCK, Allen, insurance-real estate salesman. B. in Portland, Ore., Oct. 26, 1872; s. John Wesley and Mary Corcoran (Allen) S.; gr. sc., Gresham, Ore., 1 yr.; Portland h. sc.; m. Agnes Swineford in Ketchikan, July 28, 1902; children: Allen Swineford (dec. 1920), Virginia, Curtis Gordon; sc. teacher, Multnomah Co., Ore., 2 yrs.; employe, Seattle Hardware Co.; employe, C.W. Young Hardware Co., Juneau, 1897- ; joined bro. Henry's Shattuck Insurance Co., 1900, sole owner, 1914, joined by s. Curtis, 1940; city councilman, Juneau, 1905; terr. H.R., 1929-31, Sen., 1931-35, 1947-47, pres., 1933; died in Juneau, July 1, 1960. Mem., Red Cross (treas., 28 yrs.); C. of C. (pres. many times); Elks, Moose. Democrat.

SHATTUCK, Curtis Gordon, insurance-real estate salesman. B. in Juneau, June 2, 1907; s. Allen and Agnes (Swineford) S.; gr. and h. sc., Juneau; B.A., U. Wash.; m. Mary Louise Patterson, Aug. 4, 1940; children: Allen, Roger, Sarah; reporter, Juneau EMPIRE, 1927-28, 1930; salesman, Shattuck's Insur. agency, 1930-, partner, 1940-; terr. H.R., 1945-47. Mem., SAR, Alaska C. of C. (exec. sec., 1936-40), Pioneers, Elks, Sigma Delta Chi. Democrat.

SHEAKLEY, James, lawyer, miner, merchant. B. in Sheakleyville, Pa., Apr. 24, 1829; common sc., Sheakleyville; teacher, rural scs.; learned trade of cabinetmaker but never followed it; m. Lyndia Long, 1855; children: 2 daughters (died in childhood), s. Frederick Edward; gold miner, Calif., 1851-55; ret. to family farm homestead, Pa., 1855-; sold farm and moved to Greenville, Pa.; dry goods bus., later involved in newly discovered oil operations, Pa., 1864-; U.S. Cong., 1875-77; U.S. Comr. and supt. scs. for Alaska, Wrangell, 1887-93; law stud., admitted to Alaska bar, 1888; del., Dem. Nat. Conv., Chicago, 1892; Gov., Alaska, 1893-97; employe, San Francisco C. of C., bd. of trade, Alaska, giving lectures on Alaska, 1898-; ret. to Pa., 1900, involved in oil operations, Tex. and Okla.; made trip to Alaska, 1909, to investigate oil possibilities; mayor, justice of peace, Greenville; died in his home, Dec. 11, 1917. Democrat.

SHELDON, Robert Edwards (Bobbie), businessman. B. in Snohomish, Wash., June 3, 1883; s. Robert Edwards and Flora (McCallum) S.; public sc., Snohomish, Internat. Correspondence Sc.; m. Anne Bergman; d. Frances Ruth (Mrs. William Aley, Mrs. Carl Erickson); mother died, 1897; accompanied father to Skagway enroute to Klondike goldfields,

Dec. 1897, father died, fall 1898; longshoreman, engr. in charge, White Pass & Yukon Ry. power plant, engr. on mailboat running between Skagway, Juneau, Haines, Sitka; post office employe, Skagway, until 1908; built first automobile in Alaska, 1905; operator, Northern Commercial Co.'s powerhouse, Fairbanks, 1908-13; stage bus., Richardson Highway (drove first auto over Richardson Highway, July 1913), 1913-26; employe, ARC, road comr. for 4th div., 1918; prop., tourist concession, Mt. McKinley Park, 1925-41; postmaster, Fairbanks, 1933-40; Alaska H.R., 1925-29, 1959-61, 1965-67; exec. dir., terr. unemployment compensation com., Juneau, 1941-51; ret. to Fairbanks, 1952-. Mem., Pioneers, Masons, Eastern Star, C. of C. (pres., 1936-38), 1st Fed. Savings & Loan Assn. (dir.). Democrat.

SHEPARD, H. Royal, customs official, insurance agent. B. in Vincennes, Ind., Jan. 29, 1864; m.; children: Mrs. B.B. Nieding, Royal M., John G.; dep. U.S. Customs Collector, Juneau, 1897-1913; gen. insur. bus., Juneau, 1913-40, sold bus. to Shattuck Insur. agency; represented Canadian Nat. SS and R.R.; city clerk, magistrate, assessor, Juneau; terr. H.R., 1923-25; left Juneau, 1942, made home with d. in Fresno, Calif.; died there, Aug. 31, 1944. Mem., Elks (charter mem.), Pioneers (pres.). Republican.

SHERARD, Thurman D., civil engineer. B. in 1916; dep. state highway engr., Cheyenne, Wyo., 1959; dir., state div. highways, 1959-62. Mem., Wyo. Soc. Professional Engrs. (pres.).

SHERMAN, William A., miner, barber. B. in Gratiot, Wis., 1866; public sc., Ia.; went into bus., Yankton, S. Dak., 1874; gold prospector, Fortymile dist.; Dawson, where he built first log cabin, 1896-; res., Nome, 1900-05; estab. bus., Katalla; estab. barber shop, Cordova; contract employe, AEC, Seward; prop., Service Barber shop, Anchorage, 1916-; terr. H.R., 1925-27; city councilman, Anchorage, 1924-25. Mem., Pioneers (charter mem., pres.). Democrat.

SHOUP, Arthur Glendenning, lawyer. B. in Challis, Ida., Nov. 27, 1880; s. James McCain S.; public sc., Ida.; stud., political science-law, U. Wash., 3 yrs.; m. Ethel Phillips; 3 children; m. 2d, Rose Kemp, Seattle, Aug. 28, 1915; went to Sitka with parents, 1897; dep. U.S. Marshal, Ketchikan, Sitka, 1902-10; mayor, Sitka, 3 terms; terr. H.R., from Sitka, 1913-17; supt., Pioneers' Home, Sitka, 1913-19; U.S. dist. atty., 1st jud. div., Juneau, 1921-26; pvt. law prac., San Jose, Calif., 1927-33; U.S. Comr. for northern Calif., 1933-41; died in San Jose, Apr. 9, 1942. Mem., A.B., Pioneers, Elks. Republican.

SHOUP, James McCain, U.S. Marshal, lawyer. B. in Pa., 1849; public sc., Ill.; m.; children: Arthur Glendenning, Mrs. Joseph Wager; U.S. Navy, 1865; res., Id., 1865-97; pvt. law prac., Boise; mem., const. conv. and 1st Ida. state Sen., 1889-92; first U.S. Marshal for Alaska, Sitka, 1897-1906, Juneau,

1906-09; pvt. law prac., Ketchikan, 1909-16, 1920-27; res., San Francisco, 1916-20; died in Ketchikan, Aug. 4, 1927. Republican.

SILIDES, George Constantine, civil engineer. B. in N.Y.C., June 28, 1922; s. Constantine and Hope S.; grad., Stuyvesant h. sc., N.Y.C., 1939; B.S., U.S. Military Acad., 1946; professional registered civil engr., 1952; m. Mary Ruth Ogburn in Fairbanks, June 1950; children: Mary Hope, Robert, George, Jr., David, Nicholas; m. 2d, Jeanne Aubert, 1970; went to Fairbanks, March 1947; asst. supt., Chatanika div., Fairbanks Exploration Co., 3 yrs.; gen. constr. engring. and design; estab. engring. consulting firm, 1957-; joint venture partnership of Silides & Galliett, 1962-; comr. and vice chmn., ASHA, 1969-70; state Sen., 1973-75. Episcopalian, Republican. Address: Box 746, Fairbanks 99707.

SIMPSON, Jack R., insurance adjuster. B. in Condon, Ore., Dec. 18, 1909; s. Cass A. and Helen (Parmen) S.; B.A., Willamette U., 1936; LL.B., Westminister Law Sc., Colo.; m. Nova Hedin in Portland, Ore., July 18, 1936; children: Erik J., Mark R.; law prac., Colo.; went to Anchorage, 1952-; estab. Northern Insurance Adjusters, Inc., Anchorage, Fairbanks, Juneau, Ketchikan, 1952-70, sold bus.; special asst. to Gov. Keith Miller, Juneau, 1969-70; state H.R., 1967-69; asst. claims mgr., Providence Wash. Insurance Co., Anchorage, 1971-; Rep. state finance chmn., 1965; state equal employment coordinator, 1969-70; exec. sec., Com. for Northern Operation of Rail Transportation and Highways, 1970-71. Mem., Colo. Bar, Lions, Anchorage Rep. Club (pres., 1958), United Churchmen of Alaska (pres.), Southcentral Rep. dist. com. (chmn.), 1963), Alaska Press Club. Presbyterian (elder), Republican. Address: 1127 S St., Anchorage 99501.

SINGLETON, James Keith, Jr., lawyer. B. in Oakland, Calif., Jan. 27, 1939; s. James K. and Irene Elizabeth (Lilly) S.; B.A., U. Calif., Berkeley, 1961; LL.B., Boalt Hall Sc. of Law, U. Calif., Berkeley, 1964; m. Sandra Claire Hoskins in Concord, Calif., Oct. 15, 1966; s. Matthew David; law clerk, Anchorage, summer 1963; pvt. law prac., Anchorage, 1965-70; superior ct. judge, Anchorage (also responsible for ct. matters in Glennallen, Valdez, Cordova), 1970-. Mem., Anchorage, Calif., Am. Bar Assns.; Rep. state central com., 1967-70; Rep. southcentral dist. com. (chmn., 1969-70); state boundary com. (chmn., 1966-69); Alaska Children's Services (dir., 1973-). Methodist, Republican. Address: 303 K St., Anchorage 99501.

SKINNER, Norbert H., teamster. B. in N.Y., 1928; public sc., N.Y.; unm.; employe, N.Y. Park com.; U.S. Air Force, Korean War, temporary duty at Ladd and Eilson AFB, 1954; stud., UA; radio and television announcer, Fairbanks, Juneau; worked on DEW line, Pt. Barrow, Pt. Lay, later with RCA on Ballistic Missile Early Warning System, Clear; state H.R., from Clear, 1965-67. Democrat.

SLATER, H.A., businessman. Res., Cordova; terr. H.R., 1919-21. Republican.

SLOANE, Dr. L.O., Territorial Health Commissioner, 1918-21.

SMISER, James A., lawyer. B. and reared in Columbia, Tenn.; m.; U.S. dist. atty., 1st jud. div., Juneau, 1915-21. Democrat.

SMITH, Donald Joseph, railroad executive. B. in Chicago, Ill., Apr. 18, 1919; s. James Henry and Margaret (Kavanaugh) S.; stud., Northwestern U. Inst. Management, 1957; m. Anne Gaughan Smith, July 16, 1945; children: Margaret, Terrance, Kathleen, Patricia; U.S. Army, 1942-45; apprentice (Chicago), locomotive supervisor (Little Rock and Kan. City), trainmaster (Okla., Ark., Mo.), asst. supt. (St. Paul), supt. (Fairbury, Neb., 1938-58, El Reno, Okla., 1958-60), Rock I. R.R.; gen. mgr., Alaska R.R., 1960-62; asst. gen. mgr., Missouri-Pacific R.R., Little Rock, 1962, gen. mgr., Houston, 1962-67; died in 1967. Mem., Brownsville & Matamoros Bridge Co. (v.p., dir.); Houston Belt & Terminal Co.; New Orleans Lower Coast R.R.; Southern Exploration Co., Western Townsite Co. Catholic.

SMITH, Donald Lee, businessman. B. in Anchorage, Mar. 14, 1939; s. Eugene C. and Ingeborg E. (Swanson) S.; grad., West h. sc., Anchorage, 1957; stud., UA, 1958-62; m. Nancy Lee Knight, June 11, 1959; children: Donald Lee, Jr., Kollette Elizabeth, Laura Lee, Heather; RCA Service Co., 1960s; borough assemblyman, 1965-66; state H.R.,1967-69; owner-mgr., Management Services, 1967-. Mem., Alaska Young Rep. Fed. (state chmn., 1963); Rep. southcentral dist. com. (chmn.); Mt. McKinley Jaycees (pres., 1965); Anch. C. of C., Alaska Press Club, Elks, Pioneers, Anchorage Rep. Club. Episcopalian, Republican.

SMITH, Harvey J., businessman. B. in Kearney, Neb., Apr. 18, 1898; went to Alaska as private, U.S. Army, 1923; m.; estab. bus., Anchorage; bus. agent, Fishermen's Union, which he helped organize; terr. H.R., 1939-45; settled on ranch near Chehalis, Wash., c. 1951. Democrat.

SMITH, Hoke, lawyer, journalist. B. in Newton, N.C., Sept. 2, 1855; s. Hosea Hildreth and Mary Brent (Hoke) S.; educated by father, a sc. teacher; law stud.; admitted to bar, 1873; m. Birdie Cobb Dec. 19, 1883 (dec. 1919); children: Marion, Mrs. Mary Brent Ransom, Mrs. Lucy Grant, Mrs. Callie May; m. 2d, Mazie Crawford, Aug. 27, 1924; owner-pub., Atlanta JOURNAL, 1887-96; Sec. Interior, 1893-96; Gov., Ga., 1907-09, 1911 (July-Nov.); U.S. Sen., from Ga., 1911-21; law prac., Atlanta, 1921-; died Nov. 27, 1931. Presbyterian, Democrat.

SMITH, W. Leonard, highway engineer. B. in Seattle, Wash., Jan. 12, 1894; B.S., U. Wash.; m. Miss Barbara Haering, 1924; children: Jane (Mrs. Workman), William, James; U.S. Navy, 1917-18; engr., Hammon Consolidated Mining Co., Nome, many yrs.; terr. highway engr., 1945-47; terr. H.R., from Nome, 1937-39, 1941-43; chmn., bd.

road comrs., head of Alaska highway patrol, 1947; died in Seattle hospital, Sept. 30, 1947; Mem., terr. bd. education. Democrat.

SMITH, Lynn, U.S. Marshal, miner, jeweler. B. in New Castle, Ind., Mar. 4, 1872; unm.; went to Dawson via White Pass from Ind., 1898; moved to Rampart, 1900, Fairbanks, 1904, Hot Springs, 1907, Tanana, 1910, later to Ruby and Iditarod; operated jewelry bus. in each camp to subsidize prospecting ventures; agent, NAT & T Co., Rampart, Northern Commercial Co., Ruby; dep. U.S. Marshal, Flat, Iditarod, Ruby; U.S. Marshal, 4th jud. div., Fairbanks, 1926-33; died of heart attack in Seattle, Wash., Mar. 10, 1933. Republican.

SMITH, V. Maurice, journalist, radio-television broadcaster. B. in Mt. Vernon, Ia., 1914; s. Dr. O.H. Smith, prof. emeritus, physics, DePauw U., Ind.; m.; d. Marjorie; went to Fairbanks, 1937; warden, Alaska Fire Control Service, 1940-; reporter, managing ed., JESSEN'S WEEKLY, 11 yrs.; broadcaster, KFAR-TV and radio for many yrs., gen. mgr., 1958; state H.R., 1967-69. Republican.

SMITH, Margery Goding, secretary. B. in Skagway; d. Maurice R. and Blenda E. (Lindahl) G.; m. Mr. Neil in Seward; d. Blenda G.; m. 2d, Douglas Smith in Wash., D.C.; s. Douglas; sc. teacher, Seward, during 1st m., later, Valdez and Fairbanks; exec. sec. to Del. Bartlett, Wash., D.C., 1944-59, U.S. Sen. Bartlett, 1959-68. Democrat.

SMITH, Noel, railroad executive. Asst. gen. mgr., Pa. R.R.; special asst. to Sec. Interior, July 1924, to investigate Alaska R.R.; gen. mgr., Alaska R.R., Dec. 19, 1924-1928.

SMITH, Robert L., plumbing contractor. B. in Tex., May 12, 1927; m. Mary; 2 children; U.S. Navy, 1945-48; estab. residence in Alaska, 1954; plumbing contractor, Anchorage, 1961-67; piping supt., chemical and refinery complex, Kenai, 1967-70; asst. comr. labor, Anchorage, 1971-73, comr., 1973-74, res. Mem., Anchorage Lodge F & A M; United Assn. Journeymen and Apprentices of Plumbing & Pipefitting Industries of U.S. and Can., Local No. 67. Democrat.

SMITH, Sumner S., mining engineer. B. in Portland, Ore., 1880; m.; 1 s.; grad., Coll. Mines, U. Calif., 1903; assoc. ed., *Mining & Scientific Press*, San Francisco; consulting engr., mines in Calif. and Mexico; mining engr., U.S. Bur. Mines, Ut., Wyo., Nev.; fed. mine inspector for Alaska, 1911-17; assigned to AEC, developing coal mines, Matanuska Valley, 1917-22, res.; pres., Alaska Minerals Co.; operated Hershey Mine, Kenai Peninsula; terr. H.R., from Anchorage, 1927-29; copper miner, Rainy Hollow dist., 1928; moved to Oakland, Calif., 1929.

SMITH, Walstein, G., banker. B. in Columbus, O., 1866; gr. and h. sc., Columbus; m. Alice Markley (dec. 1937); children: Walstein G., Helen (Mrs. John T. Cass, Mrs. H. Clay Scudder); rose from messenger to teller, Hayden Nat. Bak., Columbus, 1882-1904; officer, Bk. of Commerce, Anacortes,

Wash., 1904-05; cashier, banking firm of Henry Andrews & Co., later absorbed by Northwestern State Bk.. Bellingham, Wash., 1905-07; cashier, First Bk. of Katalla, 1907-13; terr. treas., Juneau, 1913-35; v.p., First Nat. Bk., Juneau, 1935-39; died in St. Ann's hospital, Juneau, Sept. 11, 1950.

SMITH, Walter Osborne (Bo), fisherman. B. in Bethel, N. Mex., Apr. 10, 1907; s. Thomas M. and Ruby S.; h. sc., Phoenix, Ariz., Visalia, Calif.; m. Itha Winchell; children: Ann Aus, Glenn W.; went to Craig, 1931; res., Ketchikan, 1944-; del., const. conv., 1955-56; state Sen., 1959-65. Mem., terr. fisheries bd., Elks. Democrat.

SNEDDEN, Charles Willis (Bill), newspaper editor-publisher. B. in Spokane, Wash., July 20, 1913; s. William A. and Alta A. S.; stud., Ore. State Coll., U. Ore., Wash. State Coll.; m. Helen Elizabeth McNeel; s. Duane McLachlan; mastered linotype operation, 1927; employe, various Puget Sound newspapers; real estate bus.; U.S. Army, 1942; owner-ed.-pub., Fairbanks NEWS-MINER, 1950-; pres., Commercial Printing Co. and Aurora Bldg., Inc. (newspaper affiliates). Mem., Fairbanks Municipal Utilities bd., 1951-54; Alaska State Employment Securities Com., 1954-57; Alaska Public Assn. (pres., 1968); Inland Empire Waterways Assn. (bd. dir., 1962, v.p., 1964); Alaska Statehood Com. (1957-59); Alaska C. of C. (pres., 1960); Pacific Northwest Trade Assn. (bd. dir.); Nat. Conf. Editorial Writers; Nat. Council, Nat. Planning Assn.; Masonic Orders (K.T., Royal Arch); Shrine, Elks. Congregationalist, Republican. Address: 514 Second Ave., Fairbanks 99701.

SNIDER, Gerrit (Heinie), miner, farmer, railroad section foreman, teamster. B. in Monnikendan, Holland, Apr. 13, 1886; s. Peter and Elizabeth S.; gr. sc., Monnikendan; went to sea, 1900; m. Alice Aldenberg in Spokane, Wash., May 20, 1915; steward on ships all over the world, 1900-08; jumped ship at N.Y.C., 1908; waiter, Davenport hotel, Spokane, 1908-09; worked aboard Alaska SS Co. ships and Yukon riverboats, and prospected for gold, 1909-14; guard, San Francisco World's Fair, 1914-15; waiter, bull-cook, watchman, laborer, section foreman, farmer, truck driver, Alaska R.R., ARC, Anchorage, Matanuska Valley, 1916-55; lived on Lake Wasilla homestead, 1925-72; fur-farmer, raising mink, martin and muskrat, 1920s; terr. H.R., 1947-49, Sen., 1951-55; del., Rep. Nat. Conv., Chicago, 1952; information aide, Alaska exhibit, Century 21 World's Fair, Seattle, 1962; died in nursing home, Anchorage, Feb. 20, 1972. Author: "So Was Alaska," 1961, "100 Alaska Stories," 1966. Mem., Pioneers (grand pres., 1953), Elks. Presbyterian, Republican.

SNODGRASS, Milton D., agronomist, farmer. B. in Jasper Co., Ind., Mar. 14, 1876; gr. and h. sc., Little River, Kan.; B.S., Kan. Agricultural Coll., 1906; hon. D.Sc., UA, 1961; m. Margaret Jane, June 7, 1907; children: Rolland, William, Mrs. Margaret E. McCarthy, Mrs. Agnes I. Reed, Mrs. Mary Hale; employe, Kan. state experimental station, Kodiak agricultural experiment station, 1907-12; cattle rancher, Kodiak I., 1912-15; estab.

Matanuska Valley experiment station, 1915; res., Seward, 1916-17; in charge of agricultural experiment stations, Fairbanks, 1917-21; farmed near Fairbanks, 1921-23; terr. Sen., 1923-25, H.R., 1953-55; in charge of agricultural experiment station, Matanuska, 1923-29; agent, Alaska R.R., instrumental in bringing 55 families to settle in Matanuska Valley colony, 1929-33, ret.; farmed his 160-acre homestead, Matanuska Valley, 1934-60; one of Alaska's first presidential electors, 1960; he and wife entered Pioneers Home, Sitka, 1966, and transferred to newly built Pioneers Home, Fairbanks, 1967; died there, Dec. 1, 1967. Received citizen-of-the-year award, Kiwanis Club, Palmer, 1964. Mem., bd. regents, UA, 1921-29; Northland Pioneer Grange, No. 1, Palmer (organizer, pres.); initiator of annual Palmer State Fair.

SNOW, Chester Kingsley, miner, journalist. B. in Norwich, N.Y., Dec. 24, 1874; stud., Southern Ia. Normal Sc., Bloomfield, Ia., 1889-92, U. Neb., 1895-97; sc. teacher, Hemingford, Neb., 1892-95; unm.; principal, Whitehood, S. Dak., 1897, res.; sailed from Seattle for Dyea, Jan. 1, 1898; moved to various gold camps, including Nome, Iditarod, Fairbanks, Ruby, 1903-11; reporter, Nome NUGGET and Nome GOLD DIGGER, early 1900s; mail contract on lower Yukon for yrs.; part-owner-operator, Ruby RECORD-CITIZEN, weekly, 1915-; dep. U.S. Marshal, Nulato and Ruby, 1911-12; terr. H.R., on non-partisan ticket, 1915-17, father of Alaska's Bone Dry law, prohibiting sale of hard liquor; underwent surgery at Mayo clinic, Rochester, Minn., 1917; died in parent's home, Alliance, O., July 30, 1918. Mem., Pioneers, Eagles, Moose. Democrat.

SOLL, Herbert D., lawyer. B. in Chicago, Ill., 1937; LL.B., U. Denver, 1959; m. Jean Patricia (div. 1971); 3 children; law clerk in state ct. system, Juneau, 1959-61; asst. dist. atty., Fairbanks, 1961-63; dist. atty., 4th jud. div., Fairbanks, 1963-64; pvt. law prac., Anchorage, 1964-66; Peace Corps, Rio de Janeiro, Brazil, 1966-69; dep. state public defender, in charge of Anchorage office, 1970-71; state public defender, 1971-. Democrat.

SOMMERS, Robert James, civil engineer. B. in Minn., 1881; m. Esther Nixon in Juneau, 1921; s. Robert James, Jr.; civil engr., Nome, 1900-; supt., ARC, Fairbanks dist., 1915-18; terr. mine inspector, 1918-19; surveyor-gen. and Sec. of Alaska, 1919-21; engr., U.S. Bur. Roads, 1921-24; engr., ARC, 1924-; estab. R.J. Sommers Constr. Co., Juneau, with George A. Parks, 1931-; died in Santa Barbara, Calif., Sept. 17, 1972. Democrat.

SOWERBY, Isaac (Ike), steamship agent, salesman. B. in Kent, N.B., Can., June 15, 1864; m.; children: Mina, Alma; joined Klondike stampede, prospecting first winter in Dawson area; lumber bus., Bennett, Y.T., 1 yr.; asst. agent, Alaska SS Co., Skagway, 1900-07, Haines, 1907-14, Juneau, 1914-; terr. H.R., 1917-21; insurance bus.; died in Seattle, Wash., July 17, 1934; funeral in Vancouver, B.C. Democrat.

SPECKING, Keith W., master guide-outfitter. B. in Hanson, Ky., July 25, 1919; m. Vera Vaughan in Anchorage, July 10, 1950; children: Glenn R., Joan L.; 1st lt., U.S. Army, 1941-45; adm. asst. to finance officer, Camp Beale, Calif., 1946-47; original settler at Rabbit Cr., Anchorage suburb, 1947; built first road across Rabbit Cr.; moved to Hope, 1953-; cost analyst, builder, master guide and outfitter; owner-operator, Alaskan Adventures, outdoor recreation; state H.R., 1971-77; pres., Hope Village Council. Presbyterian, Republican. Address: Hope 99605.

SPENCE, William N., lawyer. B. in Stewart Co., Ga., 1851; public sc., Brooks Co., Ga.; m.; children: Henry T., William, Sam Bennett, Susan, Ruth, Toy, Dorothy; state H.R., from Mitchell Co., Ga., 1881-85; solicitor-gen., Albany jud. circuit, 1885-96; circuit ct. judge, 1896-1909; cand., U.S. Cong., from Ga., 1910; U.S. dist. atty., 3d jud. div., Valdez, 1914-17; ret. to Ga., 1917; died in Albany, Ga., Oct. 25, 1919; interment in Oakview cemetery. Democrat.

SPENCES, Chester T., telegraph operator, lumberman. B. in Moscow, Ky., Sept. 30, 1883; m. Bessie Claire Buzby, Sept. 1911; children: Lois (Mrs. Chester Bryant), Elizabeth (Mrs. Robert Gleason), Thomas C., Harry Grafton, Theodore, James, Margaret (Mrs. Thomas); U.S. Army Signal Corps, 1903-11, stationed at Ft. Gibbon, Chena, Fairbanks, 1908-11; dep. U.S. Marshal, Circle, Ft. Yukon, 1911-22; res., Calif., 1922-28; logging and lumber mill bus., Fairbanks, 1928-33; dep. U.S. Marshal, Fairbanks, 1933-38; res.; lumber bus.; terr. H.R., 1939-41; died in Seattle, Wash., May 11, 1974. Democrat.

SPICKETT, John T., businessman. B. in 1858; m. Josephine C. "Lottie"; managed minstrel show on Pacific coast; arr. Juneau, 1897, with stock co.; chmn., Rep. central com., 1900-08; Canadian Pacific Ry. SS agent for yrs.; postmaster, Juneau, 1908-12; held franchise for Orpheum theater circuit, Alaska; prop., Spickett's Cigar Store, Franklin Hotel, Juneau; died in Juneau, Aug. 1, 1930. Republican.

STABLER, Howard Douglas, lawyer. B. in Bethany, O., Nov. 11, 1887; s. Clifford L. and Mary Ann (Chambers) S.; h. sc., Middletown, O.; LL.B., Hamilton Coll. Law, Chicago, 1916; m. 3d, Gladys Buehler, June 14, 1930; law prac., Spokane, Wash., 1916-18; U.S. Signal Corps, 1918, stationed in Sitka, 1919; law prac., Sitka, 1919-20; asst. U.S. dist. atty., 1st jud. div., Juneau, 1921-29; U.S. dist. atty., Juneau, 1929-33; pvt. law prac., Juneau, 1933-63; died in St. Ann's hospital, Mar. 17, 1963. Mem., Am. Leg., Vets. WWI, Pioneers (pres.), Rotary (charter mem., 1st pres.), Masons (33d degree), Eastern Star (patron), Elks, Scottish Rite (dep. to Supreme Council), Shrine. Republican.

STALEY, Howard P., state district attorney, 1st jud. div., Ketchikan, 1961-62. Democrat.

STALKER, Jacob A. (Jake), reindeer herder, seaman, miner. B. in Noorvik, 1917; 6th grade education; m. Rosie, 1941; 9 children (Bertha, Grace, Jacob, *et al.*); deckhand and mess steward on freight barge along Alaska coast; freighting bus. with run between Noatak and Kotzebue; radio operator, Nat. Guard; U.S. Army, WWII, instructor in outdoor living; mem., Alaska Scouts, 1st Combat Intelligence Platoon; state H.R., 1961-67. Democrat.

STANGROOM, Stuart L., businessman. B. in Bellingham, Wash., 1892; public sc., Bellingham, Redmond, Wash.; stud., bus. coll., Seattle; wife's maiden name, Palmberg; d. Eileen (Mrs. Arthur Harris); lumber and grocery bus.; went to Nome, 1931, assoc. with A. Polet Co.; terr. H.R., 1941-43, Sen., 1943, from Nome, res.; moved to Seattle; died in his home, Seattle, Wash., Jan. 1961. Republican.

STASER, Bruce Ingle, military officer. B. in Anchorage, Oct. 27, 1919; s. Harry I. S.; Anchorage h. sc.; stud., UA, 1937-41, U.S. Military Acad., 1941-44, parachute sc., Command & Gen. Staff Sc., 1958; M.S., U. Wis., 1960; m. Betty Jo Thies in West Point cadet chapel, June 6, 1944; children: Jeff, Merry, John; infantry unit assignments, 13 yrs.; ROTC duty, U. Calif., 1953-54; Office of Chief of Information, Wash., D.C., 3 yrs.; served in Italy and Germany; promoted to col., 1967; Plans and Programs div., Office of Asst. Sec. Defense, 2 yrs.; Inst. Land Combat, Wash., D.C., 1 yr.; sec. to Gen. Staff, HQ 6th Army, and ROTC div., dep. chief of staff for operations; chief of staff and dep. comdr., USARAL, Ft. Richardson, 1972-73; ret., U.S. Army, Apr. 30, 1973; adjt. gen., Alaska Nat. Guard, rank of major gen., May 1, 1973.

STASER, Harry Ingle, deputy U.S. Marshal, miner. B. in Newburg, Ind., Jan. 17, 1891; gr. sc., Evansville, Ind., Culver Military Acad.; stud., bus. coll., McKay Sc. Mines, Nev.; m. Barbara de Pencier; children: Bruce Ingle; Beverly de Pencier, Jean (Mrs. Redman); coal mine operator; went to Alaska, 1909; miner, Fairbanks area, 1914-, and drove stage on Richardson Highway; U.S. Army, 1917-18; gold miner, Willow Cr. dist., 1919-23; terr. H.R., 1923-25; dep. U.S. Marshal, Anchorage, 1923-31; pres. and mgr., Monarch Mining Co., Crow Cr., near Girdwood, 1931-40; died in Girdwood, Feb. 8, 1940. Republican.

STEEL, Harry G., journalist. B. in Ashland, Pa., 1868; s. Col. J. Irvin S.; unm.; ed., Ashland EVENING TELEGRAM, Maunch Chunk DAILY TIMES, Pottsville DAILY REPUBLICAN, prior to 1893, when he purchased Shamokin DAILY HERALD (all in Pa.); co-founder, Dawson DAILY NEWS, 1899; co-ed., Nome DAILY NEWS, 1900-06; clerk of dist. ct., Nome, 1901-02; co-owner-ed., Cordova DAILY ALASKAN, 1909-15; co-owner-ed., Chitina LEADER with bro. Will, 1910-11; postmaster, Cordova, 1911-16; co-owner, ALASKA PIONEER, monthly magazine, 1912; owner-ed., Alaska WEEKLY TIMES, Cordova, 1914-16; ed., Anchorage DAILY TIMES, May-Sept., 1916; ed.-pub., Cordova DAILY TIMES,

1916-36; ed., Seward DAILY GATEWAY, Jan.-Nov., 1921; del., Rep. Nat. Conv., 1924; died in Seattle, Wash., July 11, 1936. Republican.

STEEL, William Alexander, journalist. B. in Ashland, Pa., 1866; s. Col. J. Irvin; unm.; employe, several newspapers in and around Seattle, beginning with editorship of MORNING TELEGRAPH, Seattle, Wash., 1890s; co-founder, Dawson DAILY NEWS, 1899; ed., Nome DAILY NEWS, 1900-06; asst. city ed., Seattle TIMES, special rep., Tanana DAILY MINER, Fairbanks, 1906; ed., Cordova ALASKAN and Chitina LEADER, 1909-15; ed., Juneau DAILY CAPITAL, 1921-23; quartz miner near Ketchikan, office in Seattle, Wash., 1923-30; terr. Sen., 1927-31, pres., 1929 session; pvt. sec. to Del. James Wickersham, Wash., D.C., 1930-32; res., Seattle, 1932-34; died there, Aug. 21, 1934. Republican.

STEEN, Cosby E., civil engineer. B. in Emhouse, Tex., 1926; grad., Tex. A&M U., 1950; m. Betty; children: David, Dana, et al.; U.S. Army Air Corps, 1943-45; heavy constr. and employe, Tex. highway dept., 16 yrs.; asst. constr. engr., Fairbanks, 1961-62; dist. engr., Juneau, 1962-64; dist. engr., Anchorage, 1964-67; dep. comr. highways, Juneau, 1967-68, comr., 1968-69; operations mgr., Mukluk Freight Lines, 1969-70; chief engr., Kelly, Pittelko, Fritz & Forssen consulting firm, Anchorage, 1970-72; pres., Transwestern Engring. Co., Inc., civil engr. consulting firm, Anchorage, 1972-.

STEESE, Col. James Gordon, civil engineer, military officer. B. in Mt. Holly Springs, Pa., Jan. 21, 1882; s. James Andrew and Anna Zug (Schaeffer) S.; cowboy on Paddle O ranch, Mont.; B.A., 1902, M.A., 1906, Dickinson Coll.; grad., U.S. Military Acad., 1907; D.Sc., UA, 1932; unm.; U.S. Army Corps Engrs., stationed in Kan., Tex., Panama; col. in charge, personnel section, Corps Engrs., Wash., D.C., 1917-18; in charge, personnel section, gen. staff, U.S. Army, Wash.; promoted to brig. gen. during WWI, demoted to col. at end of war, 1918-20; pres., ARC, and chmn., chief engr., AEC (Alaska R.R.), Mar.-Oct., 1923, also consulting engr., Lighthouse Service, development work for NPS, river and harbor improvements, War Dept. for Alaska, 1920-27; Corps Engrs. in Africa, Mexico, South Am., 1927-34, ret.; oil bus., hdqrs., Tulsa, Okla.; mgr., Gulf Oil Corp., Columbia, Venezuela, Panama, 1934-39, moved hdqrs. to San Antonio, Tex., 1937; active military duty, Panama, South and Central Am., 1941-46; asst. gov., Panama Canal Zone, 6 mos., 1947; ret. to home, Pa.; died in Banqui, French Equatorial Africa, Jan. 11, 1958. Awarded Cong. distinguished service medal following WWI; Fellow, Royal Geographical Soc. of England; U.S. State Dept. rep., Internat. Navigation Cong., Cairo, 1926, Venice, 1931, Brussels, 1935; Internat. Geographical Cong., Warsaw, 1934, Internat. Cong. Surveyors, London, 1934 (del. chmn.).

STEPOVICH, Michael Anthony, lawyer. B. in Fairbanks, Mar. 12, 1919; s. Michael A. and Olga S., parents div., 1921; mother later became Mrs. Mark Fabianich; gr. and h. sc., Portland, Ore.; B.A.,

Gonzaga U., 1940; LL.B., U. Notre Dame, 1943; post-grad., Santa Clara Coll., 1946; m. Matilda Baricevic in Portland, Ore., Nov. 27, 1947; children: Antonia (Mrs. John Chester Gore), Maria Theresa (Mrs. G. Gregory Greulich), Michael, Peter, Christopher, Dominic, Theodore John, Nicholas Vincent, James, Laura, Nada, Andrea, Melissa; U.S. Navy, 1942-46; pvt. law prac., Fairbanks, 1948-57; city atty., Fairbanks, 1950-52; terr. H.R., 1951-53, Sen., 1953-57; Gov., Alaska, 1957-58; pvt. law prac., Fairbanks, 1958-; cand., U.S. Sen., 1958, Alaska gov., 1962, 1966. Received DeSmet medal from Gonzaga U. as "an outstanding grad. layman," 1966. Mem., Fairbanks Planning & Zoning com. (chmn., 1952-53), Pioneers, Elks, Eagles, Am. Leg., Tanana Valley Bar Assn. Catholic, Republican.

STEVENS, Theodore Fulton, lawyer. B. in Indianapolis, Ind., Nov. 18, 1923; s. George A. and Gertrude (Yost) S.; stud., Ore. State U., Mont. State U.; B.A., UCLA, 1947; LL.B., Harvard U., 1950; m. Ann Mary Cherrington in Denver, Colo., 1952; children: Susan, Elizabeth, Walter, Theodore Fulton, Jr., Ben; U.S. Army Air Corps pilot, 1943-46, awarded Air Medal, Distinguished Flying Cross and Yuan Hai (Chinese Nationalist govt.); pvt. law prac., Wash., D.C., 1950-53; U.S. dist. atty., Fairbanks, 1953-56; legislative counsel and asst. to Sec. Interior, Wash., D.C., 1956-60; solicitor, Dept. Interior, Wash., D.C., 1960-61; pvt. law prac., Anchorage, 1961-68; cand., U.S. Sen., 1962, 1968; state H.R.; appt. U.S. Sen., Dec. 23, 1968; elected U.S. Sen., 1970, 1972. Elected to Alaska Press Club's 49er Hall of Fame. Mem., Anchorage Rep. Club (pres., 1962-63), Elks, Am. Leg., VFW, Rotary, Am., Fed., Calif., Alaska, D.C. Bar Assns. Episcopalian, Republican.

STEVENS, Gilbert B., U.S. Marshal, miner. B. in Marion, O.; joined gold rush to Fairbanks, early 1900s; m. Mrs. Helen Lynch, Seward, June 1924; U.S. Marshal, 4th jud. div., Fairbanks, 1921-25; miner, Ester Cr. dist., near Fairbanks, 1940s. Democrat.

STEVENSON, Robert Douglas, accountant. B. in Seattle, Wash., Dec. 13, 1919; s. Dr. William D. and Ava D. S.; gr. and h. sc., Seattle, Wash.; B.A., U. Wash.; m. Elsie Barber, 1948; children: William Robert, James Douglas; U.S. Army Signal Corps, 1942-45, stationed at Ft. Richardson, June 1942-Sept. 1944; dep. collector, IRS, Seattle, 1945-49; agent, IRS, Juneau, 1949-53; terr. dep. tax comr., 1953-57, comr., 1957-59; dep. comr. revenue, 1959-62, comr., 1962-67, 1972-; auditor, West Coast Mortgage & Investment Co. and Security Income Corp., Seattle, 1967-68; auditor, chief, excise tax div., dep. comr. revenue, 1968-72. Mem., Western States Assn. Tax Adm. (pres., 1959), Sigma Nu, Beta Alpha Psi, Moose, Am. Leg., VFW, Elks. Presbyterian, Democrat.

STEWART, Benjamin Duane, mining engineer. B. in Missoula, Mont., Oct. 31, 1878; s. Rev. George and Isabel J. (Lombard) S.; gr. and h. sc., Missoula; B.S., U. Mont., 1902; m. Edna Ewin, May 19, 1909 (dec. 1933); children: Benjamin D., Jr., John Ewin, Jeanette, Thomas B., Mary E. (Mrs.

Robert Fellows, dec. 1949, Mrs. Charles Swithin-bank); m. 2d, Doris A. Scott, Nov. 15, 1935; topographic asst., USGS, 1900-07; engr., Fed. Mining & Smelting Co., Wallace, Ida., 1907-09; pvt. engr. prac., Missoula, 1910; consulting engr., Treadwell Gold Mining Co., 1910-15; mayor, Juneau, 1916; mgr. of mining and other interests of Charles A. Sulzer, at Sulzer, 1917-19; terr. mine inspector for Alaska, 1919-39 (comr., 1935-39), ret.; supervising engr., USGS & U.S. Bur. Mines, 1922-35; del., const. conv., 1955-56; moved to Sitka, where he managed Cathedral Apts. for a time, 1953-66; res., Sequim, Wash., 1966-. Mem., Sigma Chi, Pioneers, terr. bd. examiners for engrs. and architects (pres., 1955-61). Episcopalian, Democrat. Address: P.O. Box 881, Sequim, Wash. 98382.

STEWART, Thomas Byrd, lawyer. B. in Seattle, Wash., Jan. 1, 1919; s. Benjamin Duane and Edna (Ewin) S.; gr. and h. sc., Juneau; B.A., U. Wash., 1941; M.A., Sc. Internat. Studies, John Hopkins U., Wash., D.C., 1947; LL.B., Yale U., 1950; m. Mrs. Jane Snyder McMullin in Fairbanks, Dec. 30, 1955; children: Rebecca Luella (Mrs. William R. Stewart), Donna Elizabeth, Stephen, Mary, Caleb, Thomas; U.S. Army, 1941-45, decorated with bronze and silver stars; chief clerk, terr. H.R. special session, 1946; law clerk to dist. judge, admitted to bar, asst. atty. gen., Juneau, 1951-54; pvt. law prac., Juneau, 1955-57; state Sen., 1959-61; adm. dir., Alaska ct. system, Anchorage, 1961-67; superior ct. judge, 1st jud. dist., Juneau, 1967-. Mem., Juneau C. of C., Ski Club, Dem. central com., 1960-61, Alaska Heart Assn. (chmn., bd. dir.), Am. Judicature Soc. (bd. dir., 1962). Unitarian, Democrat. Address: 925 Calhoun Ave., Juneau, 99801.

STRAND, William C., journalist. B. in Chicago, Ill., 1912; grad., Lake Forest Acad., Ill.; stud., Brown U., Providence, R.I., Wash. U., St. Louis, Mo.; m.; d. Barbara Jeanne (Mrs. Raymond G. Larroca); staff mem., City News Bur., Chicago, 1933-37; reporter, correspondent in Wash., London, Chicago TRIBUNE, 1937-48; managing ed., Fairbanks NEWS-MINER, 1948-51; exec. ed., WASH. TIMES-HERALD, Wash., D.C., 1951-53; dir., Office Terr. & Insular Possessions, Dept. Interior, 1953-55; asst. to Sec. Interior, dir. of information, 1955-58; dir., public relations, Rep. Nat. Com., 1958-60; assoc. with NEWSWEEK, 1961-62, CHICAGO SUN-TIMES, 1962-67, Am. Pharmaceutical Assn., 1968-74; died in Washington, D.C., September 1, 1974. Republican.

STRANDBERG, Harold David, mining engineer. B. in Fairbanks, Jan. 28, 1909; s. David and Jennie Sophia (Johanson) S.; grad., h. sc., Anchorage, 1927; B.S., geology and mining, UA, 1931; m. Barbara Carlquist, Aug. 28, 1939; children: David Harold, Douglas Frank, Steven; placer miner with father and 3 bros. (Ted, Bill, Odin), Cripple Cr., Folger, Candle, Manley Hot Springs, platinum miner, Goodnews Bay, 1932-64; state H.R., 1961-68, chmn., joint H.R.-Sen. finance com., 1963-64, chmn., H.R. finance com., 1963-64, 1967-68, chmn., legislative audit com.; comr. public works, 1968-71, dep. comr., 1971-; mem., gov.'s map adv. com., 1953-64; Anchorage port com.,

1955-64; terr. bd. road comrs. Mem., Am. Inst. Mining & Metallurgy Engrs., Alaska Miners Assn. (dir. and v.p.), Anchorage Miners & Prospectors Assn., Pioneers. Presbyterian, Republican.

STRATTON, Robert Walker, Jr., businessman. B. in 1915; m. Mary Margaret; children: Robert Charles, Ruth Mary (Mrs. Daniel Edward Renshaw), Sharon, Linda; went to Alaska, 1949; owner-operator, Stratton's, Inc., Union Oil gas station, Anchorage, 1960s; state H.R., 1961-63; Union Oil wholesale distributor, Valdez, 1970s; state dir. elections, 1968-70. Mem., Lions (Spenard); bd. regents, Pacific Lutheran U.; bd. dir., 1st Fed. Savings & Loan Assn., Anchorage; YMCA (bd. mgrs.), Anchorage; Alaska State C. of C. Lutheran, Republican.

STRINGER, Herald E., lawyer. B. in Murfreesboro, Ark., Feb. 22, 1918; gr. and h. sc., Murfreesboro; B.A., Ouchita Coll., Arkadelphia, Ark.; stud., Stanford U.; LL.B., UCLA; m. Mary Ann Wentz, 1942; children: Edward Herald, David Henry; U.S. Army, 1940-45, stationed in Alaska, 1941-45; pvt. law prac., Anchorage, 1945-64; terr. H.R., 1953-55; dir., legislative div., Am. Leg., Wash., D.C., 1964-. Mem., Am. Leg. (life dept. comdr., 1950; nat. exec. com. for Alaska, 1961), VFW, Masons, Shrine, Elks, Anchorage and Am. Bar Assns., Rep. central com., C. of C., bd. examiners and appeals, Anchorage (chmn., 1962-64). Baptist, Republican.

STRONG, John Franklin Alexander, journalist. B. in Salmon Cr., N.B., Can., Oct. 15, 1856; s. Adam Robert and Janet Nicholl S.; grad., N.B. Normal Sc., Fredericton, 1874; m. Elizabeth A. Aitkens of Fredericton, Dec. 31, 1879, in Johnston, N.B.; children: Jane, Elizabeth, Robert; m. 2d, Anna Hall in Tacoma, Wash., 1896; sc. teacher, store proprietor, N.B., 1874-88; employe, various newspapers, B.C. and Wash., 1888-97; joined Klondike gold rush, employe, newspapers in Skagway, Dawson, Nome, 1897-1906; ed., newspaper in Tonapa, Nev. and Greenwater, Calif., 1906-07; estab. newspapers in Katalla, Iditarod, Juneau (ALASKA DAILY EMPIRE), 1907-13; Gov., Alaska, 1913-18, res.; moved to Seattle, Wash., spending summers there and winters in Los Angeles, Calif.; world tour, spending yr. in India, 1922-24; died of heart attack in Seattle, July 27, 1929; cremation, July 29, 1929. Mem., A.B., Nome. Democrat.

STUBBINS, William, merchant. B. in Beverly, England, c. 1864; prop., dry goods store, Douglas, 1886-1918; postmaster, 1891-95, 1899-1901, mayor, 1905, Douglas; terr. H.R., 1913-15; moved to Seattle, Wash., 1918. Independent.

SULLIVAN, George Murray, transportation executive. B. in Portland, Ore., Mar. 31, 1922; s. Harvey P. and Viola Marie (Murray) S.; gr. and h. sc., Valdez, 1939; m. Margaret Mary Eagan in Fairbanks, Dec. 30, 1947; children: Timothy Murray, Harvey, Daniel, Kevin, Colleen, George, Michael, Shannon, Casey Eagan; truck driver, Alaska Freight Lines, 1940-44; U.S. Army, transportation corps, Aleutian I., 1944-46; dep. U.S. Marshal, Nenana, 1947-52; mgr., Alaska Freight Lines, Fairbanks,

1952-56; mgr., Garrison Fast Freight, Fairbanks, 1956-59; gen. mgr., Consolidated Freightways, Inc., Alaska Div. (Anchorage), with which Garrison had merged, 1959-68; exec. asst. to chmn., Alaska Bus. Council, 1968-70; state H.R., 1964-65; mayor, Anchorage, 1967- (full-time position with salary, 1970). Named "Mayor of the Year" by the northwest region, OEO, 1971. Mem., Pioneers, Elks, Nat. League of Cities (exec. bd., 1972); K.C.; Pioneer Alaskan Lobbyists Soc.; VFW (dept. comdr., 1951); Alaska Jaycees (pres., 1951); Alaska Municipal League (pres., 1971); bs. dir., 1st Federal Savings & Loan Assn.; city councilman, Fairbanks and Anchorage; Petroleum Club. Catholic, Republican.

SULLIVAN, Harvey P., U.S. Marshal, miner, businessman. B. in Stillwater, Minn., Mar. 1, 1874; went to Dawson, 1898, Circle, Nome, 1900; miner, U.S. Marshal, Nome; m. Viola Murray in Portland, Ore., June 25, 1910 (dec. 1941); children: Marian (Mrs. Francis Burch, Mrs. Bevers), George M., Lillian (Mrs. Joseph T. Allen); U.S. Marshal, 3d jud. div., Valdez, 1909-13, 1922-33; miner, 1913-22; lived in Latouche before 2d U.S. Marshal appointment; mem., Rep com., 3d div., 1916; U.S. Comr., Valdez, 1934; prop., gen. merchandise and liquor store, Valdez, 1934-36; died in Seward hospital, Sept. 13, 1936; interred in Seward. Mem., Masons, Elks. Republican.

SULLIVAN, Leroy M., lawyer. B. in N. Dak., 1902; stud., N. Dak. State Coll., U. Ill.; LL.B., U. Tex., 1926; m. Doris Gustafson, 1931; children: James, Frank; law clerk, James Wickersham's office, Juneau, 1928-29; clerk, sec. of terr. Sen. office, 1929 session; chief clerk, terr. auditor, 1929-30; asst. U.S. dist. atty., Cordova, 1930-31; U.S. dist. atty., 2d jud. div., Nome, 1931-33; pvt. law prac., Nome, 1933-; city atty., 1936; terr. Sen., 1939-43. Republican.

SULZER, Charles August, miner. B. in Roselle, N.J., Feb. 24, 1879; s. Thomas and Lydia Jelleme S.; public sc., Roselle, Pingry Sc.; grad., Berkeley Acad., N.Y.C.; stud., U.S. Military Acad., 1900-01; fought in Spanish-Am. War, 1898-99; m. Gertrude Harrison Moore in Elizabeth, N.J., Oct. 11, 1905; s. William Stedman; gen. mgr., family-owned mining property at Sulzer, Prince of Wales I., including Jumbo copper mine and rich barium-sulphate deposit at Lime Pt., 1902-17; terr. Sen., 1915-17, res.; del. in U.S. Cong., Mar. 1917-Jan. 1919, James Wickersham declared rightful winner by U.S. Cong., and installed to serve until expiration of 65th Cong., Mar. 3, 1919; cand., del. in U.S. Cong., 1918; died, Apr. 16, 1919. Mem., Elks, A.B. (charter mem., Ketchikan camp), Moose, Eagles. Democrat.

SUNDBACK, John, miner. B. in Sweden, c. 1850; went to U.S., 1866; m.; 2 daughters; sheriff, Minnehaha Co., Dak. Terr., 1886-90s; joined Klondike gold rush to Dawson, 1899, moved to Nome after 2 mos.; prospector-miner, Seward Peninsula; mem., terr. bd. education, 1917-18; clerk of dist. ct., Nome, 1911-14, 1921-25; terr. Sen., 1917-21, pres., 1921; died following leg amputation, Seattle, Wash, July 18, 1925. Republican.

SUNDBORG, George Walter, journalist, author. B. in San Francisco, Calif., Mar. 25, 1913; s. Charles S.; gr. and h. sc., Seattle; B.A., U. Wash., 1934; m. Mary Frances Baker, Feb. 26, 1938; children: Pierre Joseph, George Walter, Jr., Rosemary (Mrs. William Bridges Hunter, III), Stephen Vincent, Mary Sarah (Mrs. William Barstow Long); city ed., GRAYS HARBOR DAILY WASHINGTONIAN, Hoquiam, Wash., Dec. 1938; editorial writer, DAILY ALASKA EMPIRE, Juneau, 1939-41; supervisor, Alaska Merit System, Juneau, 1940-41; reg. dir., Nat. Resources Planning Bd., Juneau, 1941-42, Portland, Ore., 1942-43; asst. dir., North Pacific Planning Project, U.S. State Dept., Portland, 1943-44; industrial analyst, Bonneville Power Adm., Portland, 1944-46; gen. mgr., Alaska Development Bd., 1946-47, 1951-53; exec. asst. to Gov. Gruening and consult., Development Bd., 1947-51; ed.-pub.-owner, Juneau INDEPENDENT, 1953-57; ed., Fairbanks NEWS-MINER, 1957-58; del., const. conv., 1955-56; adm. asst. to U.S. Sen. Gruening, Wash., D.C., 1959-68; asst. to dir., Bur. Outdoor Recreation, for Cong. liaison, Dept. Interior, Wash., D.C., 1969-73. Awarded citation for meritorious service by Sec. Interior, 1973. Author: "Opportunity in Alaska," 1945, "Hail Columbia," 1954, "Facts About Statehood for Alaska," 1946. Mem., Alaska State Soc., Wash., D.C. (pres.), Juneau C. of C., Rotary (pres.), Sigma Delta Chi (organizer, sec.), Alaska Visitors Assn. Catholic, Democrat. Address: 2650 39th Ave. West, Seattle, Wash. 98199.

SUNDQUIST, Richard N., miner. B. in Chicago, Ill., c. 1896; m. Beulah A. Eaden of Issaquah, Wash., in Seattle, Jan. 28, 1931; s. Lars A.; left Chicago at age 7 to join father at Candle Cr., who was a pioneer miner in that camp; terr. H.R., 1925-29, Sen., 1929-33, from Candle; died in Seattle, Wash., Aug. 4, 1967. Republican.

SUTHERLAND, Donald Alexander (Dan), U.S. Marshal, miner, fisherman. B. in Pleasant Bay, Cape Breton, Can., Apr. 17, 1869; s. John and Mary Ann (Gwinn) S.; dist. sc., Essex, Mass., until 1886; m. Hilda Evanson in Nulato, Oct. 3, 1910; s. Donald; employe, grocery stores, Boston and Salem, 1886-98; deck-hand on St. Michael-bound ship from Seattle; worked on ships and prospected in Nome area, 1898-1909; U.S. Marshal, 1st jud. div., Juneau, 1909-10; miner, Iditarod and Ruby dist., 1910-16; terr. Sen., 1913-21; fisherman, Juneau, 1916-20; del. in U.S. Cong., 1921-31; purchasing agent, Ogontz Sc., Pa., pvt. sc., later becoming part of State Coll., 1931-; died in Abbington Memorial Hospital, Phila., Pa., Mar. 23, 1955. Republican.

SVINDSETH, N.J., fisherman. B. in Norway, 1861; unm.; mem., Ore. legislature, from Clatsop Co., early 1890s; went to Alaska, 1898; terr. H.R., from Wrangell, 1913-15; died in Seattle, Wash., May 19, 1915; interment in Wrangell. Mem., A.B., Alaska Fishermen's Union. Democrat.

SWANBERG, Nels, miner. B. in Sweden, 1870; m. Charlotte Anderson, May 12, 1901; children: Nels, Jr., Grace (Mrs. Axel Edman); miner, Hope-Sunrise dist., 1896-99, Dawson, 1899-1900, Seward Peninsula, 1900-40; pres., Gold Beach Placers, Inc.,

Nome, city councilman, Nome, 1929-31; treas., Nome sc. bd., 3 yrs.; terr. H.R., 1933-35; died in Tacoma, Wash., June 22, 1961. Mem., Pioneers, Odd Fellows. Republican.

SWANSON, Leslie E. (Red), transportation executive. B. in 1919; m.; 2 sons; res., Juneau, 1946-64; moved to Nenana; sergeant-at-arms, state Sen., 1 term; lobbyist, Yutana Barge Lines, 1968; state H.R., from Nenana, 1971-73, 1975-77. Democrat. Address: Box 3, Nenana 99760.

SWEENEY, Dora M., secretary. B. in Biwabie, Minn., June 19, 1907; d. Mr. and Mrs. Alfred Lundstrom; grad., Juneau h. sc.; stud., stateside bus. coll.; m. Edward Sweeney, 1927; went to Juneau with parents, 1907; employe, BIA, 1930-40; terr. health dept., 1940-42; Shattuck Insurance agency, 1942-52, ret. from bus.; sec. of Sen., 1953; del., const. conv., 1955-56; terr. H.R., 1955-65; worked for legislative council, 1965; sergeant-at-arms, H.R., 1966; res., Sequim, Wash., 1974. Mem., Pioneers Aux. (grand sec., 1945-54), BPW (pres., 3 terms), Eastern Star, Order Rainbow Girls. Presbyterian, Democrat.

SWEET, John McCamey, geologist. B. in Parkers Landing, Pa., Sept. 29, 1924; s. John K. and Jane K. S.; B.S., Oberlin Coll.; M.S., U. Mich.; m. Mirabel Digel; children: Anne, Patricia, John, Robert, Thomas, Timothy; U.S. Marine Corps, 1943-46; oil scout, Atlantic Co. (Atlantic-Richfield), Midland, Tex., 1950-, staff geologist, exploration hdqrs., Dallas, Tex.; estab. 1st permanent dist. exploration office in Alaska (Anchorage), Atlantic Refining Co., 1962-67; dist. explorationist, Atlantic-Richfield Co., Alaska, 1967-73; state H.R., 1969-71; asst. chief geologist, Atlantic-Richfield Co., North Am. producing div., Dallas, Tex., 1973-. Mem., Petroleum Club, Masons, Scottish Rite. Presbyterian (elder), Republican.

SWINEFORD, Alfred P., journalist. B. in Ashland, O., Sept. 14, 1836; common sc., Ashland; printer's apprentice, 1851; m. Psyche Cytheria Flower in Oshkosh, Wis., Jan. 1875 (dec. 1881); d. Mrs. E.O. Stafford; m. 2d, Mrs. Wilhelmina "Minnie" Smith in Marquette, Mich., 1886 (dec. 1927); d. Agnes (Mrs. Allen Shattuck); itinerant printer, Wis. and Minn.; law stud., admitted to Minn. bar (1857), 1853-67; ed.-pub., THE MINING JOURNAL, Marquette, Mich.; state H.R., state comr. mineral statistics, Mich., 1883; del., Dem. Nat. Conv., 1872, 1884, 1867-85; Gov., Alaska, 1885-89; res., Mich., 1889-93; inspector-gen., U.S. Land Office, Wash., D.C.,1893-98; pub., Ketchikan MINING JOURNAL, 1901-05, Ketchikan MINER, 1907-08, the two papers merging in the meantime; mining interests on Prince of Wales I., 1898-1909; died in Juneau, Oct. 26, 1909; buried in Elks' plot, Evergreen cemetery, Juneau. Author: "Alaska, Its History, Climate and Natural Resources," 1898. Democrat.

T

TAGGART, Buel (Tex), businessman. B. in 1907; mgr., Fairbanks Assoc. Gen. Contractors; state comr. public works, Apr.-Dec., 1974. Democrat.

TANNER, Josiah M. (Si), U.S. Marshal, merchant. B. in Oakland Co., Mich., Feb. 22, 1850; gr. sc. education; m. Miss Juliette Valentine, 1871; 2 daughters (Mrs. Charles Schultzman), s. Fred; gold miner, Central City, Colo., 1870-74; sheriff, Harrison Co., Dunlap, Ia.; sold Ia. horses, and sheriff, Pierce Co., Wash., 1890-96; wharfinger, store mgr., Juneau, 1896-97; lighterage bus., estab. plumbing and hardware store, Skagway, 1897-1917; city councilman, 5 yrs., mayor, 1909-10, Skagway; terr. Sen., 1913-17; U.S. Marshal, 1st jud. div., Juneau, 1917-21; operated hardware bus. with son, Skagway, 1921-27; died there, Sept. 20, 1927. Mem., C. of C. (pres., 1908), Elks, Pioneers, A.B., Odd Fellows. Democrat.

TANSEY, Thomas Bernard, miner, assayer. B. in Luzerne Co., Pa., Dec. 19, 1860; unm.; coal miner in youth; went to Colo., 1878, stud. assaying between shifts; metallurgy degree, Ariz. Sc. Mines, Tombstone, 1893; prospector, Cook Inlet, 1896, Susitna, Little Susitna and Willow Cr. area; assayer, Bonanza copper mine, Kennicott, 1913-; terr. H.R., 1915-17. Mem., Odd Fellows, A.B. Independent.

TARWATER, Edgar R., banker. B. in Knoxville, Tenn., July 16, 1880; unm.; fought in Spanish-Am. War, 1898; employe, U.S. Dept. Interior, Philippines, 1899-1916; special disbursing agent, Alaska R.R., employe, Brown & Hawkins Bk., Seward, 1916-20; cashier, Bk. of Anchorage, 1925-38; real estate and insurance bus., Anchorage, 1938-44; terr. H.R., 1929-31; died in Seattle hospital, Aug. 5, 1944; buried in Neubert, Tenn. Mem., Rotary, Elks, Masons, Anchorage Golf Club (founder), Anchorage Rep. Club (pres., 1926), Alaska C. of C. (pres., 1929). Republican.

TAYLOR, Ike Pendleton, civil engineer. B. in Blackburn, Mo., Nov. 8, 1890; s. Ike P., Sr. and Sallie (Dean) T.; B.S., William Jewell Coll., Liberty, Mo., 1910; m. Laura Lewis, Feb. 18, 1918; children: Jean (Mrs. Victor G. Lien), Lewis; engr., Alaska R.R.,1916-, ARC, 1921-, dist. supt., Fairbanks dist., asst. chief engr., 1923, chief engr., 1932, comr. roads, 1932-48; ret. from fed. service, Feb. 1, 1950; died in Seattle, Wash., May 27, 1963. Awarded distinguished service medal, Dept. Interior. Mem., Elks, Kappa Sigma, Rainier Golf & Country Club, Seattle, Wash.

TAYLOR, Lytton, U.S. District Attorney for Alaska, 1894-95. Accompanied to Sitka by wife. Democrat.

TAYLOR, Warren Arthur, lawyer. B. in Chehalis, Wash., Apr. 2, 1891; s. Frank A. and Alice E. (Wilson) T.; gr. and h. sc., Bellingham, Wash.; law stud., Cordova, admitted to bar, 1927; m. Josephine Bona in Cordova, July 2, 1921; children: Elizabeth K. (Mrs. Hensley), Warren William; m. 2d, Gradelle Leigh in Anchorage, Jan. 1, 1950 (div. 1955); m. 3d, Myrtle R. Clare in Juneau, Dec. 18, 1957; constr. worker, 1909-10, fireman and locomotive engr., Copper River & Northwestern Ry., Cordova, 1910-22; U.S. Army, 1917-19; engaged in bus., studied law, dep. U.S. Marshal, Cordova, 1922-34; asst. U.S. atty., Cordova, 1934-39; pvt. law prac., Cordova, 1939-41; terr. H.R., from Cordova, 1933-35, from Kodiak, 1945-47, from Fairbanks, 1949-51, 1955-67; pvt. law prac., Kodiak, 1941-44, Fairbanks, 1944-; del., const. conv., 1955-56; cand., Alaska gov., 1962. Mem., Am. Leg. (dept. comdr., 1926), Pioneers, Masons, Alaska and Am. Bar Assns., Alaska Statehood Com., 1949-59. Protestant, Democrat.

TAYLOR, Warren William, lawyer. B. in Cordova, Jan. 13, 1926; s. Warren Arthur and Josephine (Bona) T.; B.A., UA; stud., U. Wash.; LL.B., Cumberland U., Lebanon, Tenn., 1954; m. Miss Jennings; children: Ross William, Randolph Warren, Warren Arthur, II, Karla Jo, Scott Laurence, *et al.*; U.S. Navy, 1945-46; pvt. law prac. with father, Fairbanks, 1954-59; asst. dist. atty., Fairbanks, 1959-60; state dist. atty., 4th jud. dist., Fairbanks, 1960-62; pvt. law prac., 1962-65; superior ct. judge, Fairbanks, 1965-. Mem., Pioneers, Am. Leg. Baptist, Democrat.

THIELE, Karl (Frank George), miner, cannery-operator, merchant, mail carrier. B. in Grand Rapids, Mich., May 10, 1886; went to Fairbanks in gold rush days, delivered newspapers to Ester Cr. by pony and sulky; circulation mgr., Fairbanks DAILY NEWS, 1908-09; m. Dorothy Craven in Seattle, Wash., Feb. 20, 1913; m. 2d, Mary Conly in Gov.'s mansion, Juneau, Mar. 24, 1922 (dec. 1923); s. Karl, Jr.; m. 3d, Cecelia McLaughlin in Juneau, Feb. 1, 1928 (dec. 1961); d. Rosemary Ann; joined gold rush to Iditarod, 1910; prop., dry goods store, Iditarod, pool room and stationery store, Flat; small-boat freighting bus. between Seattle and Bethel; delivered mail by dogteam to Interior villages; prop., Akiak store; U.S. Comr., Iditarod, health officer, U.S. Marshal; pvt. sec. to Gov. Bone, 1921; surveyor-gen., 1921-25; Sec. of Alaska, 1925-33; estab. Diamond K Packing Co., Wrangell, 1933-39; miner on Kugruk River, Seward Peninsula, 1939-41; died following operation, Seattle hospital, Jan. 4, 1941. Mem., Pioneers. Republican.

THOMAS, Lowell, Jr., film producer, lecturer, author. B. in London, England, Oct. 6, 1923; s. Lowell Jackson and Frances (Ryan) T.; Taft Prep Sc., Conn., 1942; B.A., Dartmouth Coll., 1948; stud., Princeton U., 1951-52; m. Mary Taylor (Tay) Pryor, May 20, 1950; children: Anne Frazier, David Lowell; U.S. Air Force pilot-instructor, B-25 light bomber, 1943-45; asst. economist, special economic assistance missions, Turkey and Iran, 1947-48; traveled throughout the world, gathering material for lectures, films and books, 1949-60; moved to An-

chorage, summer 1960; state Sen., 1967-75, majority leader, 1973-74; cand., U.S. Cong., 1962, 1964; Lt. Gov., 1974-78. Mem., bd. dir., Alaska State Bank, Salvation Army (Anchorage unit), tourism adv. bd., Western Alaska Council of Boy Scouts (twice pres.), Rotary, C. of C. (Anchorage and state), Explorers, Marco Polo and Dutch Treat (N.Y.C.), Bohemian Club (San Francisco), Alaska Press Club. Author: "Out of This World, A Journey to Tibet," 1950; "Flight to Adventure" (co-author, wife), 1956; "Silent War in Tibet," 1959; "Trail of Ninety-eight," 1962; "Famous First Flights that Changed History" (co-author, father), 1968. Episcopalian, Republican. Address: 7022 Tanaina Dr., Anchorage 99502.

THOMPSON, Morris, electronics technician. B. in Tanana, Sept. 11, 1939; s. Warren H. and Alice (Grant) T.; gr. sc., Tanana; h. sc., Mt. Edgecumbe Sc., Sitka; stud., UA, 2 yrs., RCA Inst., Los Angeles, Calif., 1 yr.; m. Thelma Mayo, Tanana, Oct. 5, 1963; children: Sheryl Lynn, Nicole Rae, Allison Mae; electronics technician, RCA's Gilmore Cr. satellite-tracking station, near Fairbanks, 1964-67; dep. dir., Alaska Rural Development Agency, Juneau, 1967-68; exec. sec., state com. on Northern Operations of Railway Transportation & Highways (NORTH), 1968-69; special asst. to Sec. Interior Hickel, Wash., D.C., 1969-71; area dir., BIA, Juneau, 1971-73; U.S. Comr., BIA, Wash., D.C., 1973-. Mem., Fairbanks Native Assn. Republican.

THOMPSON, Sidney J., U.S. Marshal, 1st judicial division, Juneau, Dec. 1951-Jan. 1953. Democrat.

THOMPSON, William Fentress, newspaper editor-publisher. B. in N.Y., June 11, 1865; s. Will H. T.; gr. sc., Howard City, Mich.; stud., Mich. Military Acad.; m. Mrs. Nell Mulrooney Noble in Yakima, Wash., 1912; children: William, Richard, Marian (Mrs. Philip Arnesen Anderson, Mrs. W.B. Bates, Mrs. Thorgaard); cook, Hudson Bay Co. stock ranch, Northcotte, Minn., traveled with circus, 1880-82; tramp printer, newspapers in Ark., Tex., 1882-87; ed. and pub., newspapers in Wash. and B.C., Can., 1887-97; reporter, ed., co-owner, YUKON SUN, Dawson, and Dawson NEWS, 1897-1906; ed., co-owner, Fairbanks DAILY NEWS, TANANA MINER (later merged with Fairbanks NEWS-MINER), 1906-26; died of pneumonia, Fairbanks, Jan. 3, 1926; buried in Pioneers plot, Fairbanks cemetery.

TILLION, Clement Vincent, fisherman, charter boat operator. B. in Brooklyn, N.Y., July 3, 1925; s. Clement Vincent and Marian (Little) T.; h. sc., 1 yr.; m. Diana Rutzebeck, 1952; children: William, Marian, Martha, Vincent; U.S. Navy, 1940-45; employed in variety of jobs, Anchorage, Fairbanks, Alaska R.R. at Cantwell, McKinley Park, 1945-48; lived on own 58-acre island, Halibut Cove, Kachemak Bay, 1948-; commercial fisherman, charter boat bus., Kachemak Bay and Cook Inlet; state H.R., 1963-75, Sen., 1975-77. Mem., Nat. Adv. Com. on Oceans & Atmosphere, 1971-75; Internat. North Pacific Fisheries Com., 1966-; Masons; various conservation organizations. Republican. Address: Box 373, Homer 99603.

TOBEY, Harold W. (Hal), lawyer. B. in 1932; admitted to Colo. bar, 1961; dep. atty. for Jefferson Co., Golden, Colo., 1965-68; asst. dist. atty., Anchorage, Apr.-May, 1968; state dist. atty., 1st jud. div., Juneau, 1968-69; state dist. atty., 3d jud. div., Anchorage, 1969-71; city atty., Anchorage, Feb.-Oct, 1971; pvt. law prac., Anchorage, Oct. 1971-.

TOBIN, Emery Fridolf, magazine publisher. B. in Roxbury, Mass., Dec. 14, 1895; s. August and Emma Louise (Ericson); gr. and h. sc., Quincy, Mass.; m. Clara Matilda Willard, Oct. 15, 1926; d. Mrs. Doris Lorraine Bordine; reporter, PATRIOT-LEDGER, Quincy and dist. mgr., Boston JOURNAL, 1916-17; U.S. Army, 1917-19; acct. and asst. mgr., New England Fish Co., Ketchikan, 1920-32; bus. mgr., Ketchikan CHRONICLE, 1932-35; founder-ed.-pub., ALASKA SPORTSMAN magazine, Ketchikan, 1935-55, Seattle, 1955-58. Received 2 awards from Freedom Found., Valley Forge, Pa. Mem., Elks, Am. Leg., Rotary, Pioneers, C. of C., Boy Scouts of Am. (scoutmaster and comr., 1925-38). Christian Science.

TOBIN, William J., journalist. B. in Joplin, Mo., July 28, 1927; s. John J. and Lucy (Shoppach) T.; public sc., Okla., Tex., Ind.; B.A., Butler U., 1948; m. Marjorie Stuhldreher in Indianapolis, Ind., Apr. 26, 1952; children: Michael, David, James; U.S. Army, 1943-45; AP staff, Indianapolis, 1948-53; field rep., AP, N.Y.C., 1953-55; reg. membership exec., AP, Louisville, Ky., 1955-56; correspondent, AP, Juneau, 1956-60; asst. chief, AP bur., Baltimore, Md., 1960-61; bur. chief, AP, Mont., 1961-63; exec. ed., Anchorage DAILY TIMES, 1963-. Received Alaska Press Club's outstanding column award, "Sat. Sundry," 1966. Mem., Alaska World Affairs Council (pres., 1967); Alaska Press Club (pres., 1968); Alaska C. of C. (dir., 1973); Anchorage C. of C. (pres., 1973); bd. trustees, Alaska Mutual Savings Bk. (Anchorage), 1973. Catholic, Republican.

TODD, Chester J., U.S. Marshal, miner, printer. B. in Highland, Ill., Oct. 13, 1861; m. (dec. 1897); children: Irma Slocum (Mrs. Richard LaDieu Clifton), Hazel (Mrs. Payne, dec. 1918); res., St. Louis, Mo., 1880s, early 1890s; miner, Cripple Cr., Colo.; went to Valdez, 1898, cont. prospecting and mining; postmaster, Valdez, 1916-19; v.p., Valdez Pub. Co., which issued PATHFINDER, monthly magazine, Valdez MINER, weekly newspaper; U.S. Marshal, 3d jud. div., 1934-39; res., Kodiak, 1939-; died in Portland, Ore., May 31, 1951. Mem., Pioneers (Igloo 7, Valdez), Eagles (charter mem., No. 1971, Valdez). Democrat.

TONER, Felix J., engineer, businessman. M. Mary Vander Leest, Juneau; 4 children (one being Kathleen Jeanne, Mrs. Steven K. Boley); dir., First Nat. Bk., Juneau; chmn., Dem. central com., 1956-60. Democrat. Address: 127 W. 7th St., Juneau 99801.

TRIPP, Herman Tilden, mining engineer. B. in Butte City, Calif., Aug. 6, 1859; m.; children: Chester, Eva Kay (Mrs. Fred Briggs Johnston), Gladys (Mrs. Gene Austin); went to Alaska, 1896; supt., Sumdum gold mine, 1897-1904; engaged in various mining ventures, mayor, Juneau, 1904-06; terr. Sen., 1913-15, H.R., 1921-23; died in Juneau, July 5, 1939. Mem., Masons (dep. inspector gen., Scottish Rite Masonic jurisdiction of Alaska, 33d degree), Pioneers. Republican.

TROY, Ethel Crocker Forgy, educator. Supt. of scs., Seward, 1913-16; m. John Weir Troy in Seattle, Wash., Nov. 27, 1916; Dem. Nat. Com., 1920-28; res., southern Calif. due to health, 1920-74; died in Los Angeles, July 1974. Democrat.

TROY, John Weir, newspaper editor-publisher. B. in Dungeness, Wash., Oct. 31, 1868; s. Smith and Laura Bass (Weir) T.; country sc., Clallam Co., Wash., h. sc., Port Townsend, Wash.; stud., Port Townsend Coll., 1 yr.; m. Minerva Lewis, Port Angeles, Wash. (div. 1911, dec. 1960); children: Helen Marian (Mrs. Robert Bender, Mrs. Alfred Monsen), Dorothy Minerva (Mrs. H.E. Morgan, Mrs. George Lingo); m. 2d, Ethel Crocker Forgy in Seattle, Wash., Nov. 27, 1916 (dec. 1974); reporter, Port Townsend ARGUS, 1886-88; dep. co. auditor and clerk, Port Townsend, 1889-97; ed.-pub., WEEKLY DEMOCRATIC LEADER, Port Angeles, 1891-97; correspondent for Seattle paper, Skagway, 1897-98; medical treatment in Wash., 1898-99; ed.-part-owner, Skagway DAILY ALASKAN, 1899-1907; sec.-publicity dir., Arctic Club, Seattle, 1907-11; ed., Alaska-Yukon Magazine, Seattle, 1911-12; ed., DAILY ALASKAN EMPIRE, Juneau, 1913-33, owner, 1914; U.S. Collector of Customs, 1919-22; Alaska Gov., 1933-39, res.; died in Juneau hospital, May 2, 1942. Mem., Pioneers, Elks, Arctic Club (Seattle), Racquet Club (Wash., D.C.), Sigma Delta Chi. Democrat.

TRUITT, James Steele, lawyer. B. in Bentonville, Ark., Oct. 16, 1858; s. James Madison and Mary Elizabeth (Pyatt) T.; public and pvt. sc., Almspring (Ark.) Acad.; law stud. under preceptor, 1918-21; m. Susia A. Oldham, Vinita, Indian Terr. (Okla.), Oct. 10, 1895; children: James G., Vella (Mrs. Moehring, Mrs. Evana); law prac., Okla.; moved to Bellingham, Wash., 1910, Anchorage, 1916; law prac., referee in bankruptcy, special master in chancery, 3d jud. div., and circuit ct. of appeals; asst. U.S. atty., 1919-21; pvt. law prac., Anchorage, 1921-33; terr. atty. gen., Juneau, 1933-41; ret. to Seattle, later to Bellingham; died there, Jan. 7, 1947. Mem., Masons. Presbyterian, Democrat.

TRUITT, Warren D., lawyer. B. in Greene Co., Ill., 1846; grad., McKendree Coll., 1868; admitted to Ill. bar, 1870, Ore. bar, 1872; elected co. judge, Polk Co., Ore., 1874; Ore. H.R., 1882-84; Presidential elector, 1884; register, U.S. Land Office, Lakeview, Ore., 1889-92; U.S. dist. judge for Alaska, Sitka, 1892-95; ret. to his home, The Dalles, Ore. Republican.

TUCKER, John Randolph, lawyer. B. in Phila., Pa., Aug. 13, 1854; s. Dr. David Hunter and Elizabeth (Dallas) T.; stud., Wash. and Lee U., U. Va.; m. Mary Singleton Hampton, Columbia, S.C., Nov. 26, 1907; circuit ct. judge, Va., 1898-1903; Va. Sen.,

1908-13, res.; dist. judge, 2d jud. div., Nome, 1913-17; pvt. law prac., Richmond, Va., 1917-; died in his home, Bedford, Va., Dec. 18, 1926. Democrat.

U

UDALL, Stewart Lee, lawyer, author. B. in St. Johns, Ariz., Jan. 31, 1920; s. Levi S. and Louise (Lee) U.; LL.B., U. Ariz., 1948; m. Ermalee Webb, Aug. 1, 1947; children: Thomas, Scott, Lynn, Lori, Denis, James; USAAF, 1944; admitted to Ariz. bar, 1948; prac. law, Tucson, 1948-54; U.S. Cong., 84th-86th Cong., 2d Dist., Ariz.; Sec. Interior, 1961-69; chmn. bd., Overview Corp., 1969-; author, "Udall on the Environment," syndicated column, 1970-. Author: "The Quiet Crisis," 1963, 1976; "Agenda for Tomorrow," 1968; "America's Natural Treasures," 1971; (with others) "The National Parks of America," 1972. Mem., Am. Bar Assn. Mormon, Democrat. Address; 1700 Penn. Ave., Wash., D.C. 20006.

ULMER, Eldon Robert, pharmacist. B. in Boise, Ida., Nov. 15, 1918; s. T.C. and Winnifred (Tarter) U.; B.S., Ida. State U., 1943; m. Lillian Virgin, May 1, 1942; children: Robert Brent, Jerry Eldon, Scott Alan, Sue Ellen, Reed Christian; U.S. Navy, 1943-46; res., Anchorage, early 1950s-; state finance chmn., Rep. party, Alaska, 1968-70; del., Rep. Nat. Conv., 1968, 1972; Rep. Nat. Com., 1972-; pres.-owner, Ulmer-Burgess, Inc., Downtown Rexall Store, Anchorage Professional Pharmacy, since early 1960s. Mem., Alaska Pharmaceutical Assn. (bd., 1968-70); Alaska Bd. Pharmacy (pres.); Anchorage Community Hospital (bd. trustees, chmn., finance com., 1968-72); Am. Cancer Soc. (nat. bd., 1969-); Anchorage Businessmen's Assn. (pres., 1966-68, v.p., 1970-72). Protestant, Republican. Address: P.O. Box 1420, Anchorage 99510.

UNDERWOOD, Martin B., law enforcement officer. B. in Hollis, Long I., N.Y., June 8, 1920; s. George B. and Elizabeth U.; B.S., Boston Coll., 1947; unm.; U.S. Navy, 1942-45; special agent, FBI, Wash., D.C., Ill., Mich., Mont., 1947-52, Anchorage, 1952-54, Fairbanks, 1954-59; comr. public safety, 1960-67; head of safety and security, UA, 1967-. Mem., Am. Assn. Motor Vehicle Adm., Internat. Assn. Chiefs Police, Internat. Assn. Arson Investigators, Farthest North Peace Officers Assn., Am. Leg., Elks, K.T. Catholic.

URION, Richard K. (Rick), home builder, salesman. B. in Woodstown, N.J., June 8, 1939; s. Howard and Alice U.; stud., Wilkes Coll., Temple U., 3 yrs.; m. Katherine (div. 1974); children: Andrew Kirby, Michael; owner, Kodiak Builders, Anchorage, 1960s; sales mgr., Alaska Fireplace Co., Anchorage, 1970s; state H.R., 1973-75. Mem., Home Builders' Assn. Alaska (past pres.). Republican. Address: Box 4-175, Anchorage 99503.

V

VALENTINE, Emory, miner, goldsmith. B. in Dowagiac, Mich., 1858; s. Joseph V.; traveled from Mich. to Colo. on pony with an overcoat for saddle and hay-rope stirrups, 1868; miner, Colo., losing leg in accident; learned goldsmith trade; m. Katherine (div. in Juneau, May 1891); m. 2d, Maude A. Gough in Juneau, Oct. 19, 1900 (dec. 1905); m. 3d, Mrs. Frank (Josephine G.) Cook in Juneau, Dec. 20, 1909 (div. in Juneau, 1915); prop., jewelry stores, Colo. and Mont., 1876-86; went to Juneau, May 1886, estab. jewelry store, bought extensive real estate, organized People's Wharf Co. and built wharf, Juneau; went to Skagway during gold rush, built wharf and engaged in wholesale lumber bus.; ret. to Juneau, living there the remainder of life; mayor, 6 terms, councilman, 1 term, Juneau; organized city fire dept. and city water system; chmn., Rep. state central com., 1912-14; Japanese vice-consul, for which he was honored with Order of the Rising Sun by Emperor; died in Juneau, Sept. 9, 1930. Republican.

VANDERLEEST, Herman Raymond (Van), pharmacist. B. in Grand Rapids, Mich., May 22, 1882; s. William and Frederika (Froling) V.; employe, Dr. Bartt Prescription Dispensary, Grand Rapids, 1897; passed Mich. State Bd. Pharmacy, 1903; m. Alexandra Pottner, Nov. 27, 1914; children: Mary Kathleen (Mrs. Felix J. Toner), Jeanne (Mrs. Gerald C. Ricke); drug clerk, 1904-06, pharmacist, 1906-08, Seattle, Wash.; pharmacist, Butler-Mauro Drug Co., Nome, 1908-14, estab. Juneau branch, 1914, eventually sole owner, ret., 1952; del., const. conv., 1955-56; died in Pioneers Home, Sitka, Nov. 5, 1964. Mem., terr. bd. pharmacy (pres.), 15 yrs.; bd., Pioneers Home, Sitka (pres.), 1936-46; Elks, Pioneers. Democrat.

VAN HOOMISSEN, Gerald J., lawyer. B. in Portland, Ore., July 10, 1934; B.A., Gonzaga U., Northwest Coll. of Law, Portland, 1958; m. Wanda Martens; 6 children; pvt. law prac., Portland, 1958-64; asst. U.S. dist. atty., Anchorage, 1964-68, Fairbanks, 1968-69; pvt. law prac., Fairbanks; superior ct. judge, Fairbanks, 1970-. Republican.

VAWTER, Cornelius Lansing, law enforcement officer. B. *c.* 1851; res., Helena, Mont.; dep. U.S. Marshal, St. Michael, 1898-1900; U.S. Marshal, 2d jud. div., Nome, 1900-01; dep. U.S. Marshal, Unga, 1901-08, Valdez, 1908-09, Fairbanks, 1909-10, Iditarod, 1911-13, Tanana, 1913-17, Ft. Gibbon, 1917-22; ret. to Calif., Feb. 1922; found oil at Santa Fe Springs, near Los Angeles; died in Los Angeles, Dec. 31, 1926.

VILAS, William Freeman, professor, lawyer. B. in Chelsea, Vt., July 9, 1840; s. Levi Baker and Esther Green (Smilie) V.; B.A., U. Wis., 1858; LL.B., U.

Albany, N.Y., 1860; admitted to bar, Wis., 1860; m. Anna Matilda Fox, Jan. 3, 1866; d. Mary Esther; fought in Civil War; state reviser of statutes, 1875-78; assisted in re-editing 20 vols. of Wis. Reports, 1875-76; prof., law, U. Wis., 1868-85, 1889-92, U. regent, 1881-85, 1898-1905; Wis. H.R., 1885; U.S. Postmaster Gen., 1885-88; Sec. Interior, 1888-89; U.S. Sen., 1891-97; died in Madison, Wis., Aug. 28, 1908; interment, Forest Hills cemetery, Madison. Democrat.

VOCHOSKA, Virgil Deane, lawyer. B. in Oxford Junction, Ia., Aug. 19, 1932; s. Otto Leonard and Louise (Webb) V.; B.A., Cornell Coll., Mt. Vernon, Ia., 1955; LL.B., U. Denver, 1958; m. Lois Ford, Anchorage, May 27, 1966; children: William Edward, Patricia Louise; legal asst., atty. gen., Juneau, 1958-60; pvt. law prac., Nome, 1960-62; state dist. atty., 2d jud. dist., Nome, 1962-64; dist. magistrate and dist. ct. judge, Anchorage, 1964-68; pvt. law prac., Anchorage, 1969-71; asst. dist. atty., Anchorage, 1971-72; dist. ct. judge, 3d jud. dist., Kodiak, 1972-. Mem., Rotary. Presbyterian, Independent. Address: Box 1367, Kodiak 99615.

VOGLER, Joseph E., miner, logger, realtor. B. in Barnes, Kan., Apr. 24, 1913; h. sc., Waterville, Kan., 1929; LL.B., 1934, J.D., 1968, U. Kan.; m. Doris Louise; children: Marilyn (Mrs. Urion), Joseph; went to Kodiak, Mar. 1942; res., Fairbanks, 1943-; pres., B.B.P. corp.; owner-op., Ketchem mines; cand., Alaska gov., 1974. Mem., Pioneers. Alaskan Independence. Address: Box 7, Fairbanks 99707.

von der HEYDT, James Arnold, lawyer, artist. B. in Miles City, Mont., July 15, 1919; gr. and h. sc., Oak Park, Ill.; B.A., Albion Coll., Mich., 1942; J.D., Northwestern U., 1951; m. Verna E. Johnson in Seattle, Wash., May 21, 1952; constr. worker, Alcan (Alaska-Canada) highways and at Nome, 1943-45; dep. U.S. Marshal, Nome, 1945-48; U.S. Comr., later U.S. dist. atty., 2d jud. div., Nome, 1951-53; pvt. law prac. and city atty., Nome, 1953-59; terr. H.R.,1957-59; superior ct. judge, presiding, Juneau, 1959-66; U.S. dist. judge, Anchorage, 1966-. Mem., Sigma Nu, Am. Ornithologists' Union, Anchorage fine Arts Museum Assn. (pres. 1969), Alaska Bar Assn. (pres., 1959). Presbyterian, Democrat. Address; Fed. Bldg., 4th & F St., Anchorage 99501.

VUKOVICH, Stephen, miner, salesman. B. in Danilograd, Montenegro, Yugoslavia, Sept. 16, 1890; s. Krsto and M. (Radovich) V.; public sc., Yugoslavia; m. Selma Walstead, Dec. 13, 1938; s. Roger Stephen; joined father in N.Y.C., 1907; laborer, Chicago wire factory, Mont. and Ida. railroads, Aberdeen, Wash., logging camp (2 yrs.); miner, Alaska-Juneau gold mine, 1914-26; U.S. Army, 1917-18; laborer in logging camp, 1926-27; prop., bowling alley and soft drink parlor, later misc. work for city and fed govt., 1927-35; estab. wholesale and retail men's and women's clothing bus., Juneau, 1936-51; terr. H.R., 1945-49; died in hotel room, Fairbanks, Oct. 8, 1951. Mem., Am. Leg., 40 & 8, Pioneers, Elks, Moose. Republican.

W

WADE, Hugh Joseph, lawyer. B. in Dougherty, Ia., June 29, 1901; s. John F. and Mary (Dougherty) W.; h. sc., Des Moines, Ia.; stud., Drake U., 3 yrs.; LL.B., U. Ia., 1924; m. Madge Case of Juneau, in Wash., D.C., June 29, 1933; children: Hugh Gerald, Suzanne (Mrs. James R. McKeown), Michael Howard (dec. 1971); law prac., Omaha, Neb., 1924-25; FBI agent, 1925-28, assigned to Alaska, 1926-28; legal staff mem., pvt. bus., Wash., D.C., 1928-34; Alaska adm., Nat. Recovery Adm., 1924-25; area dir., Fed. Social Security Adm., 1935-50; area dir., ANS, 1950-53; pvt. law prac., Anchorage, 1953-55; terr. tres., 1955-59; Sec. of State, 1959-66; reg. solicitor, Dept. Interior, Wash., D.C., Mar.-May, 1971; ret. to Tee Harbor, near Juneau. Mem., Alaska, Juneau Bar Assns., Pioneers. Catholic, Democrat.

WALKER, Arthur P., fisherman, miner, logger. B. in Calif., June 17, 1887; left farm home, 1901; employe, Alaska Central Ry., Seward, 1905-; U.S. Army, 1917-18; salmon troller, Ketchikan vicinity, 1930s; m. Martha Wheeler, Ketchikan, Apr. 1936 (div.); res., Craig, 1936-40, Pelican, 1940s; terr. H.R., from Ketchikan, 1935-37, from Craig, 1939-41; asst. to terr. comr. labor, 1942-43; terr. Sen., from Pelican, 1943-44; died in Veterans' Naval hospital, Shoemaker, Calif., Nov. 19, 1944. Mem., Alaska Trollers' Assn., Pioneers, Moose, Vets WWI. Democrat.

WALKER, George R., lawyer. B. in Akron, O.; grad., Yale U., 1878; m.; 2 sons (one named Richard); faculty mem., Jacksonville Coll., Ill.; pvt. law prac., Chicago, Ill., 1882-1903; U.S. dist. atty., Indian Terr. (Okla.), 1906-10; U.S. dist. atty., 3d jud. div., Valdez, 1910-14; ret. to former home, Okla. Republican.

WALKER, Norman Ray, pharmacist. B. in Regina, Sask., Can., July 28, 1889; s. Harry S. and Mary (Atkinson) W.; h. sc., Wash. State Coll., 1911; m. Josephine O'Keefe, 1916; children: Florence Mary (Mrs. John J. O'Shea), William Woodrow; moved from Can. to ranch, Glasgow, Mont., later went to sea as deck hand bound for Orient, 1901-; pharmacist, Seattle, Wash., 1911-13; went to Alaska, 1913; prop., Walker Drug Co., Ketchikan, 1916-49; naturalized U.S. citizen, Seattle, Wash., 1918; U.S. Army, 1918-19; mayor, Ketchikan, 1930-32; terr. Sen., 1933-49; died in Ketchikan, Apr. 4, 1949. Mem., Alaska Bd. Pharmacy (pres.), Nat. Bd. Pharmacy, Selective Service Bd., 1943-45, Am. Leg., Rotary (pres.), Elks, Eagles (pres.), Wash. State Press Club (Seattle). Democrat.

WALSH, Michael Joseph, miner. B. in Balinade, Co. Cork, Ireland, Apr. 8, 1882; emigrated to U.S., 1901; m. W. Louise Forsythe in Nome, Aug. 1, 1909 (dec. 1971); children: Joseph, Eileen (Mrs. Julian R. Taylor), James, Pearse, Ann, Kevin, Kathleen (Mrs. David Farley), Noreen (Mrs.Wills), Patricia (Mrs. Holbrook), Mary Erin (Mrs. Maurice King, dec. 1944); gold prospector, Nome, 1906-63; city clerk, Nome, 1931-44; terr. H.R., 1945-47; del., const. conv., 1955-56; hon. LL.D., UA, 1958; died in Nome, Apr. 1, 1963. Mem., terr. bd. education 1934-42; bd. regents, UA, 1943-59; Pioneers (grand pres., 1954); Alaska Statehood Com., 1958-59. Catholic, Democrat.

WALSH, Pearse M. (Pete), miner, airlines executive. B. in Nome, Jan. 16, 1919; h. sc., Nome, 1936; stud., UA, 1939-40; m. Mary Ellen Sprole, Aug. 24, 1946; children: Daniel, John, Brian; U.S. Army Air Corps, 1941-45; agent, Pan-Am. World Airways, San Francisco, Seattle, Nome, 1945-57; state Sen., 1961-67; station mgr., Alaska Airlines, Nome, 1966-71; employe, Lost River Mining Corp. and prospecting on own, 1971-. Mem., state planning com., 1959; Alaska C. of C. (bd. dir.); Nome light & power bd. (pres., 1955-58); Pioneers (pres., Nome Igloo, 1956); Northwest Alaska C. of C. (pres., 1960-63). Catholic, Democrat.

WALSH, Walter Edward, lawyer. B. in Fulton Co., Ind., Dec. 15, 1898; s. John J. and Anna (Hosey) W.; LL.B., Valparaiso U., 1922; admitted to Mo. bar, 1923, Alaska bar, 1945; m. Blanche; 1 d.; pvt. law prac., Kan. City, Mo., 1923-42; chief enforcement atty., OPA, Juneau, 1944-; reg. atty., ANS, and asst. reg. solicitor, Dept. Interior, 1951-59; superior ct. judge, 1st jud. div., Ketchikan, 1959-67; ret. to Milwaukie, Ore.; died there, Oct. 3, 1969. Democrat.

WALTERS, Benjamin O., Jr., lawyer. B. in Ventura, Calif., Oct. 4, 1934; s. Benjamin O. and Minnie M. (McColpin) W.; h. sc., Homer, 1952; A.A., Ventura Coll., 1960; B.A., U. Calif., Berkeley, 1962; J.D., U. Calif. Sc. of Law (Boalt Hall), 1965; m. Annetta M. Loffswold, Ventura, Aug. 11, 1957; children: Bonnie, Benjamin O., III, Andrew G.; went to Homer to join father, 1949; asst. atty. gen., Juneau, 1965-67; state dist. atty., 1st jud. dist., Ketchikan, 1967-68; asst. dist. atty., Anchorage, 1968-70; pvt. law prac., Anchorage, 1970-. Mem., Spenard Rotary Club, Elks. Methodist. Address: 360 K St., Suite 301, Anchorage 99501.

WANAMAKER, James N., lawyer. B. in Seattle, Wash., June 2, 1935; s. Lemuel A. and Pearl A. (Anderson) W.; B.A., 1957, LL.B., 1959, U. Wash.; m. Kalliroi Y. Todolou, Juneau, Dec. 15, 1961; children: Catherine, James, Caroline, John; asst. atty. gen., Juneau, 1960-62; asst. state dist. atty., Anchorage, 1962-63; chief, state law dept.'s consumer protection div., Anchorage, 1963-64; state dist. atty., 3d jud. div., Anchorage, 1964-65; pvt. law prac., Anchorage, 1965-. Mem., Southcentral Timber Development, Inc. (dir.); Anchorage Charter Com.; Alaska Nat. Guard; Anchorage Bar

Assn. (pres., 1973); state bd. education (vice chmn.), 1971-. Democrat. Address: 750 W. Second Ave., Anchorage.

WARD, Robert W., businessman. B. in Addy, Wash., Nov. 26, 1929; h. sc., Metaline Falls, Wash.; m. Peggie Garske of Ione, Wash., 1949 (div.); children: Karen, Robert, Jr., Kenneth; USFS employe, logging for Dimond Match Co., constr. and contracting, 1946-54; supt., electrical dept., Ketchikan Pulp Co., 1954-66; city councilman, Ketchikan, 1961; chmn., Gateway-Ketchikan Borough, 1963; comr. adm., 1966-69; Sec. of State, 1969-70; mem., Alaska Power Com., Dept. Interior, 1971-74; pres., Alaska div., Arctic Gas Pipeline Co., Anchorage, 1973-. Received Alaska Jaycees "Key Man" award, 1958. Mem., Alaska Municipal League (pres., 1964), Ketchikan Pulp Co. Fed.Credit Union (pres., 1964). Republican.

WARDELL, Thomas M., lawyer. B. in Boise, Ida.; B.A., San Jose State Coll., Calif.; J.D., U. Calif. Hastings Law Coll., 1963; asst. atty. gen., Juneau, 1965-68, dep. atty. gen., 1968-70; state dist. atty., 3d jud. div., Kenai-Kodiak, 1971-.

WARREN, Clifford E., painting contractor. B. in Seattle, Wash., Jan. 25, 1919; s. John L. and Esther W.; h. sc., West Seattle; m. June Crate, Tacoma, Wash., May 20, 1938; went to Anchorage, Apr. 1949; estab. Warren Painting Co.; chmn., Dem. state central com., 1970-72; Dem. Nat. Com., 1972-. Mem., Masons, Shrine, Bartlett Dem. Club, Wash. Athletic Club (Seattle). Democrat. Address: Box 1124, Anchorage, Alaska 99510.

WARREN, Roscoe R. (Bud), fisherman. B. in Gardiner, Mont., 1905; m.; 3 children; went to Alaska, c. 1936; bus. agent, Cook Inlet fishermen's union; journeyman sheet metal and automotive worker; terr. H.R., 1946-47, served only in "extraordinary session," 1946. Democrat.

WARWICK, Andrew S. (Andy), accountant. B. in Fairbanks, Jan. 6, 1943; stud., Ore. State U., U. Ore.; B.B.A., UA, 1966; m. Judith Peters in Anchorage; d. Sydney Elizabeth; U.S. Navy; employe, accounting firm, Anchorage, 1968-69; moved to Fairbanks, 1969; acct., Burgess Constr. Co., later Alaska Airco; state H.R., 1971-75; cand., lt. gov., 1974; comr. adm., 1974-78. Democrat (1970), Republican (1972). Address: 518 Fulton St., Fairbanks 99701.

WASKEY, Frank Hinman, miner, merchant. B. in Lake City, Minn., Apr. 20, 1875; s. George W. and Julia Amelia (Hurd) W.; gr. sc., Madison, S. Dak., Minneapolis, Minn.; h. sc., Minneapolis; m. Edna Norma Blodgett, Aug. 10, 1904; children: John Blodgett, Robert; m. 2d, Josie Livona Moody in Dillingham, June 29, 1924; children: Frank Hinman, Jr., Roberta Faith, Susan (Mrs. Carl E. Howe), June (Mrs. Don R. Goe); salesman, Minneapolis, 1892-98; prospector, Hope area, 1898-1900; prospector-miner, Nome, Iditarod, Marshall, Kuskokwim, striking it rich several times, 1900-30; Alaska's first del. in U.S. Cong., Dec. 1906-Mar. 1907, short term; pres., Nome Bk. & Trust Co.,

1908; prop., trading post, Dillingham, 1930-56; ret. to Oakville, Wash., where he cont. to trade in Eskimo artifacts; died in Oakville, Jan. 25, 1964; burial at Shelton, Wash. Seventh Day Adventist, Democrat.

WATSON, Harry Glover, government administrator. B. in Thayer, Mo., 1884; s. Alexander Wilson and Eliza Lucretia (Bond) W.; h. sc.; stud., bus. coll., 2 yrs.; m. Lillian G. Smith, Nov. 11, 1925 (dec. 1967); U.S. Customs Inspector, Seattle, Wash., 1905-06; chief clerk, N.A.T. & T. Co., St. Michael, 1906-09; gen. agent, Merchants Yukon Line, St. Michael, Iditarod, 1910-12; gen. agent, Northern Navigation and Northern Commercial Co., Dikeman, 1912-15; owner-operator, Northern Aerograph Co., mining-prospecting firm, Dikeman, Marshall, 1916-20; dep. clerk of ct., 4th jud. div., 1920-22; supt., riverboat service, Alaska R.R., 1923-25; terr. H.R., 1925; sec. to Gov., Juneau, 1925-39; sec., Alaska Miners Assn., Fairbanks, 1940-41; budget officer, CAA (FAA), Anchorage, 1942-54, ret.; died in Anchorage, Jan. 1964. Mem., Pioneers (he and wife were king and queen regents, Fur Rendezvous, Anchorage, 1960), Elks, Masons. Episcopalian, Republican.

WAUGAMAN, William I., miner, game guide. B. in Pa., 1916; B.S., Pa. State U., 1940; m. Florence "Flora"; children: William I., Jr., Richard, Edward, Linda, Debra; gold miner, Fairbanks dist., 1940-43; U.S. Army, 1943-45, 1948-53; gen. mgr., Usibelli coal mine, Healy, 1953-; co-owner, Cripple Cr. Lodge, Ester; owner, Wood River Guides & Outfitters, Fairbanks; state Sen., 1967-69. Mem., bd. dir., Fairbanks C. of C.; First Nat. Bk., Fairbanks; Alaska Goldpanners; v.p., Alaska C. of C.; Nat. Rifle Assn.; Tanana Valley Sportsmen's Assn. Republican.

WAUGH, William H., president, Alaska Road Commission, 1917-20.

WEBB, Jack G., government administrator, aviator. B. in San Diego, Calif., 1914; m. Dorothy "Dottie"; children: Jack, Marilynne; pilot, 1936-; dist. flight supervisor, FAA, Los Angeles, Calif., 1942, later transferred to Wash., D.C., Okla. City, Atlanta, Ga.; dir., Nat. Aviation Facilities Experimental Center, Atlantic City, N.J., 1965-70; reg. adm., FAA, Anchorage, 1970-72; dir., Pacific reg., FAA, Hawaii, 1972-.

WEISE, Jack E., state Senator, from Bethel, 1959-63. Republican.

WELLS, James K., hunter, fisherman. B. in Deering, c. 1907; terr. H.R., from Noorvik, 1951-53. Democrat.

WENNBLOOM, Noel K., lawyer. Native of Neb.; asst. dist. atty., dist. atty., 3d jud. div., Anchorage, 1942-46; m. in Anchorage; ret. to Neb. Democrat.

WERNER, John R., businessman. B. in Seward, June 27, 1943; s. Jack and Esther (Hanninen) W.; gr. and h. sc., Seward; B.A., U. Wash., 1965; M.B.A., Wayne State U., Detroit, 1970; m. Cheryl Ann, Mt. Clemens, Mich., June 10, 1967; children: Jeffrey, Dustin; capt., U.S. Air Force; dep. comr., dept. economic development, 1970-73; special asst. to Gov. Egan, Anchorage, 1973-74; chmn., Alaska Pipeline Com., Anchorage. Catholic, Democrat. Address: 338 Denali St., Anchorage 99501.

WERNER, John R. (Jack), businessman. B. near Everett, Wash., 1918; grad., h. sc., Lake Stevens, Wash.; moved to Ketchikan, 1936; m. in Bethel, 1939; children: Catherine, John R., Jr., Larry; moved to Seward, 1940, operated grocery and meat market, cold storage plant, furniture and appliance co., Seward; life insurance salesman; terr. Sen., 1955-57; v.p., Japanese-Am. Development Co., fish freezing plant, Seward, 1968-. Mem., Alaska Life Underwriters Assn. (charter, dir., 1953), Seward Dem. Club (pres.), Kiwanis, Elks, SPEBSQA (pres., Anchorage). Presbyterian, Democrat.

WEST, Roy Owen, lawyer. B. in Georgetown, Ill., Oct. 27, 1868; s. Pleasant and Helen Anna (Yapp) W.; B.A., DePauw U., 1890; law stud.; admitted to bar, 1890; m. Louisa Augustus, June 11, 1898 (dec.); 2 children; m. 2d, Louise McWilliams, June 8, 1904; law prac., Chicago, 1890-; asst. atty., Cook Co., 1893; city atty., Chicago, 1895-97; mem., Cook Co. bd. assessments, 1898-1914; mem., Cook Co., Rep. com., 1900-28; chmn., Ill. Rep. state central com., 1904-14; sec., Rep. state central com., 1924-28; del., Rep. Nat. Convs., 1908, 1912, 1916, 1928; Sec. Interior, 1928-29; chmn., nat. Rep. party, 1932; special asst. to U.S. Atty. Gen., 1941-53; died in Chicago, Nov. 29, 1958. Mem., bd. trustees, DePauw U. (pres., 1928). Methodist, Republican.

WESTDAHL, John L., heavy equipment operator, salesman. B. in Fish Village, June 17, 1918; s. Theresa W.; m. Judy of Bethel, c. 1953; children: Anna Marie, Patricia; father died, 1935, and son left home to work in mining camps, 1935-43; merchant seaman, 1943-45; itinerant constr. worker and at one time insurance salesman, 1946-63; moved to St. Mary's, 1963; state H.R., 1967-68; found dead in hotel room, Anchorage, Feb. 18, 1968. Catholic, Democrat.

WHALEY, Frank H., aviator, miner, photographer. B. in Davis, W. Va., Aug. 6, 1906; s. Frank H. and Buena Vista W.; stud., Naval Prep. Sc., San Diego, flying sc., Chicago; instructor, 3 yrs.; commercial pilot's license, 1928; m. Neva Brownfield in Seattle, Wash., 1931; children: Frank B., Nina (Mrs. Chris von Imhof); flight sc. and charter service, Boeing Field, Seattle, 1929-33; bush pilot, Nome and Fairbanks, gold miner during summer seasons, 1933-55; terr. H.R., 1941-45, Sen., 1945-47; exec. dir., Alaska Visitors Assn., 1955-57; interline and tour mgr., asst. v.p., Wien Airlines, Fairbanks, 1957-71, ret.; filmed 13 documentaries on Arctic and Eskimo way of life. Awarded Air Medal by Pres. Truman for rescue mission. Mem., Alaska Miners' Assn. (bd. dir.), Alaska Travel Promotion Assn. (dir.), Gov.'s Tourist Adv. Bd. Democrat.

WHITE, Albert, U.S. Marshal, lawyer, merchant, real estate broker. B. in San Francisco, Calif., Nov. 2, 1890; s. Albert and Kate (Cills) W.; public sc., San Francisco; prop., saloon and pool hall, inherited from father, Valdez, 1908-17; m.; city councilman, 2 terms; pres., C. of C., 1 term; res., Ida., 1917-25; m. Margaret Nefsy in Boise, Ida., Oct. 5, 1922; s. George (dec. 1936); chmn., Rep. state central com., 1918; dep. collector of internal revenue, 1921; special agent, dept. justice, Boise, 1922; prohibition adm. for Ida., Mont., Wyo., 1924; FBI agent, San Francisco, 1925; U.S. Marshal, 1st jud. div., Juneau, 1926-34; admitted to Alaska bar, 1929; pvt. law prac., Juneau, 1934-63; chmn., Rep. central com., 1933-36; cand., del. in Cong., 1938; gen. counsel, Rep. party, Alaska, 1938-52; prop., Bon Marche dry goods store, Juneau; real estate broker; sold bus. and moved to Calif., 1963; died in Seattle, Wash., Jan. 28, 1972; buried in family plot, Green Lawns cemetery, San Francisco. Republican.

WHITE, Barrie Moseley, businessman. B. in Little Falls, N.Y., Oct. 13, 1923; s. Barrie M. and Barbara (Beebe) W.; St. Paul's Sc., Concord, N.H.; stud., Harvard U.; m. Daphne Milbank; children: Deborah Mary, Pamela, Sara Ellen, Barrie M., III; m. 2d, Mrs. June (Sewell) Faulkner in Anchorage, Mar. 17, 1966; U.S. Army Air Corps, 1944-45; went to Anchorage, 1947; estab. Alvest, Inc., investment corp.; pres., Anchorage Sports Arena, Inc., 1965-72; del., const. conv., 1955-56. Mem., Operation Statehood (pres.), Alaska Title Guaranty Co. (dir.), Elks, Greater Anchorage, Inc. (v.p.). Republican. Address: 838 W. 4th Ave., Anchorage 99501.

WHITE, Elmer John (Stroller), journalist. B. in O., Nov. 28, 1859; public sc., O.; sc. teacher and employe, newspapers; m. Josephine "Josie" Keys, Dec. 1891 (dec. 1956); children: Lenore "Lena", Albert; sc. teacher, 2 yrs., ed., weekly newspaper, 6 yrs., Fla., 1881-89; employe, newspapers, Puget Sound area, 1889-98; joined Klondike stampede; employe, Skagway NEWS, Bennett NEWS, KLONDIKE NUGGET (Dawson), Dawson DAILY NEWS, Dawson FREE PRESS, 1898-1904; ed.-pub., Whitehorse (Y.T.) STAR; U.S. vice-consul, 1904-16; ed.-pub., Douglas ISLAND NEWS, moved plant to Juneau, 1921, and named changed to STROLLER'S WEEKLY, 1916-30; chief of terr. bur. publicity, Juneau, 1918-21; terr. H.R., speaker, 1919-21; died in Juneau, Sept. 28, 1930. A 5,000-foot mountain on northwest side of Mendenhall glacier, 15 mi. from Juneau, was named Mt. Stroller White by nat. geographic bd., Oct. 7, 1931. Democrat.

WHITE, Jack Harold, salesman. B. in Bellingham, Wash., May 25, 1910; s. Charles D. and Mary W.; gr. and h. sc., Seattle, Wash.; stud., Heald Engr. Coll., San Francisco; m. Wilma "Willie" Hansen, Sept. 5, 1936; U.S. Navy, 1934-41; employe, radio intelligence div., FCC, Fairbanks, 1941-43, Juneau, 1943-46, Anchorage, 1946-48; wholesale and retail radio bus., Anchorage, 1948-53; city councilman, Anchorage, 1951-56; estab. Jack White Real Estate & Insurance Agency, Anchorage, 1953-; sold insur. div. to Allen T. Archer Co., Los Angeles, 1968. Mem., Yukon Power for Am., Inc. (pres., 1965),

Anchorage Insurance Agents Assn. (pres.), Anchorage (dir.) and Alaska C. of C., Masons, Shrine, Elks, Lions. Protestant, Republican.

WHITE, Margaret Nefsy, merchant. B. in Sundance, Wyo., Oct. 11, 1896; d. Frank and Bertha (Alden) Nefsy; gr. and h. sc.; m. Albert White in Boise, Ida., Oct. 5, 1922; s. George (dec. 1936); went to Juneau with husband, 1926; co-owner-operator, Bon Marche dept. store, Juneau, 1934-55; postmaster, Juneau, 1955-63; Rep. Nat. Com., 1935-55; sold bus. interests, moved to Calif., 1963-; died in Monrovia, Calif., May 5, 1974. Mem., Eastern Star. Republican.

WHITEHEAD, William Massie, physician. B. in Lovington, Va., Oct. 21, 1905; s. S.B. and Susan (Massie) W.; M.D., U. Va., 1931; internship, Virginia Mason Hospital, Seattle, Wash., 1931-32; m. Dorothy Johnson in Wrangell, 1934; children: Virginia Ann (Mrs. Dickerson Regan, div.), Page Massie (Mrs. Wesley Merrill), Stuart Baldwin, Suellen Baldwin, Anne Effinger; ship's doctor aboard Am. Mail line vessels, 1932-34; pvt. prac., Wrangell, 1934-35, Juneau, 1935-66; estab. Juneau Medical & Surgery Clinic; state H.R., 1963-65; died of heart attack on hunting trip, Nov. 12, 1966. Received community service award from state medical assn., 1966. Mem., Rotary (pres.), Juneau city council, bd. med. examiners (1943-64), Juneau C. of C. (pres.), terr. med. assn. (pres., 1945), terr. bd. education (1945-59), state jud. council (chmn., 1959-66), bd. regents, UA (1965-66). Democrat.

WHITMAN, Reginald Norman, railroad executive. B. in Jasmin, Sask., Can., Oct. 15, 1909; s. Norman L. and Irene (Haverlock) W.; stud., St. Joseph Coll., Yorkton, Sask.; grad., advanced management program, Harvard U., 1958; m. Opal Vales, Jan. 31, 1932; children: James, Richard, Donna (Mrs. Ronald Throener); employe, Great Northern R.R., 1929-69; U.S. Army, 1943-44; gen. mgr., Alaska R.R., 1955-56; fed. R.R. adm., Dept. Transportation, 1969-70; chmn. bd., pres., Mo.-Kan.-Tex. R.R., Dallas, Tex., 1970-. Mem., Alaska North Com., 1967-69, Nat. Defense Transportation Assn., Am. Leg. Catholic, Republican. Address: 701 Commerce St., Dallas, Tex. 75202.

WHITTAKER, Richard L., lawyer. B. in Princeton, Ill., Mar. 3, 1931; s. Marion and Louise (Walker) W.; h. sc., Ophir, Ore.; B.S., U. Ore.; J.D., Northwestern Coll. of Law, Portland, Ore.; m. Judith Feinberg, Kodiak, May 6, 1957; children: Jed, Louise, Josh, Juno, Jake, Jonah; Alaskan res., 1952; U.S. Army, 1952-54; newsman on Aleutian Chain, Kodiak, Ketchikan; reporter, Anchorage TIMES, 1957; law clerk for U.S. dist. judge, Fairbanks, 1964; state dist. atty., Ketchikan, 1964-66; pvt. law prac., Ketchikan, 1966-; Dem. state central com., 1968-74; state H.R., 1971-73; gen. counsel and v.p., Alaska Timber Corp.; city atty., Saxman, Hydaburg, Kake, Yakutat, town of Metlakatla, Klukwan village. Mem., Southeastern Alaska Community Action Program, Inc. (pres.); ANB (pres., Ketchikan, 1973-74); Ketchikan Gateway Sc.

Bd., 1973-74; Ketchikan Community Council (chmn., 1968); Alaska and Am. Bar Assns. Democrat. Address: Box 13, Ketchikan 99901.

WICKERSHAM, James, lawyer, historian, ethnologist, author. B. in Patoka, Ill., Aug. 24, 1857; s. Alexander and Mary Jane (McHaney) W.; public sc., Patoka; law stud., Springfield, Ill.; LL.D., UA, 1935; admitted to Ill. bar, 1880; m. Deborah Susan Bell, Oct. 27, 1880 (dec. 1926); children: Darrel Palmer, Arthur James, Howard Sullivan; m. 2d, Mrs. Grace Vrooman (Harry) Bishop, June 1928; law clerk, U.S. Census Bur., Springfield, 1880-83; probate judge, Pierce Co., Tacoma, Wash., 1884-88; city atty., Tacoma, 1892-98; Wash. state H.R., 1898-1900; U.S. dist. judge, 3d jud. div., Eagle, Fairbanks, Valdez, 1900-07, res.; pvt. law prac., Fairbanks, 1907-09; del. in U.S. Cong., 1909-21, 1931-33; pvt. law prac., Juneau, 1921-31, 1933-39; died in Juneau, Oct. 24, 1939. Mem., A.B., Elks (1st pres., Nome lodge, 1902), Moose, Masons, Pioneers (v.p.), Alaska Geographic Soc. (1900), Am. Anthropological Assn., Asiatic Soc. of Japan (life), SAR, Am. Ethnological Soc., Linguistic Soc. Am. (founder), Wash. State Hist. Soc. (charter). Author: "Old Yukon: Tales, Trails & Trials"; ed., "Alaska Territory Law Reports," 7 vols. Protestant, Republican.

WIDMARK, Alfred E., merchant. B. in Haines; grad., Sheldon Jackson h. sc.; B.S., Ore. State Coll.; m.; 6 children; merchant and mayor, Klawock; state H.R., 1961-63. Mem., ANB (past grand pres.). Republican.

WIEN, Ada Bering, secretary. B. in Nome, 1907; d. Mr. and Mrs. Arthurs, pioneer gold miners; gr. and h. sc., Nome; stud., Mills Coll., Oakland, Calif., bus. coll., Seattle, Wash.; m. Noel Wien in Nome, May 19, 1929; children: Noel Merrill, Jean Carolyn (Mrs. Edwin A. Rozanski), Richard Allan; ct. reporter and sec. to dist. judge, Nome, until 1929; moved to Fairbanks; office adm., Wien Alaska Airlines, Inc., Fairbanks, 1929-40, ret.; del., const. conv., 1955-56. Mem., Eastern Star, Sourdough Dance Club, Toastmistress Club (pres.). Presbyterian, Republican.

WIGGINS, William C., carpenter, construction contractor. B. in Galesburg, Ill., Sept. 11, 1900; s. Edward T. and Minnie M. W.; B.A., Chico State Teachers' Coll., 1923; post-grad., U. Calif.; m. Bernice; children: Stratton T., Nancy (Mrs. Frank S. Anderson); sc. teacher, Calif., 1923-30; fruit rancher, upper Napa Valley, Calif., 1930-50; carpenter, M-K Constr. Co., Anchorage, then organized own contracting firm, 1951-; state H.R., 1963-65, 1967-68. Mem., Manpower Training Adv. Com. (state chmn.), Senior Citizens Com. (1968-), Odd Fellows. Methodist, Republican.

WILBUR, Alden L., businessman. B. in Seattle, Wash., Feb. 19, 1909; s. Alden L. and Agnes W.; gr. sc., Fairbanks, Lincoln h. sc., Seattle; stud., heating and plumbing training sc., Seattle, 1931; m.; 2 children; went to Fairbanks with parents, 1914; joined father in A.L. Wilbur & Son heating and plumbing bus., Fairbanks, 1932-45; city council-

man, Fairbanks, 1941; U.S. Army, 1942-45; when father died, 1945, he was joined by bro.-in-law, Kenneth Bell, firm's name changed to Wilbur-Bell Plumbing and Heating Co., 1947-; terr. H.R., 1951-55. Mem., Jaycees (pres., 1940), Am. Leg., Elks, Eagles (pres.). Republican.

WILBUR, Ray Lyman, educator, physician. B. in Boonesboro, Ia., Apr. 13, 1875; s. Dwight Locke and Edna Maria (Lyman) W.; h. sc., Riverside, Calif.; B.A., 1896, M.A., 1897, Stanford U.; M.D., Cooper Med. Sc., 1899; m. Marguerite May Blake, Dec. 5, 1898; 3 sons; dean, Stanford Med. Sc., 1911-16, pres., 1916-43, lifetime chancellor, 1943; chief, Conservation Div., Food Adm., 1917; U.S. del., 6th Pan-Am. Cong., Havana, 1928; Sec. Interior, 1929-33; ret. to Stanford, cont. work in medicine; died in Stanford, Calif., June 26, 1949. Received Dr. William F. Snow medal for distinguished service to humanity, 1943. Mem., Am. Soc. Hygiene Assn. (pres., 1936). Congregationalist, Republican.

WILCOX, Charles Herbert, journalist. B. in Danbury, Conn., Sept. 1, 1867; m.; children: John, Charles; went to Alaska, 1898; ed., Valdez DAILY PROSPECTOR, 1912-14, having absorbed Valdez MINER, a weekly, Aug. 1912; co-pub., Cordova WEEKLY and DAILY TIMES, 1914-16; terr. H.R., from Valdez, 1925-27, speaker; ed., Valdez MINER, 1920s; chief dep. U.S. Marshal and dep. clerk of ct., Valdez, 1933-; moved to Anchorage when ct. hdqrs. transferred there, 1941-; died in Valdez, Feb. 3, 1948. Democrat.

WILDER, Claire Almon, U.S. Marshal, journalist. B. in Lamont, Ia., Jan. 12, 1893; s. James and Ximena Adel (Truman) W.; public sc., Ia. and N. Dak.; m. Gertrude Ethel Mace, Oct. 23, 1921; children: William W., Jane Claire, Betty Mae (Mrs. E.L. Clemons); U.S. Army, 1916-19; newspaper employe, Mont., Ore., Wash., 1920-37; staff mem., ALASKA PRESS, Juneau, 1937-40; owner-operator, Petersburg PRESS, 1940-53, sold paper to son-in-law; U.S. Marshal, 1st jud. div., 1954-59; died in Ariz., Sept. 1974. Mem., Rotary, Am. Leg., Elks, Masons. Protestant, Republican.

WILLIAMS, J. Gerald, lawyer. B. in Fraser, Ia., Apr. 8, 1907; s. Frank Eldon and Mary (Allen) W.; gr. sc., Gebo, Wyo.; h. sc., Thermopolis, Wyo.; B.A., 1929, LL.B., 1941, U. Wash.; m. Harriet Ann Sey in Douglas, June 30, 1930 (dec. 1970); children: Catherine Ann (Mrs. Ralph Bruce MacMillan), James Douglas; m. 2d, Marcella Loretta Luedtke in Anchorage, Nov. 6, 1971; sc. teacher, McGrath, Hoonah, Unga, Hope, Seldovia, Juneau, also U.S. Comr., Hoonah, 1930-40; asst. dist. atty., Anchorage, 1942-43; pvt. law prac., Anchorage, 1943-48; atty. gen., 1949-59; cand., Alaska gov., 1958; fed. referee in bankruptcy for state, 1962-74, succeeded by son. Mem., Western Reg. Assn., Atty. Gens. (chmn., 1958), Masons, Shrine, Amaranth (royal patron, 1961-62), Pioneers (hist., 1962), Elks, Moose, Lions (pres., Juneau). Presbyterian, Democrat. Address: 308 G St., Anchorage 99501.

WILLIAMS, Llewellyn Morris, journalist. B. in Fedora, S. Dak., May 23, 1895; s. William and Jane (Morgan) W.; stud., Ore. Agricultural Coll. (Ore. State U.); m. Winifred Eugenia Dow, Apr. 14, 1923; children: Llewellyn M., Jr., Jane (Mrs. Valentine Ferguson), Susan (Mrs. Susan Coonjohn); U.S. Navy, 1918-19; reporter to ed., Tacoma LEDGER and NEWS-TRIBUNE, Tacoma, Wash., 1919-22; ed.-pub., weekly newspaper, Hermiston, Ore., 1922-23; reporter, Spokane (Wash.) CHRONICLE, 1923-25, OLYMPIAN, Olympia, Wash., 1925-27; ed., Tillamook (Ore.) HEADLIGHT, 1927-28; reporter, Tacoma LEDGER and Tacoma NEWS-TRIBUNE, 1928-34; chief editorial writer, ALASKA DAILY EMPIRE, Juneau, 1934-39; ed.-pub., Wrangell SENTINEL, weekly, 1939-47, 1951-65; mayor, Wrangell, 1942, 1952; postmaster, Wrangell, 1942-44; Sec. of Alaska, Juneau, 1944-51; pub., Wrangell SENTINEL, until retirement, 1965; died in his home, Wrangell, Dec. 29, 1972. Mem., Am. Leg., Elks, Pioneers, Wrangell C. of C. (sec.). Democrat.

WILLIAMS, Llewellyn Morris, Jr., journalist. B. in Spokane, Wash., Nov. 26, 1924; s. Llewellyn M. and Winifred Eugenia (Dow) W.; h. sc., Wrangell, Randles Naval Prep. Sc., Wash., D.C.; m. Dorothy M. Baum, July 2, 1953; children: Christina, Kathryn, Lew, III; U.S. Army, 1943-45; ed., Wrangell SENTINEL, 1946-49; ed., ALASKA SUNDAY PRESS, Juneau, 1950; ed. and asst. to pub. (father), Wrangell SENTINEL, 1951-56; ed.-pub., Petersburg PRESS, 1956-66; mayor, Petersburg, 5 yrs.; managing ed., Ketchikan DAILY NEWS, 1966-; owner, Sitka SENTINEL, 1968-74. Mem., Alaska Public Assn. (pres.), Dem. state central com., C. of C. (dir., Wrangell, Petersburg, Ketchikan), Elks, Am. Leg., Alaska Judicial Council, Wrangell and Petersburg fire depts., Rotary, Silver Beaver in Boy Scouts.

WILLIAMS, Louis Littlepage, U.S. Marshal. B. in Boonville, Mo., Jan. 31, 1857; s. Marcus and Mary (Littlepage) W.; public sc., Boonville; m. Mary Spahr, March 17, 1887 (dec. 1911); dep. sheriff, Cooper Co., as a boy; U.S. Marshal, western dist., Mo., then U.S. Comr., 1st jud. div., Juneau, 1886-90; Alaskan rep., World's Columbian Exposition, Chicago, 1893; U.S. Marshal for Alaska, Sitka, 1894-97; Dem. Nat. Com., 1894-1908; ret. to Boonville, 1908-10; died of heart attack in hotel room, St. Louis, Mo., Jan. 22, 1910. Democrat.

WILLIAMSON, Fred S., U.S. Marshal, carpenter. B. in Wash. Co., Me., 1906; h. sc. education, special training in bookkeeping; m.; went to Anchorage from Longview, Wash., to work as carpenter for J.B. Warrack Constr. Co., 1944-53; U.S. Marshal, 3d jud. div., Anchorage, 1953-60; U.S. Marshal for Alaska, 1960-61. Mem., Employment Securities Com., Anchorage Carpenters' Union (pres., 4 yrs.), Anchorage Rep. Club (pres., 1952). Republican.

WILLIS, John R., collector of customs, 1908-13; U.S. Customs employe, 13-1/2 yrs.; employe, B.M. Behrends Bk., Juneau, 1913-.

WILSON, Emmitt, banker, B. in 1937; exec., Alaska Nat. Bk., Fairbanks; dep. comr. commerce, 1970-73, comr., 1973-75. Democrat.

WILSON, James W., banker. B. in Pocatello, Ida., Nov. 20, 1916; stud., Ut. State Agriculture Coll., U. Ut.; m. Wanda Peterson, 1938; children: Allyn, Carol Jean, James, Gerald; mgr., farm co-operative, Wash.; mgr., Matanuska Valley Farmers Cooperative Assn., Palmer, 1948-53; comr. agriculture, 1953-59; dir., div. agriculture, dept. natural resources, 1959-62; v.p., Matanuska Valley Bk., 1962-. Address: Palmer 99645.

WILSON, John A., miner, mineral surveyor. B. in Forest City, Ia., Aug. 31, 1879; grad., bus. coll., Minneapolis, Minn., 1898; stud., mining and engring., U. Wash., 1908, 1920; worked in Ut., 1898-1900; prospector-miner, Nome, 1900-08; surveyor, mostly on mineral claims; terr. road comr., 2d div., 1917-19; terr. H.R., 1923-24; died in fire, Meeghan roadhouse, Bluff, Sept. 17, 1924. Mem., Pioneers (pres.), Moose, Miners' Union (sec., pres.). Independent.

WILSON, I. Lavell, mechanic, aviator, guide. B. in Freewater, Ore., Nov. 24, 1937; grad., Sheldon Jackson h. sc.; stud., UA and Brigham Young U.; m. Catherine; 4 children; Alaskan res., 1949-; state H.R., from Tok, 1973-75. Mem., Operating Engrs., Local No. 302, Tok Dog Mushers Assn. (pres.), C. of C. (bd. dir.). Republican.

WINN, Grover Cleveland (Ki), lawyer. B. in Wiota, Wis., Jan. 3, 1886; s. Col. William and Anna W.; public sc., Juneau, LL.B., U. Wash., 1910; m. Bessie Louise Anderson, Feb. 19, 1912 (dec. 1949); children: Barbara (Mrs. William J. Roberts), Elizabeth "Suzy" (Mrs. Russell R. Hermann), William; went to Juneau with parents, Sept. 1893; U.S. Comr., Juneau, 1910-13; pvt. law prac., 1913-; terr. H.R., 1929-33; mem., Juneau sc. bd., 1931-40; died in Sitka, May 18, 1943. Mem., Delta Chi, Pioneers. Republican.

WINSOR, Paul, government administrator. B. in Onecta, Kan., Jan. 19, 1912; B.A., Whittier Coll., Calif.; stud., U. Calif., Long Beach; m. Charlotte Seymour Hapgood, 1936; children: Stephanie (Mrs. Irving), Brian, Lucinda; engaged in banking on Pacific Coast before and following WWII; U.S. Army Air Corps, 1943-45; sc. teacher and principal, Calif., 1945-49; sc. teacher, BIA, Hooper Bay; BIA adm., Bethel, 1950-56; estab. BIA office, Fairbanks, 1956-57; area field rep., BIA, Anchorage, 1957-59; comr. health and welfare, Juneau, 1960-63; BIA area dir., Minneapolis, Minn.

WIRTH, Francis X. (Frank), law enforcement officer, businessman. B. in Indianapolis, Ind., July 10, 1920; public sc., Helena, Mont.; stud., bus. coll., Everett, Wash.; m. Sylvia; children: Rita Eleanor, Cecelia Marie; m. 2d, Anchorage, 1972; U.S. Navy, received disability discharge, and employe, Everett Pacific shipyard, 1942-43; dep. U.S. Marshal, Fairbanks and points along Yukon and Kuskokwim Rivers, 1944-53; city councilman, Nenana, 1947-48; chief of detectives, Fairbanks city police dept., 1953-58; terr. H.R., 1957-58; chief of police, Sitka, 1958-59; prop., hotel and bar, Fairbanks, 1962; estab. Wirth Investigations, pvt. detective agency, Anchorage; Anchorage Borough Assemblyman, Mar.-May, 1972, res. Democrat. Address: 8060 Lake Otis Parkway, Anchorage.

WITTEMYER, John, lawyer. B. in 1940; law clerk, supreme ct. justice, Juneau, 1965-66; asst. dist. atty., Anchorage, 1966-67; state dist. atty., 1st jud. div., Juneau, Jan.-Aug., 1967.

WOHLFORTH, Eric Evan, lawyer. B. in Ridgefield, Conn., 1932; B.A., Princeton U., 1954; LL.B., U. Va., 1957; m. Caroline; children: Eric Evan, Jr., Charles; joined Hawkins, Delafield & Wood law firm, N.Y., 1957, went to Alaska after 1964 earthquake on behalf of firm; bond counsel, Greater Anchorage Area borough and ASHA, 1966-70; comr. revenue, 1970-72, res.; pvt. law prac., Anchorage, 1972-. Address: 645 G St., Anchorage 99501.

WOLD, Sigurd, miner, businessman. B. in Duluth, Minn., Apr. 24, 1896; public sc., Duluth; m.; d. Robin Louise; U.S. Army, 1917-18; worked in Wash., 1918-20; cannery worker, Excursion Inlet and Cordova, summer 1920; employe, Kennecott copper mine, winters, 1920-22; prop., Alaska House, rooming house and restaurant, McCarthy; taxi and transfer bus., expanding to warehouse storage, delivery of wood, coal, ice, 1922-37; sawmill operator, Fairbanks, 1937-42; storage and transfer bus., Fairbanks, 1942-62, ret.; state H.R., 1965-67. Mem., Rotary, C. of C., Nat. Defense Transportation Assn. (dir.), Tanana Hist. Soc., Am. Leg. (post comdr.), Masons, Elks, Pioneers (dir.), Alaska Carriers' Assn., Selective Service Bd. (16 yrs.). Republican.

WOOD, Joseph K., lawyer. U.S. dist. atty., 2d jud. div., Nome, 1900-02. Republican.

WOOD, Dr. William Ransom, educator. B. in Jacksonville, Ill., Feb. 3, 1907; s. William James and Elizabeth (Ransom) W.; B.A., Ill. Coll., 1927; M.A., 1936, Ph.D., 1939, U. Ia.; LL.D., Ill. Coll., 1960; m. Margaret Osborn, 1930 (dec. 1942); s. William Osborn; m. 2d, Dorothy Jane Irving, Mar. 18, 1944; children: Mark Irving, Karen Jane (Mrs. Parrish); sc. teacher, Mich., Ia., Ill., 1928-46; asst. supt., Evanston Township Scs., 1948-50; comdr., U.S. Naval Reserves, 1943-46; U.S. Office Education, Wash., D.C., 1950-53; v.p., U. Nev., 1954-60; pres., UA, 1960-73; education and bus. consult., exec. dir., Fairbanks Industrial Development Corp., 1973-. Mem., Rotary, Navy League, AAAS, Arctic Inst. North Am. (v.p.), Internat. Assn. U. Presidents. Methodist.

WOOFTER, Clarence Jefferson, telegraph operator. B. in Auburn, W. Va., Aug. 9, 1885; grad., W. Va. State Normal Sc., Mt. State bus. coll., Parkersburg, W.Va.; stud., W. Va. U., Morgantown; m. Miss Klondy E. Nelson in Juneau, Jan. 13, 1920 (div.); d. Virginia Olive; m. 2d, Mrs. Mina King Mezger, Fairbanks, Jan. 16, 1933; telegraph operator, several eastern railroads before joining U.S. Army

Signal Corps, 1904; ACS, Fairbanks, 1905-17; U.S. Army, 1917-18; Signal Corps, Juneau, 1918-21; ct. librarian, dist. ct., Juneau, 1921-22; chief dep. clerk, dist. ct. and registrar, U.S. Land Office, Nome, 1922-31; linotype operator, Nome NUGGET; terr. H.R., 1929-31; re-enlisted in Signal Corps, in charge Fairbanks office, 1931-45, Nome, Jan.-Sept., 1946, res.; died in Fairbanks, early 1968. Mem., Am. Leg. (comdr.), Pioneers (pres., sec.), Elks (exalted ruler), Odd Fellows, Moose, Eagles, Masons. Republican.

WORK, Hubert, physician. B. in Marion Center, Pa., July 3, 1860; s. Moses Thompson W.; stud., Pa. State Normal Sc., U. Mich. Med. Sc., 1882-84; M.D., U. Pa., 1885; m. Laura M. Arbuckle, 1887 (dec. 1924); children: Philip, Doris, Robert; m. 2d, Ethel Reed Gano, Dec. 1933; medicine prac., Greely, Colo., 1885-96; founded Woodcroft Hospital for Mental & Nervous Diseases, Pueblo, Colo., 1896-; del.-at-large, Rep. Nat. Conv., 1908; chmn., Rep. state central com., Colo., 1912; U.S. Army Med. Corps, WWI; pres., Am. Med. Assn., 1920; nat. com., 1920; asst. U.S. Postmaster Gen., 1921-22, Postmaster Gen., 1922-23; Sec. Interior, 1923-28; chmn., Rep. Nat. Com., 1928-29; died in South Denver, Colo., Dec. 14, 1942. Presbyterian, Republican.

WORTH, William E., merchant. B. in Provincetown, Mass., c. 1893; m. Mrs. May Gibson in Wrangell, 1934; employe, Petersburg Mercantile Co. and other firms, estab. own bus., 1912-39; terr. H.R., 1927-29; mercantile bus., Kodiak, 1939-53; city councilman, Kodiak, 1951-53, res.; left Alaska. Republican.

WRIGHT, Donald R., teamster, heavy equipment operator. B. in Nenana, Nov. 24, 1929; s. Arthur R. and Myrtle R. W.; grad., Lathrop h. sc., Fairbanks, 1947; m. Carol Adams, 1952; children: Darlene, Donald, George, Gareth; employed on riverboats, 1944-49; teamster and heavy equipment operator, own trucking service and other firms, 1949-67; lobbyist, Native Land Claims legislation, Wash., D.C., 1968-71; cand., U.S. Cong., 1968; cand., Alaska gov., 1974. Mem., Operating Engrs., teamsters, United Mine Workers labor unions; Cook Inlet Native Assn. (pres., 1967-68); Alaska Dog Mushers Assn. (pres.); AFN (pres., 1970-72); Nat. Cong. Am. Indians (v.p.). Democrat. Address (1974): Anchorage and Kenai.

WRIGHT, Dr. Joshua J., dentist. B. in Georgetown, S.C., Aug. 6, 1929; s. Joshua and Louise W.; gr. and h. sc., Georgetown; B.S., 1952, D.D.S., 1956, Howard U., Wash., D.C.; m. Lillie E. Mitchell, 1957; children: Joshua, III, Jacqueline, Rodney; U.S. Navy, 22 mos.; staff mem., Public Health Service hospital, Mt. Edgecumbe, Sitka, 1956-58; pvt. dental prac., Anchorage, 1958-; state H.R., 1970-73. Mem., Rotary, NAACP, Masons (grand master), Shrine, Anchorage Dental Soc. (pres., 1963), Alaska Dental Soc. (pres., 1967), Alaska Bd. Examiners (chmn., 1967-68), Anchorage Borough Sc. Bd. (1969-72). Presbyterian, Democrat. Address: 1033 W. Fireweed Lane, Anchorage 99503.

WRIGHT, Jules, trucking contractor. B. in Nenana, Aug. 21, 1933; s. Arthur R. and Myrtle R. W.; gr. sc., Nenana h. sc., Fairbanks; m. Marge; children: Robert, Allen, Julie; U.S. Army, 1952-53; owner-operator, Tundra Contractors, Inc., Fairbanks; state H.R., 1967-69. Mem., Fairbanks Native Assn. (pres.). Republican.

1958. Mem., Central Labor Council, Bldg. Trades Council, Laborers' Local (pres.), Salvation Army adv. bd. (1951-56), city planning com., Elks. Democrat.

Y

YANDELL, Robert K., lawyer. B. in Ga., 1897; grad., San Gabriel Coll., Calif., 1948; LL.B., LL.M., Pacific Coast U., Los Angeles; boxer before joining U.S. Army, 1917-20; law prac., Jackson, Miss., 1953-59; went to Alaska, 1959; asst. dist. atty., Anchorage, 1960-61; superior ct. probate master and ct. trustee, Anchorage, 1961-66; pvt. law prac., Anchorage, 1966-67; asst. dist. atty., Mar.-Sept., 1967; state dist. atty., 3d jud. div., Anchorage, 1967-68; headed new exec. office of complaints dept., 1968-71, ret. Awarded hon. state trooper badge upon retirement.

YEAGER, George McClellan, lawyer. B. in Lawrence Co., Pa., Oct. 11, 1926; s. Harry D. and Anna (Graham) Y.; B.A., B.S., Kent State U., 1950; LL.B., Western Reserve U., 1953; m. Jeanne F. Thompson, Mar. 18, 1949; children: George E., Sherry A., Linda M., Ellen D.; U.S. Army, 1944-46; asst. U.S. atty., Fairbanks, 1953-56; U.S. atty., 4th jud. div., Fairbanks, 1956-60; U.S. atty., Dist. Alaska, Anchorage, 1960-61; pvt. law prac., Fairbanks, 1961-. Mem., Fed., Alaska Bar Assns., U.S. Jr. C. of C. (dir., 1956-57), Alaska (pres., 1960), Fairbanks Jr. C. of C., Am. Leg. Republican.

YOUNG, Donald E., school teacher, riverboat captain. B. in Meridian, Calif., June 9, 1933; A.A., Yuba Jr. Coll., 1952; B.A., Chico State Coll., 1958; m. Lula Fredson in Ft. Yukon, Feb. 22, 1963; children: Joni, Dawn; U.S. Army, 1955-56; sc. teacher, Ft. Yukon, 1960-68, city councilman, 1960-64, mayor, 1964-68, Ft. Yukon; state H.R., 1967-71, state Sen., 1971-73, res.; riverboat capt., Yukon River, 1969-72; U.S. Cong., 1973-77. Mem., Nat. Education Assn., Alaska exec. bd. (1963-67); Ft. Yukon Dog Mushers Assn., Elks, Lions, Masons, Jaycees. Episcopalian, Republican.

YOUNG, Russell Kennedy, labor union official. B. in Passaic, N.J., Jan. 31, 1905; grad., h. sc., 1925; law stud. at nights, U. Newark, N.J., 1925-28; m.; children: Russell K., Jr., Robert, d. (m.); insurance investigator, N.J., N.Y., 1928-37; employe, Heyden Chemical Corp., installing cost systems, Garfield, N.J., 1937-46; auditor, U.S. dist. engrs., Anchorage, 1947-48; bus. agent, Laborers' Local Union No. 341, 1947-56; appt. Pres.'s conf. on labor legislation, 1953; terr. H.R., 1955-59; mem., B.R.B. Assoc. engrs. and manufacturers rep., 1956-57; Mars Employment Service, 1957-; cand., terr. labor comr.,

Z

ZAHRADNICEK, William T., educator. B. in Bison, Okla., Nov. 17, 1903; public sc., Atkinson, Neb.; B.A., Wayne State Teachers' Coll., 1934; M.A., U. Neb., 1947; m. Ita; s. William T.; supt. sc., Johnstown, Colo., 1930-39; supt. sc., Anselmo, Neb., 1939-42; education adm., U.S. Bur. Prisons, 1942-45; supt. sc., Monta Vista, Colo., 1945-47; sc. teacher, Anchorage, 1947-48; supt. sc., Telluride, Colo., 1948-49; supt., Palmer Ind. sc. dist., 1949-59; supt. on-base scs., Ft. Richardson, 1959-60; ret. to Palmer sc. system, 1960-63; city councilman, Palmer; state comr. educ., 1963-67; h. sc. principal, Palmer, 1967-70, ret.; pres., Kuskokwim Development Corp., 1970; died in Providence Hospital, Anchorage, June 5, 1974. Mem., Masons, Phi Delta Kappa, Kiwanis. Democrat.

ZIEGLER, Adolph Holton, lawyer. B. in Longwood, Md., Dec. 20, 1889; s. J.J. and Pauline (Keller) Z.; h. sc., Easton, Md.; stud., Bryant & Sadler's bus. coll.; law stud., Juneau; admitted to Alaska bar, 1915; m. Lillian Windfohr in Baltimore, Md., June 27, 1917; s. Robert Holton; m. 2d, Katherine Woll in Chehalis, Wash., July 28, 1936; ct. reporter, Easton, 1912-13; law stud., Z.R. Cheney office, 1913-15, law partner, 1915-17, Juneau; U.S. Navy, 1917-18; pvt. law prac., Ketchikan, 1919-70; mayor, Ketchikan, 1937-38; terr. H.R., 1929-33, 1935-37; cand., del. in U.S. Cong., 1932, 1944; died in Seattle hospital, May 18, 1972. Mem., terr. bd. education (pres., 1931-); 1st Nat. Bk. Ketchikan (bd. dir., pres.); Elks (exalted ruler, dist. dep. Alaska); Masons, Shrine, Pioneers. Episcopalian, Democrat.

ZIEGLER, Robert Holton, lawyer. B. in Baltimore, Md., Mar. 27, 1921; s. Adolph H. and Lillian (Windfohr) Z.; public sc., Ketchikan; LL.B., U. Va.; m. Betsy (div. 1972); children: Robert, Ann; m. 2d, Paula Kathryn Sampson, Ketchikan, Dec. 6, 1974; U.S. Army, 1943-45; joined father in law partnership, Ketchikan, 1946-; terr. H.R., 1957-59; state Sen., 1965-76. Mem., Alaska Bar Assn. (pres., bd. govs.); Rotary (pres.); Elks (exalted ruler). Democrat.

APPENDIX

Attorneys General

Cobb, John H. (Terr. Counsel)*	1913-16	Moody, Ralph	1960-62
Grigsby, George B.	1916-19	Hayes, George	1962-64
Murphy, Jeremiah C.	1919-20	Colver, Warren	1964-66
Rustgard, John	1920-33	Burr, Donald A.	1966-67
Truitt, James S.	1933-41	Boyko, Edgar Paul	1967-68
Roden, Henry	1941-45	Edwards, G. Kent	1968-70
Rivers, Ralph J.	1945-49	Havelock, John	1970-74
Williams, J. Gerald	1949-59	Gorsuch, Norman	1974 (Oct.-Dec.)
Rader, John	1959-60	Gross, Avrum	1974-

*Office of attorney general created by 1915 legislature.

Commissioners and Directors of Territorial and State Departments

Administration
Auditor
1929-32 Cole, Cash
1932-50 Boyle, Frank A.
1950-53 Moore, Neil

Commissioners
1959-66 Guertin, Floyd
1966-69 Ward, Robert
1969-70 Downes, Thomas
1971-74 Henri, Joseph
1974 (Apr.-Dec.) Freer, Richard
1974 Warwick, Andrew S.

Commerce
Commissioners
1959-65 Romick, A.H.
1965-66 Courtney, E.N.
1966-69 Sharrock, George
1969-70 Kubley, Walter
1970-73 Kadow, Kenneth
1973-75 Wilson, Emmitt

Community & Regional Affairs
Commissioners
1972-74 Mallott, Byron
1974 McAnerny, Mrs. Lee

Economic Development & Planning
(created in 1962)
Commissioners
1964-65 Roloff, Henry
1965-67 Dickson, William
1967-70 Murkowski, Frank
1970-71 Buness, Everett
1971-74 Ryan, Irene
1974-75 Edmondson, A. Cameron

Education
Commissioners
1917-29 Henderson, Lester D.
1929-31 Breuer, Leo W.
1931-33 Keller, William K.
1933-40 Karnes, Anthony E.
1941-51 Ryan, James C.
1951-53 Erickson, Everett R.
1953-59 Dafoe, Don
1959 (Apr.-Oct.) Matthews, Howard A.
1959-63 Norby, Theo J.

1963-67 Zahradnicek, William T.
1967-71 Hartman, Clifford R.
1971- Lind, Marshall L.

Environmental Conservation
Commissioners
1971-74 Brewer, Max C.
1974- Mueller, Ernest

Fish & Game
Commissioners
1949-61 Anderson, Clarence L.

Military Affairs
Adjutants General
1949-51 Alexander, Joseph D. (Army advisor)
1951-53 Johnson, Lars L.
1953-56 Noyes, John R.
1956-57 Farmer, Elvis
1957-64 Carroll, Thomas P.
1964 (Apr.-July) Reger, Fred O.
1964-67, 1971-73 Elmore, William S.
1967-71, 1974- Necrason, Conrad F.
1973-74 Staser, Bruce I.

Natural Resources
General Manager, Alaska Development Board
1946 Clark, Henry W.
1946-47, 1951-53 Sundborg, George W.

Exec. Director, Alaska Resource Development Board
1954-55 Baird, Alexander
1955-59 Anderson, Al

State Commissioners
1959-67 Holdsworth, Phil
1961-67 Kirkness, Walter
1967-68 Nelson, Urban C.
1968-69 Reetz, August F.
1969-72 Noerenberg, Wallace
1972- Brooks, James W.

Health & Social Services
Commissioner of Health
1918-21 Sloane, Dr. L.O.
1922-33 DeVighne, Dr. H.C.
1933-43 Council, Dr. W.W.
1944-45 Carter, Dr. C.C.

1945-56 Albrecht, Dr. C. Earl
1956-57 Hayman, Dr. Charles R.
1957-60 Gibson, Harry V.

Director of Public Welfare
1941-49 Maynard, Russell
1949-60 Harmon, Henry A.

Commissioners of Health & Welfare
1960-63 Winsor, Paul
1963-67 Browning, Dr. Levi M.
1967-68 Chapman, Dr. John
1968-69 McDonald, J. Scott
1969-70 Betit, Joseph
1970-71 Hall, Robert A.
1971- McGinnis, Frederick

Highways
Alaska Road Commission Presidents
1905-17 Richardson, Wilds P.
1917-20 Waugh, William H.
1920 Gotwals, John C.
1920-27 Steese, James G.
1927-32 Elliott, Malcolm
1932-48 Taylor, Ike P.
1948-51 Noyes, John R.
1951-56 Ghiglione, Angelo F.

Territorial Highway Engineers (elected)
1931-45 Hesse, William H.
1945-47 Smith, W. Leonard
1947-53, 1957-60 Metcalf, Frank A.
1953-57 Reed, Irving M.

State Commissioners
1959-67 Downing, Richard (comr. of
  public works)
1959-62 Sherard, Thurman D. (dir. of
  highways)
1962 Johnson, Sam
1962-66 McKinnon, Donald A.
1967-68 Gonnason, Warren C.
1968-69 Steen, Cosby E.
1969-71 Beardsley, Robert L.
1971-74 Campbell, Bruce A.
1974- Parker, Walter

Labor
Commissioners
1941-42 Haas, Michael J.
1942-46 Sharpe, Walter P.
1946-59, 1970-72 Benson, Henry A.
1959-60 Dischner, Lewis
1960-66 Johnson, Gil
1967-70 Moore, Thomas J.
1972-74 Smith, Robert L.
1974 (July-Dec.) Alexander, John
1974- Orbeck, Edmund N.
1967-70 Kelly, Thomas E.
1970-75 Herbert, Charles F.

Public Safety
Superintendants, Territory Highway Patrol
1957-60 Metcalf, Frank A. (terr. highway engr.)
1959 (Sept.-Nov.) Fitzgerald, James M.

Commissioners
1960-67 Underwood, Martin B.
1967-70 Personett, Mel J.
1970-74 Chapple, Emery, Jr.

Public Works
Commissioners
1959-67 Downing, Richard A.
1967-68 MacClanahan, George R.
1968-71 Strandberg, Harold
1971-73 Easley, George W.
1974 Taggart, Buel "Tex"

Revenue
Territorial Treasurers
1913-35 Smith, Walstein G.
1935-49 Olson, Oscar
1949-55 Roden, Henry
1955-59 Wade, Hugh

State Commissioners
1959-62 Gatz, Peter
1962-67, 1972-74 Stevenson, Robert D.
1967 (Feb.-Oct.) Rettig, Ron L.
1967-70 Morrison, George A.
1970-72 Wohlforth, Eric E.

Delegates to Constitution Convention

Armstrong, Robert Rolland	Juneau	Hinckel, Jack	Kodiak
Awes, Dorothy J. (Mrs. Ragnar Haaland)	Anchorage	Hurley, James J.	Palmer
Barr, Frank	Fairbanks	Johnson, Maurice Theodore	Fairbanks
Boswell, John C.	Fairbanks	Kilcher, Yule F.	Homer
Buckalew, Seaborn Jesse	Anchorage	King, Leonard H.	Haines
Coghill, John Bruce	Nenana	Knight, William Wellington	Sitka
Collins, Ernest Bilbe	Fairbanks	Laws, William W.	Nome
Cooper, George D.	Fairbanks	Lee, Eldor R.	Petersburg
Cross, John Milton	Kotzebue	Londborg, Maynard D.	Unalakleet
Davis, Edward V.	Anchorage	McCutcheon, Stephan Douglas	Anchorage
Doogan, James Patrick	Fairbanks	McLaughlin, George M.	Anchorage
Egan, William Allen	Valdez	McNealy, Robert James	Fairbanks
Emberg, Truman C.	Dillingham	McNees, John A.	Nome
Fischer, Helen Marie (Mrs. Edward A.)	Anchorage	Marston, Marvin R. "Muktuk"	Anchorage
Fischer, Victor	Anchorage	Metcalf, Irwin Logan	Seward
Gray, Douglas	Douglas	Nerland, Arthur Leslie	Fairbanks
Harris, Thomas C.	Valdez	Nolan, James	Wrangell
Hellenthal, John Simon	Anchorage	Nordale, Katherine Driscoll	Juneau
Hermann, Mildred (Mrs. Russell R.)	Juneau	Peratrovich, Frank	Klawock
Hilscher, Herbert Henry	Anchorage	Poulson, Chris Peter	Anchorage

WHO'S WHO IN ALASKAN POLITICS

Reader, Peter L.	Nome	Sundborg, George Walter	Juneau
Riley, Burke	Haines	Sweeney, Dora M. (Mrs. Edward)	Juneau
Rivers, Ralph Julian	Fairbanks	Taylor, Warren Arthur	Fairbanks
Rivers, Victor Claudius	Anchorage	Vanderleest, Herman Raymond	Juneau
Robertson, Ralph Elliott "Bob"	Juneau	Walsh, Michael Joseph	Nome
Rosswog, John H.	Cordova	White, Barrie Moseley	Anchorage
Smith, Walter Osborne "Bo"	Ketchikan	Wien, Ada Bering (Mrs. Noel)	Fairbanks
Stewart, Benjamin Duane	Sitka		

District Attorneys: Territorial, State and U.S.

District of Alaska, hdqrs. Sitka
Haskett, Edward W., 1884-85
Ball, Mottrone Dulany, 1885-87
Grant, Whitaker M., 1887-89
Johnson, Charles S., 1889-94
Taylor, Lytton, 1894-95
Bennett, Burton E., 1895-98
Frederich, Gen. Robert A., 1898-1902 (hdqrs. Juneau after 1900)

Three judicial districts created June 6, 1900
First district hdqrs. Juneau
Lyons, Thomas R., 1902-03
Boyce, John J., 1903-10
Rustgard, John, 1910-13
Reagan, John J., 1913-15
Smiser, James A., 1915-21
Shoup, Arthur G., 1921-26
Harding, Justin W., 1926-29
Stabler, Howard D., 1929-33
Holzheimer, William A., 1933-42
Gemmill, Lynn J., 1944 (Feb.-May)
Jernberg, Robert L., 1944-45
Tollefson, Robert L., 1945-46
Gilmore, Patrick J., Jr., 1946-54
Munson, Theodore E., 1954-56
Connor, Roger G., 1956-59

Second district hdqrs. Nome
Wood, Joseph K., 1900-02
McGinn, John L., 1902 (Jan.-May); 1903-04
Grigsby, Melvin, 1902-04
Hoyt, Henry M., 1904-07
Grigsby, George B., 1908-10
Rodey, Bernard S., 1910-13
Saxton, H.M., 1913-17
Mundy, G.M., 1917-18
Lomen, Gudbrand J., 1918-19
Clements, J.M., 1919-21
Harrison, Fred R., 1921-29

Hart, Julius H., 1929-31
Sullivan, Leroy M., 1931-33
O'Neill, Hugh, 1934-39
Clasby, Charles J., 1939-44
Bingham, Frank C., 1944-51
von der Heydt, James A., 1951-53
Hermann, Russell R., 1953-60

Third district hdqrs., Eagle, Fairbanks, Valdez Anchorage
Post, Alfred M., 1900-01
Harlan, Nathan V., 1901-18
Crossley, James J., 1908-09 (transferred to 4th dist.)
Murane, Cornelius D., 1909-10
Walker, George R., 1910-14
Spence, William N., 1914-17
Munley, William A., 1917-21
Duggan, Sherman, 1921-25
Foster, Frank H., 1925-26
Coppernoll, W.D., 1926-29
Cuddy, Warren N., 1929-33
Kehoe, Joseph W., 1934-42
Wennbloom, Noel K., 1942-46
Plummer, Raymond E., 1946-49
Cooper, J. Earl, 1949-52
Buckalew, Seaborn J., 1952-53
Plummer, William T., 1953-60

Fourth district created, 1909, hdqrs. Fairbanks
Crossley, James J., 1909-14
Roth, Rhinehart F., 1914-21
Erwin, Guy Burton, 1921-24
Hurley, Julien A., 1924-33
Rivers, Ralph J., 1933-44
Arend, Harry O., 1944-49
Hepp, Everett W., 1950-52
McNealy, Robert J., 1952-53
Stevens, Theodore, 1954-56
Yeager, George M., 1956-60

State District Attorneys

First judicial district
Juneau
Asher, Jack O'Hair, 1960-67
Wittemyer, John, 1967 (Jan.-Aug.)
Birch, Ronald G., 1967-68
Tobey, Harold W. "Hal", 1968-69
Fraties, Gail R., 1969-70
Balfe, Joseph D., 1971-73
Hickey, Daniel W., 1973-

Ketchikan
Staley, Howard P., 1961-62
Craddick, Marrs A., 1962-63
Fenton, Thomas E., Jr., 1963-64

Whittaker, Richard L., 1964-66
Walters, Benjamin O., 1967-68
Hawley, William H., Jr., 1969-71
Brown, Harold M., 1971-73
Currall, Geoffrey, 1973-

Second judicial district
Nome
Erwin, Robert B., 1960-62
Vochoska, Virgil D., 1962-64
Mason, John D., 1964-65
Crane, Fred D., 1965-69
Garrison, William W., 1970-

Third judicial district
Anchorage
Colver, Warren C., 1960 (Jan.-Apr.)
Hayes, George, 1960-62
Merbs, James C., 1962-63
Erwin, Robert C., 1963-64
Wanamaker, James N., 1964-65
Brubaker, John, 1965-66
Curran, Thomas E., Jr., 1966-67
Opland, Robert N., 1967 (June-Sept.)
Yandell, R.K., 1967-68
Bailey, Douglas, 1968-69
Tobey, Harold W. "Hal", 1969-71
Buckalew, Seaborn J., 1971-73
Balfe, Joseph D., 1973-

Kenai & Kodiak
Wardell, Thomas M., 1971-

Fourth judicial district
Fairbanks
Taylor, Warren Wm., 1960-62
Erwin, Robert B., 1962-63
Soll, Herbert D., 1963-64
Fenton, Thomas E., Jr., 1964-67
Hodges, H. Jay, 1967-68
Crane, Fred D., 1968 (May-Sept.)
Van Hoomissen, Gerald, 1968-69
Cooper, Stephen, 1969-71
Clayton, Monroe N., 1971-74
Chandler, Catherine, 1974-75

U.S. District Attorneys Since Statehood

Anchorage Headquarters
Plummer, William T., 1960 (Jan.-June)
Yeager, George M., 1960-61
Colver, Warren C., 1961-64
Cella, Joseph J., 1964 (June-Oct.)

McVeigh, Richard L., 1964-68
Frankel, Marvin W., 1968-69
Bailey, Douglas B., 1969-71
Edwards, G. Kent, 1971-

Governors

Kinkead, John Henry, 1884-85
Swineford, Alfred P., 1885-89
Knapp, Lyman Enos, 1889-93
Sheakley, James, 1893-97
Brady, John Green, 1897-1906
Hoggatt, Wilford Bacon, 1906-09
Clark, Walter Eli, 1909-13
Strong, John Franklin Alexander, 1913-18
Riggs, Thomas, 1918-21
Bone, Scott Cordelle, 1921-25

Parks, George Alexander, 1925-33
Troy, John Weir, 1933-39
Gruening, Ernest, 1939-53
Heintzleman, Frank, 1953-57
Stepovich, Michael Anthony, 1957-58
Egan, William Allen, 1959-66, 1970-74
Hickel, Walter Joseph, 1966-69
Miller, Keith Harvey, 1969-70
Hammond, Jay Sterner, 1974-78

Judges: Territorial, State and U.S.

District of Alaska, hdqrs. Sitka
McAllister, Ward, 1884-85
Dawne, Edward J., 1885 (Aug.-Dec.)
Dawson, Lafayette, 1885-88
Reatley, John H., 1888-89
Bugbee, John S., 1889-92
Truitt, Warren D., 1892-95
Delaney, Arthur K., 1895-97
Johnson, Charles S., 1897-1900

Gore, Lester O., 1932-34
Morison, J.H.S., 1935.44
Kehoe, Joseph W., 1944-51
Cooper, J. Earl, 1952-53
Hodge, Walter H., 1954-60

Three judicial districts created June 6, 1900
First district, Juneau
Brown, Melville C., 1900-04
Gunnison, Royal Arch, 1904-09
Lyons, Thomas R., 1909-13
Jennings, Robert W., 1913-21
Reed, Thomas Milburne, 1921-28
Harding, Justin W., 1929-34
Alexander, George Forest, 1934-47
Folta, George W., 1947-55
Kelly, Raymond John, 1955-60

Third district, Eagle, Fairbanks, Valdez, Anchorage
Wickersham, James, 1900-07
Reid, Silas H., 1908-09
Cushman, Edward E., 1909-12
Overfield, Peter D., 1912-13
Brown, Frederick M., 1913-21
Ritchie, Elmer E., 1921-27
Hill, E. Coke, 1927-32
Clegg, Cecil H., 1932-34
Hellenthal, Simon, 1935-45
Dimond, Anthony J., 1945-53
McCarrey, J.L., 1953-60

Second district, Nome
Noyes, Arthur H., 1900-02
Moore, Alfred S., 1902-10
Murane, Cornelius D., 1910-13
Tucker, John Randolph Jr., 1913-17
Holzheimer, William A., 1917-21
Lomen, Gudbrand J., 1921-32

Fourth district, Fairbanks
Overfield, Peter D., 1909-12
Fuller, Frederick E., 1912-14
Bunnell, Charles E., 1915-21
Clegg, Cecil H., 1921-34 (moved to 3d dist., 1932)
Hill, E. Coke, 1932-35
Pratt, Harry Emerson, 1935-54
Forbes, Vernon D., 1954-60

State Judiciary
(State court system officially began functioning
February 20, 1960)

State Supreme Court
Nesbett, Buell A., 1960-70 (chief justice)
Dimond, John H., 1960-71
Hodge, Walter H., 1960 (Feb.-Mar.)
Arend, Harry O., 1960-65
Rabinowitz, Jay A., 1965- (chief justice, 1972-)
Boney, George F., 1968-72 (chief justice, 1970-72)
Connor, Roger G., 1968-
Erwin, Robert G., 1970-
Boochever, Robert, 1972-
Fitzgerald, James M., 1972-75

State Superior Court
Arend, Harry O., 1960 (Feb.-Mar.)
Cooper, J. Earl, 1960-62
Davis, Edward V., 1960-73
Fitzgerald, James M., 1960-72
Gilbert, Hubert A., 1960-74
Hepp, Everett, W., 1960-75

von der Heydt, James, 1960-66
Walsh, Walter, 1960-68
Rabinowitz, Jay A., 1960-65
Moody, Ralph E., 1962-
Sanders, William H., 1964-
Taylor, Warren William, 1965-
Stewart, Thomas B., 1966-
Butcher, Harold J., 1967-
Lewis, Eben H., 1967-
Occhipinti, C.J., 1968-
Burke, Edmond W., 1970-
Carlson, Victor D., 1970-
Hanson, James A., 1970-
Singleton, James K., 1970-
von Hoomissen, Gerald J., 1970-
Kalamarides, Peter J., 1972-
Schulz, Thomas E., 1973-
Buckalew, Seaborn J.,1973-

U.S. District Judges

Hodge, Walter H., 1960-66
Plummer, Raymond E., 1961-73

von der Heydt, James, 1966-
Fitzgerald, James, 1975-

U.S. Marshals: Territorial and Since Statehood

District of Alaska, Sitka
Hillyer, Munson C., 1884-85
Atkins, Barton, 1885-89
Porter, Orville T., 1889-94
Williams, Louis L., 1894-97
Shoup, James McCain, 1897-1900

Three judicial districts created, 1900
First district, Juneau
Shoup, James McCain, 1900-09
Sutherland, Dan, 1909-10
Faulkner, Herbert L., 1911-14
Bishop, Harry A., 1914-17
Tanner, Josiah M., 1917-21
Beaumont, George D., 1921-25
White, Albert, 1926-34
Mahoney, William T., 1934-50
Hellan, Walter G., 1950-51
Thompson, Sidney J., 1951-53
Byington, Glen, 1953 (Feb.-Mar. 1954)
Wilder, Claire A., 1954-60

Second district, Nome
Vawter, Cornelius L., 1900-01
Richards, Frank H., 1901-04
Dunn, John H., 1904-05
Powell, Thomas Calder, 1905-13
Jordan, Emmet R., 1913-21
Griffith, Morris W., 1921-25
Jones, Charles D., 1925-33

Gaffney, Thomas, 1934-37
Mozee, Benjamin B., 1938-55
Oliver, Robert W., 1955-60

Third district, Eagle, Fairbanks, Valdez, Anchorage
Perry, George C., 1900-08
Love, Henry K., 1908-09
Sullivan, Harvey P., 1909-13, 1921-33
Brenneman, F.R., 1913-21
Todd, Chester J., 1934-39
Patterson, James H., 1939-48
Herring, Paul Clint, 1948-50
Metcalf, Irwin L., 1951 (June-Sept.)
Huntley, Walter, 1951-54
Williamson, Fred A., 1954-60

Fourth district, Fairbanks (new district created, 1909)
Love, Henry K., 1909-13
Erwin, Lewis T., 1913-21
Stevens, Gilbert B., 1921-25
Smith, Lynn, 1925-33
Carlson, M.O., 1933 (Mar.-June)
McDonald, Joseph A., 1933-46
Nichols, Stanley J., 1946-51
McRoberts, Ted, Dec. '50-Apr. '51, Aug. '51-
Oct. '51, July '53-Oct. '53
Barr, Frank, 1951 (Apr.-Aug.)
Chapados, Francis X., 1951-53
Dorsh, Albert F., 1954-60

U.S. Marshals Since Statehood

Williamson, Fred S., 1960-61
Bayer, George A., 1961-69

Miller, Norman, 1969 (Aug.-Dec.)
Olson, Robert D., 1969-78

National Committeemen and Committeewomen

DEMOCRAT
1894-97 Louis L. Williams, Sitka
1897-1904 Arthur K. Delaney, Juneau
1905-08 Louis L. Williams, Sitka
1908-09 William W. Casey, Juneau
1909-12 Alfred J. Daly, Nome and Fairbanks
1912-13 Charles E. Davidson, Fairbanks
1913-16 Zina Reville Cheney, Juneau
1916-28 Thomas J. Donohoe, Valdez and Cordova
1920-28 Mrs. John W. Troy, Juneau
1928-34 James J. Connors, Juneau
1928-40 Mrs. William A. Holzheimer, Juneau
1935-40 John A. "Jack" Hellenthal, Juneau
1940-44 Oscar G. Olson, Juneau
1940-44 Mrs. Bertha Perrine, Palmer
1944-48 Mrs. Harriett Hess, Fairbanks
1944-52 Howard Lyng, Nome
1948-52 Mrs. Essie R. Dale, Fairbanks
1952-53 Stanley J. McCutcheon, Anchorage
1952-53 Mrs. Louise Miller, Ketchikan
1953-54 Mrs. Essie R. Dale, Fairbanks
1953-56 Raymond E. Plummer, Anchorage
1954-56 Mrs. Katherine D. Nordale, Juneau
1956-63 Mrs. Helen Fischer, Anchorage
1956-72 Alex Miller, Fairbanks
1963-72 Mrs. Alice Harrigan, Sitka

1972- Clifford E. Warren, Anchorage
1972- Mrs. Bettye Fahrenkamp, Fairbanks
REPUBLICAN
1889- Miner W. Bruce, Juneau
1900-08 John G. Heid, Juneau
1908-12 Louis P. Shackleford, Juneau
1912-16 William S. Bayless, Juneau
1916-20 Cornelius D. Murane
1920-24 John C. McBride, Juneau
1924-28 George Sexton, Seward
1928-32 Austin E. Lathrop, Fairbanks
1928-32 Mrs. Forest J. Hunt, Ketchikan
1932-34 Mrs. Pauline Reed, Anchorage
1932-49 Edward A. Rasmuson, Skagway
1935-54 Mrs. Margaret White, Juneau
1949-50 Austin E. Lathrop, Fairbanks
1952-54 Robert J. McKanna, Fairbanks
1954-58 Mrs. Doris Barnes, Wrangell
1954-64 Walter J. Hickel, Anchorage
1958-64 Mrs. Tillie Reeve, Anchorage
1964-68 Mrs. Doris Barnes, Wrangell
1964-69 Lloyd Burgess, Fairbanks
1968-70 Mrs. Margee Fitzpatrick, Anchorage
1969-72 Robert A. Davenny
1970- Mrs. Edith Holm, Fairbanks
1972- Eldon Ulmer, Anchorage

Representation in the U.S. Congress: Delegates, Senators, Representatives

Territorial Delegates
1906-07 Frank H. Waskey, Nome
1907-09 Thomas Cale, Fairbanks
1909-21 James Wickersham
(Charles A. Sulzer, 1917-19, and George B. Grigsby, 1919-21, sat as delegates but each was declared illegally elected by the U.S. House and

that Wickersham was the rightful winner.)
1921-31 Dan A. Sutherland, Fairbanks and Juneau
1931-33 James Wickersham
1933-44 Anthony J. Dimond, Valdez
1944-59 Edward L. (Bob) Bartlett

After Statehood

U.S. Senate
1959-68 Edward L. (Bob) Bartlett
1959-69 Ernest Gruening
1968- Ted Stevens
1969- Mike Gravel

U.S. House of Representatives
1959-66 Ralph J. Rivers
1967-71 Howard W. Pollock
1971-72 Nick Begich
1973- Don Young

Secretaries of Alaska (Lieutenant Governor)

(Lieutenant Governor)*
1884-87 Lewis, Andrew T.
1887-90 Hayden, Henry E.
1890-93 Peckinpaugh, Nicholas R.
1893-97 Rogers, Charles D.
1897 (July-Aug.) Elliot, Albert D.
1897-1913 Diston, William Langmead
1913-18 Davidson, Charles E.
1919-21 Sommers, Robert James
1921-33 Theile, Karl
1934-38 Griffin, Edward W. "Ned"

1939-44 Bartlett, Edward L. "Bob"
1944-51 Williams, Llewellyn M.
1951-52 Kehoe, Joseph W.
1952-53 Riley, Burke
1953-59 Hendrickson, Waino
1959-66 Wade, Hugh Joseph
1966-69 Miller, Keith Harvey
1969-70 Ward, Robert W.
1970-74 Boucher, Henry Aristide "Red"
1974-78 Thomas, Lowell Jr.
*Title changed to Lieutenant Governor, 1970.

Secretaries of the Interior

Administration	Secretary	Date
Grover Cleveland	Lucius Lamar	1885-88
	William Vilas	1888-89
Benjamin Harrison	John Noble	1889-93
Grover Cleveland	Hoke Smith	1893-96
	David Francis	1896-97
William McKinley	Cornelius Bliss	1897-98
	Ethan Hitchcock	1898-1901
Theodore Roosevelt	Ethan Hitchcock	1901-07
	James Garfield	1907-09
William Taft	Richard Ballinger	1909-11
	Walter Fisher	1911-13
Woodrow Wilson	Franklin Lane	1913-20
	John Payne	1920-21
Warren Harding	Albert Fall	1921-23
	Hubert Work	1923-25
Calvin Coolidge	Hubert Work	1925-28
	Roy West	1928-29
Herbert Hoover	Ray Wilbur	1929-33
Franklin Roosevelt	Harold Ickes	1933-45
Harry Truman	Harold Ickes	1945-46
	Julius Krug	1946-49
	Oscar Chapman	1949-53
Dwight Eisenhower	Douglas McKay	1953-56
	Fred Seaton	1956-61
John Kennedy	Stewart Udall	1961-63
Lyndon Johnson	Stewart Udall	1963-68
Richard Nixon	Walter Hickel	1968-70
	Rogers Morton	1971-74
Gerald Ford	Rogers Morton	1974-

Miscellaneous Categories

Alaska Railroad General Managers

1919-23 Mears, Col. Frederick
1923 (Mar.-Oct.) Steese, Col. James Gordon
1923-24 Landis, Lee H.
1924-28 Smith, Noel W.
1928-45 Ohlson, Col. Otto F.
1946-53 Johnson, Col. John P.
1953-55 Kalbaugh, Frank E.

1955-56 Whitman, Reginald N.
1956-58 Lloyd, John H.
1958-60 Anderson, Robert H.
1960-62 Smith, Donald J.
1962-71 Manley, John E.
1971- Johnston, Walker S.

Regional Administrators, Federal Aviation Agency

1939-45 Hoppin, Marshal C.
1945-55 Plett, Walter P.
1955-63 Hulen, Allen D.
1963-65 Rogers, James G.
1965-67 Gary, George M.

1967-70 Brown, Lyle K.
1970-72 Webb, Jack
1972-73 Cresswell, Thomas J.
1973- Brown, Lyle K.

University of Alaska Presidents

1921-49 Bunnell, Charles E.
1949-53 Moore, Terris
1953-60 Patty, Ernest N.

1960-73 Wood, William R.
1973- Hiatt, Robert W.

Bureau of Indian Affairs Area Directors (Name changed from Alaska Native Service, 1953)

19 -50 Foster, Don
1950-53 Wade, Hugh
1954-58 Olsen, William H.
1958-61 Hawkins, James E.

1961-65 Bennett, Robert L.
1968-71 Richmond, Charles A.
1971-73 Thompson, Morris
1973- Antioquia, Clarence "Clay"

Collector of Customs

1884-87 French, Peter
1887-90 Delaney, Arthur K.
1890-91 Pracht, Max
1891-93 Hatch, Edwin T.
1893-97 Moore, Benjamin P.
1897-1902 Ivey, Capt. Joseph W.
1902-05 Jarvis, Capt. David H.
1905-08 Hobart, Clarence L.
1908-13 Willis, John R.

1913-18 Pugh, John Fraser
1919-22 Troy, John Weir
1922-33 McBride, John C.
1933-51 Connors, James J.
1951-53 Nordale, Mrs. Katherine
1955-61 Heisel, Walter B.
1961-65 Knight, William W.
1965- Bailey, Joseph

Newspaper Editors and Publishers; Radio and TV Executives

Andrews, Clinton
Atwood, Robert
Boucher, Emily
Branstedt, Al
Brown, Norman
Cernick, Clifford
Frame, John
Friend, Elmer
Hiebert, August
Russell, Edward

Ryan, John
Snedden, Charles
Steel, William and Harry
Sundborg, George
Tobin, Emery
Tobin, William
Troy, John
Thompson, W.F.
Williams, Llewellyn Sr. and Jr.